D1564397

The Illusion
of Democracy
in Dependent Nations

A joint study of the

Center for International Studies,
Massachusetts Institute of Technology,

and the

Centro de Estudios del Desarrollo,
Universidad Central de Venezuela

Volume 3 of THE POLITICS OF CHANGE IN VENEZUELA

The Illusion of Democracy in Dependent Nations

José A. Silva Michelena

THE M.I.T. PRESS
Cambridge, Massachusetts, and London, England

ISBN 0 262 19 069 9 (hardcover)

Library of Congress catalog card number: 77-103902

ACKNOWLEDGMENTS

The planning stage of this work started in 1962 when Jorge Ahumada's restless imagination began to conceive the CENDES research program, of which this study is only a part. In the years that have elapsed since the idea became a well-formulated project, scores of people have participated, making it a truly collective, interinstitutional effort. In the first volume, *A Strategy for Research on Social Policy*, the special contributions of many persons were acknowledged explicitly. Thus I need here only to reiterate my gratitude to them.

The unquestioning cooperation that I received from the Center for International Studies of M.I.T. made it possible for me to carry this work to its final stage. James Dorsey and Kathy Gallery, acting as godfather and godmother, solicitously materialized whatever I needed, always with a pleasant smile despite my importunate demands. The essential role that the ADMINS tool of analysis plays in this book is only a token of the unlimited collaboration that I received from Stuart McIntosh and David Griffel, creators of that system. Carol Sudhalter translated the first two chapters.

The collaboration of CENDES was effected, most of all, through the willingness of its director, Luis Lander, to take over my responsibilities at CENDES. Carlos Domingo, whose keen knowledge of computers can be matched only by his disinterested willingness to help friends, made it possible for me to do some of the analysis on which this study rests.

I realized how much intellectual support was given to me by my friend and adviser, Frank Bonilla, only when in October 1967 I departed for Caracas with a suitcase full of tables and came back in June 1968 with just 22 pages added to those which already had been written. Since the day of my return, his constant intellectual stimulation has helped me.

Martha Gillmor not only did the editing but also translated this book from "Spanglish" to English. The blend of a sharp, critical editor's eye with the warmth of her friendship made the task of correcting the original typescript a pleasure.

Financial support for this study was received from the Central University of Venezuela, the Central Planning Office of Venezuela, and the Ford Foundation.

José A. Silva Michelena

CENDES
Universidad Central de Venezuela
September 1969

CONTENTS

List of Figures   viii

List of Tables   ix

Chapter 1   The Diagnostic Approach   1

Chapter 2   The Historical Process   33

Chapter 3   The Twentieth Century   50

Chapter 4   The Impact of Change on the Social Structure   78

Chapter 5   The Social Psychology of Venezuelans: Normative
               Orientations   113

Chapter 6   Psychological States   154

Chapter 7   Evaluations: Priorities, Measures, and Agents   172

Chapter 8   Political Capacity   217

Chapter 9   Synthesis   243

Chapter 10   Democracy and Dependency   264

Appendix A   List of Variables   282

Appendix B   Sources for Figure 3.1   283

Appendix C   A Note on the Analytic Tool   286

Bibliography   299

Index   307

LIST OF FIGURES

1.1 Representation of CONVEN Samples in a Social Space   12

1.2 Integrated Analytical Scheme for CONVEN, VENELITE, and VENUTOPIA I   18

1.3 Clusters of Variables: Urban Groups of Low Socioeconomic Status   28

1.4 Empiricoconceptual Subsystems of Variables: Urban Groups of Low Socioeconomic Status   30

3.1 Venezuela: Correlation between the Principal Economic and Political Crises (1600–1989)   73

7.1 Sets of System Evaluations   178

7.2 Constraint within and among Evaluations of Institutional Sets of Roles   185

7.3 Clusters Based on Evaluation of Systems   214

7.4 Clusters Based on Evaluation of Roles   215

8.1 Clusters Based on System Antagonisms   239

8.2 Clusters Based on Role Antagonisms   240

9.1 The Structure of Politics in Venezuela   249

B.1 Value of Coffee Exports   285

C.1 Analysis Plan   293

C.2 ADFORM Statements and Marginals for Income and Occupational Prestige of Respondents   294

C.3 Construction of an Index and Category File of Respondents of Middle Socioeconomic Status Using the COUNT Command   295

C.4 An Example of the Kendall Tau Generator   297

LIST OF TABLES

1.1   Correlation between Power-Centralizing Dictatorships and Per Capita Income   4

1.2   Social Aggregates for Which Multiple Regression Analysis Was Done   20

1.3   Beta Weights Matrix for Urban Groups of Low Socioeconomic Status   22

1.4   Reordered Matrix of Clusters of Figure 1.3   29

1.5   Urban Groups of Low Socioeconomic Status, Empiricoconceptual Subsystems   31

2.1   Changes in Key Groups of the Venezuelan Social Structure: Sixteenth, Seventeenth, and Nineteenth Centuries   35

2.2   The Regional Nature of Venezuelan Politics   45

3.1   Distribution of the Labor Force by Economic Sector: Venezuela, 1920–1968 (thousands of persons)   55

4.1   Percentage of People Living Outside Birth State   79

4.2   Class Status of Sample Groups   87

4.3   Impact of Horizontal Mobility on the Social Structure   92

4.4   Vertical Mobility: Educational and Occupational   97

4.5   Four Best Predictors of Education and Occupational Prestige (beta weights)   99

4.6   Residential and Vertical Mobility   101

4.7   Newness of Occupational Status by Socioeconomic Status   102

4.8   Relationship between Newness to an Occupational Status and Other Background Factors   103

4.9   Experience of Change of Venezuelan Groups (percentages)   105

4.10   Functions of Public Communication in Different Types of Societies   107

4.11   Socioeconomic Status, Experience of Change, and Communication (percentages)   109
4.12   Social Location, Experience of Change, and Communication   110
5.1   Index of Style of Evaluation: Kendall Tau Rank Correlation Coefficients   119
5.2   Indicators of Nationalism in Venezuela (percentages)   123
5.3   Interrelation of Nationalism and Its Components   127
5.4   What Individuals Would Do to Try to Influence National Government (percentages)   129
5.5   Operational Definitions of Styles of Sanctioning   134
5.6   Ideology and Style of Sanctioning   137
5.7   Relationship between Sanctioning Styles and Other Normative Orientations of Venezuelans   138
5.8   Building Types of Ideological Orientation   141
5.9   Correlates of Ideology   143
5.10   Capacity to Defer Gratification and Familism (percentages) 147
5.11   Correlates of Capacity to Defer Gratification and Familism 148
5.12   The Normative Orientations of Venezuelans   152
6.1   Correlates of Personal Maladjustment   160
6.2   Percentage Distribution of Personally Maladjusted Individuals (NEURA) by Functional Sphere and by Status   161
6.3   Variables Associated with Paranoid State (NEURA)   162
6.4   Definition of Three Basic Types According to the Relationship of Their Level of Aspiration and of Achievement   166
6.5   Psychological States of Venezuelan Groups (percentages)   168
6.6   Correlates of Levels of Satisfaction and Placidness   169
6.7   Four Best Predictors of Level of Satisfaction by Status Aggregates   171
7.1   Foci of the Problems   176
7.2   Perception of Problems in Systemic Areas (percentages)   177
7.3   Systems Constraint: Kendall Tau Rank Correlation Matrix   178
7.4   Correlates of System Evaluations   179
7.5   Evaluations and Best Predictors of Evaluations   180
7.6   Evaluation of Roles   182
7.7   Constraint among Role Evaluations   184
7.8   Correlates of Role Evaluation   186
7.9   Role Evaluation by Institutional Sphere (percentages)   187
7.10   Evaluation of the Political System (percentages)   189
7.11   Degree of Constraint of Evaluation of Systems, Roles, and Politics   194

7.12 Evaluation of the Political System and Some Characteristics   195
7.13 Most Beneficial and Most Prejudicial Foreign Influences (percentages)   197
7.14 Interrelation among Different Evaluations of Foreign Influence   198
7.15 Correlates of Evaluation of Foreign Influence   199
7.16 Preferred Instruments for Solving National and Work Problems: Examples of Typical Answers   201
7.17 Type of Measures Preferred by Sample Groups (percentages)   202
7.18 Characteristics of Measures to Solve System and Role Problems   203
7.19 Type of Measures Recommended and Social Characteristics   204
7.20 Priority of Goals (average ranks)   207
7.21 Patterns of Policy Priorities for Venezuela (by rank)   209
7.22 Principal Responsibility for Implementing the Recommended Action (percentages)   212
8.1 The Political Capacity of Venezuelans (percentages)   223
8.2 Cooperation in Venezuela (percentages)   229
8.3 Intercorrelations among Dimensions of Political Capacity   230
8.4 Sample Groups by Political Capacity and Institutional Loci   232
8.5 Political Capacity and Evaluation of System and Roles   233
8.6 Political Capacity and Evaluation of the Political System   234
8.7 Measures and Political Capacity   236
8.8 Level at Which a Cluster of Antagonistic Groups Was Defined (Systems and Roles)   241
9.1 Characteristics and Evaluations of Venezuelan Groups   246
9.2 Intercorrelations among Characteristics and Evaluations   248
9.3 Ideology, Characteristics, and Evaluations   251
9.4 Policy Sets Which Guided VENUTOPIA Experiments   255
9.5 Evolution of Social Conflicts under Three Hypotheses of Social Policies   257
B.1 Exports of Cacao   283
B.2 Nominal Value of Petroleum Exports   284
C.1 Marginals from the Cross-Tabulation Program (Student Leaders)   290
C.2 Marginal from ADMINS System, Same Group, Same Question, but with Codes Conceptually Resequenced   290
C.3 Example of Tabular Output of ADMINS System   296

1   THE DIAGNOSTIC APPROACH

Building analytical models that predict a society's future along a given road of development is a centuries-old intellectual activity. Plato's *Republic* can be read as an alternative to the society of his times. Sir Thomas More's brief but penetrating introductory notes to his *Utopia* are a classic example of a sociopolitical diagnostic of a global society. And it is not by chance that the Marxist analysis of social change concludes with a new alternative. This current of thought, however, has not been brought much beyond the point at which those authors left it.

The new positivist style at the end of the last century sparked social thinkers, especially in the United States, to examine rather meticulously not the whole society but its component parts in order to establish explicative rather than normative propositions. Over the last fifteen years, however, another significant change has occurred in the social sciences. The trend toward compartmentalizing knowledge has given way to the study of more comprehensive themes. This change has had a twofold effect. It has spurred certain social scientists to use, more and more, the data of diverse relevant sciences to explain a given theme;[1] and it has led to greater comparative efforts.[2] Another current of thought, stimulated perhaps by the anticolonial and national liberation movements, has been a renewal of interest in social dynamics. Thus, as the idea of progress most captivated the minds of thinkers in the last century, today the theme of development

---

[1] C. Wright Mills, *The Sociological Imagination* (New York: Oxford University Press, 1959), pp. 139–140.
[2] Gabriel A. Almond and G. B. Powell, *Comparative Politics: A Developmental Approach* (Boston: Little, Brown, 1966), pp. 1–15.

draws more attention; at the same time there is a renewed interest in scrutiny of the future.[3]

The new trend has been beneficial to the political sciences. It has led, according to Almond and Powell, to criticism and defeat of the old parochial, configurative, formalistic approach and to the emergence of a new one, more comprehensive in its field of attention, more realistic and precise, tending to seek out a new theoretical order.[4] Although these authors and others of the time have made strides that could be considered a revolution in political science, even the best of these contributions have been schematic, giving more attention to categorizations per se than to dynamics or relations among categories. This is true especially in the case of political development, or modernization. Various symptoms suggest that the theme has not yet been crystallized. First, a mere summary review of the literature will show plainly that no conceptual consensus has been reached. As concepts, "modernization" and "political development" are interchanged as often as they are differentiated. Second, and indeed notable, is the multitude of definitions and the variety of analytic approaches. One author in a recently published work succeeded in bringing together some ten definitions of these concepts,[5] and another — after an exhaustive analysis of relevant literature — distinguished not less than five approaches.[6] The curious thing is that very few of these approaches have been subjected to rigorous empirical test.

Still, this analytical and conceptual diversity lies more in form than in content. Examining each of the approaches in its essence, we find that for the most part the methods converge on a broad treatment of a few sociopolitical processes: identity, rationalization of authority, structural differentiation, and political participation and capacity.[7] We shall explore briefly the meaning of these key terms.

[3] There are a growing number of publications that hold exploration of the future to be a primary objective. Among these the following are worth mention here: Nigel Calder, *The World in 1984* (London: Penguin Books, 1964), 2 vols.; Bertrand de Jouvenel, *Futuribles* (Geneva: Droz, 1963), 2 vols.; Dennis Gabor, *Inventing the Future* (New York: Knopf, 1964); Arthur C. Clarke, *Profiles of the Future* (New York: Harper & Row, 1962). Also, efforts are being made in the United States to create an "Institute for Study of the Future," which would coordinate those already existing (about 26). Last, it is worth mentioning that the Interamerican Planning Society chose for the theme of its congress held in Lima in 1968: "America in the Year 2000."

[4] Almond and Powell, *Comparative Politics*, pp. 1–15.

[5] Lucian Pye, *Aspects of Political Development* (Boston: Little, Brown, 1966).

[6] Robert A. Packenham, "Approaches to the Study of Political Development," *World Politics*, vol. 17, no. 1 (October 1964).

[7] See, for example, S. P. Huntington, "Political Development and Political Decay,"

The term "identity" is used to describe the process by which a population defines for itself a common territory, acquires political autonomy, and socially and economically integrates the population that lives within these boundaries. These acts do not necessarily follow a predetermined order. It is, in fact, the peculiar forms that these processes have taken across the world that have drawn specialists' attention. Both the identification and the analysis of these periods of identity crisis have, in turn, helped ascertain levels of development reached by different societies. Thus, from a universal point of view, it is certain that the earlier a nation solves the problem of territorial boundaries, the higher the country's stage of development is likely to be.[8] However, as can be seen in the case of Latin America, mere political independence does not guarantee development. One of the basic identity problems to be resolved is that of social integration, that is, elimination of cultural, social, and ethnic barriers on the basis of which numerically important groups are segregated from national life. Again, the further along a country is in solving the problem, the higher its probable level of development.

These processes of redefining identity generally have occurred in connection with changes in the system of authority, that is, a rationalization of authority. Thus in the particular case of Latin America, Silvert indicates that

> Every country underwent a "time of trouble" after independence, and every one has had at least one great integrating dictator. . . . These men are to Latin America as Louis XIV to France or Ivan the Terrible to Russia: they broke the power of the local *caciques* and established centralized control over the territories of their nascent nation-states. . . . Where the integrating dictatorship came early, as in Chile, national life subsequently has tended to develop with comparative ease; yet other countries, such as Venezuela, show a procession of *caudillos* persisting unto yesterday's headlines.[9]

If we consider the more developed Latin American countries — those in which the 1965 per capita income was $400 or more, including Argentina, Colombia, Costa Rica, Chile, Mexico, Panama, Uruguay, and Venezuela —

World Politics, vol. 17, no. 3 (April 1965), and "Political Modernization: America vs. Europe," *World Politics,* vol. 18, no. 3 (April 1966); Almond and Powell, *Comparative Politics,* especially Chapter 11; R. E. Ward and D. A. Rustow, eds., *Political Modernization in Japan and Turkey* (Princeton, N.J.: Princeton University Press, 1964), Introduction; and Pye, *Aspects of Political Development,* pp. 46–48.

[8] Dankwart A. Rustow, *A World of Nations: Problems of Political Modernization* (Washington, D.C.: Brookings Institution, 1967).

[9] Kalman H. Silvert, *The Conflict Society: Reaction and Revolution in Latin America* (New Orleans, La.: Hauser Press, 1961), pp. 12–13.

we discover that every country except Panama and Venezuela went through a power-centralizing dictatorship before 1910. Of the remaining twelve Latin American countries classified as underdeveloped, in contrast, only Ecuador (and even here there are doubts) had a power-centralizing dictator before 1910 (see Table 1.1). Naturally, these data do not prove Silvert's

TABLE 1.1   Correlation between Power-Centralizing Dictatorships and Per Capita Income

Countries with per capita income of greater than $400 (1965)		
Country	Power-Centralizing Dictator	Period
Argentina	Juan Manuel de Rosas	1829–1852
Colombia	Rafael Nuñez	1880–1894
Costa Rica	Tomás Guardia	1870–1882
Chile	Diego Portales	1830–1850
Mexico	Porfirio Díaz	1877–1910
Panama	José Remón	1952–1955
Uruguay	J. Batlle y Ordoñez	1903–1907
Venezuela	Juan V. Gómez	1908–1936

Countries with per capita income of less than $400 (1965)		
Country	Power-Centralizing Dictator	Period
Brazil	Getulio Vargas	1930–1945
Bolivia	(no definite leader)	
Cuba	Fulgencio Batista	1934–1944
Ecuador	García Moreno	1859–1875?
	Eloy Alfaro	1895–1911
Guatemala	Jorge Ubico	1920–1944
Haiti	F. Duvalier (?)	1956–present
Honduras	Tiburcio Carías	1932–1948
Nicaragua	A. Somoza (?)	1937–1956
Paraguay	Alfredo Stroessner (?)	1954–present
Peru	A. B. Leguía	1919–1930
Dominican Republic	R. L. Trujillo (?)	1930–1961
El Salvador	Maximiliano Hernández	1930–1944

SOURCE: Paul Rosenstein-Rodan, "Latin American Development: Results and Prospects," mimeographed (Cambridge, Mass.: M.I.T., 1967), Table 1, p. 2.

hypothesis; the criteria for defining a centralizing caudillo are not well enough established for this, and the tendency to accept the authority of caudillos, so characteristic of Latin America, makes it all the more difficult to test the hypothesis unequivocally.

Perhaps the most effective criterion for distinguishing the power-centralizing caudillo is the extent to which the man in question was able to organize and equip an army on a national scale. The existence of a national army probably indicates that the given country at a given moment was already feeling a certain economic prosperity, or at least holding enough fiscal income to maintain and equip a national army that effectively could cover all the country's territory. These dictators were neither enlightened despots nor democratic Caesars but more often ambitious, little-educated, implacable men, who knew how to take advantage of an occasional turn toward economic prosperity to consolidate their power over other regional caudillos. Thus it is understandable that in Latin America the national concentration of power did not significantly foster the growth of rationalization of authority. Many authors have shown that the attempt to establish universal, affectively neutral standards — which are functionally specific and oriented to the achievement of explicit national goals — encounters serious obstacles in the inherited inclinations toward *personalismo, caudillismo,* and nepotism.

Nevertheless, one of the most extraordinary paradoxes of Latin America is that during these periods of extreme concentration of power and of iron political control, in many countries the conditions for structural differentiation were created. Thus after this stage of concentrated control passed, political participation and social mobility in general could expand significantly.[10] The relative economic prosperity that allowed the organization of the army on a national basis also allowed some investment of funds in public works and especially in the improvement and expansion of transport routes, all of which not only helped unify the country but also rendered public administration structurally more complex. Thus, too, the growth of private sectors of the economy was stimulated, giving place to the formation of new social strata such as the bourgeoisie and the industrial workers. Once the dictatorial period had passed, the new demands arising from these social groups created pressure toward expanding political participation. Moreover, in most cases there were no significant reforms in the antiquated, inefficient agrarian system; the bulk of investment was made instead in large cities and especially in the capital. As a result, migration from rural to urban areas was accelerated, helping in turn to increase pressure for greater political participation.

This development, as noted, is indeed far from the classic democratic

[10] Seymour Martin Lipset, "Values, Education, and Entrepreneurship," in Seymour Martin Lipset and Aldo Solari, eds., *Elites in Latin America* (New York: Oxford University Press, 1967).

model according to which greater participation will mean greater loyalty to the system.[11] In fact, the contrary is true: In Latin America new opportunities for participation increased *in spite of* the prevailing political system. As a result, new loyalties were bestowed almost exclusively on political parties and leaders and not on the system, or else were not generated at all, creating conditions for anomic participation of the urban masses such as riots or demonstrations with no political goal.

The pattern of development set forth in preceding paragraphs provides a useful conceptual frame of interpretation for the general process of development of a country, and we shall use it for this purpose in Chapters 2 and 3. But it must be stated that this pattern proves inadequate when applied to particular countries, for three reasons. First, the order of these processes varies from nation to nation, and the way the variations affect the development process is not well established. Second, none of them is completed all at once or permanently. In the majority of Latin American nations, the crises of authority, identity, and participation seem to recur with obstinate frequency, though not necessarily taking the same form each time. Third, in the long run one surely can assert that authority has been increasingly rationalized and democratized, that a higher level of social equality has been reached, and that the institutional structure has been rendered more complex. Yet such changes certainly have been very limited, perhaps because periods of political decay have been so frequent — periods, that is, of ritualization of authority, restriction of political participation, and limitation of social equality. Argentina and Brazil are the latest examples.

These are complex phenomena. To try to understand them by paying attention to just a few factors is like attempting to analyze a chimera. There are two conditions among others that seem to have special relevance. One is external — the influence of the United States. The other, internal, is the degree to which the normative orientations of the different groups of the population are in consonance with the institutional processes mentioned here.

The economic and political influence of the United States on Venezuela and on Latin America in general (excepting Mexico) became important only in this century. In the final chapter we attempt to give a global picture of the importance of Latin America's dependency relationship with the United States. Here we want to add only that an analysis of the most

[11] See Gabriel A. Almond and Sidney Verba, *The Civic Culture: Political Attitudes and Democracy in Five Nations* (Princeton, N.J.: Princeton University Press, 1963).

decisive events of the last fifty years leads to a conclusion that, though not really explanatory, is important for its predictive value: Whenever a Latin American country has been confronted internally by a critical situation that did or would affect the economic or political interests of the United States, U.S. policy has been that of direct or indirect intervention in favor of the more conservative faction.[12] The intervention of the Marines in the Dominican Republic, the active role played by the U.S. ambassador in the overthrow of Goulart, and the open U.S. support of Eduardo Frei in Chile in financing his electoral campaign are recent and dramatic examples that this tendency is not likely to change.

In the preceding paragraphs the analysis has been confined to a strictly institutional plane. This has been done purposely in order to highlight at this point the cultural plane: the combination of value orientations that coexist with the institutional processes. Herein, we must first take into account that a given institutional process affects different groups or individuals in different ways. What probably contribute most to these differences in effect are status criteria (education, income, and occupation). Second, we can postulate that identity, authority, and equality are tightly bound to these various group orientations toward the nation. Nationalism, seen from this angle, is defined as a particular combination of patriotism, nationalist ideology, and a generalized sense of national identification that expresses itself in a combination of orientations such as (1) secularism, (2) commitment to the nation and citizenship, (3) a sense of openness of society, and (4) acceptance of the state as a supreme secular value.[13]

Patriotism is no more than the emotional expression of the national identity process. It is a feeling of love, commitment, and devotion evoked by certain symbols such as the flag, independence day, a national hero, or the fatherland. Rationalization of authority finds its counterpart in the degree of secularism existing in different social groups, that is, in the number of areas of social life which they consider to be outside the control of the Church, of magic, or of other idea systems related to the supernatural. But perhaps still more important as an element of nationalism is a view of the state as a supreme value, in that its intervention is accepted as the legiti-

---

[12] Bryce Wood, *The Making of the Good Neighbor Policy* (New York: Columbia University Press, 1962).

[13] This concept of nationalism was suggested by Silvert and Bonilla. See Kalman H. Silvert and Frank Bonilla, "The Process of National Development," mimeographed (Cambridge, Mass.: M.I.T., 1965), pp. 11–24. One empirical proof of these concepts is found in Frank Bonilla and José A. Silva Michelena, eds., *A Strategy for Research on Social Policy* (Cambridge, Mass.: The M.I.T. Press, 1967), Chapter 3; hereafter cited as *SRSP*.

mate regulator or arbiter in all areas of social life. The correlate of the social equalization process is the sense of openness of society: the extent to which one does not sense social barriers holding back any citizen of any social origin from reaching positions of prestige. Finally, we shall postulate that there is usually a connection between participation and the feelings of citizenship and political efficacy. All this does not imply a necessary one-to-one correspondence between levels of institutional development and this combination of value orientations. Marion Levy already has indicated that any absolute correspondence between structures and values would render the global system too fragile, because any change whatever would then endanger it.[14] Thus, what one normally finds is a kind of incongruity. But as has been shown by Marx, this incongruence has limits beyond which serious disruptions occur for the whole society or for important sectors of it. One of the fundamental premises here is that in societies undergoing a rapid change process, the conflicts arising from the contradiction between structure and value levels tend to be not only more frequent but sharper. Later we shall return to this point.

The analytical usefulness of this institutional versus evaluative comparison stands out in viewing any Latin American nation. Here the actual objectives of social equality, participation, and self-affirmation which some key groups acting within the national polity set forth clash somewhat with an antiquated social structure. Moreover, the clashes are not just of this type. Technology imported from more advanced nations, especially from the United States, and forms of economic organization and politicoeconomic domination that come with it incite further clashes, for they must now operate within a social system based on different operative principles. Perhaps the most important consequence of this phenomenon is fluctuation in export. On the one hand, conditions prevailing in the world market tend to limit less-developed countries such as those of Latin America to the export of only a few primary products. On the other hand, the value curve of these products' export follows a logistic (S-shaped) trajectory. Each historic period is marked by the prevalence of one product whose export grows slowly at first, then reaches a point of rapid increase, and later declines. On the product's exhaustion, an economic crisis arises, lasting until the country can substitute another product. The technical reasons for this phenomenon are outlined in the following paragraph:

[14] Marion Levy, Jr., *Modernization and the Structure of Societies* (Princeton, N.J.: Princeton University Press, 1966), p. 26.

First, . . . it is a proven empirical fact that almost all the goods, considered individually, follow an asymptotic law of growth. . . . Second, in the case of primary products, the primary resources from which they are obtained . . . are, in the long run, of growing costs. Third, as a historic fact, technological innovations have notoriously reduced the input of raw materials per unit of output, so that the income effect on the demand for these raw materials in developed countries has in part been compensated for by a substitution effect.[15]

When each of these economic crises occurs, it is usually reflected in the discontent of certain groups that, in turn, induce new crises of identity, participation, and authority.

The processes mentioned, then, are useful in making a diagnosis of any country if one performs a careful historic investigation. Their primary usefulness lies in providing an analytical global model of the society, permitting a prognosis of the direction in which the country is heading. But since, in this investigation, our interest is in establishing the tightest connections that exist between politics and policy, we find this perspective limited in two respects. First, policies and their effects must be considered at most in the middle run, but the approach just described is essentially long-run. To try to use it to assess policy would be like attempting to measure a fraction of an inch with a yardstick. Second, policy measures are directed at specific sectors of the population rather than at the country as a whole. How structural changes over the course of history have affected specific key population group values is a subject requiring more information than is usually available.

Another theme pertinent to development is that of political capacity. Eisenstadt suggests that one can call a political system "developed" in the proportion that it can satisfactorily absorb the demands the population sets before it and, at the same time, stimulate the population to set forth new demands.[16] Again, this idea forces one into a long-range view of political capacity, for, though catching the pith of the matter, it tells little about the concrete form in which the process occurs and about what variables intervene and what their specific effects are. In just this respect the contribution of Hirschman helps to fill a gap.[17] He shows clearly (1) the importance that

[15] Jorge Ahumada, "Conferencia No. 5, Teoría del desarrollo económico," mimeographed (Caracas: CENDES, September 25, 1964), pp. 5–6.

[16] S. N. Eisenstadt, "Bureaucracy and Political Development," in Joseph G. La Palombara, ed., *Bureaucracy and Political Development* (Princeton, N.J.: Princeton University Press, 1963), p. 96.

[17] Albert O. Hirschman, *Journeys toward Progress: Studies of Economic Policy-Making in Latin America* (New York: Twentieth Century Fund, 1963), especially p. 227.

ideological orientation and rhetorical style hold in the formation of solutions to national problems and (2) the role both play in the dynamics of decision making.

A more general approach to the problem is that offered by Fals Borda by way of his subversion concept, "that condition that reflects in a social system its internal inconsistencies, spotlighted by newly revered goals that a society wishes to reach." [18] Thus, in a given social system, a utopia is externally introduced or internally generated, whereupon its antivalues, counternorms, counterorganizations, and technical innovations throw a challenge at the values, norms, institutions, or techniques in force. The tensions culminate when the old tradition is subverted and the utopian objectives are partially realized through a new social outlook expressed in a new social order.

Both Hirschman and Fals Borda show the importance of evaluative elements in founding social conflicts and their effect on the extent to which policy is realized. Nevertheless, both approaches turn out to be too general for our purposes. Our interest is to calibrate a country's capacity to decide on and carry out objectives such as those postulated in a national development plan. This requires a knowledge more refined and reference to agents more concrete than the great social aggregates used in the conceptual schemes of these authors.

For this reason the diagnostic approach, besides taking into account the general historical frame and focusing on the evaluative elements, defines these elements in relation to a set of specific agents.

The selection of those groups to be considered "key" should be based on a minute analysis of the process of political development, seen from a historical perspective. The object of this analysis is to discover the significant periods, those marked by identity, participation, and authority crises. In each of these periods one can identify (1) groups linked to the interests representative of the status quo and (2) groups emerging, in the sense that they are linked to structures in formation. In each of these stages one also can find groups or social strata that control and influence national policy and groups whose participation must be taken into account if and when policies are carried out.

It was mentioned previously that one consequence of the development process is the growing structural differentiation of society. This differentiation implies that in the proportion that more recent periods are con-

[18] Orlando Fals Borda, *La subversión en Colombia: El cambio social en la historia* (Bogotá: Tercer Mundo, 1967), pp. 28–29.

sidered one must differentiate and modify criteria to define the social agents. Thus, in the first decades of the colonial period perhaps it was enough to distinguish groups according to ethnic criteria, but by the end of the same period it became indispensable to take into account economic activity. Otherwise, understanding the antagonisms, for instance, between white Venezuelans and the Spanish would have been most difficult. Today, we must consider each individual's location in a social position defined at least by class status; the functional sector where he fulfills his principal activity (political, economic, cultural, or military); the specific institutions to which he belongs (government, parties, industry, commerce, education, religion, air force, or navy); the degree of political participation; and the type of life, defined according to the level of assimilation to urban behavior standards.

Figure 1.1 shows the groups that were selected for inclusion in this investigation. The attempt in the graph has been to place each group in a social position defined by the dimensions described in the preceding paragraph. Where this arrangement is perhaps most suggestive is in tracing channels and patterns of mobility by status and functional spheres. The arrows have been drawn precisely to emphasize these points. From each of these groups a sample was drawn up following various probabilistic models.[19] Information was obtained for each individual of each one of the key groups, allowing confirmation of the a priori criteria of selection. In addition, a great variety of data was obtained relative to the individual's social locality, change experience, normative orientation, and psychological state, his evaluation of structures, roles, and priorities, and his political capacity. Specific variables studied under each of these headings will be named later. We shall now consider the combination of normative orientations that, as Hirschman and Fals Borda suggest, are indispensable to understanding political change.

One of the fundamental hypotheses from the beginning of this study is that in situations of rapid change, as in Venezuela, contradictions are created within the cultural level. These tend to generate conflicts that in turn affect the formulation and practice of a policy for development. These contradictions are what Ahumada termed "cultural heterogeneity":[20] when

[19] A complete report on the sample procedures used in each case is published, along with the answers to each question, by the Center of Development Studies of the Central University of Venezuela. See *Estudio de conflictos y consenso, serie de resultados parciales*, vols. 1–15 (Caracas: Imprenta Universitaria, 1965–1968).

[20] Jorge Ahumada, "Hypothesis for Diagnosing Social Change: The Venezuelan Case," *International Social Science Journal*, vol. 16, no. 2 (1964), pp. 192–202.

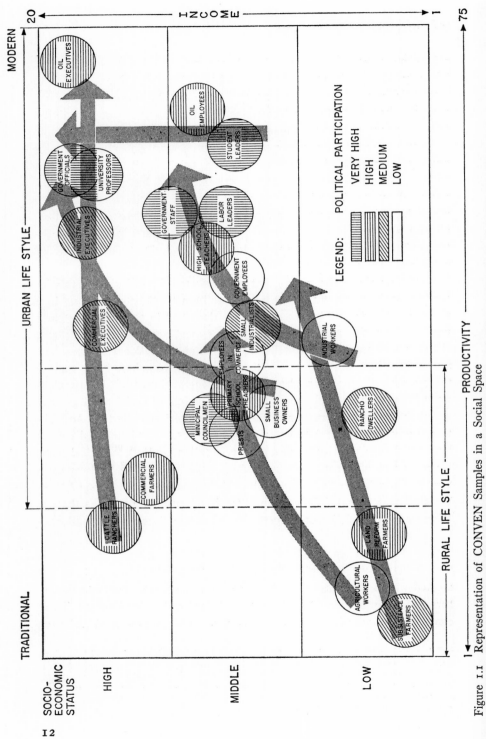

Figure 1.1 Representation of CONVEN Samples in a Social Space

12

individuals occupying a more or less similar level in the hierarchical structure of the society show appreciable differences in their normative orientations. Because of rapid change, positions available within a determined level of power expand much more quickly than does the number of individuals that the society can adequately socialize to occupy these positions.

Frequent political changes, intensity of rural-urban movement, and sustained economic growth, together with the endemic lag of socializing institutions (school, family, and church), produce a situation in which these clashes permeate all social groups, affecting even individual psychological integrity. This means, on the one hand, that in each institution, new or old, one is likely to find within one hierarchical level important sectors that hold divergent orientations toward the nation, or that vary considerably in feeling of political efficacy (that is, the degree to which one feels able to do something about injustice committed by authority). On the other hand, it means that on the individual level we shall probably not find a correspondence between various dimensions of nationalism. As a case in point, many primary and secondary school teachers and student leaders seem to have a low level of secularism, which is incongruent with their measure of acceptance of the state as a social value in the economic area.[21] This is perhaps why, in Venezuela, policies regarding religious education tend to stimulate conflict.

The importance of nationalism and political efficacy in relation to the development process was shown in previous paragraphs. We shall thus explore other normative orientations that appear to play a very important role in setting up conflicts. Perhaps most important among these orientations is the concrete (positive-negative) way in which a group evaluates itself and its social environment. There are data to substantiate the statement that this evaluative dimension is not only dominant in but also generalizable

[21] *SRSP*, p. 72.

NOTE: Figure 1.1 seeks to represent the initial, intuitive judgments of the research team regarding the location of the sample groups in a space defined primarily by the dimensions of socioeconomic status and traditionalism-modernism. The research itself includes numerous alternative concepts linked to appropriate empirical indicators of these dimensions. The two ratios shown here — 20:1 for income and 75:1 for productivity — are noted to convey a sense of the sizable social distances these dimensions cover in Venezuela. In developed countries both ratios are closer to 4:1. The overlap of rural and urban on the chart is meant to portray the interpenetration of rural and urban life styles both in the largest cities and the small towns. The arrows suggest a variety of paths and stages in upward movement through this social space for groups and individuals. The values for the categories of political participation are: very high, 40 percent or more; high, between 25 and 40 percent; medium, between 15 and 25 percent; low, less than 15 percent.

to the majority of judgments, for, as demonstrated, it can be associated with almost any other dimension of meaning.[22] Moreover, it seems that evaluative judgments on political objects begin to be made at a very early age, at least before other kinds of judgments are made.[23] This may be because man, meeting a new situation, seeks to establish some evaluative relationship between the objects he perceives and his own feeling of identity, as is evident in the burgeoning literature about underdeveloped nations.

If, then, one supposes that the changes occurring in society affect variously the sundry value and structure orientations, it is understandable that evaluations are sharpened in times of rapid change. Still more, the problem of establishing one's identity becomes critical when (as a result of the change) many people are virtually uprooted from their social environment and grouped with persons of very different evaluative orientations. Perhaps this is one reason why ideology plays such a conspicuous role in these periods of rapid change: in such periods, evaluative differences seem to promote and intensify antagonism among various social groups.

Any individual's way of evaluating a given situation depends, of course, on the place he occupies in the social structure. Thus, it has been shown that the higher a group's status, the likelier it will be that its style of evaluation will be rational — the group having greater breadth of perception, more and better information, a more secular normative orientation, and greater innovative leanings.[24] Within each class, however, the rationality level of any group's evaluative style will be in direct relation to the urban life experience and social origin of group members. Furthermore, rationality will tend to be greater in those individuals whose principal activity unfolds around the political or cultural field.

The greatest differences in evaluative style will tend to occur among groups of middle socioeconomic status and the slightest differences within the lowest socioeconomic groups. The higher the degree of cultural heterogeneity of a class, the less consensus there is among evaluations by members of groups in that class. This greater evaluative sophistication is tied also to greater individual political capacity. For these reasons, the increase

[22] Charles E. Osgood, George J. Suci, and Percy H. Tannenbaum, *The Measurement of Meaning* (Urbana, Ill.: University of Illinois Press, 1957), pp. 188 ff.

[23] Robert D. Hess and Judith Torney, "The Development of Basic Attitude Values toward Government and Citizenship during the Elementary School Years," part 3, multilith (Chicago: University of Chicago Press, 1965).

[24] An empirical check of this and the subsequent propositions can be found in José A. Silva Michelena, "Desarrollo cultural y heterogeneidad cultural en Venezuela," *Revista Latinoamericana de sociología,* February 1967.

in the middle class, at least while cultural heterogeneity exists, signifies more rather than fewer political conflicts. After all, it is only when two groups have similar amounts of power that evaluative differences are converted into socially significant antagonism.

Why certain relatively secure groups feel dissatisfaction with the existing conditions can also be explained partially by the difference between their aspirations (wants) and what they consider they have gained (gets). Lerner, one of the sociologists who has made greatest use of this theory, states that when people repeatedly desire more than they can possibly obtain,

> . . . the resulting frustration produces among the people either regression or aggression as a response. The regressive response leads people to drop their expectations, to withdraw from the public arena into the private narcosis of resignation and apathy. The aggressive response leads people to persist in their excessive expectations, to renounce the existing arena of public action, and to erupt in personal violence and public agitation.[25]

In a preliminary proof of this theory through analysis of data for the 24 sample groups that are the subject of this study, we arrived at the conclusion that the want-get ratio actually *is* negatively related to the levels of satisfaction manifested by each of these groups.[26] However, we also found that levels of satisfaction were directly related to socioeconomic status. As socioeconomic status is also strongly associated with political activism, it is logical to suppose that in a situation of imbalance between needs and gains, the response in lower-status groups will tend more frequently to be regressive, whereas in the higher-status groups the aggressive response will tend to be strongest.

This theory may also explain why antagonisms tend to be sharper among higher-status groups. However, it is obvious that this explanation in itself is not enough. At equal status levels and levels of political activism the predisposition to antagonism between groups or individuals depends on the sanctioning style — the specific manner in which an individual thinks he should resolve a conflict situation or correct deviant conduct. Some are more inclined than others to use legal or institutional processes. Others will tend simply to do nothing in the face of such situations. Finally, others will favor the application of noninstitutional sanctions. If the premises estab-

[25] Daniel Lerner, "Conflict and Consensus in Guayana," in F. Bonilla and J. A. Silva Michelena, eds., *Studying the Venezuelan Polity,* mimeographed (Cambridge, Mass.: C.I.S., M.I.T., 1966), p. 511. This is an earlier version of *SRSP.*

[26] José A. Silva Michelena, "Satisfaction, Personal Adjustment, and Incongruencies in Venezuelan Society," mimeographed (Cambridge, Mass.: C.I.S., M.I.T., 1966).

lished by the theory of the want-get ratio are true, it should be true that those whose gains are consistently less than their needs will be more inclined to favor noninstitutional sanctions, whether of the aggressive type (killing, striking a blow) or of the regressive type (doing nothing).

It must be emphasized that the reasoning in the preceding statements does not imply a value judgment. There are times in a given society when it is functional to go against certain established norms and even against the current social order. It is not necessary to revert to the example of Hitler's Germany to support this reasoning. The political history of Latin American countries shows that noninstitutional processes, frequently of the violent type, have been the most effective instrument of social change, permitting the sweeping away of obstacles that could not otherwise be eliminated.

Plan of Analysis

The body of assertions just presented can be said to constitute the pith of the diagnostic approach. Included are, albeit with only a preliminary backing, the principal formulations of Ahumada.[27] Yet these are no more than a tiny part of the complex network of interrelations that one must establish in order to construct an analytical model of a national political system like the one under consideration which has as its objective the examination of how social conflicts obstruct or incite, as the case may be, "the nation's capacity to satisfy human needs on a large scale and at the same time diminish the repressive and deprivational features of the present system or any alternative that may evolve in the near future." [28]

Obviously, to carry out this task, we must know much more about the social background and experience of change of individuals, not only because these affect their normative orientations and psychological states, but also because it is assumed that variations in these mediating dispositions influence the specific evaluation that individuals make of social systems or institutions, of their own roles, and of themselves. We postulate that divergent evaluations, depending on the political capacity of the individuals, constitute the primary source of social conflicts which in the short or middle run affect the process of formulating and carrying out of a development policy.

[27] Ahumada, "Hypothesis for Diagnosing Social Change."
[28] *SRSP*, pp. 26–27.

By saying that this type of conflict has meaning only if we look at it in terms of political capacity of the agents, and if we recognize explicitly that evaluations change with social location and experience of change of the actors, we locate the analysis within a basically structural context. These ideas were discussed more extensively in the "Integrated Analytical Scheme" presented in *SRSP*. The flow of this type of analysis is reproduced in Figure 1.2. However, at that time we failed to consider two vitally important points. The first has to do with the empirical basis of the conceptual plan, and the second with the definition of specific relations that define the global structure.

A bias often found in sociological analysis is the following: when even the smallest of surveys yields data on a multitude of variables, the analysis is usually made on the implicit presumption that only a few of them — usually occupation, education, age, and sex — are important to consider when exploring relations among most of the variables. Although this presupposition provides a convenient guide for analysis, no one has taken the trouble to prove it. This would not be so serious if the consequences ended here. But if we consider the risks run by adopting this method of a priori selection of variables, we see that the problem is not so trivial. First, we can commit the error of establishing relations as significant when really, if we considered all available variables, the significance would not hold. Moreover, we also run the risk of bypassing relations among variables that may be vital for explaining the problem under study.

In speaking of "families of concepts" in the analytical plan, we are presupposing, specifically, that the variables included in each square of Figure 1.2 are more closely related to each other than to other variables. Yet, although this new supposition avoids the simplistic assumptions of the preceding one, it introduces a new and equally risky assumption: that families of concepts correspond to empirical subsystems.[29] Therefore, to proceed in the analysis with some confidence, we must test the validity of this hypothesis.

The procedure we have followed develops in stages. First, we must ascertain which variables are related, and to what degree. Since we assumed that there can be a multidirectional relation of varying intensity between two or more variables, each variable had to be considered as a

---

[29] This definition of system, as well as the subsequent analysis, was suggested by Professor Carlos Domingo in an informal seminar held at M.I.T. in 1967. However, the responsibility for any errors rests entirely with us.

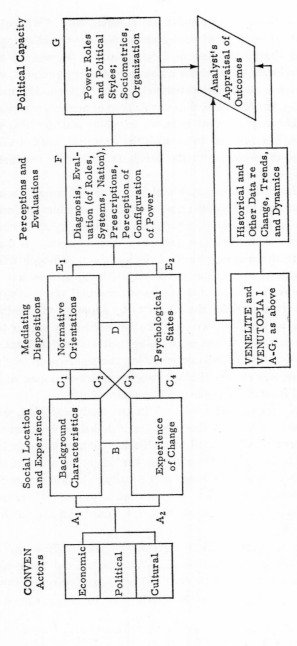

Figure 1.2 Integrated Analytical Scheme for CONVEN, VENELITE, and VENUTOPIA I
NOTE: Letters indicate families of propositions or conventional laws; boxes are families of concepts.

dependent variable once and as an independent variable in the remaining cases, because there *is* the possibility that a variable is related to all other variables. Thus at least all relations of importance are explored. The technique that we have followed to achieve our objective is multiple regression by successive steps. The program selects independent variables in strict order, based on the magnitude of the partial correlation coefficient.[30] In this case, the number of variables to consider as predictors was set at four, because it was empirically proved that adding new variables contributed very little to reducing the unexplained variance. That is, the network of interrelations became excessively complicated without really gaining much in terms of precision in the prediction.

As a result of this procedure a group of equations is obtained that indicate, for each variable, which four can best predict it. Because it is possible that the form and even the structure of these relations vary significantly for social aggregates whose socioeconomic status and styles of life are quite diverse, it is necessary to repeat the process as many times as there are detectable homogeneous aggregates. Thus, for example, it becomes intuitively obvious that the laws (equations of multiple regression in this case) governing evaluation of campesinos are of a different form than those that govern university professors.[31] As the emphasis in the analysis of this book lies more in comparison between groups than in the detailed study of each sample group, performing the calculation for only the six aggregates shown in Table 1.2 was considered adequate.

[30] The program is called *SLURP* and was developed by Professor K. Jones of Harvard University.

[31] We must remember that the equation of multiple regression, using matrix notation, is in the form

$$Y_i = \sum_j b_{ij} Y_{j+a},$$

where Y_i is the dependent variable; b_{ij} represents the slope of the independent variable being considered (N.GR. maintaining all the rest constant); Y_j are the independent variables; and a is the point of origin of the curve of regression (when $Y_j = 0$). The beta weights (B_{ij}) are a standardization of b_{ij} that allows comparison of variables measured in different units (years, bolivares, etc.) and can be obtained by "multiplying b_{ij} that is comparable by the ratio of standard deviations of the independent variables [noncontrolled] to those of the dependent variables." Mathematically,

$$B_{ij} = b_{ij} \frac{s_j}{s_i}.$$

"The beta weights indicate, therefore, the amount of change that should occur in the dependent variable in a standard unit of change in the independent variable, when all the rest remain constant." See Hubert M. Blalock, *Social Statistics* (New York: McGraw-Hill, 1960), pp. 343–346.

TABLE 1.2   Social Aggregates for Which Multiple Regression Analysis Was Done

High Socioeconomic Status		Medium Socioeconomic Status[a]		Low Socioeconomic Status	
Urban	Rural	High	Low	Urban	Rural
DMAKER	CATLER	GSTAFF	SMALIN	WORKEC	PEASAN
OILEXE	FARMER	LICEOS	SHOPOW	WORKEE	LANREF
INDEXC		PRIEST	SCHOOL	WORKEW	AGWORK
INDEXE		STUDEN	CLERKS		
INDEXW		COUNCL	COLLAR		
UNPROF		LABORL	MPLOIL		
COMEXC					

NOTE: The symbols used in this table are abbreviations of the complete names of the 24 sample groups analyzed in this study. See Appendix A.

[a] This group of social aggregates is divided into high and low rather than urban-rural because the middle class is mostly urban.

With the idea of clarifying the procedure followed, we present in a more detailed manner the case of urban groups of low socioeconomic status. Table 1.3 contains the matrix of beta weights, the quantity of change that can be expected to occur in each dependent variable (columns) for each unit of change that occurs in each independent variable (rows). Thus, for example, if one wishes to predict the level of satisfaction (SATISF) that these groups experience, it suffices to know how they evaluate their families (FAMILY), the educational system (EDUCAT), the economy (ECNOMY), and the level of their aspirations (WANTS) as these will account for approximately 61 percent of the variance, which is certainly more than one might expect to account for by looking at variables such as age, income, or years of education.

Once this matrix of interrelations is calculated, the next step is to identify the empirical subsystems, the real structure of the aggregate. This implies that one will differentiate the groups within which variables have more relation to one another than to variables of other groups. Various procedures exist for carrying out this type of analysis. The procedure chosen for this study is the so-called "cluster analysis." The medium is the method proposed by Alexander.[32] This procedure consists, in essence, of minimizing

[32] Christopher Alexander, *Notes on the Synthesis of Forms* (Cambridge, Mass.: Harvard University Press, 1964).

that which in information theory is known as "redundancy of information," and which can be expressed intuitively as the number of interconnections that, on separating a group of variables in two, are cut.[33]

The method presupposes (1) that the important element is the strength of the relation and therefore does not take into account its direction, and (2) that the input matrix is symmetrical (for example, the evaluation made by urban groups of low socioeconomic status of their country's international relations (FOREL) depends on the group's level of information (LEVINF) but not vice versa). We must therefore make the necessary transformations to convert it into an input acceptable for Alexander's program.

This was achieved by adding the absolute values of the symmetrical elements of the matrix and then dividing them into three.[34] The program of partitions first divides at random all the variables (48 in this case) into two groups. Then each resulting cluster is divided into two parts in an effort to minimize the redundancy of information (RED). The partitions of each resulting cluster continue successively until one arrives at a cluster of two variables. Figure 1.3 represents the tree of partitions which, however, reaches only the third of the five levels that the program worked out. Note how the redundancy of information decreases as the level descends. The relations between the sixteen resulting groups can be better appreciated in Table 1.4, which is simply the input matrix with variables reordered according to the degree of relation among them. Our interest is in determining whether these clusters form empirical subsystems that correspond to any of the families of concepts of the analytical plan presented in Figure 1.2.

Until now we have had only various clustered groups of variables which can be considered as nodules or parts of fuller subsystems. Consequently, in order to be able to identify these subsystems, it is necessary to rearrange

---

[33] The mathematical expression of the redundancy of information is

$$R = \frac{C - C \times N}{M(U - C)}$$

when C = number of unions cut,
N = existing unions, total number,
M = maximum number of unions cut, and
U = number of possible unions.

[34] The mean of symmetrical beta weights was able to be taken, but nevertheless it was decided to divide this into three to reduce the resulting value to two real numbers and thus facilitate the printing of the results on the console.

TABLE 1.3 Beta Weights Matrix for Urban Groups of Low Socioeconomic Status

Variables[a]	1	2	3	4	5	6	7	8	9	10	11	12	13	14	15	16
1 AGE					−0.01	−0.01										
2 OCPRGS	−0.94	0.10	0.45	0.93			0.53	0.69								
3 YRSEDU					0.68	0.71			0.12		0.14					
4 INCOME	1.14	0.11					0.26									
5 FATHED			1.17			−1.01										
6 EDUMOB			1.15		−0.93								0.58			
7 GENMOB		0.14	−0.14	0.35				0.57								
8 OCCMOB		0.10					0.38									
9 FAMILY											0.67					
10 BARRIO																
11 EDUCAT									0.17							
12 POLITY				0.10												
13 ECNOMY										0.14	0.27	0.09				0.16
14 CHURCH																
15 FOREL																
16 BUSNES																
17 PEASAN																
18 LABORL																
19 GOVOFF												0.07				0.16
20 JUDGES																
21 POLTCO																0.33
22 TEACHR																
23 TALKER														0.17		
24 PRIEST																
25 STUDEN																

26 SOLDIR														
27 POLICE														0.18
28 CITIZN										−0.31	−0.35			0.35
29 DK														
30 MASNED			0.10	0.11										
31 LEVINF					−0.15									0.62
32 WORDOM														
33 POLPAR											−0.19			0.41
34 OPTPES														0.19
35 POLEFF														0.23
36 NATION														
37 PROLEFF														
38 PRORIG						0.05								
39 URBANX						−0.07								
40 LOCALM														
41 RELIG													0.99	
42 RANGEV							−0.33						0.30	
43 INTERP														
44 COOP								0.27						
45 GETS	−0.60											1.11		
46 SATISF								1.42	−1.64			0.45		
47 SECULR	−0.40													
48 WANTS		0.22						0.21				−0.40		
Multiple R's	0.35	0.86	0.97	0.97	0.82	0.84	0.79	0.74	0.26	0.41	0.41	0.44	0.30	0.45

[a] Coding names are variables. For a complete name of each variable see Appendix A.

TABLE 1.3 (*Continued*)

Variables[a]	17	18	19	20	21	22	23	24	25	26	27	28	29	30	31	32
1 AGE																
2 OCPRGS					−0.75											
3 YRSEDU												0.10		0.38	0.19	
4 INCOME																
5 FATHED															0.15	
6 EDUMOB																
7 GENMOB																
8 OCCMOB																0.15
9 FAMILY																
10 BARRIO																
11 EDUCAT																
12 POLITY												−0.17				
13 ECNOMY																
14 CHURCH								0.14								
15 FOREL																
16 BUSNES				0.15		0.16				0.17						
17 PEASAN				0.27		0.15	0.12	0.33	0.17		0.14		−0.07			
18 LABORL					0.29		0.09			0.11	0.39					
19 GOVOFF		0.20	0.16	0.22	0.16					0.29	0.12					
20 JUDGES	0.14						0.23	0.16								
21 POLTCO		0.29	0.14						0.13							
22 TEACHR	0.15								0.24							
23 TALKER		0.15		0.28					0.15							
24 PRIEST	0.22															
25 STUDEN				0.15		0.10	0.12									

No.	Label	Values
26	SOLDIR	0.19
27	POLICE	0.19 0.31
28	CITIZN	0.24 0.35
29	DK	−0.17 −0.36 −0.56
30	MASNED	0.14 0.26
31	LEVINF	
32	WORDOM	0.11 0.20 0.22 0.23
33	POLPAR	
34	OPTPES	0.12
35	POLEFF	
36	NATION	−0.17
37	PROLEFF	−0.17
38	PRORIG	
39	URBANX	0.11
40	LOCALM	
41	RELIG	0.64
42	RANGEV	0.20
43	INTERP	
44	COOP	0.07
45	GETS	
46	SATISF	
47	SECULR	
48	WANTS	

TABLE 1.3 (Continued)

Variables[a]	33	34	35	36	37	38	39	40	41	42	43	44	45	46	47	48
1 AGE																
2 OCPRGS					0.27											
3 YRSEDU							0.21	0.06								
4 INCOME						−0.13					0.11	0.20				0.32
5 FATHED							0.14									
6 EDUMOB	0.09															
7 GENMOB																
8 OCCMOB							−0.10									
9 FAMILY												0.06		0.33		
10 BARRIO										−0.05						
11 EDUCAT																−0.07
12 POLITY	−0.11													−0.11		
13 ECNOMY									0.06			0.08	0.42	0.09		
14 CHURCH									0.11							
15 FOREL			0.04													
16 BUSNES								0.02								
17 PEASAN																
18 LABORL																
19 GOVOFF										−0.03						
20 JUDGES															0.04	
21 POLTCO																
22 TEACHR																
23 TALKER																
24 PRIEST									0.06				0.04			
25 STUDEN								−0.03								

		C1	C2	C3	C4	C5	C6	C7	C8	C9	C10	C11	C12	C13	C14
26	SOLDIR														
27	POLICE														
28	CITIZN														
29	DK	−0.35	−0.40	−0.20	−0.26	−0.28				−0.11					0.17
30	MASNED	0.14	0.14												
31	LEVINF	0.34	0.34	0.16					0.34						
32	WORDOM	0.36	0.34							0.09					
33	POLPAR	0.34								0.17					
34	OPTPES											0.14	0.10		
35	POLEFF	0.16													
36	NATION				0.25									0.75	
37	PROLEFF	0.18			0.39				0.17						
38	PRORIG			0.24											
39	URBANX														
40	LOCALM					−0.44	−0.29								
41	RELIG													−0.13	
42	RANGEV														
43	INTERP														
44	COOP	0.11													
45	GETS	0.14													
46	SATISF							−0.08						−0.23	
47	SECULR	0.23										0.21	−0.20		
48	WANTS														
Multiple R's		0.45	0.59	0.53	0.48	0.46	0.37	0.46	0.41	0.33	0.35	0.77	0.78	0.49	0.54

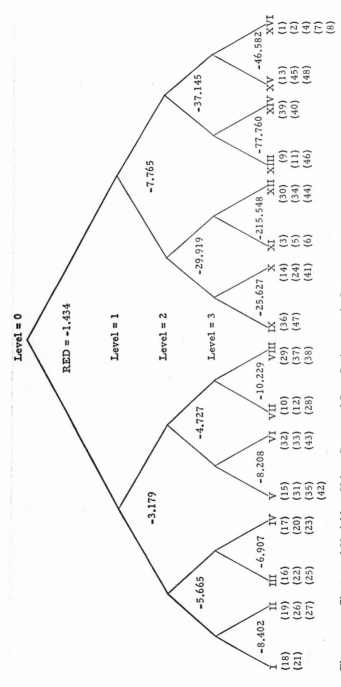

Figure 1.3   Clusters of Variables: Urban Groups of Low Socioeconomic Status

NOTE: The numbers refer to the variables that appear in Table 1.3, and RED is the redundancy of information.

TABLE 1.4   Reordered Matrix of Clusters of Figure 1.3

Number of Clusters																
VIII	0	4	0	0	2	0	0	0	0	0	0	0	1	1	1	0
IX	4	0	1	0	0	0	0	0	0	0	2	0	0	0	0	0
X	0	1	0	0	2	0	0	0	0	0	0	0	0	0	0	0
III	0	0	0	0	3	1	1	0	0	0	0	0	0	0	0	0
IV	2	0	2	3	0	2	2	0	0	0	0	0	0	0	0	0
I	0	0	0	1	2	0	3	0	2	0	0	0	0	0	0	0
II	0	0	0	1	2	3	0	0	0	0	0	0	0	0	0	0
XI	0	0	0	0	0	0	0	0	3	1	0	1	0	2	0	0
XVI	0	0	0	0	0	2	0	3	0	0	4	0	0	0	0	0
XIII	0	0	0	0	0	0	0	1	0	0	5	0	0	0	0	0
XV	0	2	0	0	0	0	0	0	4	5	0	0	0	1	0	0
XIV	0	0	0	0	0	0	0	1	0	0	0	0	0	0	0	0
VII	1	0	0	0	0	2	0	0	0	0	0	0	0	1	1	1
XII	1	0	0	0	0	0	0	2	0	0	1	0	1	0	0	1
V	1	0	0	0	0	0	0	0	0	0	0	0	1	0	0	3
VI	0	0	0	0	0	0	0	0	0	0	0	0	1	1	3	0

NOTE: See Figure 1.4.

them according to the degree of relation that exists among them. The best way to do so is to determine the strength of interconnections existing among clusters and then make a new cluster analysis. Table 1.4 is the input matrix showing the level of relation between each pair of clusters, reordered according to the strength of this relation. The figures contained in Table 1.4 are simply the mean of values calculated in the previous step, those indicating the relation between the variables interconnecting each pair of clusters. Figure 1.4 is another, perhaps clearer, way of representing the result of this last analysis. The lines connecting the clusters indicate the strength of the relation between them. With all this information we can proceed to test the hypothesis that there are empirical subsystems that correspond to families of concepts.

To test this hypothesis, let us suppose that each group of clusters is a random sample taken from the universe (A) of 48 variables. Because the number of variables of each type (B) in each sample of size (C) is known a priori, the number of variables (D) that are of type (B) can easily be determined. With these data we can estimate the exact probability, following the method of Fisher,[35] that the event under consideration (D) has occurred. Thus, for instance, the proof that the empirical subsystem W

[35] Blalock, *Social Statistics*, pp. 221–225.

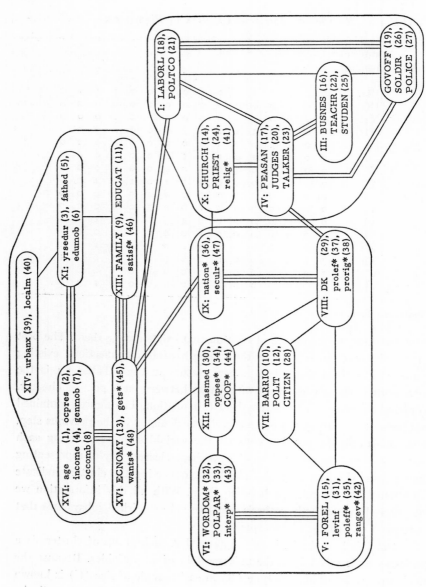

Figure 1.4 Empiricoconceptual Subsystems of Variables: Urban Groups of Low Socioeconomic Status

(Figure 1.4) corresponds to the conceptual family social location and experience of change (see Table 1.5) is the small probability (0.00006) that, if a sample of 16 variables is taken of a universe of 48, having a total of 12 variables of this type, 10 of them will be chosen at random. Following this procedure, we succeeded in identifying the other two empiricoconceptual subsystems that appear in Figure 1.4: mediating dispositions (Y) and evaluations (Z).

TABLE 1.5 *Urban Groups of Low Socioeconomic Status, Empiricoconceptual Subsystems*

| Subsystem | Total Variables ($A = 48$) | | | | |
	Number of Variables in each Type B	Size of Sample of Variables C	Size of Intersection of B and C D	Fisher Exact Test E	Area to the Right of E F
Social location and experience of change	12	16	10	0.00	1.00
Mediating dispositions	12	18	8	0.017	0.980
Evaluations	21	14	13	0.00	1.00

This proof was carried out for each of the six class aggregates presented in Table 1.2 with similar results although, as one would expect, minor variations occurred from group to group as to the specific variables that remained within each subsystem.

KEY TO FIGURE 1.4: *Social location* and *experience of change* variables are printed in lowercase letters.
  Mediating disposition variables are printed in lowercase letters followed by an asterisk.
  Evaluation variables are printed in capitals.
  Political capacity variables are printed in capitals followed by an asterisk.
  Each *small cluster* is circled and labeled by a roman numeral (see Table 1.4). The arabic number in parentheses following each variable is the number of the variable.
  Subsystems W, Y, and *Z* are indicated by the large circles enclosing the small clusters.
  The *straight lines* connecting small clusters (ranging from 1 to 5) correspond to the degrees of association as listed in Table 1.4. Associations rank from 0 to 5.

We can therefore assert that the analytical scheme, having been empirically backed up, constitutes an efficient guide for analysis of the data. Specifically (1) it indicates which variables to look at if we wish to predict the value of another variable, and (2) it has enormous value for an investigation oriented toward throwing light on a development policy. Thus, for example, to know that educational changes (such as those expressed in the educational level of individuals and their parents, and in educational mobility) are related to changes individuals undergo in age, prestige, income, and occupational and residential mobility is useful because all these factors influence primarily the evaluation individuals make of the economy, family, and the educational system. Furthermore, these evaluations, after all, are what most influence their achievements, aspirations, and level of satisfaction.

Nevertheless, we ought not to carry these conclusions beyond their proper limits. These relations were derived from the starting hypothesis that they were linear, and we know that this is a very rough approximation of reality. So we shall consider these results preliminary. The task that remains is to examine carefully the relations within and between clusters in order to determine their nature in a more qualitative way. In Chapters 4 through 8 the intent is to carry out this task. As stated earlier, an effort is made in Chapters 2 and 3 to construct, on the basis of norms established in the first part of the chapter, the historical frame that provides an interpretative context for the survey data. Chapter 9 contains a summary of the results and an indication of their implications for the political future of Venezuela. Finally, as mentioned before, Chapter 10 places the findings in a larger context and analyzes the dependency relationship between Latin America and the United States.

2   THE HISTORICAL PROCESS [1]

The panoramic view of Venezuelan social and political development presented in this chapter and the following one, in addition to furnishing the reader with the historical background necessary for interpreting later chapters, tries to answer, though necessarily in an incomplete way, two of the most important questions of the diagnostic approach: What has been the role of different social classes and strategic groups in Venezuelan social change? What historic elements are important in the present political culture? The political scientist is as much interested in the objective facts that the historian gathers as in the overall view that he presents. From the former it is possible to establish important lines of change and continuity: the regional distribution of different social strata (ethnic or occupational), changes in sources and distribution of power, and key points in the process of structural differentiation. The historian provides insights about how historic facts become implanted in the minds of individual citizens today, and how these facts come to shape the citizens' value orientations.

The recorded history of Venezuela goes back about four centuries but only in the past forty years has there been a sudden and violent acceleration of significant structural modifications. This does not mean, of course, that before 1926 there were no structural changes in the society. On the contrary, we shall see that the history of the country was one of permanent struggle, during the course of which new social groups emerged, grew, and disappeared. In this sense, the most important changes were the disappearance of slavery and of ethnic criteria for determining social strata and their replacement by class criteria.

[1] I would like to express my gratitude to Professor Germán Carrera Damas for his valuable criticisms and comments on this chapter.

From the time the conquistadores realized that El Dorado was not to be found in Venezuela until well into the first half of this century, the country was considered poor, with few resources. Nevertheless, historically, Venezuelans tended to feel that "from today's misery one looks to the golden utopian promise of tomorrow" [2] — an optimism about the future that has lasted up to our own time. Despite this optimism, the wealth that came from the discovery of oil was strange and unfamiliar to a country whose directing elite had considered land the most valuable social asset and whose nationalism did not go beyond a ritual veneration of the men who gave the country its independence. As a result, the elite of the country had neither the entrepreneurial drive nor a unifying spirit of nationalism directed toward the future. These conditions, deeply rooted in Venezuela's history, have hindered the economic and political development of the country.

Colonial Society

Venezuela at the time of its discovery by the Europeans was populated by indigenous tribes of differing degrees of technological advancement and complexity of social organization. The Timoto-Cuicas, inhabitants of the Andean zone, had the most complex culture; yet they had mastered only a few technical skills: in agriculture, they had developed terracing and irrigation; in production, they had learned to weave cotton and make garments of it. Although they had some military and clerical organization, they had built neither fortresses nor temples, in marked contrast to Mexico, for example,[3] which had developed a significant architecture. The simple level of the culture in Venezuela probably accounted for the fact that the Spanish colonizers who came there were few in number and relatively low in social status.[4]

[2] Mariano Picón Salas, "La aventura venezolana," *150 años de vida republicana (1811–1961)* (Caracas: Ediciones de la Presidencia de la República, 1963). For a characterization of the poverty of Venezuela, see Arturo Uslar Pietri, *Del hacer y deshacer de Venezuela* (Caracas: Publicaciones del Ateneo de Caracas, 1962), pp. 29–36.

[3] For a description of the different cultural areas, see Miguel Acosta Saignes, *Estudios de etnología antigua de Venezuela* (Caracas: Imprenta de la Universidad Central de Venezuela, 1961). See also Federico Brito Figueroa, *La estructura económica de Venezuela colonial* (Caracas: Imprenta de la Universidad Central de Venezuela, 1963), chap. 1.

[4] One Venezuelan historian who writes about the "anti-Spanish reaction that was prevalent among us at the time of Independence" says, "It is certain that among us [the conquistadores], there were no *Mayorazgos* nor *Grandes* of Spain; those who came were the *segundones* and notorious *hidalgos*." Mario Briceño-Iragorry, "Discurso de recepción como individuo de número de la Academia Nacional de la Historia,"

This combination of an almost neolithic culture and the social level of Spanish colonizers who entered the country profoundly influenced the social configuration of the colony. In spite of all the criteria of caste that were so deeply rooted in the normative orientations of the population, the Spanish colonizers in Venezuela, unlike those in other Latin American countries, were neither psychologically nor socially able to establish a rigid social structure. These conditions were probably also significant in the colonial authorities' failure to establish a well-developed bureaucracy that would have given political and administrative unity to the colony.

The statistics that historians have compiled imply a definition of what is considered relevant in historical analysis. Thus, population categories supply a definition of the groups that statisticians of the time, as well as the historians who report these statistics, consider keys to the understanding of the social structure. In this sense, the data presented in Table 2.1

TABLE 2.1   Changes in Key Groups
of the Venezuelan Social Structure:
Sixteenth, Seventeenth, and Nineteenth Centuries

	Middle of the Century		
Key Groups	Sixteenth	Seventeenth	Nineteenth
Total	*312,000*	*370,000*	*897,000*
Whites	2,000	30,000	180,000
Pardos	5,000	30,000	407,000
Negroes	5,000	30,000	150,000
Indians	300,000	280,000	160,000

SOURCE: Angel Rosemblat, cited by Federico Brito Figueroa, *La estructura social y demográfica de Venezuela colonial* (Caracas: Ediciones Historia, 1961).

may be understood as historically seasoned criteria, indicative of the important changes that have occurred in the ethnic composition of the population. One of these changes was the mixture of the different ethnic groups, as attested to by the fact that the group of pardos produced by the mixture of the whites with other ethnic groups grew as much as the white population itself. Nevertheless, this does not mean that there was no rigidity in the social system or that ethnic criteria were the only ones im-

Historia de la historiografía venezolana, G. Carrera Damas, ed. (Caracas: Imprenta de la Universidad Central de Venezuela, 1961), p. 64.

portant in the social system. In fact, economic relations were another key dimension for defining social class. Not only did relationships among the various ethnic strata take place in the political and social levels of colonial society; they took definite form from the economic sphere as well.

At the end of the colonial period the top of the economic pyramid consisted of the merchants and the landowners, primarily Spanish and white Venezuelans, respectively; the administrators and government officials, who were exclusively Spanish; and the high clergy, who were considered as powerful as, and sometimes more powerful than, the Crown. At the next lower level were the artisans, small tradesmen, and clerks (some of whom owned land), and the "marginal whites" or white subjects whose purity of blood was doubted.[5] Some pardos were in these occupational categories; others were day laborers, servants, and unskilled workers. The members of the last group, although legally free, were under the *de facto* economic domination of their employers. Most of the rest of the population worked in agriculture. This group included the different categories of Indians, freed slaves, and indigenous Venezuelans who held positions equivalent to indentured servants. Finally there were the slaves, a group composed principally of Negroes but also of some pardos and Indians.[6]

The strict legal norms that prescribed certain conduct for each ethnic stratum slowly lost their force as a consequence of the mixture of the ethnic groups, the relative prosperity that some of these groups obtained, and, in large measure, because of the political and administrative weaknesses of the colony.

An indication of this lack of political and administrative capacity is the fact that the Intendencia del Ejército y Real Hacienda was not created until 1776; the Capitanía General de Venezuela, not until one year later; and the Real Audiencia de Caracas, nine years after this. For a period of almost three hundred years there were no effective mechanisms for the centralization of the army, government income, political power, and the administration of justice. This situation, combined with the pattern of large landholding (*repartimientos* and *encomiendas*), hindered the growth of urban areas of any significant size and stimulated the formation of regional centers of power around a few landlords.[7]

---

[5] The civil and ecclesiastic authorities had various ways of investigating the purity of blood as far back as three or four generations.

[6] *Castas* was the term used to designate the pardos and other mixed groups during the colonial period.

[7] Politically and economically the most important provinces were Caracas, Maracaibo, Coro, Puerto Cabello, Mérida, Barinas, Cumaná, and Angostura.

The impact on the socioeconomic system of the introduction of Negro slaves into the Spanish colonies is one of the most debated aspects of Spanish-American history; of course, we cannot deal here with such a complex matter in full. However, we shall single out the cultural and economic factors that operated to rationalize the importation of slaves. In the first place, as Carrera Damas points out,

> In general, the notion seems to prevail that it was the rapid depopulation of the conquered lands and the inefficiency of the Indians as a labor force — which badly hampered the conquerors' profits — and therefore determined the importation of slaves. This gave origin to a productive business in which even the European kingdoms competed. Spanish pride, however, shielded itself in the fact that "no Spaniard was a Negro slaver." [8]

The institution of American slavery, south and north, was radically different in its origins from classical slavery, because the material use of the slave was as a commercial good of an expanding world capitalist system rather than as a product of the conquered lands.

A second factor, which increased the need to employ a slave labor force, was the Spaniard's contempt for manual labor:

> His [the Spaniard's] idea of manliness was the soldier; even the mystics and religious men ended up being "gentlemen in a divine style.". . . Thus, it should not come as a surprise that the giant efforts of Fray Bartolomé de las Casas to organize an agricultural colony in Cumaná failed because the agricultural workers he brought from Spain decided "to feel like gentlemen" and went away with the conquerors to steal.[9]

Although the combination of economic profit and ethnic prejudice made it possible for the Spaniards to reconcile slavery with their Christian faith, this very same faith, linked as it was to the missionary zeal for the Indians, served as an escape hatch for Spanish-American Christianity. The latter was colored by a certain ethical humanism and a moral idealism that, from early colonial times (in 1542 enslavement of the Indian was prohibited by Carlos V), induced the Spanish to protect the natives, even though this protection existed mainly on a formal ethical level.

All of these factors determined that slavery in Latin America would be quite different from classical Roman slavery. Therefore, the apparently

[8] Germán Carrera Damas, "La sociedad colonial: Formación y dinámica," mimeographed (Caracas: CENDES, January 1968), p. 13.

[9] Orlando Fals Borda, *La subversión en Colombia: El cambio social en la historia,* p. 79.

rapid increase of the Negro population, which Table 2.1 suggests, cannot be interpreted as the consolidation of the slave mode of production in the country; rather, it should be interpreted as another indicator of the consolidation of a colonial system linked to the more global process involved in the expansion of a world capitalist system.

The emergence of cacao estates during the seventeenth century in the hot coastal areas and low valleys of the country ensured that the Negroes, who were used as slaves on the haciendas, would be located principally in these areas. In addition to these changes in population distribution, however, the growing of cacao had other, perhaps more important consequences for the social structure. It consolidated the social system of the hacienda and, as a result, made the social stratification more rigid. It influenced as well the emergence of "courtly" aspirations in the estate owners who, in order to legitimize their new style of living, hastened to buy titles of nobility and to imitate the ways of the Spanish court. The members of this new class lived primarily in the cities of Caracas and Valencia. But even though the economy of the country depended primarily on cacao, the Venezuelan estates were never characterized by the social rigidity or the opulence of the Peruvian and Mexican haciendas.[10]

The features just described characterize the structural framework within which the social tensions leading to the rupture of colonial society were generated. In the first two decades of the eighteenth century there had been many severe revolts among the slave population; as a result there arose a nomadic group of rebellious Negroes who lived in the mountains.[11] There were two important consequences of these social movements. First, they were the expression of the social hostilities that had arisen among the rural masses — *free* Indians, day laborers, mulattoes, *free* Negroes, and so forth — who had been submitted to emancipated servitude by landlords; these slaveholders, without legally being owners, were able to submit these masses to forms of *extraeconomic* coercion because of their monopoly over the land, means of production, and political institutions in the urban centers.[12] Second, these revolts motivated the landlords to organize their own guards and patrols for the purpose of control. Both of

[10] By the eighteenth century, revenue from cacao constituted 75 percent of the value of Venezuela's exports. See Julio Cotler, "Visión panorámica del proceso histórico social de Venezuela," mimeographed (Caracas: CENDES, 1963), p. 6.

[11] By 1721, the number of these *cimarrones*, as they were called at the time, reached 20,000, or more than 10 percent of the total Negro population. From that time forward the Negro revolts increased in frequency and the number of slaves who took part also grew. See Brito Figueroa, *La estructura económica de Venezuela colonial*, pp. 350–361.

[12] Ibid., p. 359.

these consequences prepared the masses and the elite for later participation in the struggle for independence.

The political and administrative exclusiveness and the rigid commercial control imposed by Spain and strengthened by the operations of the Guipuzcoana Company (to which the Crown had granted commercial control) helped to sharpen the antagonism between the Spaniards and the Venezuelans and between the tradesmen and the landowners. It is difficult to determine the degree of overlap that existed among these social categories, but it may be said that the sector in which the conflicts were cumulative (Venezuelan landowners and Spanish tradesmen) was much larger than that which experienced cross-pressures (Venezuelan tradesmen and Spanish landowners).[13]

The conflict between the first two groups recurred continually as a consequence of the monopolistic policies imposed by the Guipuzcoana Company, culminating in 1749 with the revolt of Juan Francisco de León. This revolt, which lasted three years, resulted in the formation of an army of more than 8,000 men who, on one occasion, occupied Caracas and forced the governor to grant their requests — which they made "in the name of the nobility and the masses." [14] De León was finally defeated militarily and imprisoned, but his protest had one important consequence: the Venezuelans were given the opportunity to participate in the affairs of the Guipuzcoana Company. Naturally, this helped reduce the tensions between the conflicting groups, but it also marked the beginning of the end of Spanish administrative control.

Although the tensions between the Venezuelans and the Spanish lessened, and the loyalties of the former to the Crown were reaffirmed by increments in production, in exports, and in income that followed the policy of "Venezuelanization" of the Guipuzcoana Company, there was no corresponding lessening in the antagonism between producers and tradesmen. On the contrary, difficulties increased sharply because, in practice, the merchants effectively absorbed the profits the producers had expected to gain from the opportunity to trade with nations other than Spain. The underlying motives and the sharpness of the conflict may be seen easily in the report that was presented in 1797 by the Count of San Javier, Manuel Felipe de Tovar, Martín Jérez, and Martín de Herrera, "representing the estate owners of the province of Caracas," to the Consulate of Caracas:

[13] Ibid., pp. 278–284, and Eduardo Arcila Farías, *Economía colonial de Venezuela* (Mexico: Fondo de Cultura Económica, 1946), pp. 361–372.
[14] Arcila Farías, *Economía colonial de Venezuela*, p. 227.

Many problems having befallen us, we have patiently suffered the ruinous effects that were expected. The Intendencia, through neutral commerce, has secured a way to save us from hunger, nudity, and begging at least. But our tradesmen, who are more cruel than can be imagined, do everything in their power to snatch from us this only saving feature, that Heaven has given us. And when we see our opportunity being taken away, when we feel that our own tradesmen have been given the best channel to gain their interests with security and double effectiveness, no one should doubt that their opposition stems from an innate desire to keep the fruits of our labor subjugated, and laborers dominated and humiliated — from a desire so vehement and disordered that it blinds them and they do not recognize their true advantages. No one should doubt that it stems from pernicious anger, through which they see the prosperity of this province and its agricultural inhabitants. No one should doubt, finally, that it precedes and is a known effect of the old and continuous monopoly under which a few men with the title of tradesmen have oppressed these countries.[15]

Additional measures taken by the king expanded the conflict to other social groups and undermined the loyalty of the upper strata of the population. Among these measures perhaps the most significant was the law called "Gracias al Sacar," which gave the pardos the opportunity to rid themselves of this classification by payment of a certain sum. One Venezuelan writer describes the consequences of this policy:

Thanks to this law, which legally made him white, the pardo was able to enjoy certain privileges, among which was that the women were able to use parasols on the street and have pews in the church — things which at that time had decisive importance. In addition, pardos were able to hold certain offices and perform certain functions that customarily had been closed to them. Some saw in this a kind of reduction of their privileges. Therefore it influenced the upper classes' alienation from the king and their regarding the royal authority with hostility; but, on the other hand, it helped the king enjoy popular prestige with the masses. This is one of the causes that helps explain the curious phenomenon of the conduct of the Venezuelan masses at the outbreak of the wars for independence. The majority were loyal to the Crown and only later adopted the cause of independence.[16]

In summary, at the end of the eighteenth century Venezuela was going through a period in which the existing social order was crumbling. To this situation were attached external ideological influences to give political expression to the conflicts. Thus, the exclusion of the white Venezuelans from political decision making had undermined their loyalty to Spain and

[15] Cited by Brito Figueroa, *La estructura económica de Venezuela colonial,* pp. 389–391.
[16] Uslar Pietri, *Del hacer y deshacer de Venezuela,* pp. 47–48.

to the established norms. This alienation was reinforced by the fact that among themselves they had formed an important nucleus of well-educated persons who, in their reading and European travels, had encountered the ideology that had inspired the French and North American revolutions. This ideological articulation of their own aspirations made them desire even more to participate in political decision making. When this was denied them, their discontent with the colonial government was strengthened, and thus was closed the circle that finally brought them to their struggle for emancipation from Spain, affirming the sense of national identity generated in the process.

The War Period

One should not conclude, however, that because different social levels were suddenly dragged into an armed struggle for the emancipation of their territory, these social levels acquired a national conscience. On the contrary, if the period between 1810 and 1830 is seen as the culmination of the crises of colonial society, it follows that in such a period all tensions generated during its formation should emerge.[17] Thus, if it is true that the principal aspect of the struggle was criollos against Spaniards, one should not forget that tensions among pardos, slaves, and criollos could permit a concerted and common effort only when, on the one side, the criollos gave definitive signs of abandoning their slaveholding and other discriminatory inclinations and, on the other side, the mass of the population was convinced that the Spaniards wanted only the return of the former regime. It was unrealistic of the patriots of the first republic (1810–1812) to expect popular support for their cause when at the same time they passed measures such as restricted suffrage (*sufragio censitario*), the Rule of the Llanos (which established a system of almost forced labor for the pardos), and reestablishment of the national guard and patrols to control and repress the slaves.

In the following years (1812–1815) the critical internal factors were

[17] In this tight summary of Venezuelan history, we can hope only to point out what, according to our criteria, were the two most important social processes that were defined in the period between 1810 and 1830: first, the articulation, although temporary, of the interests of two opposing but Venezuelan classes, criollos and pardos; second, the role of provincialism in the definition of the national consciousness. Other social processes as well as the military campaigns are better known; therefore we make no attempt to summarize them here. Finally, it should be acknowledged that this section closely follows Professor Germán Carrera Damas's approach. See Carrera Damas, "La sociedad colonial," sec. 4.

defined and demarcated. However, at the end of this time the interests of the criollos and the popular masses were still in opposition. Not until the period between 1815 and 1821 did these interests merge as a result of two conditions: (1) the massive desertion of the popular base of the formerly successful Boves and Morales army, because of the repressive elements of Morillo's pacification policy; and (2) both the criollos' abandonment of their former slave policies and the net effects of their new policy of persuading the slaves that their basic condition would indeed change (decree of June 1816) and the lessening of discriminatory treatment of the pardos by allowing them to be incorporated into the upper ranks of the liberation army. For the first time, then, the Venezuelan army became a truly popular army not only in its social composition but also in its military tactics.

This articulation of interests, however, proved to last only as long as the need to maintain a fighting army. Once the armed struggle was over, the expected redistribution of land never took place, and the criollos, with a few exceptions such as José Antonio Páez, grabbed all the positions of economic and political power.

Unlike the definition of classes, the other important social processes, such as provincial and federalist drives, remained latent throughout the war period. Federalism, though an important issue in the first decade of the nineteenth century, was covert, only to reappear later with unusual strength, linked to the drive to secede from Gran Colombia and, in the second half of the century, during the process that led to the Federal War. The secessionist tendencies of the Venezuelans are better understood in light of the fact that, in the formation of Gran Colombia, the most important provinces of Venezuela were not represented. Caracas, Maracaibo, Coro, and Barquisimeto had been under the control of the Spaniards since 1814 and therefore could not be incorporated. But once independence was won, these provinces made certain demands that led to a crisis of participation. The end result was a negative definition (by separation) of a national consciousness. On the ashes of Gran Colombia a new and difficult process of positive definition of the national consciousness began.

The Republic until 1900

The Venezuelan political situation between 1830 and the end of the century may be summarized by the famous sentence of one of its presidents, Guzmán Blanco: "The country is like a dry hide, you step on it on one end and it pops up on the other." It is true that between 1830 and 1845 there was a period of relative peace; however, one Venezuelan historian points out that between 1830 and 1900 there were "39 significant revolutions and 127 minor revolts; in total, 166 revolts, which together lasted 8,847 days."[18] Between the years 1858 and 1899 alone there were 418 battles in the country, that is, an average of 10 per year.[19] The characterization that Gil Fortoul gives the forms of government during this period helps to clarify this panorama of political instability: "From 1830 to 1861 the government was an oligarchy; it was both dictatorial and anarchic from 1861 to 1863; during the Federation, a military anarchy, and after that alternatively autocratic and eclectic."[20]

How can we reconcile these facts with the glorious struggle for independence? How is it possible that the "superheroes" who gave the call for liberty throughout South America were not able to put their country in order when the struggle was finished? The reason for asking these questions is not to embarrass the Venezuelan historians who have written about these "heroes" but to clarify one basic fact: The economic and social structure of the country changed very little as a result of the wars for independence. In the first place, the regional distribution of power was maintained, though it became concentrated in the hands of military landlords. Some of them had land before independence; others took it from the royalists or received it from the government; and still others, through a series of perhaps questionable maneuvers, dispossessed ex-soldiers of the lands they had been given for their services in the war. The system of slavery was maintained until 1854; and once the war had ended in the Department of Venezuela, civil power remained in the hands of the Mantuano revolutionaries of 1810, none of whom — because of the administrative exclusiveness of the Crown — had had any governing experience. On the whole, then, the social structure remained very much the same. Obviously there were important changes in the Constitution and in the legal system in general; nevertheless, these quickly became dead letters.

After 1826 the disputes between the civil government in Caracas and General Páez became increasingly important. General Páez had been one

[18] Antonio Arraiz, cited by Juan Liscano, "Aspectos de la vida social y política de Venezuela," *150 años de vida republicana (1811–1961)*, p. 191.
[19] Armando Córdova and Manuel Felipe Garaicochea, "Inversiones extranjeras y desarrollo económico, primera parte," mimeographed (Caracas: Publicaciones del Instituto de Investigaciones de la Facultad de Economía, 1966), p. 47.
[20] José Gil Fortoul, *Historia constitucional de Venezuela*, vol. 2, 5th ed. (Caracas: Ediciones Sales, 1964), p. 319.

of the major figures during the wars for independence. The tensions between Páez and the other two military commanders (Mariño in Occidente
and Bermúdez in Oriente) also heightened to such an extent that the
chief military commander (General Carlos Soublette) had occasion to write
to Bolívar: "I regret that you are so far away at this time, and I am
afraid that we are becoming involved in an increasingly worsening situation.
You leave me in Venezuela, and you know that I cannot manage this world.
To lighten my cares there remain with me, Páez, and Mariño, with great
military commands, independent of each other and subject to God alone,
because you have told me nothing." [21]

The third and final element in this combination of political tensions was
the desire for separation (from Gran Colombia) that some influential persons of Caracas harbored because of the dominance of Bogotá in the central government. The loyalty of Páez to Bogotá contributed to his bad
relationships with the city and *intendencia* of Caracas. Thus at the end of
1825, Páez, against the wishes of the city and not without causing ill will,
issued a statement concerning the recruitment policy of the central government in Bogotá. The city council of Caracas complained to the House of
Representatives and the Senate, and as a result Páez was relieved of his
duties. However, his loyalties to Gran Colombia were apparently not very
strong, for, encouraged by support from his home city of Valencia and
other municipalities, he declared himself in rebellion against the government in Bogotá. The municipality of Caracas, which "had caused the problem, then hastened to name him commander general. The explanation for
this apparently contradictory behavior is that Páez, after denying the
authority of Bogotá, identified with the interests of the Venezuelan separa-
tists, who, in turn, saw in him the military figure they needed to take such
a consequential step." [22] Thus, civil power was subordinated to military
force and prestige; this situation continued in the country during almost
all of the next 150 years.

Páez, in spite of his great prestige, was not capable of reconcentrating his
power on a national scale, even though some measures were taken toward
this end. Laws passed in 1830 and 1836 created a national militia. In
principle, all male citizens between the ages of eighteen and forty-five were
to serve in the army; however, most of the recruits were from the lower
classes, and the army was not present in some regions. Nor was the mili-

---

[21] Ibid., vol. 1, p. 451.
[22] J. M. Siso Martínez, "Ciento cincuenta años de vida republicana," *150 años de vida republicana (1811–1961)*, p. 98.

tary hierarchical organization adequate. As a consequence, any regional leader was able to do his own recruiting and form his own army to fight the central government. Table 2.2 traces the successive regional distributions of power in the Venezuelan political process from 1830 to 1958.

TABLE 2.2   The Regional Nature of Venezuelan Politics

Regional Source of Power	Caudillo	Period
Llanos[a]	Páez	1830–1839 and 1861–1863
Eastern area	Monagas	1843–1855 and 1868–1869
Coro[b]	Falcón	1863–1868
Andes[c]	Castro	1899–1908
	Gómez	1908–1936
	López Contreras	1936–1940
	Medina Angarita	1940–1945
	Pérez Jiménez	1948–1958

[a] Llanos indicates the plains area.
[b] Coro is a province.
[c] Andes refers to the Andean mountain region.

As each successive regional group took over central power, the leveling process in social relations was accelerated. The *llaneros,* for example, had an equalitarian tradition dating back to colonial times; when they penetrated the most exclusive circles of the oligarchies of Caracas and Valencia, their attitudes helped to reaffirm *de facto* the leveling tendencies of the independence movement. Later, the freeing of the slaves, the frequent battles, and especially the War of the Federation, which can be interpreted as crises of equality, helped strengthen tendencies that were, after all, inherent in Venezuelan history. The colonial past, although influenced by criteria of caste, was never characterized by the rigid social stratification that would have evolved if the country had been settled heavily by Spanish nobility. The complex interactions of all these forces created in the Venezuelan the predisposition, later reinforced by the rapid economic growth of the past forty years, to view his society as open, an important characteristic of a modern orientation toward the nation.

The most significant aspect of regional dispersion was its consequences for the formation of the Venezuelans' orientation toward their nation. The regional factor was operative in their conception of political and administrative limits, the emotions that the independence wars awakened in them, and also the degree to which they had internalized a combination of social values such as secularism, civic responsibility, the open society, and the acceptance of the power of the state in diverse areas of social life.[23]

Thus, a nation that in the course of thirty years had changed its loyalties from the Spanish Crown to the superstate of Gran Colombia and then to the Department of Venezuela necessarily experienced much confusion with respect to its feeling of identification, and as a result Venezuela became plagued by internal divisions. Perhaps the most natural reaction in this situation was to strengthen local loyalties as the only road to salvation before a sense of national identity could be attained. The constant political struggles that characterized the remaining years of the nineteenth century without doubt have their roots in the delayed formation of a national conscience that could serve as a base from which to project the attainments of the past.[24] In other words, it became impossible to see the state as the supreme social value. Instead, there developed an almost exclusively affective attitude toward the nation, an attitude that fosters a kind of patriotism that, after sanctification through the course of time, becomes a kind of emotional but neither practical nor productive superpatriotism.

The same factor was operative in delaying the crystallization and effective functioning of Venezuela's traditional secular tendencies. The 1830 constitution, though formulated by the conservative oligarchy, affirmed the supremacy of the state over the Catholic Church. This incited a dispute between the Venezuelan clergy — headed by the archbishops of Caracas, Mérida, and Guayana — and the government. These archbishops were exiled, but not until 1841 did the new archbishop accept the prerogatives of civil power. As Gil Fortoul notes,

> The vigilance with which successive governments maintained the right of patronage saved the State from clerical reactions that had occurred in other American republics, and maintaining the Catholic Church within a permanent spiritual jurisdiction, assured the religious freedom that Venezuelan citizens have always enjoyed — a freedom which helps them achieve, without disturbance or conflict, the complete and definitive separation of the State and the Church.[25]

[23] For an extensive explanation of this concept, see Silva Michelena, *SRSP,* chap. 3.
[24] Germán Carrera Damas, "La conciencia nacional como meta," in Elena Hochman, ed., *Venezuela Primero* (Caracas: Imprenta de la Universidad Central de Venezuela, 1963).
[25] The oath to which the prelates had to swear, and which was the center of the conflict, is as follows: "I . . . Archbishop or Bishop of . . . , swear that I shall never consider annulled, either directly or indirectly, nor in any way affected the oath of obedience to the Constitution, the Laws, and the Government of the Republic to which I have sworn before my presentation to His Holiness, by my oath of obedience to the Vatican to which I had to swear at the time of my consecration,

Although the conflicts between the Church and the state never reached proportions equal to those in other American countries, later accounts reveal that conflicts for supremacy between these two powers were always latent and occasionally surfaced, creating delicate situations for one or the other institution. Such cumulative tensions lay behind the conflict between the government of Guzmán Blanco and the Church, which culminated with the closing of convents and seminaries, the establishment of civil registry and marriage, and other measures that tended more effectively to concentrate power in the hands of the state. As a result the balance definitively swung toward civil power. But as will be seen, in the substrata of Venezuelan political culture there is still a latent religious orientation in the sense that the Church has retained certain powers that in most modern nations are reserved to the state.

Let us focus our attention now on the economic characteristics of the society. It is as futile to try to establish a one-to-one correlation between economic facts and political and social facts as it is to deny any relationship between them. We have already noted the significant changes resulting from the emergence of cacao estates not only in the structure and distribution of the population but also in the social and political role of the different social strata that, together with other factors already mentioned, led to the wars of independence. Historians have pointed repeatedly to the influence of the cattle industry in the formation of a very important social type in Venezuela: the *llanero*. But a given product and its production and export curve are not always the independent variable. The disappearance of tobacco, for example, was occasioned more by the administrative weakness and incapacity of the governing elite in the newly constituted Venezuelan Republic than by the saturation of the foreign market. Venezuelan tobacco (*barinas*) was considered to be of very high quality in Europe, where it had had a secure market since the mid-seventeenth century. For this reason, as soon as the war was over, Simón Bolívar proposed a subsidy aimed at restoring and exceeding previous levels of production. The income resulting from these exports was to be used exclusively to pay the foreign debt that had been incurred to finance the war. And, indeed, production increased rapidly, but the funds were not destined to be allocated as Bolívar had planned; instead, they were squandered or distributed among military commanders. By 1832 the governing officials had lost all interest in the plan as such and withdrew the subsidy. In consequence the tobacco yield

nor for any later action for whatever motive. May God help me." Gil Fortoul, *Historia constitucional de Venezuela*, vol. 2, p. 60.

descended from 22,000 *quintales* in 1820 to 1,200 *quintales* in 1840 and almost disappeared in succeeding years.[26]

The history of the national bank provides another example of the lack of centralization of power and of the absence of institutional stability and coherent policy. In 1830 a law was passed creating a national bank, but it was never actually established. Between 1830 and 1890 no less than seven private banks were established, of which only one remains today. Not until 1939 was the Banco Central, which has responsibility for printing currency, created. Until that time each bank issued its own bank notes.[27]

In other cases, as in that of the substitution of coffee for cacao as a principal export product, a complex combination of external and internal factors intervened. At the end of the seventeenth century the production and export of cacao had reached a peak as a consequence of the elimination of the privileges of the Guipuzcoana Company and the free trade provisions of 1789.[28] With the start of the wars for independence, however, access to markets diminished because of the shortage of ships; this gave the advantage to coffee because it could be stored conveniently (it does not spoil easily) at a time when the world demand for this product was increasing. When the wars ended and new lands could be opened to production, the cultivation of coffee spread, especially in the Andean region. The residents of the *llanos,* who had been living in poverty, migrated to the Andean coffee-growing regions, thus giving these regions greater demographic importance than they had enjoyed before. The population shift also created a relatively prosperous social group from which Cipriano Castro emerged. He, like many other youths of his region, class, and time, was educated in the more or less liberal ideas of the schools of Barranquilla (Colombia).

By the end of the nineteenth century the price of coffee in the world market had decreased. This economic stress added to the degeneration of national politics as purposeless governments came to power through coups or farcical elections following the "illustrious" dictatorship of Guzmán Blanco. Castro, of whom it has been said that he reached power by "defeat

[26] Eduardo Arcila Farías, "Evolución de la economía en Venezuela," *Venezuela independiente* (Caracas: Fundación Mendoza, Editorial Sucre, 1962), p. 361. "The income from tobacco, which should have been used to repay foreign debts, was used in very different ways. The military officers considered themselves sufficiently powerful to disregard orders, and they often forcefully took the funds from tobacco administrators. The officials responsible for this income were defenseless to resist this military pressure."

[27] Ibid., p. 397.

[28] Arcila Farías, *Economía colonial de Venezuela,* pp. 254–270.

after defeat," was only the first of a series of Andean caudillos who governed the country almost up to the present.[29]

At the beginning of this century Venezuela could be described as typically underdeveloped. It was essentially a one-product economy from whose export the country derived the major part of its income. Approximately 85 percent of the work force was involved in agriculture, and the per capita rate of growth of the economy was almost stationary (0.3 percent), as it had been since the beginning of the republic's life and as it continued to be during the first quarter of the twentieth century.[30]

Because the economic route was closed, the only remaining road to upward social mobility was through participation in armed bands or political revolts, for education continued to be the privilege of a very small elite. Even though a central government existed nominally, its power was challenged permanently by various regional caudillos who periodically succeeded in overthrowing it. Cultural power — exercised by the intellectuals and the newspapers — was strictly controlled by the central government or by caudillos who aspired to power. Although the legislation to create an army dated from early times, the armed forces were always factional, never national, in character. Finally, the existing political parties, like the government itself, never penetrated the masses and never became more than semiprogrammatic. This was the situation in Venezuela when the Minister of War, General Juan Vicente Gómez, gained control in 1908.

[29] Domingo Alberto Rangel, *Los andinos en el poder* (Mérida: Talleres Gráficos Universitarios, 1965).

[30] Lecture by Dr. Bernardo Ferrán at the Center for Development Studies (CENDES), Universidad Central de Venezuela, 1962.

3   THE TWENTIETH CENTURY

National Concentration of Power

The dictator Juan Vicente Gómez ruled Venezuela longer than any other in its history (1908–1936). The sources of his power were essentially the same as those of his predecessors: the army, the latifundio, and the personal qualities that distinguished him as an ambitious caudillo. In spite of the imprisonments, exiles, and revolts that occurred during this period, his rule was undoubtedly the most politically stable that the country had experienced since 1800. It is not without justification that his eulogists proclaimed Gómez as the man who had succeeded in imposing "peace and order" on the country.

How did this uncultured man successfully eliminate regional leaders and effectively concentrate power in his own hands? One of the most important factors was his ability to enlarge his bases of power and make them more effective. To accomplish this he took advantage of the discovery and exploitation of oil, a new export product that, fortunately, substituted for the declining exports of coffee and cacao. This combination of an agrarian-based dictatorship in a country with one of the most technologically and organizationally advanced foreign industries was a determining factor in the later development of Venezuela.

Gómez, on assuming power, enjoyed the general approval and support of the population, whereas Castro's administration, in addition to its general disorder, had been faced with the problem of a diminishing national income because of the general crisis in agricultural production and, more specifically, the decrease in coffee production. The price of coffee declined notably in 1903, but it had been decreasing erratically since the end of the

50

nineteenth century when Andean rulers had gained power.[1] By 1908 Castro's government also had earned the antagonism of several foreign powers, thus culminating a process that had begun in the second year of his administration. In 1900 he had ordered the imprisonment of certain financiers who had dared to protest his fiscal measures. This action created a panic among the bankers. Apparently behind Castro's policy was his desire for revenge against those who, months before, had refused to subscribe to a government loan. After the imprisonments a revolution was organized and directed by one of the bankers who had help not only from certain foreign companies but also from a heterogeneous coalition of old and new regional leaders who wanted to gain control of the government. A Venezuelan historian notes,

> The groups cannot be more significant. Liberals of all factions, *guzmancistas, crespistas,* autonomists, and traditional conservatives, make up this fusion. . . . Those from the east are under the command of Domingo Monagas, Nicolás Rolando, and Horacio and Alejandro Ducharne; those from the central part of the country are under Hernández Ron, Crespo Torres, Blanco Fombona, and Ortega Martínez; those from Guayana are led by Zoila Vidal, "El Caribe"; the Andeans, by Juan Pablo and Manuel Peñalosa; and those from Coro, by Gregorio Riera and Amabile Solagnie. And there are many minor commanders who aspire to top posts in this new war.[2]

In spite of the fact that his forces completely defeated the insurgents, Castro did not bother to consolidate his power. Rather, he repeated his earlier pattern in office: He surrounded himself with a central oligarchy whose members knew how to take advantage of his Bacchic weaknesses. This move, in turn, created problems for him among his own group of Andeans, who felt that their leader was being unduly influenced by the very same people against whom they had fought.

Shortly afterward Venezuela was blockaded by German, English, and Italian ships; these countries demanded payment of debts approximately equivalent to two-thirds of the Venezuelan fiscal income.[3] The president issued a proclamation appealing to Venezuelan nationalism and received some fervent responses in the principal cities, but the movement lost momentum when the United States, aided by pressure from other Latin

[1] See Eduardo Arcila Farías, "Evolución de la economía en Venezuela," pp. 417–418; also Appendix C.1.
[2] J. M. Siso Martínez, "Ciento cincuenta años de vida republicana," p. 132.
[3] The foreign debt was 21,421,798 bolivares. Ibid., p. 133. The fiscal income in 1901–1902 was 31,650,000 bolivares. Arcila Farías, "Evolución de la economía en Venezuela," p. 411.

American countries, persuaded Venezuela to submit the matter to arbitration. In 1904 a decision favorable to the European powers was announced; but even this did not mobilize effective nationalistic feelings among Venezuelan citizens. Four years later the United States itself, together with France and Holland, was to be involved in payment claims against Castro. The relative apathy demonstrated by Venezuelans at that time, in the face of possible foreign conflicts, resulted not only from the lack of crystallization of the national conscience but also from the weakness of the central government.[4] This apathy toward the nation made it possible in 1899 for Venezuela — represented by a judge of the Supreme Court of the United States — to accept a decision that gave Great Britain rights to a large part of Guayana and, later, to cede La Guajira (part of Venezuelan territory) to Colombia without significant protest from any part of the population.

For all of these reasons, signs of general delight were shown when France cooperated with Gómez to prevent Castro — who had been having health treatments in Europe — from reentering Venezuela. There was no opposition when Gómez proceeded to open the country to foreign oil companies, which for some time had been operating in the country through Venezuelan figureheads. As a result, foreign companies (principally Shell and Standard Oil) were able to intensify their exploitation of oil. These companies gave only small benefits to the country, but these benefits were sufficient to allow the newly "elected" constitutional president (1910) to consolidate his power. From this time forward, foreign capital became an increasingly powerful economic and political force in Venezuela.[5]

Gómez brought about this central concentration of power with considerable efficiency. He put the land of the central valleys under his own control or under that of his friends; thus he eliminated possible or real enemies of the central oligarchy. In this task, and in the management of his farms, he was aided by the formation of a regular army that was organized on the Prussian model.[6] The establishment of a central staff with permanent regional commands allowed Gómez to control the country militarily to an extent that had never been possible before. The army also offered his com-

---

[4] During the nineteenth century Venezuela was involved in various international disputes, first with *la Nueva Granada,* and then with Europe and North America. In no case was a national protest or sentiment expressed that exceeded a few resounding words pronounced in the isolated halls of Congress. See José Gil Fortoul, *Historia constitucional de Venezuela,* vol. 2, chap. 5.

[5] Rómulo Betancourt, *Venezuela: Política y petroleo* (Mexico: Fondo de Cultura Económica, 1956). See especially chaps. 1 and 2.

[6] A Chilean officer was brought to the country to help with this task. By that time the Chilean army already had been organized on the Prussian model.

patriots of Tachira a "natural" path to social advancement, thus guaranteeing their loyalty.[7]

New sources of income provided the dictator with the necessary funds to consolidate his power in the short run; at the same time, however, conditions were created that would, in the long run, destroy Gómez's traditional bases of power and the relationships among the various social classes. This matter is important enough to merit a more detailed consideration.

Parallel to the process of political concentration just described, the economic expansion generated by the exploitation of oil aided the integration and strengthening of the internal market. This economic development was possible not only because the circulation of money increased but also because new channels of communication developed. Both of these factors, in turn, facilitated national political control. Government expansion of transportation and public works had another important effect: It took laborers away from agriculture.

Venezuelan agriculturalists initially had succeeded in satisfying growth in internal demand by using idle lands more extensively and by taking advantage of disguised unemployment. Soon, however, the situation worsened, because the prevailing agricultural structure offered no innovative solutions (a problem reinforced by the semifeudal system of government) and because the agricultural surpluses were controlled by commercial exporters (a situation that had existed since colonial times).[8] Landowners were negatively affected by the exodus of agricultural labor, and in 1926 they demanded that the government halt public works programs so that laborers would return to the fields.[9] This action indicates that the attitudes of the Venezuelan landowners were nearer those of their colonial ancestors — who on the eve of independence and in the face of this same kind of labor exodus had asked the Spanish authorities to take measures to force workers to return to the farms — than to those few of their contemporaries who decided to intensify their cultivation through the use of capital.[10]

This situation, added to the demand for land in urban areas and the investments in the infrastructure, raised the price of land and increased the opportunity cost of agricultural production. The increasing fluctuation

[7] See Domingo Alberto Rangel, *Los andinos en el poder,* especially chaps. 10 and 11.
[8] See Armando Córdova and M. F. Garaicochea, "Inversiones extranjeras y desarrollo económico, primera parte," pp. 58–59.
[9] U.S. Department of Commerce, *Commerce Yearbook, 1926.* Cited by Córdova and Garaicochea, ibid., p. 30.
[10] Federico Brito Figueroa, *La estructura económica de Venezuela colonial,* pp. 391–392.

in the world price of coffee acted as another depressing factor. Although the government tried to help resolve this crisis by extending credit through the Banco Agrícola, this only aggravated the problem of absentee ownership, for recipients of this credit used it to establish themselves permanently in the cities. This, then, is the paradox: When the most typically *latifundista* government is in power, and when the traditional bases of power are most significant, the landowning class loses its effective power and prestige.

The merchants, however, did not suffer from the decline in agricultural production. They rapidly transformed themselves from agricultural exporters into importers of manufactured products from economically more advanced countries, a transformation that did not require the development of new attitudes or abilities. The capital they accumulated as a result of their activities in finance, imports, exports, and distribution of both foreign and domestic products was used for urban land speculation, investment in the stock market in New York, or simply for pleasure trips to Europe. The entrepreneurs needed for the development of national industry would not emerge from this class either.

The economic growth generated by petroleum increased the need for broader distribution facilities for both domestic and foreign products. Thus, there appeared a group of small businessmen in the relatively few cities of the country. The growth of the petroleum industry was, of course, more beneficial to some persons than to others. Those who did not benefit had no choice but to use local products; consequently, the artisan class also increased notably. These precapitalist producers never were successful enough, however, to create national industries whose products could compete with imported goods. Those who did establish industries usually followed traditional production methods.[11]

Among the groups who benefited directly from the economic expansion were, of course, the employees of the oil companies. As may be seen in Table 3.1, their number was small, but their strategic power was obvious, as their 1936 general strike for more benefits demonstrated.[12] Because of this kind of aggressiveness, and also because of the nature of the industry itself, petroleum employees succeeded in obtaining salaries higher than those paid in any other sector of the economy. But the other effect of this

[11] Córdova and Garaicochea, "Inversiones extranjeras," pp. 63–65. Córdova emphasizes this point and mentions an interesting law of correspondence between the development of productive forces and the pattern of consumption.

[12] Rodolfo Quintero, "Las bases económicas y sociales de una aristocracia obrera en Venezuela," *Economía y ciencias sociales*, vol. 5, no. 2 (April–June 1963), p. 95.

TABLE *3.1* Distribution of the Labor Force by Economic Sector: Venezuela, 1920–1968 (thousands of persons)

Sector	1920[a] N	%	1936[b] N	%	1950[b] N	%	1958[b] N	%	1968[c] N	%
Petroleum	2.0	0.3	13.8	1.2	42.7	2.7	44.3	2.1	35	1.2
Mining	—		1.6	0.2	5.7	0.3	11.5	0.5	12	0.4
Industry	20.0	3.1	51.0	4.7	92.6	5.8	155.8	7.3	} 445	15.4
Crafts	35.6	5.6	96.6	9.0	114.3	7.1	99.3	4.7		
Commerce	51.1	8.0	64.3	6.0	149.7	9.4	236.7	11.0	396	13.7
Construction	8.0	1.3	24.4	2.3	91.1	5.7	179.6	8.3	199	6.9
Transportation	16.0	2.5	25.0	2.3	52.3	3.3	82.5	3.9	152	5.3
Electricity and water	—		—		5.0	0.3	10.5	0.5	41	1.4
Public services	13.4	2.1	56.2	4.0	113.3	7.1	173.2	8.1		
Domestic services	35.0	5.5	108.3	10.0	149.4	9.3	193.0	9.0	} 799	27.6
Others	—		15.4	1.4	79.1	4.9	132.1	6.2		
Agriculture	437.0	71.6	625.0	57.9	704.7	44.1	824.4	38.4	813	28.1
Total	638.6		1,081.6		1,598.9		2,142.9		2,892	

NOTE: The unemployed are excluded. The unemployment rates for other years are as follows:

Year	1951	1959	1962	1968
Thousands of persons	127	251	374	219
Percentage of the work force	6.8	10.5	14.4	7.0

SOURCES:
[a] Córdova and Garaicochea, "Inversiones extranjeras," pp. 52 and 56.
[b] Armando Córdova, "Consideraciones acerca del tipo de desarollo alcanzado por la economía venezolana," *Economia y ciencias sociales*, vol. 5, no. 2 (April–June 1963), p. 44.
[c] *Venezuela, Plan de la Nación 1966–1968, CORDIPLAN.*

demonstration was that salaries in all sectors increased to levels that did not correspond to real productivity.

The small number of oil company employees suggests that there were other sectors of the economy that also absorbed the agricultural workers, landowners, and small merchants who migrated to the cities. Many of the women entered domestic service, and most of the men became employed in the lowest ranks of public administration (janitors and so forth); there were few who were able to enter the new and relatively undynamic industrial sector of the economy. Members of higher-class families found employment in commerce or enlarged the upper ranks of the expanding governmental bureaucracy.

The increasing number of government employees merely reflected the more fundamental change in the government's role in national life. The state was the only mechanism for channeling into the national economy an increasingly larger income deriving from the exploitation of oil.[13] The Gómez bureaucracy, however, functioned within strict limits. The dictator handled the bureaucracy almost as his personal estate, without specific objectives and without converting it into a concrete entity that could, in turn, transform the country's traditional paternalistic orientation toward the government into a more modern and functional one in which the state would be considered the supreme secular entity. The trend was in the opposite direction, perhaps because of the extreme religious fervor of the Andeans, who were again in control of the military. The Church was therefore able to regain many of the influential positions that it had lost since the Guzmán administration. It was with good reason that the Pope conferred a prestigious honor on Gómez.

A more important manifestation of the Church's position, however, was the rapid growth of private educational institutions operated by religious associations, especially the Jesuits and the Brothers of La Salle. Members of the new rising middle class as well as the older oligarchy — of whom only some were still considered powerful — sent their children to these schools. From these students came not only many of the founders of the Christian Democratic movement but also many of the members of the economic and political elites.[14]

There were, of course, public schools, which the majority of the children of the petite bourgeoisie attended. From this group and especially from those who studied with Rómulo Gallegos — future president of the republic — emerged the leaders who, acting as members of the Student Federation of the Central University of Venezuela, repeated in 1928 the student demonstrations of 1912, but with more significant political consequences. These student movements brought to the surface the discontent that characterized other sectors of the population; this discontent, in turn, made the students aware of the need to expand their organizations to include the interests of

[13] Córdova and Garaicochea, "Inversiones extranjeras," p. 44. "The revenue from the public sector grew from 10 percent of the national income in 1920 to 20 percent in 1936."

[14] The Minister of Interior Relations under Pérez Jiménez relates these facts in detail. See L. Vallenilla Lanz, *Escrito de memoria* (Paris: Imprimerie Lang Grandemange, 1961).

these other groups, who had never found adequate means for expression either in other organizations or in the press. Both channels were strictly controlled.

The student movements were also the first political manifestation of the change that had come about in the sources of government power. In essence these students were very different from the intellectuals who had emerged and flourished earlier in the Gómez administration. He had contemptuously called them *plumíferos* (eggheads). An indication of his control over them is the fact that the person who directed the "corral" (as Gómez disparagingly referred to the group of intellectuals who served him) was Ezequiel Vivas, an Andean of very little education.[15]

By the end of the second decade of this century fundamental changes had been realized in Venezuela's economic and social structure, but it would not be until after the death of Gómez, at the end of 1935, that these transformations were to have any important political consequences.

The Dissociation of Power

Although Gómez effected a national concentration of power, he did not erase regional loyalties as a criterion for transmission of power. The fact that the army had been used as an avenue of ascent, principally by Andeans, helped to strengthen this regional primacy. Therefore it was not surprising that the person who replaced Gómez was his Minister of War, General López Contreras, who — once his term was finished in 1940 — was succeeded, in turn, by his Minister of War. Nor was it surprising that both successors were from Táchira and had begun their careers as members of Castro's army. Finally, these regional sentiments played an important part in the rise of General Marcos Pérez Jiménez as the leader of the 1948 military movement that overthrew the government of Rómulo Gallegos.[16] How, then, did this same military group ally itself three years earlier with

---

[15] See Rangel, *Los andinos,* chap. 12.

[16] One of the ministers of Pérez Jiménez — and an important coordinator of the bloodless coup of 1948 — relates that General Medina, in his exile, advised him while they were walking through Central Park in New York, "Don't conspire with just anyone, Laureano. It would be sad if you were to be put in jail. Try to work with those who can actually overthrow those people, without too much force, without blood. Pérez Jiménez surely has ambitions. Encourage him. I think that his possibilities for success are better than those of Delgado Chalbaud. Don't forget that he is *paisa* [a term used by Andeans meaning "from the Andean region"] and that most of the government officials are from my part of the country. Your friend Carlos, whose father is from Mérida and whose mother is from Caracas, was educated in Paris and he will always be considered an intruder." Lanz, *Escrito de memoria,* p. 270.

the party of Gallegos (Acción Democrática) to overthrow Medina? The answer leads to the identification of two processes that affect the entire social structure and that were direct consequences of the changes that had taken place in the preceding years: intrainstitutional differentiation and the incorporation into the political process of new social groups.

The institutionalization of the army had advanced sufficiently so that a group of young career officers had emerged; many of these men had completed their education outside Venezuela. These new officers, however, saw their path blocked by the older supporters of Gómez who, though ranking higher, had had no professional training. In other words, a basic heterogeneity had been created within the armed forces, but at the same time there were no adequate means to counteract resultant dissociational effects. On the contrary, the young officers, in spite of having increased remuneration, felt that they had much less prestige than they deserved; this greatly undermined their loyalty to their superiors.

Parallel to this process, new groups were being incorporated into the political sphere. In fact, on returning from exile with a better-defined ideological orientation, many of the student leaders who had participated in the protests of 1928 founded various political organizations.[17] These groups soon became a force that added coherence to the demands of the established and emerging labor organizations. An indication of the success of this process was what happened ten months after Gómez's death, when the Committee of Democratic Defense, supported by the Workers' Front and the Workers' National Front, was prevented from forming the Democratic National Party (PDN), the "unique party of the left."

The activities toward increased political participation that had begun in 1928 and intensified with the death of Gómez were not successful until

---

[17] El Bloque of April 1936 was formed with the support of the following organizations: the Student Federation of Venezuela (FEV), which had led the successes of 1912 and 1928; the National Association of Laborers (ANDE), the first labor group organized during the period; the National Republican Union (UNR), a short-lived party composed principally of young progressive managers; the Progressive Republican Party (PRP), which had been joined by a group of former student leaders of a predominantly socialist orientation; and the militants of the Movement of Venezuelan Organization (ORVE), in which militant former student leaders were also active and which had emerged not as a political party but with the goal of becoming a coalition of the various classes. Two months after it had been created, the oil unions and the National Democratic Block (BND), which had begun in Maracaibo, were added to it, thus forming the Committee of Democratic Defense that between June 9 and 13 paralyzed the country with a general strike in which a large proportion of the population participated. A concise description of these events may be found in J. D. Martz, *Acción Democrática: Evolution of a Modern Political Party in Venezuela* (Princeton, N.J.: Princeton University Press, 1966).

years later, because the new leaders of the middle class had no well-defined strategy, especially in terms of their basic objectives. Perhaps for this reason they committed a series of tactical errors that antagonized many of the old supporters of Gómez (of the extreme right) and forced the government to put a stop to public participation. In 1936, after Caracas police had fired on a crowd gathered in the Bolívar Plaza, there was a huge and vociferous march of the opposition toward the presidential palace. In a fiery speech before an excited audience, Jóvito Villalba, one of the most popular political leaders, declaimed, "Law is the refuge of the rheumatics." These actions antagonized the ruling classes and the government and gave them an excuse to accuse the opposition of trying to subvert the public order through violence. The opposition's final error lay in carrying the general strike in June beyond its extreme limits, converting triumph into defeat by giving the government what seemed to be a legitimate excuse for repression.

As a result of the anti-Communist panic of the ruling classes, the government was able to take a series of measures that ultimately destroyed the initial force of the opposition. It prevented the formation of the PDN; it further restricted the vote for the nomination of municipal representatives (the only elections in which there was a direct vote); it jailed and then exiled not only the leaders of the opposition who had been elected to office in prison but also other important political leaders, particularly Communists. Finally, in 1937 it blocked all attempts by other organizations (such as the Venezuelan Democratic Party — PDV) to gain recognition. These organizations had been formed principally by citizens associated with the exiled groups.

Such measures, however, were unable to stop the drive for political participation that had arisen throughout Venezuela. Although the political exiles were not able to return to Venezuela until 1941, in the intervening period there were successful underground efforts to incorporate new segments of the population, especially from the interior of the country, into the political process. The new groups had among their objectives the expansion of political activity into all sectors of the nation. These efforts were strengthened by the liberal ideas of the new president, General Medina Angarita, who was influenced by Roosevelt's democratic programs, the economic prosperity resulting from the wartime increase in the petroleum exports, and the need (because of the economic restrictions of war) to create national industries.

Perhaps because of the benefits they received from this situation, the economic leaders of the country remained dependent on military power. The economic sectors were composed of businessmen who had no direct interest in politics; they had had no interest since the early dissolution of the UNR. The apolitical attitude of the economic sector made the political structure less adaptive; it also prevented the economic elite from seeing the necessity to yield to popular pressure by altering the criteria for selection of governments. This group probably believed, as did many of the older officials, that the political structure of the country would permit the same kind of power transfer that López Contreras had effected. A paragraph written by General Medina three years after his overthrow characterizes this aspect of that elite's political culture:

> . . . never did I manifest any political aspirations, nor did I attempt in any way to become a presidential candidate. My respect for the law, which left no room for any kind of compromise; the constancy of the professional order; my patriotism and my dedication to the service of my country — perhaps these caused General López Contreras to recommend my candidacy to his political friends, who had the power to elect the President of the country.[18]

The dissociation of political power from the military was achieved between 1945 and 1948. In 1948 the recently elected President Rómulo Gallegos was overthrown in a bloodless military coup led by his own Minister of Defense and the chiefs of the General Staff. The structural changes that had been effected in the political system were revealed during this new dictatorship. In contrast to its predecessors, this government was forced to consider, when making its political decisions, a systematic and somewhat coordinated opposition of political parties together with their allied student organizations and labor unions. Moreover, as will be seen, the government had to confront the opposition of powerful sectors of both the economy and its own armed forces. But before considering this phase of the Venezuelan political process, the principal consequences for the political system of the events between 1945 and 1948 will be discussed in more detail.

In the first place, popular political participation was institutionalized by means of direct universal suffrage by secret ballot; there was no electoral discrimination of any kind except an age limit, which was lowered from twenty-one to eighteen years of age. This lower age limit is of great significance for a country such as Venezuela; a large proportion of its

[18] Isaías Medina Angarita, *Cuatro años de democracia* (Caracas: Pensamiento Vivo, 1963), p. 17.

population is young, and most of the youth (especially those who attend high school) become interested in politics at a very early age.

Second, avenues for the expression of interests were expanded and made more accessible. This process, however, was not realized autonomously. The growth of the peasant and labor organizations — the only ones that expanded significantly — was stimulated almost exclusively by the political sector. (This does not mean that there was no class consciousness that encouraged these people to organize themselves in order to defend their interests against landlords and employers, nor that there were no ideological differences between various unions. On the contrary, these differences were accentuated by the unions' expansion.) Nevertheless, the interesting point is that if leaders of the political parties had not also become union leaders, this strengthening of the labor unions (with the possible exception of those of the oil industry) would probably not have occurred nearly so early in Venezuela's history.[19]

Finally, the activities of the state also increased notably, as the government took a decidedly more active role in the development of production and services. This resulted in the creation of a new autonomous agency for the encouragement of industrial growth and the strengthening of the agency for agrarian reform and modernization of social services. Especially important in this process was the fact that the "50-50" petroleum decree increased the government's income, thus giving its activities wider and more effective scope.[20]

The political system underwent a twofold change: Political participation was expanded and institutionalized, and there was a change in governmental administration. It would seem then that the basic conditions for political stability had been created. Nevertheless, the administration of Venezuela's first popularly elected president lasted only nine months. An examination of some of the conditions that usually produce political stability will help to explain this fact.

The first condition is that citizens not only participate in the political process themselves but believe that others too have the right to participate.

[19] The operations and functions of rural unions are summarized by John Mathiason in "The Venezuelan Campesino" in *SRSP*.

[20] In 1943, before the reform of the petroleum laws (which was made in that same year), the income from petroleum was approximately 155 million bolivares. By 1948, it had increased to 1,110 million bolivares. See International Bank for Reconstruction and Development, *The Economic Development of Venezuela* (Baltimore: Johns Hopkins Press, 1961), p. 482.

They must feel that *something* should be done to protest injustices of governmental authority.[21] In summary, citizens should both feel politically efficacious and act in politically effective ways.

A second condition, also deeply rooted in a nation's political culture, is the degree of legitimacy that citizens grant their government. Universal suffrage, of course, confers some legitimacy, but alone it is neither a necessary nor even a sufficient condition for legitimacy. What really confers legitimacy on a government is the belief that the system it represents is the ideal political form; that is, *the form* is considered valuable in itself, and the form is defined by legally constituted procedures that the citizenry will protect.

Most Venezuelans in 1948 lacked these normative orientations, partly because of the colonial paternalism that had been reinforced by later regional caudillos. The new powerful government became, in the minds of the masses, the new great paterfamilias, not a modern secular state. This feeling obviously also indicated a lack of political efficacy among the political groups that were the sources of support for Acción Democrática. This fact seems to be confirmed by the few protests elicited when it was overthrown — those that were forthcoming reflected a loyalty to the party rather than loyalty toward the democratic system that the party had been trying to establish. Similarly, important members of Venezuela's elite did not maintain loyalties toward the democratic system. A lawyer who was a member of the economic elite made an illuminating comment on this score:

> We shall deal with the problem of governmental legitimacy again. A *de facto* situation will legitimize itself, in the long run, if it is useful. The opposite also happens. An administration elected by universal suffrage becomes illegitimate if it does not fulfill the hopes of that majority which brought it to power. The Gallegos administration is *legal* perhaps, at least after the elections, but it becomes less legitimate every day because of its ineptitude.[22]

Finally, it could not be expected that the new constitution — in spite of better representation in the constitutional assembly — could confer legitimacy overnight on a system designed to govern citizens who since 1830 had seen an average of one constitution every five years.

The third condition refers to the organization of the government, the adaptability of the system, and the capacity of the government to respond efficiently to the demands of the population. Part of the problem is, of

---

[21] Gabriel A. Almond and Sidney Verba, *The Civic Culture* (Princeton, N.J.: Princeton University Press, 1963).

[22] Lanz, *Escrito de memoria,* pp. 279–280.

course, the ability of the people themselves to transmit their demands to the government in an efficient manner. Theoretically, if the citizens use institutionalized channels to transmit their demands, then whether or not their loyalties toward the government become strengthened depends on the efficiency with which the government responds to those demands. The process is apparently circular and cumulative.[23]

We have seen that at this time there were many organized groups (political parties and unions) that articulated and transmitted the demands of the population; nevertheless, the government proceeded with sectarian judgment to give preferential treatment to organizations controlled by Acción Democrática. This greatly influenced the process of recruitment of new members of the growing bureaucracy; thus, the channels of communication between other organized groups and the government were obstructed. Of equal consequence for the system was the absence of organizations to serve the interests of the petite and high bourgeoisie. Certainly the membership of the newly created Committee of the Independent Electoral Political Organization (COPEI) included a large number of these people, but because of the organization's religious cast it could not be truly representative of all the members of the bourgeoisie, many of whom were secular in their orientation.

In addition to differences in ideological orientation, two other factors helped to sharpen the antagonism between the bourgeoisie and the government. On the one hand, ethnic discrimination — the norm in colonial society — was a relatively strong, although latent, characteristic of these social classes. Many of the clerks who composed the middle class, and a large number of upper-middle-class persons as well, were extremely apprehensive about the equalitarian encouragement Acción Democrática was giving the "rabble" and the "Negroes" to occupy high government offices and interact with the best families of Caracas.[24] The survival of a nonsecular attitude toward the state also influenced the antagonism between the middle classes and the government, especially in the field of education. Thus, governmental acts that strengthened public education and gave more

---

[23] Almond and Verba, *The Civic Culture.*

[24] Vallenilla Lanz cites various anecdotes that validate these comments. Significant in this respect is this reflection, which he made while in pseudo-exile in Cali: "I carefully read *El Siglo* and *El Tiempo* from Bogotá every day. Eduardo Santos's newspaper calls Rómulo Betancourt *Doctor* and Roberto García Peña applauds Venezuela's *democratic advance.* He neglects to mention that there are political prisoners and exiles. I examine the society columns with interest and they surprise me. Every day a Restrepo marries a *Londoño*" [a sarcastic way of referring to class miscegenation]. *Escrito de memoria*, p. 242.

state control to private education brought massive organized protests by directors of Catholic schools. These incidents gave Venezuelans the impression that Acción Democrática was anti-Catholic.

The fourth condition concerning political stability is perhaps the most important — the institutionalization of the armed forces. Although a system of seniority had been introduced and criteria for selection and promotion were well defined, officers of high rank still considered themselves the supreme arbiters of the national destiny. In addition, the agreement between Acción Democrática and the army was circumstantial, not programmatic or ideological, and in their short period of cogovernment nothing had been done to strengthen the relationship between them. On the contrary, regional loyalties still persisted within the higher military command.

The cumulative effects of these conditions brought about the downfall of Acción Democrática and the beginning of a new period of military government that lasted until 1958.

The Last of the Military Dictators?

Between 1948 and 1958 Venezuela's gross national product and national income increased at the very high annual rate of 8 percent. The economic policy of the new government emphasized construction, especially road construction and building in the cities, but industry also expanded greatly (the value of the industrial product tripled). In spite of the establishment of basic industries such as petrochemical plants, iron and steel works, and a huge hydroelectric plant, the principal growth was in light industry. Internal consumption also increased at a high annual rate (7 percent) and commercial agriculture (especially production of sugar, tobacco, cotton, rice, cattle, and milk) prospered. Moreover, there was a notable expansion of services. In summary, the country experienced what was termed the "oil boom."

At the same time, however, a series of structural maladjustments was created. These are well known, but by way of illustration and because of their social and political consequences, some will be mentioned: unequal distribution of income, inequalities in the production and employment structures, and inequalities in the system of finance. Thus, whereas the national per capita income was approximately 2,500 bolivares, the per capita income of the rural peasants was only about 125 bolivares.[25] Similarly,

[25] At that time 3.35 bolivares equaled one dollar. See Córdova and Garaicochea, "Inversiones extranjeras," p. 22. The income of the rural peasant was estimated by

traditional agriculture contributed only 3 percent to the GNP, but it employed 31 percent of the nation's active population; petroleum contributed a little more than 29 percent of the GNP, while employing only about 2 percent of the work force.[26] The banking system allowed practically no industrial credit, but it favored speculative ventures. The government financed its public works projects by internal borrowing; these debts were then canceled by new income receipts.

Perhaps the greatest structural maladjustments were created in the political and social sectors. The state continued its process of rapid expansion to such an extent that by 1958 it employed more than 8 percent of Venezuela's work force (see Table 3.1). The government built and managed basic industries, sugar refineries, agricultural colonies, a luxury hotel chain, huge residential centers, and, of course, all the services traditionally managed by the government.[27] The government did not, however, establish rational administrative policies; rather, the old practices of embezzlement and nepotism were maintained and perfected.

Participation in politics and unions was so much restricted that legal political parties and labor organizations almost disappeared. Those that remained were government sponsored or had nonmilitant participants. Government "ideologists" affirmed the virtues of apoliticalism, and the government tried to instill loyalty through civic parades held during "patriotism week," which pompously commemorated the fifth of July, Venezuela's day of independence. Government employees, students of both public and private schools, and at least some representatives of university and labor organizations were forced to attend these parades. Imbued with the idea that "to govern is to populate," but also hoping to change Venezuelan political attitudes, the government greatly encouraged immigration, especially from Spain and Italy. The number of these new inhabitants eventually grew to constitute 10 percent of the population.

A look at the educational system, municipal government, and the judicial system also gives evidence of the maladjustments in Venezuela's social structure. The increased complexity of the country began to require certain technical abilities that the educational system was unable to provide. The illiteracy rate remained high (52 percent in 1958), and there were schools for only 60 percent of the school-age population. The content of

---

G. W. Hill, J. A. Silva Michelena, and R. O. Hill in "La vida rural en Venezuela," in *Revista de sanidad y asistencia social,* vol. 24, nos. 1 and 2 (January–April 1959).
[26] Córdova and Garaicochea, "Inversiones extranjeras," pp. 44–45.
[27] IBRD, *Economic Development of Venezuela,* pp. 84 ff.

education remained rather "bookish" and impractical and tended to channel students toward careers in law, humanities, medicine, and civil engineering.

The elimination of provincial political activity made the institutions of local government even more innocuous, changing these into small offices for the administration of the relatively few municipal services. Finally, the judicial system remained dependent on the executive, and, on the local level, appointment to office continued to be made on the basis of particularistic criteria; thus, most local judges were incompetent and subject to local influences. The juridical structure remained unaltered in spite of the significant changes that the country had undergone. For example, the penal code, which was drawn up in 1920 for a society that was 85 percent rural, remained unchanged even though by 1950 the larger part of Venezuela's population lived in the cities.

This process of rapid urbanization was the product of a combination of factors. First, except for the few and low-paying jobs in new agricultural enterprises, the agricultural structure maintained the semifeudal pattern in which the rural peasant was scarcely able to subsist. Thus, new highways and the expansion of transportation and mass communications stimulated new aspirations in the rural masses who, because of their long history of bellicose mobilization, were relatively unbound by community ties. Furthermore, the huge investments in public works that were being made in the cities opened, even though temporarily, immediate possibilities for unskilled laborers. In consequence, the rural-urban distribution of the population was reversed in the short period of 25 years — a process that took Chile 32 years and Argentina five decades.[28]

With this phenomenon, and the kind of industrialization that goes with it, a new social type appeared: the uprooted rural migrant to the city. This migrant is a completely marginal person not only in the sense that he is not integrated into the dynamic sector of the economy but also in the ecological and psychological sense. These persons did not retain their rural identification, but neither were they able to rid themselves of old patterns of thought and conduct or totally assimilate the ways of urban life. Their political attitude tended to be apathetic, and when they were

[28] In Argentina the percentage of the urban population increased from 39.5 in 1895 to 65.7 in 1947. In Chile the percentage increase was from 46.0 to 60.2 between 1920 and 1952, whereas in Venezuela the urban population increased from 34.7 percent to 67.5 percent of the total population between 1936 and 1961. The figures for Argentina and Chile may be found in Roger Vekeman, S.J. and J. L. Segundo, "Tipología socioeconómica de los paises latinoamericanos," *Revista interamericana de ciencias sociales,* special issue, vol. 2 (1963). The data for Venezuela were taken from the respective national censuses.

politically active, they tended to participate anomically in groups or to support independent personalities rather than party candidates, as they had done after the overthrow of Pérez Jiménez.

Industry was able to employ relatively few of the increasing number of unskilled workers in the cities; therefore there was no great differentiation between the few industrial workers and the other rural migrants. For this reason, place of origin and residence (rural-urban) became the most important criteria for analyzing the conduct and psychology of lower-class individuals. In the middle classes the situation was somewhat different. In this group ideas and political conduct could be expected to vary according to employment. Political leadership continued to spring primarily from the cultural sphere, and this copenetration of political and cultural activities was accentuated between 1948 and 1958, principally because of the lack of political freedom in Venezuela at that time. This does not mean, however, that both sectors did not become increasingly differentiated internally. In the first place, the expansion of the official bureaucracy itself gave more people the opportunity to become active in the political sphere without necessarily having to belong to any political party. Second, the number of persons participating in strictly party activities, in spite of secrecy and repression, continued to increase.

By way of contrast, persons working in the economic sphere, as for example employees of commercial houses or small merchants, remained relatively inactive politically even though the proportion of the population that worked in commerce almost doubled between 1936 and 1958 (see Table 3.1).

In upper-class strata there were also important changes. Employers' organizations were consolidated at both the national and regional levels. The Federation of Chambers of Commerce and Production (FEDECAMARAS), after its founding in 1944, rapidly expanded its functions of coordinating and defending the interests of its members and in this way encouraged a class consciousness among this group. The large and prosperous commercial houses retained their predominance, although by the end of the 1950s the manufacturing and agricultural industries also had gained importance. The fact that internal tensions were not created to threaten this process of institutionalization of economic power permitted the so-called "managerial class" to play an active role in the overthrow of the dictator. We shall examine more closely the factors that brought the downfall of Pérez Jiménez.

The Venezuelan economic crisis was a first and major factor, originating in the declining rate of growth of petroleum exports. The termination of European reconstruction, the end of the expansion of the use of the diesel engine in the United States, and the resolution of the Korean and Suez Canal conflicts stabilized the world demand for petroleum; this had a direct repercussion on Venezuela's national income. In 1956 the government, trying to meet its debts by internal borrowing, gave new concessions that did bring additional income to the government. The following year, however, it was not able to repeat this policy. The government owed almost two billion bolivares to the private sector of the economy.[29] This led some Venezuelan capitalists to participate in conspiratorial activities being planned in those sectors of the army that had not been included among Pérez Jiménez's close friends. Finally, the unification of the underground political forces helped to coordinate the economic, military, and political leaders who opposed the dictator; this coordination made a three-day general strike possible. The strike concluded with Pérez Jiménez's flight on January 23, 1958.

The Past Ten Years

The climate of unity and general content following the overthrow of Pérez Jiménez led the principal political parties (AD, COPEI, and URD) to conclude the pact of Punto Fijo by which the parties agreed to govern by coalition, regardless of who should be victorious in the elections scheduled for December of 1958. What they called "the spirit of January 23," however, disappeared as rapidly as it had emerged. Conflicts first became apparent in the political sphere. The URD party left the coalition because it disapproved of President Rómulo Betancourt's condemnation of Cuba.

The principal leaders of Acción Democrática, in contrast, who were perhaps influenced by their experiences of 1948, had been following a policy of friendship toward the United States and toward Venezuela's economic sector, and a policy of attack on the Communist Party. These policies were followed in spite of growing opposition from the younger members of the party, who had not only developed friendships with Communists during the clandestine struggle but had also been taking a more radical ideological position than that of the older directors of the party. These internal controversies led to a schism within Acción Democrática and to the formation of a new party, the Movement of the Revolutionary Left

[29] *IBRD, Economic Development of Venezuela,* p. 105.

(MIR). This incorporation of young activists into the leftist opposition soon was reflected in more virulent opposition and in the increased political participation of the marginal inhabitants of the cities. The young leaders had worked among these people to overthrow Pérez Jiménez and therefore enjoyed great prestige among them. The growing virulence also stemmed from the miserable conditions created by the high rates of unemployment caused by the economic crisis and distortions in the occupational structure. In 1962 the unemployment rate was over 14 percent; it is estimated that the average rate in the cities was as high as 17 percent, and it is probably true that it was as high as 25 percent in the "marginal" neighborhoods of the cities. Anti *adequismo* sentiments (feelings against AD) in Caracas were another contributing factor to the fervent popular support given to the opposition groups.

Paralleling López Contreras and his actions after Jóvito Villalba's speech in 1936, Betancourt, on the basis of an editorial published in the newspaper of the MIR, accused the left of planning the subversion of the constitutional order and seized the newspaper. The opposition mobilized its followers and the masses of Caracas. The police and the army acted to reestablish public order, but by the end of 1961 the conflict was open and armed. The fighting broke out first in the cities, especially in the outlying neighborhoods, where the Tactical Combat Units (UTC) of the Armed Forces of National Liberation (FALN) had their headquarters. This organization had been created by the leftist parties for the purpose of taking power and was inspired by Fidel Castro's tactics. When it was defeated in the urban centers, the conflict was transferred to rural areas where guerrilla camps were established. Although at this writing it has not been completely eradicated, this rural effort was also relatively unsuccessful.

There are many factors that contributed to the defeat of the FALN, but there is little information available on which to base an analysis of the movement. Nevertheless, for the purposes of this chapter several interesting factors should be mentioned. I quote here from an analysis by a member of the FALN:

1. The first is infantile subjectivism of petty-bourgeois origin — the swollen enthusiasm due to a long chain of successes which we gained for a time and which made us appear each day, in Venezuela as well as abroad, like an almost mythological force of immeasurable power, and which gave the impression that at any moment we would be able to throw Rómulo Betancourt out of the Palacio de Miraflores.

2. The second cause, which on many occasions had facilitated the blows delivered by the repressive apparatus, is the open liberalism, profoundly rooted in our organization and in almost all our cadres and militants, which has led us to abandon revolutionary vigilance.

3. For quite a long time the FALN and the revolutionary parties have been operating in accordance with a more or less fixed schema, with procedures that have become almost clichés. This has permitted the government, once an attack has been opened, to foresee the next ones and to prepare to meet them.[30]

An additional important factor was the failure of the rural peasants to support the FALN. This hindered the establishment of lines of effective communication between different centers of operation and aided the forces of the government.

This bitter struggle produced divisions and disorder in almost all of the labor unions and political parties. The ideological conflict deeply penetrated the political-cultural groups and even the economic sector, although with less intensity. This ideological conflict, however, was only one of the symptoms — perhaps the most severe — of the heterogeneity of value orientations among the different middle- and upper-class groups. These differences were possibly related to dissimilar experiences of change and to the divergent political activities of groups within the same position or status.[31]

The almost innumerable divisions, regroupings, and realignments that have characterized Venezuelan politics during the past few years have created a political situation prone to impasse, now that there is no political party with a clear majority. The most obvious result is, of course, that it has become necessary to govern by coalition — which has proved very unstable because of the heterogeneity of the normative patterns existing within and among the different parties. Even, for example, when the same party wins two consecutive elections, the coalition that existed in the first period will not necessarily be re-formed. This happened when the AD-COPEI coalition during Betancourt's regime was supplanted by the coalition of AD with URD.[32]

In spite of this situation of permanent transition of political and institutional compromises and loyalties, the processes of consolidation of economic

[30] FALN, "Our Errors," *Studies on the Left,* vol. 4, no. 4 (1964), pp. 129–130.
[31] See Chapter 1 for a more rigorous formulation of this concept.
[32] It should be remembered that both AD periods began with a coalition among three parties, and at approximately the midpoint of their governments the number of parties constituting the coalitions was reduced to two. Thus, URD left the Betancourt government and the Frente Nacional Democrático (FND) left Leoni's government. In 1969, COPEI was making an effort to govern alone; however, this party has made some selective, limited agreements with economic and political groups.

power and of increasing articulation of the interests of various middle groups have continued. Thus, the Venezuelan Independent Association (AVI) was founded by a group of businessmen associated with FEDECA- MARAS, and open political negotiation exists in permanent form between this organization and the government. In the middle class, ANDE and the National Union of Public Employees (UNEP) have been strengthened, and a multitude of small commercial and industrial associations, new associations and unions of professional and technical personnel, and the Venezuelan Association of Executives have emerged.

The army is more difficult to evaluate. On the one hand, its directors continually emphasize in the press that it has been institutionalized. On the other hand, each political group tries to capture the sympathies of the military officers. The key questions, of course, are: Have the army and other national groups developed a strong loyalty to the political system and eliminated regional sentiments? To what extent do patterns of attitudes favorable to a new traditional dictatorship still exist among the population? To what degree did party officials and those sympathetic to revolutionary solutions place all their hopes on the uprisings of Carúpano and Puerto Cabello in 1962?

In summary, then, the Venezuelan political system is characterized today by the lack of a crystallization of its institutions and by the cultural heterogeneity that exists within them and among the different social strata. The presence and interaction of both circumstances have two principal effects. First, they limit the adaptive capacity of the system, that is, the promptness with which the various institutions are able to absorb and satisfy the new demands of the population. Second, they considerably expand the number of policy alternatives. Both of these effects, in turn, make the task of defining social objectives more difficult. A brief examination of the future prospects of the country will help clarify the implications of these problems.

1984: A New Revolutionary Crisis?

To predict the future of a political system is a task for which the novelist is still better qualified than the social scientist. Nevertheless, this is an indispensable exercise in an investigation such as this one which has among its objectives the provision of a rational basis for decision making. Lacking an Orwellian imagination, however, we shall limit ourselves to pointing out a series of events that are likely to occur and to indicating how the present situation may influence the form these events will take.

By approximately 1984 Venezuela will again be at a crossroads. In the past, as may be seen in Figure 3.1, when there has been a leveling or a decline in the export of the economy's principal product — cacao, coffee, or petroleum — the country has experienced a period of intense conflict that became a critical point in Venezuela's political history. The decline in cacao prices at the end of the eighteenth century was undoubtedly a factor that precipitated the wars for independence. The Andean rise to power was stimulated by the critical economic situation that affected Táchira at the end of the nineteenth century as a result of the sudden decrease in coffee prices. The economic crisis in the country between 1957 and 1963 originated in the falling petroleum prices and the decreasing rate of growth in petroleum exports. The government that emerged at this time succeeded in strengthening and stabilizing the economy, as is indicated by the rate of growth of the gross national product and by the reduction in unemployment.[33] The government's policy was based principally upon the restimulation of the construction industry and upon the initiation of two processes that may become extremely important forces in the national economy: the modernization of agriculture and substitution of imports. It is of prime importance to make these two processes compatible. If the modernization of agriculture frees more rural workers than industry can absorb, the problem of unemployment and the plight of the marginal population in general will become more severe. At the same time, inadequate agricultural production creates inflationary pressures and makes the financing of industry and of agriculture itself more difficult. Thus, in order to obtain equilibrium in economic growth, the public and private institutional capacity must be used to stimulate both sectors in a *coordinated* manner. As has been mentioned earlier, however, Venezuelan institutions are not characterized by their adaptive capacities. Apparently this has been the main obstacle that agrarian reform has encountered, and it has prevented this process from being as efficient as had been desired.[34]

The prognostic curve presented in Figure 3.1 is imaginary; its only purpose is to call attention to the fact that substitution of imports is a process that, by definition, exhausts itself.

Basing our opinion on the experiences of other Latin American countries,

[33] "Second Message to the Congress," by Dr. Raúl Leoni, Constitutional President of the Republic, March 11, 1966, p. xi.

[34] Alejandro M. Osorio, *Factor limitante del desarrollo agropecuario* (Caracas: Imprenta Nacional, 1966).

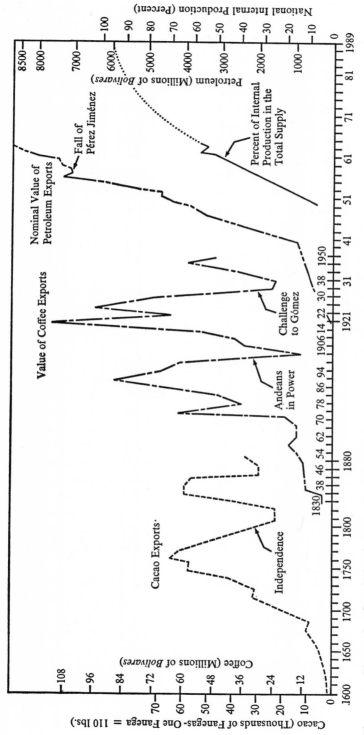

Figure 3.1 Venezuela: Correlation between the Principal Economic and Political Crises (1600–1989)

NOTE: See Appendix B for sources of this figure.

we estimate that this condition will be reached in about fifteen or twenty years, taking into account the peculiarity that as time advances the process becomes more complex and difficult. In other words, by 1984 the economy will again reach one of its critical points. Whether or not the country can successfully pass this critical period depends on the efficiency with which industrialization has been realized. If the new industries are capable of competing successfully in world markets, then perhaps the bases will have been created for further outward expansion; if not, the future is one of a long period of stagnation, such as has characterized Argentina and Chile for some thirty years. The magnitude of the effort that must be made is described by the chief of Venezuela's Central Office of Coordination and Planning:

> If we want to achieve by 1980 a degree of industrial development which will correspond to our level of income, similar to industrialized nations, or increase the industrial component of the national product to 30%, it will be necessary to reach an annual cumulative growth rate of over 11% in the industrial sector, and an over-all growth rate of 7%.[35]

The inherent difficulties in reaching these goals are more evident if one realizes that in the easiest stage of the process of import substitution, which was completed in Venezuela between 1957 and 1964, the industrial product grew to 8.4 percent. The economic requisites are, of course, many; nevertheless, these do not present all of the difficulties inherent in this process. It is also imperative that the Latin American Common Market be consolidated and perfected. From a national point of view this requires not only that the governments take adequate measures but also that members of the managerial classes themselves acquire attitudes that will permit active collaboration in this process. This implies an orientation toward the nation which allows them to view the state not as an enemy but as an entity capable of productively directing their activities.

Similarly, the working class not only must have a consciousness of the goals toward which they are working but must receive the technical training necessary to elevate their productivity substantially. In other words, the government, with the participation of pertinent organizations, will have to elaborate and put into practice a social policy that will induce attitude changes — so that efficient groups will emerge in existing industries and so that activities will develop in whatever new industries may be formed. To

---

[35] Héctor Hurtado, *Etapa difícil y compleja del desarrollo industrial* (Caracas: Imprenta Nacional, 1966).

design such a policy it is necessary above all to know the present relevant attitudes and value orientations in various national groups.

Industrial development is not the only factor to be dealt with, however, in an evaluation of Venezuela's situation in 1984; precisely at that time the principal oil concessions will lapse.[36] The policy of the present government leads one to assume that if a similar government is in power in 1984, these concessions will not be renewed. But the nature of the negotiations that take place and the advantages Venezuela will derive from them do not depend solely on the kind of government in power. Another important factor is the negotiating power the Venezuelan government will actually have at the time; it is quite obvious that if the Venezuelan Petroleum Company and the Venezuelan Corporation of Guayana meet their goals successfully, and if industrialization and modernization of agriculture are realized efficiently, the government's position will be much stronger simply because there will be greater capacity to absorb whatever fluctuation may occur in the production and prices of petroleum.

An even more fundamental and dramatic factor, because of its global implications, is the possible exhaustion of Venezuela's oil reserves. In 1965 it was estimated that the theoretical duration of reserves was 13.7 years at the present rate of production (3.5 million barrels per day). The official estimations are optimistic:

> It can be anticipated that, for a period difficult to determine, Venezuela will be able to add at least sufficient new petroleum to its reserves to replace future production.[37]

This optimism is based on the possibilities of finding oil not yet discovered and of increasing the recovery from existing oil deposits, and on the technological advances in the industry that might make economically feasible the exploitation of a heavy oil that exists in large quantities in the eastern regions of the country.[38] If the country has the political and technical capacity to transform these possibilities into realities, there is no doubt that its bargaining power will be strengthened; if the reverse occurs, the consequences could be catastrophic.

Other factors that influence the negotiating capacity of the government are its own heterogeneity, the nature of the political opposition it en-

[36] Interview 138163, VENELITE, pp. 31–32.
[37] Manuel Pérez Guerrero, *Petróleo y hechos* (Caracas: Imprenta Nacional, 1965), pp. 21–22.
[38] Ibid., pp. 20–26.

counters, and the attitudes of the various national groups. If cultural
heterogeneity is still high, the opposition to the government will be powerful
and total, and the Venezuelan masses will continue as apathetic toward
international events as they have been in the past; the government will then
be in a very weak position to negotiate. The opposite characteristics will
help to strengthen the government's position. Perhaps the only caution
that should be exercised is with regard to the relative strength and the
political attitudes of the leftist groups. Paradoxically, if these groups are
strong enough to threaten the government but not strong enough to overthrow it, the position of the government may be strengthened with regard
to the internal groups opposed to the policy of no concessions.

Last, though not least important, is the policy of the United States
toward Latin America, and particularly toward Venezuela. This policy is
important because the danger exists, if the policy continues to be one of
intervention (even when a socialist government does not exist), that it
may lead to an invasion of the country. This is especially true in view of the
enormous and increasing importance of North American economic interests
in the area. North American policy is also important because the increasing
political, social, and cultural influence that the United States exerts may
hinder the formation of the attitudes necessary to harmonious and autonomous development.

Although in the past few years the government of the United States,
with the object of winning the Cold War, has launched what is termed the
"ideological offensive," [39] we assume that the "policy" of the United States
does not imply an explicit and unified set of norms for application in each
situation. Such a rigid policy would deny the complexity of the situation.
The epoch in which the imperialists built colonies in their image has ended,
not only because strong opposition emerged in the colonies and because of a
more guilty national conscience, but also because the dominant nations
themselves, and especially the United States, contain influential groups who
see their economic interests damaged by such a deterministic policy.

It also would be very simplistic to think that because North American
interests largely control mass media and because the majority of magazines,

[39] The "ideological offensive" is an operation by which conscious and coordinated
efforts are made to know and influence the positions of different nations of the
world. The majority of these efforts are centralized in the Department of Defense
and may lead to the overmilitarization of United States foreign policy. See U.S.
House of Representatives, Committee on Foreign Affairs, Subcommittee on International Organizations and Movements, Behavioral Sciences and the National Security,
Report no. 4 on Winning the Cold War, *The U.S. Ideological Offensive* (Washington,
D.C.: Government Printing Office, December 6, 1965).

films, and television productions originate in the United States, that country will exercise an absolute control over the minds of Venezuelans. Nevertheless, the communications opportunities that artificial satellites offer are entirely new, and if at present we know very little about the influence that these media exert, we can measure even less the future implications of this technological revolution in communications. Neil Hurley, a shrewd observer of Latin America, points out,

> As long as nations can control the *reception* of space signals through a central ground station, the problem of "psychic invasion" of any given people is excluded. The question of "controlling the signal," however, will present itself sooner or later — when nations gain the technical capacity to broadcast directly from a satellite to a receiver in a home or a village anywhere on the globe. With third and fourth generation satellites, we run the risk of information fallout not unlike the spread of radioactive dust after a nuclear explosion. The Orwellian specter of "mind control" is not as far-fetched as might be supposed.[40]

Venezuela was one of the first five Latin American nations to sign the COMSAT agreement to create, eventually, an *inter-American* common market of communications. This, of course, makes Hurley's warning more relevant. But in the last analysis, the effect of the "fallout" of communications will depend on the attitudinal predispositions of the population.

The following chapters will present a detailed study of Venezuelans' experience of change, of their value orientations, and of evaluations of those social groups that have played an important role in Venezuela's recent history — as protagonists or as objects of politics. Whether or not a crisis will occur in 1984 and whether or not the country will successfully resolve that crisis depends to a great extent on the political capacity of these groups to work efficiently and constructively, that is, whether or not they can manage the conflict so that it does not exceed the limits that any of the parties may set. However, this capacity is obviously conditioned by the real possibilities of the system to tolerate or make the necessary structural changes.

The historical exploration that has been made here reveals that this is the weak point in the functioning and organization of Venezuelan society. Venezuela's history exudes violence; nevertheless, new nationalistic attitudes and new organizations to articulate these attitudes are expanding. This trend should give better adaptive capacity to the political system. We shall turn our attention, then, to an examination of these factors.

[40] Neil P. Hurley, "Satellite Communications," *America,* August 27, 1966, p. 205.

4 THE IMPACT OF CHANGE ON THE SOCIAL STRUCTURE

Introduction

The most salient feature of the past forty years of Venezuelan history is also the one that makes it most unique: the extent to which the country has changed. The preceding chapter describes generally how the structure of the economy was radically transformed after the beginning of the exploitation of oil in the 1920s. One of the many aspects of these changes, which will be emphasized here, is the modification of the structure of employment. New positions were opened up even at the highest levels of prestige, but still more significant, in terms of figures, was the reduction in the proportion of people employed in agriculture.[1] In what occupations are these people now? At what level? This movement, of course, also meant a shift in place of residence. Thus, another way of expressing the extent of change is to say that the rural-urban ratio was reversed in the period 1920–1969.[2] But perhaps a better global indicator of the increase in the residential mobility of the Venezuelan population are the figures shown in Table 4.1.

However, these general figures, though useful, are of little value for the policy maker. In the first place, it is possible that, in spite of so thorough a change, some groups may remain relatively unaltered. Second, the same process of change may differently affect people placed in the same position of the social hierarchy. We must remember Ahumada's root hypothesis,

[1] In 1920, 72 percent of the labor population was engaged in agricultural activities; 48 years later the figure was only 31 percent. See Ministerio de Fomento, Dirección General de Estadísticas y Censos Nacionales, *Venezuela: Indicadores socio-económicos* (Caracas: Ministerio de Fomento, 1968).

[2] In 1920, 26 percent of the population lived in urban areas; in 1969 it was estimated that this percentage was 75. Ibid.

TABLE 4.1   Percentage of People Living Outside Birth State

Census Year	Percent
1920	3.9
1936	11.2
1941	14.2
1950	18.0
1961	20.4

Source: URVEN study data (Caracas: CENDES, 1968), unpublished.

that the political capacity of the country has been impaired by the cultural heterogeneity of key groups of the population.[3] This heterogeneity was assumed to be related to both upward and residential mobility, which brought together, in view of the rigidity of the socialization agencies, people with different normative orientations. The aim of this chapter is to determine the extent and the way in which each of the important groups of the Venezuelan population has been affected in transiting the main avenues of change. In order to do this the following groups of variables will be considered: background characteristics, especially prestige, income, and education; experience of change; and a set of communication variables. We leave for the next chapter the exploration of how the experience of change has affected individual psychological orientations.

Social Classes

There is no area of sociological theory as simultaneously controversial and important as the theory of social classes. It may remain so for years to come. Unfortunately, the subject is even less well defined with respect to underdeveloped countries, such as the Latin American nations, where theories elaborated to explain the situation of developing nations have been applied almost mechanically. We cannot deal exhaustively with this subject here, first, because only recently have sociologists begun to investigate the subject from the perspective of underdeveloped, dependent nations and, second, because proper treatment of the subject of social classes requires a separate study. Nevertheless, we hope to make a modest beginning toward the empirical study of social classes in underdeveloped nations. In order to do so we must, of course, start from a critical base of classical ideas.

[3] Jorge Ahumada, "Hypothesis for Diagnosing Social Change: The Venezuelan Case," pp. 192–202.

The two most outstanding theorists in the past hundred years — Marx and Weber — left their treatment of social stratification at a point where they had just begun to attack the problem. Marx showed us that the kind of relationship established between man and man with respect to the means of production is a key criterion for differentiating any society into classes. However, even in the day of the *Communist Manifesto* it became evident that this single criterion was not enough for understanding social conflicts in an ever more complex industrial society. Marx himself introduced other criteria of classification such as "workers" and "nonworkers," large and small business, national and foreign capitalists, and whether or not they employed salaried workers.[4]

Marx also introduced the concepts of class consciousness and relative dissatisfaction to explain why organized discontent may appear when some economic equalization in the social classes has reached a certain stage:

> A notable advance in the amount paid as wages presupposes a rapid increase of productive capital. The rapid increase of productive capital calls forth just as rapid an increase in wealth, luxury, social wants, and social comforts. Therefore, although the comforts of the laborer have risen, the social satisfaction which they give has fallen in comparison with these augmented comforts of the capitalists, which are unattainable for the laborer, and in comparison with the scale of general development society has reached. Our wants and their satisfaction have their origin in society, and not in relation to the objects which satisfy them. Since their nature is social, it is therefore relative.[5]

Nevertheless, it became apparent that although in the long run and from a broad historical perspective conflicts based on other criteria seemed unimportant as compared to that of class struggle, when a closer and narrower view was taken, new criteria for stratifying were needed. It was to fill this gap that Weber introduced his concept of "class status":

> . . . the typical probability that a given state of (a) provision with goods, (b) external conditions of life, and (c) subjective satisfaction or frustration will be possessed by an individual or a group. These probabilities define class status insofar as they are dependent on the kind and extent of control or lack of it which the individual has over goods or services and existing possibilities of their exploitation for the attainment of income or receipts within a given economic order.[6]

[4] See Stanislaw Ossowski, *Class Structure in the Social Consciousness* (New York: Free Press, 1963), chap. 5.

[5] Robert Freedman, ed., *Marx on Economics* (New York: Harvest Books, Harcourt, Brace, 1961), pp. 70–71.

[6] Max Weber, *The Theory of Social and Economic Organization* (Glencoe, Ill.: Free Press, 1947), p. 424.

However, Weber immediately saw that this treatment was inadequate. Opportunity for exploitation of services, authority, prestige of birth, sphere of occupation, and interchange of individuals could not be fitted readily in the schema of class status. Concepts such as "acquisition class," "stratum stand," "social strata," "social status," and "social class" were introduced by Weber to cover such an array of problems. Later on, Parsons emphasized, though excessively, the valuational aspect of social stratification: " . . . the broad rank-order of precedence will be below the paramount value-pattern, the order of relative strategic importance of the exigencies relating to the other three major functional problem contexts of the system." [7] But Parsons also stressed the fact that stratification is given within a multidimensional social space (functional spheres of activity such as the cultural, political, and economic).

Another criterion to be taken into account is what Marx called the historical specificity of the social classes. Weber also allowed for variations depending on the overall economic system:

Acquisition classes are favoured by an economic system oriented to market situations, whereas social strata develop and subsist most readily where economic organization is of a monopolistic and liturgical character and where the economic needs of corporate groups are met on a feudal or patrimonial basis.[8]

This is, perhaps, the main reason why placing groups in a system of stratification is an even more complex task in an underdeveloped society. Underdevelopment may be understood as the coexistence in one single structure of different economic systems as defined by the means of control of production, such as communal, capitalist, and state capitalist.[9] The problem therefore is one of identifying several stratification criteria that may or may not be common to all collectivities. In what specific way do these different criteria operate? How are they related to one another?

We can just hint at a solution to a theoretical problem that sociologists concerned with Latin American and other dependent areas only recently have begun to approach. The elaboration of a theory of social classes in dependent countries can be generated only after a profound reexamination of historical formation, one that is aimed at characterizing changes in the means of control of production in Latin America as a whole and showing

[7] Talcott Parsons, *Essays in Sociological Theory* (Glencoe, Ill.: Free Press, 1954), p. 406.

[8] Weber, *Social and Economic Organization*, p. 428.

[9] Armando Córdova and Héctor Silva Michelena, *Aspectos teóricos del subdesarrollo* (Caracas: Imprenta Universitaria, 1966).

precisely the role of these changes in the productive forces of society. Our point of departure from classical theory is the hypothesis that, in the course of its development, Latin America has experienced diverse stages of dependency but all of them framed within the context of the world capitalist system.

That is, the control of production developed during the colonial period was basically capitalist, but to emphasize the particular character of this stage we shall call it the *colonial-exporter stage*. Plantation and mining enterprises were essentially capitalist ventures that performed the complementary and subsidiary function of transferring profits to the economy of the dominant country. What has confused scholars for a long time is that, owing to the low level of development of the productive forces then, the form these exploitations took was similar to precapitalist forms. This tended to conceal the reality that it was indeed a dependent primitive capitalism, a historically new formation, that was growing.

After the political emancipation of the Latin American countries, the bourgeoisie (criollos) — who never intended to change the means of control of production — made efforts to engage the country in the new capitalist system that was expanding as a result of the industrial revolution. But because this revolution was occurring in England rather than in the original dominant centers, Spain and Portugal, such engagement was difficult and less significant for Latin America in comparison to the English colonies.

Along with this geographic shift in the center of dominance, important changes in the economy of the dependent countries took place: The method of commercialization of primary export products became more competitive and open, and new capitalist forms of production were introduced both in agriculture and in industry. This represented a significant advance in the dependent development of the productive forces and therefore in the life style of those classes associated with this process, but not necessarily in the life style of classes still associated with the colonial-exporter stage.

During the twentieth century a new displacement of the dominant center has taken place, with the United States now in control. The monopoly phase of capitalism was initiated, and it took advantage of investment opportunities created in the periphery during the development of primary-export capitalism. The appropriation of profits was accomplished this time by means of import substitution that, along with Latin American enterprises, was controlled by a few, but key, strategic internationally financed industries.

Where the process is now most advanced (Argentina, Brazil, Chile), it led to the progressive denationalization of industries and to a further dependent development of the productive forces. It created a small sector of the population able to afford an affluent life style, but it also produced an increasing mass of marginal people who converged on those cities which were growth poles of the economy.

In each of the previously mentioned stages of development of dependent capitalism, many different social classes emerged. Their way of life was determined more by the level of development of the productive forces than by qualitative changes in the means of control of production. Because this development took place in overlapping rather than in clear-cut stages, we find today a heterogeneous social structure. Thus, great numbers of subsistence farmers, artisans, and small shopkeepers use a technology appropriate to the stage of colonial-exporter capitalism. *Latifundistas* (owners of large, extensively exploited estates) are a fading expression of the loss of importance of such ways of production.

Agricultural workers, owners of small industries, and owners of medium-sized commercial enterprises are associated with the primary-export stage. Owners of large industries and commercial organizations, whether national or foreign, the middle classes (privileged or not), industrial workers, government officials, and the marginal population were the new classes that emerged with the growth and maturity of dependent capitalist society. Thus, the historical development of dependent capitalism has generated a class structure that is heterogeneous with regard to life styles associated with a certain level of development of the productive forces, but not heterogeneous with respect to the means of control of production. The insistence on seeing these class differences through lenses ground to focus on quite different situations, such as those that exist in the dominant center countries, has induced theorist and practitioner alike to make mistakes with serious political consequences — for example, to assign a historically revolutionary role to an invented "national bourgeoisie" or to believe that the first step toward a Latin American revolution had to be the elimination of a nonexistent feudalism.

It should be stressed that historically different classes are associated with different life styles, but that in each stage there is a style that, in the social consciousness, is taken as a referent; therefore, people fight to reach it. This, of course, does not imply that each class does not have a consciousness of its own, but rather it implies that each social layer or class generally struggles to reach the new style of life associated with each new development of the productive forces of society. This takes place not because class consciousness is independent of the social situation but, on the contrary, as Marx suggested in the earlier cited passage, because social wants and their satisfactions are of a social nature and are therefore relative.

Consequently, the approach taken here relies to an important extent on the concept of socioeconomic status. The basic assumption is that income, education, and occupational prestige may be used for drawing the basic profile or describing the hierarchy of societies in the same stage of development as Venezuela. The implication is that the values people attach to certain factors are more or less stable for extended periods of time, and these values express themselves in the life styles people strive to achieve. Presently, the overarching process of change in Venezuela is urbanization; therefore, the extent to which a group has assimilated urban ways of life serves to define its position in the social hierarchy. Seen along this dimension, then, cultural heterogeneity becomes a more meaningful concept.

Still another general dimension of social stratification, which crosscuts all the previously mentioned criteria, is the institutional locus, or functional sphere of activity. The importance of this dimension may best be conveyed through an example: University professors, high government officials, and executives of large manufacturing firms have the same style of life and same socioeconomic status, and yet the fact that each acts in different functional spheres (cultural, political, and economic) has important consequences both attitudinally and behaviorally. The interconnection between socioeconomic status and sphere is made clear by Bonilla: "Embedded within the more embracing concepts of class and situs, occupation stands as a first order of social differentiation on a vertical axis of status and a horizontal dimension of institutional locus." [10]

Socioeconomic status, style of life, and institutional sphere are theoretically and empirically among the most important criteria of stratification. Nevertheless, there are in Venezuela — as in most underdeveloped countries — certain peculiarities that also must be taken into account because they significantly affect the social structure. First, the fact that oil, the most strategic product of the country, is exploited almost exclusively by foreign companies introduces new sources of positions, images, and values that, in turn, affect the social hierarchy. The Venezuelan case is not as acute

---

[10] Frank Bonilla, "Occupation as a Unit of Cross-National Political Analysis," paper prepared for the Joint ESOMAR-WAPOR Conference, August 20–24, 1967, Vienna, Austria (Cambridge, Mass.: Center for International Studies, M.I.T., June 1968), p. 2.

as the Puerto Rican, where Americanization is the key value that defines the style of life for which people strive. Nevertheless, it does give the Venezuelan social structure a certain flavor that makes it reminiscent of a colonial society.

Second, ownership of the means of production was not used as a criterion for defining sample groups within the manufacturing industry. Only the position of individuals within the enterprise (executives and nonexecutives) was considered. This, however, does not mean that this criterion is not to be an important one. On the contrary, in the overall study design it was used for defining the economic elite.[11] Here property relations were used only at the middle level (small businessmen and owners of small industries) and for choosing the upper-status rural groups.

Finally, other groups such as student and labor leaders must be considered because, within the Venezuelan context, they are collectivities with enough historical relevance and political influence to merit special attention. A few words also should be said with regard to the *rancho* dwellers. Obviously not an occupational or income group, they were included because it was assumed that unemployment was greatest in the *ranchos* — hence their importance for understanding certain kinds of conflicts in this rapidly urbanizing dependent society.

A combined application of all these criteria of stratification yields the results displayed in Figure 1.1. Some of these criteria are qualitative. In the analysis that follows, socioeconomic status will be used as a master independent variable, but it may be assumed that other criteria will be taken into account in a selective fashion.[12] There are two main reasons for choosing socioeconomic status as a testing variable. The first is that socioeconomic status can be computed from the interview data alone. This maximizes its comparability with other variables. A second reason is that,

---

[11] *SRSP*, pp. xiv–xvii.

[12] In this text socioeconomic status is defined as a combination of income, occupational prestige, and education. Figures that will appear in the remaining tables are the percentages of respondents classified as having a high socioeconomic status (HIRSES). That these variables can properly be combined in a higher index is shown by the high rank correlations among them and by the still higher correlation among the variables and the index:

	HIRSES	High Education	High Income
High education	0.56		
High income	0.73	0.33	
High prestige	0.76	0.36	0.65

The smallest of these coefficients is significant at the 0.03 level. All the correlation coefficients used throughout this book are Kendall's tau, unless otherwise specified.

not only conceptually but empirically, it is closely related to the more encompassing concept of class status.

Socioeconomic status is, as has been noted, a major component of class status, but this does not guarantee that one can be used as a substitute for the other. Therefore, this second assumption must be tested. An index of class status may be built by adding the rank into which each group is ordered according to the following variables: level of decision making (an indicator of degree of control over goods and services); socioeconomic status; and a subjective indicator of class, which in this case is the percentage of individuals who declare that they belong to at least two of the following categories: upper or middle class, the rich or modest means, and the upper or petite bourgeoisie. These operations are shown in Table 4.2, where we see that in fact there is a close relationship between socioeconomic status and the index of class status ($Rs = 0.98$).

There are two points in Table 4.2 that, before concluding this section, should be brought to the attention of the reader. In the first place, staff in government rank *very high* in socioeconomic status and class identification; however, they are considered as belonging to merely a *high* level of decision making. Second, contrariwise, owners of cattle ranches and agricultural entrepreneurs who are rather low in socioeconomic status and class identification are, nevertheless, classified among those belonging to a very high level of decision making. This apparent inconsistency is, in part, a result of applying multidimensional criteria of stratification. Staff in government are second to the group of government decision makers, whereas owners of cattle ranches and agricultural entrepreneurs figure at the top of the decision-making hierarchy in the agricultural sector.[13]

Experience of Change

Having placed the sample groups in a social grid, we now turn to the question of origin. Do high-status groups come primarily from high-status groups? What avenues have those individuals used who have managed to ascend in the social hierarchy? Analytical answers to these questions

[13] At this point it should be made clear that top rural groups are probably underrepresented, in a status sense. The sampling scheme used assumed administrators and owners of cattle ranches and agricultural enterprises as part of the same universe. However, it was later realized that administrators are, in their characteristics, very much like the traditional subsistence farmers. For an explanation of the sampling procedures, see CENDES, *Muestra de ganaderos y empresarios agrícolas: Resultados parciales* (Caracas: Imprenta Universitaria, 1967).

TABLE 4.2   Class Status of Sample Groups

Sample Groups	Decision-Making Level	High Socio-economic Status		Identified with High or Middle Groups		Class Status	
		%	Rank	%	Rank	Sum of Ranks	Rank
High government officials	Very high	100	(1.5)	89	(3.5)	9.0	(1.0)
University professors	" "	100	(1.5)	87	(5.0)	10.5	(2.5)
Oil industry executives	" "	98	(5.5)	94	(1.0)	10.5	(2.5)
Commercial executives	" "	98	(5.5)	89	(3.5)	13.0	(4.0)
Industrial executives	" "	96	(8.5)	82	(6.0)	18.5	(5.5)
Owners of cattle ranches	" "	80	(11.0)	70	(10.0)	25.0	(7.0)
Agricultural entrepreneurs	" "	56	(16.0)	65	(13.0)	33.0	(11.0)
Staff in government	High	99	(3.0)	90	(2.0)	18.5	(5.5)
Secondary school teachers	"	96	(8.5)	80	(7.0)	29.0	(8.0)
Students	"	98	(5.5)	68	(11.5)	30.5	(9.0)
Primary school teachers	"	86	(10.0)	71	(9.0)	32.5	(10.0)
Government employees	"	61	(14.0)	77	(8.0)	35.5	(12.0)
Priests	"	98	(5.5)	44	(17.5)	36.5	(13.0)
Municipal council members	"	63	(12.5)	50	(16.0)	42.0	(14.0)
Owners of small industry	"	60	(15.0)	63	(14.0)	42.5	(15.0)
White-collar workers in commerce	"	42	(18.5)	68	(11.5)	43.5	(16.0)
Labor leaders	"	63	(12.5)	22	(20.0)	46.0	(17.0)
Oil industry employees	"	42	(18.5)	52	(15.0)	47.0	(18.0)
Small business owners	"	54	(17.0)	44	(17.5)	48.0	(19.0)
Industrial workers	Low	16	(20.0)	41	(19.0)	59.5	(20.0)
Rancho dwellers	"	14	(21.0)	16	(21.0)	62.5	(21.0)
Wage workers in agriculture	Very low	4	(22.0)	15	(22.0)	67.0	(22.0)
Traditional subsistence farmers	" "	0	(24.0)	9	(23.0)	70.0	(23.5)
Farmers in land reform settlements	" "	1	(23.0)	5	(24.0)	70.0	(23.5)

usually have been given in terms of large categories such as manual and nonmanual work.[14] These studies have shown a great deal about the dynamics of society. However, we can say with Germani that

> Only one conclusion about the social consequences of mobility is likely to encounter general agreement: an enormous variety of social and individual con-

[14] S. M. Miller, "Comparative Social Mobility," *Current Sociology,* vol. 9, no. 1 (1960). Seymour Martin Lipset and Reinhard Bendix, *Social Mobility and Industrial Society* (Berkeley: University of California Press, 1959).

sequences can be imputed to social mobility. . . . An adequate analysis of the consequences of mobility — either social or individual — requires both a theory, that is, a series of clearly specified, logically interrelated hypotheses, and relevant data. Unfortunately neither theory nor empirical evidence is adequate at present.[15]

One of our core hypotheses is that at all status levels, groups entering new occupations include large numbers of individuals with much experience of change. In order to test this major hypothesis we first must establish the extent to which each strategic group has been affected by the variety of changes going on in Venezuela. Among these changes perhaps the most important are the classical residential migration, both national and international, and vertical mobility; however, we shall also take into consideration some more specific types of change such as the time that each individual has spent in his present status. Let us first consider residential mobility.

Horizontal Mobility: Residence

Discussions of residential mobility usually have as referent a geographical unit or a low-status group. The first trend is a consequence of census statistics, which tell how many people move from one place to another but tell nothing about the social status of the migrants. The second has been conditioned by the fact that low-status groups are the only visible migrants to the cities.[16] They are visible in a literal sense and also because they long have been the objects of social policies. For instance, in Venezuela in 1801, one such situation was vividly described by the prior Vicente Linares:

> The first need that must be remedied is the lack of laborers for the country works and for the preparation of fruits, because even with the precariousness of the crops it is not possible to find anyone to work even if we offer an exorbitant salary. This in spite of the abundancy of idle people who abound in their misery without any other occupation but to beg . . . which evidently prejudices not only the society but the state itself; in this capital *there are no less than ten thousand persons who live without doing any work, capable*

---

[15] Gino Germani, "Social and Political Consequences of Mobility," in Neil Smelser and Seymour Martin Lipset, eds., *Social Structure and Mobility in Economic Development* (Chicago: Aldine, 1966), p. 364.

[16] Visibility here means the degree of differentiation among the social strata. For a discussion of the concept, see Gino Germani, "Clase social subjetiva e indicadores objetivos de estratificación," mimeographed (Buenos Aires: Instituto de Sociología, 1963), pp. 7–8.

of producing what is necessary for subsistence; with respect to the beggars, every Saturday of each week one thousand two hundred of them hang around the Episcopal Palace, among whom there are only a few who are disabled; and the number of bashful people that beg during the night being excessive, it should not be strange that, inquiring into this matter through the *alcaldes de barrio,*[17] it would be found that half of this population lives from the work of the other half.[18]

Obviously, such a statement represents an interested overestimation of the phenomenon that it describes; however, it helped to induce the political authorities, representative of the metropolitan state, to take measures to deport those who were capable of working to rural areas in need of workers. In spite of the diligence of the officials, the city soon was to see the same picture.[19]

Venezuelan history includes other events, not circumscribed by a class, that affected mobility patterns among wider sectors of the population. One such event, of course, is war. There are statistics about population movements caused by the wars of independence. Without citing them, it is safe to assume that the wars, more than any other factor, were responsible for the movement of masses of Venezuelans not only throughout the country but also outside its colonial limits. Unquestionably these wars must have had lasting effects on the population, but this factor alone — or together with later revolts and internal wars, including the War of Federation — did not create a permanent impulse to migrate to the cities. After 1830 there were other, more important factors accounting for the population migration from the hinterland to the city, perhaps the most important of which was the spread of malaria.[20] Nevertheless, the impact was not truly significant. The population of Caracas between 1830 and 1930 grew at almost the same rate as the total population. Only after the exploitation of oil began in 1925 were the "pull" forces set in motion. Marginal populations became so visible in so short a period that thirty years later the government, as a means of solving this "problem," was launching a program of massive construction of low-cost apartment buildings and forcing the people to move out of the hills of Caracas.

After the fall of Pérez Jiménez (1958), the sudden wave of migrants

[17] Selectman to whom the mayor delegates his function in a section of the city.
[18] Archivo General de la Nación, Real Consulado, *Libro de Actas,* no. 4, fs. 22, ss. Cited by Federico Brito Figueroa, *La estructura económica de Venezuela colonial,* pp. 391–392.
[19] Brito Figueroa, *La estructura económica,* p. 392.
[20] G. Carrera Damas, "Apuntes de clase," mimeographed (Caracas: CENDES, 1968).

occupying several hills throughout Caracas and the outskirts of the principal cities of the country coincided with a growing concern about solving the problem of the "misery belts," as the newspapers called the zone of *ranchos*. The Venezuelan authorities tried to implement acts reminiscent of those of the metropolitan delegates of 1800. Fortunately, it was quickly realized that to return the *rancho* dwellers to the rural areas was a far more complex task than simply putting them into trucks and driving them off to the newly established land reform settlements.

Today, at least among the most sophisticated circles, there is a better understanding of the problem, but the phenomenon of rural-urban migration is still predominately considered, even by the knowledgeable academicians, as a "social problem" that must be solved, presumably by stopping or reducing it.[21] Recently some social scientists have begun to speak of the "positive" effects of the marginal settlements as a factor contributing to the urban development of the country.[22] But the most significant fact is that they continue to discuss migration as if it were a phenomenon confined to the lower-status groups.

In this section a different perspective will be taken, and the impact of migration on groups located at all levels of the social hierarchy will be explored. According to Table 4.3, it is evident first that in *all* groups, regardless of rank in the social structure, migration has been significantly widespread. Of the urban occupations (90 percent or more living in towns of 10,000 inhabitants or more) the range is from 19 percent in the group of industrial executives of the central region to 52 percent among *rancho* dwellers, the median being 36 percent.

Second, among those groups where between 50 and 90 percent live in urban areas, the impact is still higher. The median is 38 percent, but it should be taken into account that the real base (the total number of people actually living in urban places) is less than 100; thus the relative impact of rural-urban migration in these groups is actually higher than it appears to be.

Still another differential impact of migration that may have consequences for the future is apparent from the figures of Table 4.3 indicating

[21] Philip R. Hauser, ed., *Seminar on Urbanization Problems in America* (New York: International Documents Service, 1961).

[22] See William Mangin, "Latin American Squatter Settlements: A Problem and a Solution," *Latin American Research Review*, vol. 2, no. 3 (Summer 1967), pp. 65–98; John C. Turner, "La marginalidad urbana, calamidad o solución?" *Desarrollo económico*, vol. 3, nos. 3 and 4 (1966), pp. 8–14, and "Asentamientos urbanos no regulados," *Cuadernos de la sociedad venezolana de planificación*, no. 36 (December 1966).

the percentage of people that have lived (six months or more) in three or four places or states, and that may be taken as a measure of intensity of residential mobility. What is most striking about these figures is the large proportion of peasants on the move. We know that residential mobility follows a definite pattern: People move from a small village into a larger one and continue to do so until they reach the largest city.[23] The finding that between 33 and 43 percent of rural workers already have lived in three or four places suggests that these moves are a prelude to migration to the cities, and thus the flow of people toward the cities can be expected to continue. Moreover, it is clear that living in a city not only does not stop residential mobility but expands its range. Middle- and upper-status urbanites, more than any other group, seem to move from one state to another frequently.

Table 4.3 also reveals the impact of international movement on the social structure. Perhaps the most significant fact to be noted here is that immigrants from other countries have had access to certain occupations in proportions well beyond what might be anticipated in a group that constitutes only 8 percent of the total population.[24] We can say that the higher the socioeconomic status of a group, the higher will be the proportion of foreign-born individuals in that group ($Rs = 0.54$, $p < 0.01$). However, this generalization is even more applicable if we take into consideration only the economic groups in which, for example, more than 60 percent of the industrial executives of the central region, where the biggest factories mobility is still higher if we consider the number of people, including the cultural and political groups, who have lived in foreign countries for more than six months. An extreme case is that of priests, two-thirds of whom are foreigners. Most immigrants within each group were born in Spain, Portugal, or Italy, with the exception of oil industry executives, most of whom were born in other parts of Europe or in the United States.

So far we have considered migration only within one generation. If we compare the figures of the first column of Table 4.3 (where, for each group, the proportion of the informants' fathers born in urban and foreign places are shown) with the respective proportions of urban and foreign-

[23] G. W. Hill, José A. Silva Michelena and R. O. Hill, "La vida rural en Venezuela."

[24] See Levi Marrero, *Venezuela y sus recursos* (Madrid: Editorial Mediterraneo, 1964), p. 232. The proportion of foreign-born in the labor force is not known. The 8 percent cited here includes only the foreign-born people living in Venezuela in 1962 who have not become citizens. Since 1958 the inflow of immigrants has almost stopped.

TABLE 4.3 Impact of Horizontal Mobility on the Social Structure

Sample Groups	Father's Place of Birth Urban	Father's Place of Birth Foreign	Urban-Born Informants	Urban Residence	Rural-Urban Migration	Intensity of Mobility: Lived in 3 or 4 Places	Intensity of Mobility: Lived in 3 or 4 States	Foreign Experience Born	Foreign Experience Lived	Causes of Migration Economic	Causes of Migration Educational	Causes of Migration Others (1)
High government officials	34	13	68	100	32	50	28	10	24	25	37	27
University professors	34	35	74	99	24	57	21	23	41	26	35	26
Oil industry executives	25	29	64	88	35	79	30	26	45	62	6	28
Industrial executives												
Central region	16	64	81	99	19	46	8	62	64	50	6	32
Western region	23	55	64	100	36	68	14	46	51	55	0	27
Eastern region	16	32	37	79	47	84	26	32	37	90	0	11
Commercial executives	23	51	74	99	25	48	14	45	51	52	7	27
Owners of cattle ranches	25	25	22	43	29	46	7	7	8	53	10	16
Agricultural entrepreneurs	4	14	19	30	18	37	9	11	14	44	7	24
Staff in government	35	20	65	98	36	50	29	9	19	30	19	35
Secondary school teachers	26	27	59	95	38	63	32	20	27	40	25	23
Priests	5	71	55	54	22	91	13	65	69	16	15	67
Student leaders	36	12	73	96	26	48	34	4	9	8	45	20
Municipal councilmen	13	4	17	41	33	44	17	0	3	40	11	24
Owners of small industries	21	38	49	83	37	44	15	26	28	48	4	27

Small business owners	13	44	52	87	37	39	10	37	39	58	2	24
Primary school teachers	20	7	38	71	39	41	17	2	2	26	18	30
Government employees	37	16	64	99	36	34	21	2	3	25	12	34
Labor leaders	32	8	48	98	50	51	27	1	3	39	5	37
White-collar workers in commerce	27	21	63	98	35	28	9	17	18	33	9	28
Oil industry employees	20	7	31	88	63	58	19	4	7	57	1	32
Industrial workers												
Western region	42	21	62	99	37	30	4	12	18	41	2	26
Eastern region	24	11	37	86	49	44	13	5	6	46	5	27
Central region	18	32	53	98	45	25	8	23	24	42	2	32
Rancho dwellers	24	19	46	97	52	21	7	7	8	28	3	44
Wage workers in agriculture	4	14	7	9	8	33	5	6	6	49	0	18
Traditional subsistence farmers	5	15	7	7	8	42	4	1	1	52	0	24
Farmers in land reform settlements	7	18	9	1	0	43	4	5	5	52	0	22

SOURCE: CENDES, UCV, *Estudio de conflictos y consenso, Serie de resultados parciales.*

born informants, we have still another indicator of horizontal mobility: intergenerational residential mobility. The most relevant fact to be noted here is that, aside from foreigners, today's urbanites are predominantly of rural origin.

Migration has been uniformly and extensively experienced by all social groups. Even a substantial proportion of peasants have lived for some time in three or four different places. This means that social status is not related to horizontal mobility. Indeed, when we build indexes of horizontal mobility (HORMOB) and foreign experience (FOREX), we find that these variables do not correlate significantly with socioeconomic status.[25] However, internal and international migration experiences do tend to reinforce each other (tau = 0.43, $p <$ 0.00).*

Our informants give two main motives when asked why they moved from one place to another: search for economic or for educational gains. However, between one-fourth and one-third of most groups also gave other reasons such as political, family, or health.

A closer look at Table 4.3 reveals two important generalizations. (1) The higher the percentage of individuals in a group giving educational reasons as the principal motive to migrate, the greater the likelihood that it will be a high-status group. However, the percentage giving economic or other reasons has no relationship to socioeconomic status. (2) Economic groups, when asked the reason for migrating, also tend to give economic motives as a modal answer. Cultural and political groups tend to give other causes as a modal reply. There are, however, two exceptions to this rule: Secondary school teachers mention economic motives more often, and, surprisingly, *rancho* dwellers mention primarily family or health reasons.

---

[25] The index of horizontal mobility takes into account the three types of internal migration discussed in the text, namely, intergenerational and intragenerational rural-urban migration and intensity of mobility (from place to place and from state to state). The index of foreign experience is also a combination of intergenerational and intragenerational international migration. For an explanation of how the index was built, see the methodological appendix. The Kendall tau coefficients among these indexes and socioeconomic status were

Socioeconomic status of	Horizontal mobility (HORMOB)	Foreign experience (FOREX)
Father (HIFSES)	0.23	0.19
Informant (HIRSES)	0.25	0.22

The highest coefficient is significant only at the 0.09 level.

* Throughout the text $p <$ 0.00 and $p =$ 0.00 indicate probabilities of more than zero and less than 0.005, rounded to two significant digits by the computer.—ed.

That the majority of groups, when asked, mention economic or educational motives for migration may also be taken as an indication that they aspire to move upward in the social ladder; or to put it another way, they foresee that to stay in one place also means to stay in the same social position. But is it so? In order to answer this question, we must first examine the impact of vertical mobility in greater detail.

Vertical Mobility

Vertical mobility, change of status in the social hierarchy, is considered a key variable in sociological theory. However, as is the case with stratification theory, no clear-cut principle has been established. Some scholars have stressed the importance of vertical mobility as both a condition and a result of economic development.[26] Others, notwithstanding, have argued that such a relationship may not exist,[27] and still others have contended that vertical mobility is compatible with agrarian societies.[28] Politically also, mobility has been singled out as a crucial variable; thus a growing proportion of declassed people from the middle class has been noted as an important condition in the emergence of fascist-type regimes.[29] Yet Puerto Rico, a democratic commonwealth, has the highest rate of downward mobility ever registered,[30] and

a comparison with rates in eleven other European nations and Japan indicates that the two countries with the highest rate of downward mobility from the "elite" strata are the two among them that are currently in the process of emerging industrially — Italy with 36 percent moving downward into manual positions from the elite strata, and Japan with a downward rate of 27 percent.[31]

These rates of downward mobility apparently have not had important political consequences in either Japan or Italy. Moreover, the existence of economic and educational mobility in the face of political rigidity has been

[26] Gino Germani, "Estrategia para estimular la movilidad social," in Edgar De Vries and José Medina Echavarría, eds., *Aspectos sociales del desarrollo económico en América Latina,* vol. 1 (Paris: UNESCO, 1963).

[27] Neil Smelser and Seymour Martin Lipset, "Social Structure, Mobility and Development" in Smelser and Lipset, eds., *Social Structure and Mobility,* p. 20.

[28] Gerhard E. Lenski, *Power and Privilege* (New York: McGraw-Hill, 1966), pp. 289–295.

[29] Seymour Martin Lipset, *Political Man* (Garden City, N.Y.: Doubleday, 1960), p. 136.

[30] Melvin Tumin and Arnold S. Feldman, *Social Class and Social Change in Puerto Rico* (Princeton, N.J.: Princeton University Press, 1961), p. 441.

[31] Smelser and Lipset, eds., *Social Structure and Mobility,* p. 47.

interpreted as providing a favorable climate for the emergence of revolutionary elites.[32]

In the following chapters we shall explore in a variety of ways the effects of vertical mobility on the social psychology of Venezuelans; in this section we shall attempt to answer only the following questions: How much has the social hierarchy been altered as a consequence of vertical mobility? Are horizontal migrants more likely to have experienced upward mobility?

To answer the first question appropriately one must have data gathered at least within an interval of 25 to 30 years. Lacking such data, we shall give a tentative answer by comparing the education and occupation of our informants' fathers with their own education and occupation. Such a procedure has been questioned methodologically because, among other arguments, there is no reason to believe that fathers of people living today constitute a representative sample of those who lived a generation ago.[33] Nevertheless, the data in Table 4.4 are quite suggestive. The first factor to note is that those people who have reached the top educational and occupational levels come from families where the father has also reached the top, which suggests that from one generation to the other the Venezuelan social hierarchy, in spite of all changes, has hardly been altered. A more refined measure of the extent to which the social structure has been influenced by mobility is the coefficient of correlation between the socioeconomic status of fathers and that of sons. We can assume that the higher the correlation, the less the social structure has been altered.[34] In Venezuela this correlation is high (tau = 0.72; $p < 0.00$) because the probability that chance is the determinant in a person holding the same position in the social hierarchy that his father did is very small. This, of course, does not mean that the sample groups have not experienced relative vertical mobility but does indicate that whatever experience of change they have had contributed little to changing the social structure

Stability of the social structure, measured through comparison of the occupations of fathers and sons, has been established for other countries that are economically more advanced than Venezuela.[35] Some have questioned this conclusion on the basis that comparison of the occupational

[32] Harold D. Lasswell and Daniel Lerner, *World Revolutionary Elites* (Cambridge, Mass.: M.I.T. Press, 1965), pp. 458–459.

[33] Otis Dudley Duncan, "Methodological Issues in the Analysis of Social Mobility" in Smelser and Lipset, eds., *Social Structure and Mobility,* pp. 54–63. See also Natalie Rogoff Ramsy, "Changes in Rates and Forms of Mobility," in ibid., p. 215.

[34] Duncan, "Methodological Issues," pp. 63–70.

[35] Ibid., p. 70; Miller, "Comparative Social Mobility."

TABLE 4.4 Vertical Mobility: Educational and Occupational

Sample Groups	Educational Mobility			Occupational Prestige			
	Mean Years of Education		Percentage Experiencing Upward Educational Mobility	of Informant	of Informant's Father	Percentage Experiencing Upward Intergenerational Mobility	Percentage Experiencing Upward Intragenerational Mobility
	of Informant	of Informant's Father					
High government officials	15	6	77	5	3	79	9
University professors	15	6	78	5	3	67	22
Oil industry executives	12	5	71	5	3	74	33
Industrial executives			66			79	52
Central region	10	4	—	5	3	—	—
Western region	9	5	—	5	3	—	—
Eastern region	7	3	—	4	2	—	—
Commercial executives	9	4	66	5	3	83	57
Owners of cattle ranches	5	2	61	4	2	65	51
Agricultural entrepreneurs	6	2	56	3	2	67	39
Staff in government	13	5	72	5	3	73	35
Secondary school teachers	13	5	86	4	3	54	39
Priests	16	4	87	4	2	85	0
Student leaders	14	6	81	4	3	15	0
Municipal councilmen	7	2	75	4	2	75	42
Owners of small industries	6	3	63	4	2	75	58
Owners of small shops	5	2	67	4	2	82	59
Primary school teachers	10	2	88	3	2	49	3
Government employees	9	4	69	3	3	28	10
Labor leaders	7	2	70	3	2	63	46
White-collar workers in commerce	8	3	74	3	2	38	7
Oil industry employees	6	2	79	2	2	44	22
Industrial workers			68			28	14
Central region	6	2	—	2	2	—	—
Western region	6	2	—	2	2	—	—
Eastern region	5	1	—	2	2	—	—
Rancho dwellers	3	1	53	2	2	12	6
Wage workers in agriculture	1	0	32	1	1	16	10
Traditional subsistence farmers	1	0	25	1	1	10	8
Peasants in land reform settlements	1	1	21	1	1	3	2

status of fathers and sons is not a good measure of mobility. On the assumption that "the channels for mobility are multiplying as modernizing societies develop and as rich countries become richer," it has been suggested that other indicators of mobility should be used.[36] We compare not only occupations but socioeconomic status, which is an index of occupational prestige, education, and income. It is true, however, that such comparisons offer no direct measure of mobility. In order to test the hypothesis that mobility has not significantly altered the social structure, we have built an index of vertical mobility that tells us the percentage of people within each group experiencing upward or downward mobility and the percentage remaining static. This index is a combination of intergenerational and intragenerational occupational mobility and educational mobility.

These indexes reveal how intensive and widespread the experience of upward mobility has been for all Venezuelan groups (see Table 4.4), but note that it has been so regardless of the group position in the social structure. The majority of the population has moved upward but in such a way that their relative ranking has changed very little. This is confirmed by the fact that there is no correlation between upward mobility and the socioeconomic status of origin (tau = 0.08) or present status (tau = 0.13).

A more sophisticated statistical analysis, however, yields some interesting results. Seeking to establish what variables could be taken as predictors of basic stratification variables (education and occupational prestige), we selected, by means of the multiple regression technique, the four best predictors among forty different characteristics and, as Table 4.5 reveals, educational mobility stands out as a very important variable.[37] Is this fact in contradiction with the previous findings?

Perhaps the best way to answer the question is to look at the data from a different perspective (see Table 4.4). Consider, for instance, the case of government decision makers. Their fathers had, on the mean, six years of education, whereas they themselves had a much higher level, fifteen years on the mean. Obviously, they have moved upward, but at the same time they have remained in the same relative social position. Similarly, peasants have, on the mean, one more year of education than their fathers, who were illiterates. A modest gain, but still they remain in the same relative social position. When we consider all groups, the conclusion becomes rather obvious: All groups have experienced some upward educational mobility,

[36] Harold L. Wilensky, "Measures and Effects of Mobility," in Smelser and Lipset, eds., *Social Structure and Mobility*, p. 129.

[37] A description of the procedure used may be found in José A. Silva Michelena, "Venutopia I: An Experimental Model of a National Polity," in *SRSP*, pp. 344–345.

TABLE 4.5 *Four Best Predictors of Education and Occupational Prestige (beta weights)*

		Four Best Predictors of			
Clusters of Groups		Education		Prestige	
High	Urban	FATHED	(2.47)	YRSED	(0.08)
		EDUMOB	(2.42)	GENMOB	(0.23)
		GENMOB	(−0.15)	OCCMOB	(0.19)
		POLPAR	(0.11)	ECNOMY	(−0.03)
	Rural	FATHED	(1.45)	YRSEDU	(0.10)
		EDUMOB	(1.39)	GENMOB	(0.40)
		LEVINF	(0.08)	OCCMOB	(0.31)
		LOCALM	(0.15)	URBEX	(0.10)
Middle	Upper	FATHED	(1.58)	YRSED	(0.07)
		EDUMOB	(1.58)	GENMOB	(0.39)
		MASMED	(−0.09)	OCCMOB	(0.13)
		POLPAR	(0.05)	ECNOMY	(−0.04)
	Lower	FATHED	(2.23)	YRSED	(0.11)
		EDUMOB	(2.18)	INCOME	(0.04)
		ECNOMY	(−0.16)	GENMOB	(0.45)
		POLPAR	(−0.05)	OCCMOB	(0.15)
Low	Urban	OCPRES	(0.45)	YRSEDU	(0.10)
		FATHED	(1.17)	INCOME	(0.11)
		EDUMOB	(1.15)	GENMOB	(0.14)
		GENMOB	(−0.14)	OCCMOB	(0.10)
	Rural	FATHED	(1.00)	YRSEDU	(0.08)
		EDUMOB	(0.94)	INCOME	(0.07)
		MASMED	(0.04)	GENMOB	(0.29)
		URBEX	(0.06)	INTERP	(−0.01)

but the distribution of gains is highly dependent on the social status. The higher the socioeconomic status of origin of a group, the higher the net gain. In this sense, then, either the social structure has not changed at all or, if it has, the change is in a regressive direction.

This generalization holds even if we control by sphere of activity. That is, within each institutional locus, be it cultural, political, or economic, the higher the status of a group, the higher the absolute vertical mobility experienced by that group. Table 4.4 reveals some interesting facts from this perspective. First, note that for each status level, the socioeconomic background of the fathers of those who are now engaged in educational or political activities is consistently higher than the socioeconomic status of the fathers of those who have chosen to work within the economic sphere. In other words, individuals born in high-status families generally prefer a political or cultural career. Perhaps the most obvious cases are those of government clerks and student leaders. The first of these groups has fathers with as high a socioeconomic status as the fathers of industrial executives of the central region. Student leaders, together with government decision makers and university professors, come from the top-ranking families. This pattern seems to reverse what has been reported for the Venezuelan elite, that economic leaders are more likely to come from higher-status families than cultural leaders, and the latter, in turn, come from higher-status families than political leaders.[38]

This last finding may be interpreted in various ways. The interpretation that seems most viable is that individuals born in relatively high-status families prefer cultural and political careers both because they are culturally prescribed and because it is perceived that the economic elite is more exclusive.

If we now focus on the quantity of vertical mobility (the difference between the educational and occupational level of informants and those of their fathers), we again note that high- and middle-status cultural and political groups have experienced a higher leap than the economic groups; moreover, the difference is much higher with respect to educational mobility than to occupational mobility. This finding suggests that education is the channel that offered more opportunity for upward mobility for those who were already relatively high in the social hierarchy. Two exceptions may be noted here: Priests and teachers come from families of a rather low-status background, and, as is revealed by the analysis of elite career patterns, because they chose these avenues, some of them were able to reach the highest levels in the Venezuelan society.[39] But such successful cases are exceptional; the rule is that individuals born in low-status families have, as the main avenue of ascendance, the economic sphere, and it is very unlikely that they will reach the top levels within that sphere.

Are Horizontal and Vertical Mobility Associated?

We have found that migration, both national and international, has significantly contributed to the formation of present key economic groups, and that these groups contain significant proportions of people who have

[38] Frank Bonilla, *The Failure of Elites*, vol. 2 of *The Politics of Change in Venezuela* (Cambridge, Mass.: M.I.T. Press, 1970).
[39] Ibid.

ascended in the social hierarchy. Several authors have indicated that rural-urban migrants are more educated and alert than those who stay in the villages.[40] It also has been suggested that people who emigrate from one country to another are high achievers.[41] Both of these findings lead to the conclusion that horizontal mobility is associated with vertical mobility. However, in the case of Venezuela this conclusion is not supported by the data. As Table 4.6 indicates, neither internal migration nor international experience (birth or travel) has had a significant impact on upward vertical mobility.

TABLE 4.6   Residential and Vertical Mobility

| | Upward Vertical Mobility | |
Residential Mobility	Tau	Probability of Error
Horizontal mobility	0.11	0.45
Foreign experience	0.24	0.10

Other Forms of Occupational Mobility

Inter- or intragenerational occupational mobility are not, of course, the only forms of occupational mobility. A person may frequently change from one job to another without changing his status, or he may change once in his work life and go up or down the prestige scale. Searing, using the Robot technique, a statistical technique for multivariate analysis, was able to establish that in Venezuela time in present position ranks fourteenth in predictive scope (number of attitudes predicted) among 37 other social background factors; it ranks higher than parents' primary occupation, region of birth, size of town, informant's first occupation, and occupational mobility. The same study shows that time spent in present position in Israel ranks ninth in scope among 18 other social background variables, and that in the United States the same variable ranks seventh among 56 other background factors.[42] In order to assess the impact of what may

[40] Gideon Sjoberg, "Rural-Urban Balance and Models of Economic Development," in Smelser and Lipset, eds., Social Structure and Mobility, p. 243.

[41] "To begin with, moving up in social status frequently implies the geographical mobility we have found to characterize high n-achievement." David C. McClelland, The Achieving Society (Princeton, N.J.: Van Nostrand, 1961), pp. 313–322.

[42] Donad D. Searing, "Elite Socialization in Comparative Perspective," mimeographed (Chapel Hill: University of North Carolina, March 1968).

be called newness of an occupational status, we have built an index that combines the mean number of years spent by the informant in the first, previous to present, and present jobs with the frequencies of job changes and time spent without employment during the last five years.

Table 4.7 illustrates, again, the pervasiveness of the change experience. With the exception of owners of small industries, all groups that are less than 40 percent new in their status either are rural or belong to special sample groups where change of job is hardly an applicable concept, for example, *rancho* inhabitants, student leaders, and priests.

TABLE 4.7   Newness of Occupational Status by Socioeconomic Status

SES	0–19	20–39	40–59	60 and above
		Percentage in New Status		
High		Cattle owners Agricultural entrepreneurs	*University professors *Industrial executives	*Government decision makers *Oil executives *Commercial executives
Middle	Priests Student leaders	Owners of small industries	*Secondary school teachers *Municipal councilmen Owners of small shops *Primary school teachers Government clerks *Labor leaders *Clerks in commerce *Oil industry employees	*Staff in government
Low	*Rancho* inhabitants	Wage workers in agriculture Traditional peasants Land reform peasants	*Industrial workers	

NOTE: An asterisk (*) means that the distribution observed has a probability of 0.95 or more of not being due to chance. This measure is similar to a Fisher exact test but generalized for an *n*-dimensional table. See Stuart McIntosh and David Griffel, "ADMINS: A Progress Report," mimeographed (Cambridge, Mass.: Center for International Studies, M.I.T., 1967).

Table 4.8 shows that frequent changes of job, time spent in each job, and/or job instability, as measured by the index of newness of occupational status, are not associated with the sweeping residential changes experienced by the Venezuelan population in the recent past. These variables are, instead, related to the upward experience of change and to the basic stratification variables, namely, present socioeconomic status and status of origin.

TABLE 4.8 *Relationship between Newness to an Occupational Status and Other Background Factors*

Background Factors	Newness of Occupational Status	
	Tau	p
Horizontal mobility	0.17	0.25
Foreign experience	0.10	0.51
Upward vertical mobility	0.36	0.01
Father's socioeconomic status	0.44	0.00
Respondent's socioeconomic status	0.43	0.00

Experience of Change: Overview

In the preceding pages we have explored the way in which different forms of change have directly influenced the Venezuelan social structure, as represented in the sample groups. The most general conclusion is that every group, regardless of its position in the social hierarchy, has been extensively and intensively affected by residential changes. However, this nomadic tendency of Venezuelans has not significantly affected the social hierarchy.

Venezuelans have also moved upward in significant proportions. Although the mean is no more than suggestive here, as an illustration we shall note that, on the one hand, about 70 percent of all the interviewees have experienced upward educational mobility, nearly 53 percent have moved upward with respect to the occupational prestige of their fathers, and almost one-fourth have experienced upward occupational changes in their own lives.

On the other hand, the percentage of people that have experienced any type of downward mobility is, in all groups except two, equal to or lower than the rates reported for other developing or industrial nations.[43] Among

[43] Miller, "Comparative Social Mobility," p. 32.

both oil industry employees and industrial workers, 30 percent now have a lower-status job than their fathers did. This fact, however, should not surprise anyone because both of these occupations are literally new in the country. Forty years ago, there were hardly any industrial workers or oil industry employees. Emerging occupations such as these are more likely to draw people coming from the rural middle sectors or from modest occupations that, nevertheless, have a relatively higher prestige level. However, such massive mobility has not greatly altered the social structure that existed when the informants' fathers were at the peak of their careers. Quantitatively, then, change has been enormous, but relatively most people are in the same position their fathers were about thirty years ago.

Venezuelans change jobs frequently, and between 1958 and 1963, when we interviewed them, job changes had been extensive, especially in the political and cultural spheres. Moreover, at that time, there was a high incidence of unemployment that particularly hit the lower-status groups. Between one-fourth and one-third of the industrial workers had been unemployed once or twice during that period. Even 13 percent of the industrial executives reported being unemployed once in the five years previous to the interview. All these factors make Venezuelans rather new in their current status. This newness of status is not due to residential changes but rather to upward mobility; at the same time, the higher the status of a group, the higher the proportion of people new in their occupational status.

All these dimensions of mobility have been summarized in a global index of experience of change (CHANEX). This index tells us the proportion of people in each group that has experienced change in at least two of the mobility dimensions mentioned here (see Table 4.9).

That this index of experience of change (CHANEX) is a good one is demonstrated not only by its validity, as shown by the high Kendall tau correlation coefficient that it has with the indexes of upward vertical mobility (VERTUP), foreign experience (FOREX), horizontal mobility (HORMOB = 0.49), and status newness (NEWSTA = 0.58), but also by its reliability as established by the high Kendall tau correlation between CHANEX and another index of experience of change computed using a different method (EXCHAN = 0.78).[44] Therefore, from now on, CHANEX will be used as a global measure of the impact of change on the Venezuelan sample groups.

As an overall conclusion, drawn from the comparison of the global experience of change of Venezuelan and past and present socioeconomic

[44] This was the method applied to build the index of class status (Table 4.2).

TABLE 4.9 Experience of Change of Venezuelan Groups (percentages)

Sample Groups	(N)	HIRSES	HIFSES	VERTUP	FOREX	HORMOB	HEWSTA	CHANEX
						Dimensions of Change		
High government officials	(100)	100	97	12	18	78	83	75
University professors	(190)	100	95	17	35	85	57	70
Oil industry executives	(224)	98	86	18	31	95	67	78
Industrial executives	(200)	96	83	27	60	91	51	79
Commercial executives	(176)	98	86	28	51	90	60	80
Owners of cattle ranches	(178)	80	56	18	12	66	22	32
Agricultural entrepreneurs	(174)	56	48	25	20	57	22	33
Staff in government	(162)	99	95	21	19	78	75	72
Secondary school teachers	(183)	96	88	24	26	85	58	68
Priests	(193)	98	76	0*	70	93	0	70
Student leaders	(197)	90	95	0*	11	83	0	11
Municipal council members	(152)	63	61	26	4	66	55	52
Owners of small industry	(200)	60	65	22	38	88	33	64
Small business owners	(179)	54	51	30	42	84	45	68
Primary school teachers	(202)	86	73	3	7	75	54	48
Government employees	(141)	61	82	6	16	71	43	39
Labor leaders	(220)	63	61	25	8	83	56	60
White-collar workers in commerce	(180)	42	73	6	23	84	49	53
Oil industry employees	(211)	42	48	18	8	92	55	59
Industrial workers	(666)	16	52	8	28	86	48	58
Rancho dwellers	(258)	14	36	4	13	91	18	28
Wage workers in agriculture	(168)	4	18	5	14	35	30	23
Traditional subsistence farmers	(182)	0	12	4	10	38	20	21
Farmers in land reform settlements	(191)	1	19	1	17	41	33	28

* No upward vertical mobility is shown for these groups because the index shows the percentage of people in each group that has experienced inter- and intragenerational educational and occupational mobility. This definition, of course, leaves out priests and student leaders for whom no intraoccupational mobility was recorded. This index, it is recognized, is a rather restrictive one.

status, we can state that the higher the status of a group, the more likely it is that it has been affected by at least two factors of change (tau of CHANEX with father's SES $= 0.51$, and tau of CHANEX with respondent's SES $= 0.50$).

The view that emerges from our study of social stratification and mobility gives an idea of how some objective changes have affected key Venezuelan groups; these findings establish a basis for studying the impact of social stratification as measured by socioeconomic status and experience of change on the social psychology of Venezuelans. But, before taking up that task, let us explore one more background variable closely related to attitudes and opinions.

Mental mobility

People do not necessarily have to move physically to widen their experience of change. The peasant who has never left his village may receive information via mass media, most probably the radio. Exactly how much attitudinal change is experienced through exposure to mass media is still an unanswered question. Research in developed societies generally indicates that, except for some residual situations, the effect of mass media is to reinforce those attitudes and beliefs already held.[45] It has been suggested, however, that when a person has not formed an attitude or an opinion about an issue, the effectiveness of mass media is increased. Similarly, whereas it has been reported that in developed societies the function of mass media, among others, is to provide respite, security, vicarious interaction, and reinforced apathy, in the developing nations the *emphasis* is put on inducing new styles of living, of evaluation, and of leadership.[46] These differences are graphically depicted in Table 4.10. In this table the dividing line is dotted to suggest that the difference is in emphasis, *not* that these functions are exclusive.

Other types of literature contend that mass media exposure is dysfunc-

---

[45] Joseph T. Klapper, *The Effects of Mass Communication* (Glencoe, Ill.: Free Press, 1960).

[46] Ibid., *passim*. See also Lucian Pye, ed., *Communications and Political Development* (Princeton, N.J.: Princeton University Press, 1963), especially Ithiel de Sola Pool, "Mass Media and Politics in the Modernization Process" and Daniel Lerner, "Toward a Communication Theory of Modernization"; Daniel Lerner, *The Passing of Traditional Society* (Glencoe, Ill.: Free Press, 1958); and Frederick Frey, *The Mass Media and Rural Development in Turkey,* Report no. 3, Rural Development Research Project (Cambridge, Mass.: Center for International Studies, M.I.T., 1966), especially pp. 195–200.

TABLE 4.10 Functions of Public Communication in Different Types of Societies

Type of Society	Systemic Area		
	Cultural (Personality)	Social	Political
Developed	Respite Security Emotional release Stimulus of imagination	Prestige Vicarious interaction Social contacts	Reinforcement of apathy
Developing	Empathy Need-achievement New styles of evaluation	New styles of living New roles	New styles of leadership Participation Social control Policy instrument Political development

tional because it introduces values, attitudes, and desires not in accordance with the stage of development of the country, its culture, and the means available to the government to cope with these new demands. In this sense, mass communication, because it is mostly imported, helps to increase cleavages, cultural dependency, and asynchronisms.[47]

From this survey of the literature it may be concluded that, disruptive or not, in the underdeveloped societies mass communication functions primarily in the service of change; this change, however, seems to fall more in the realm of desires and information than in that of specific actions.[48] So far the discussion has used nations as the unit of reference, but looking more closely at the structure of any underdeveloped society, we see immediately that although some sectors of the population are very similar in background characteristics to those of a developed society, others are in quite a backward stage.

These sectors are embedded in the social structure in a manner roughly corresponding to different economic systems. Some people in Venezuela work in one of the most advanced industries of the world, the oil industry.

[47] See, for instance, Antonio Pascuali, El aparato singular (Caracas: Imprenta Universitaria, 1967) and Eduardo Santoro, "Los medios de comunicación de masas," mimeographed (Caracas: UCV, Escuela de Psicología, 1967).
[48] Klapper, Effects of Mass Communication, chaps. 1, 3.

Others manage state services and enterprises, while still others are engaged in quite modern industrial plants. But at the same time, there is a large sector of the population, such as the traditional peasants, working in precapitalist systems.[49] According to the previous discussion, we can expect that people working in the most advanced sectors will use mass media more as they are used in the developed countries, whereas people living in less advanced systems will be affected more in the sense suggested in the lower section of Table 4.10. But before studying the relationship between mass media, attitudes, and opinion, we must first examine the extent to which Venezuelan groups have been exposed to mass media and their effect, as well as the effect of other background variables on the information level of these groups.

As Table 4.11 indicates, all middle- and upper-status Venezuelan groups have a high exposure to several media (MASHI). The fact that as few as 22 percent of *rancho* inhabitants, 9 percent of agricultural wage workers, 3 and 1 percent of traditional and land reform peasants, respectively, are classified as having a high exposure to mass media should not mislead the reader, because "high" here means those persons who either read the newspaper every day and a magazine at least a few times a week, and/or listen to the radio every day and watch television at least a few times a week, and go to the movies a few times a month or more often. Indeed, the Venezuelan campesino is among the most exposed peasant of the world. As reported in *SRSP,* about half of the peasants listen to the radio daily; nearly three-quarters of them (although infrequently) have gone to the movies; and about one-third, in spite of the relatively high rate of illiteracy (about 50 percent), have had some exposure to newspaper reading. Moreover, we asked people to mention their regular sources of information about political affairs. From this data we built an index of the quantity of sources used (2SOURC). This index shows, for each group, the percentage of persons who declared that they obtained their political information regularly from two or more of the following sets of sources: (1) mass media (commercial newspapers, magazines, radio, and television); (2) political parties (party newspapers and party meetings); and (3) friends or relatives.

If we look at the distribution of this index (2SOURC), we see that a strikingly large proportion of peasants (Table 4.11) reported that they regularly obtained information from at least two of the previously men-

[49] For a systematic differentiation of the economic systems in underdeveloped economies, see Córdova and H. Silva Michelena, *Aspectos teóricos del subdesorrollo, passim.*

TABLE 4.11 Socioeconomic Status, Experience of Change, and Communication (percentages)

Sample Groups	(N)	NIVHI	MASHI	2SOURC	HIRSES	CHANEX
High government officials	(100)	87	89	27	100	75
University professors	(190)	88	86	15	100	70
Oil industry executives	(224)	79	89	10	98	78
Industrial executives	(200)	65	77	4	96	79
Commercial executives	(176)	72	82	7	98	80
Owners of cattle ranches	(178)	47	47	9	80	32
Agricultural entrepreneurs	(174)	43	51	12	56	33
Staff in government	(162)	81	88	17	99	72
Secondary school teachers	(183)	69	77	16	96	68
Priests	(193)	75	74	6	98	70
Student leaders	(197)	86	86	42	90	11
Municipal council members	(152)	64	71	32	63	52
Owners of small industry	(200)	56	51	9	60	64
Small business owners	(179)	40	44	4	54	68
Primary school teachers	(202)	40	52	18	86	48
Government employees	(141)	49	72	10	61	39
Labor leaders	(220)	76	80	44	63	60
White-collar workers in commerce	(180)	47	66	6	42	53
Oil industry employees	(211)	50	71	17	42	59
Industrial workers	(666)	29	47	4	16	58
Rancho dwellers	(258)	16	22	5	14	28
Wage workers in agriculture	(168)	5	9	6	4	23
Traditional subsistence farmers	(182)	4	3	13	0	21
Farmers in land reform settlements	(191)	3	1	13	1	28

tioned sets of sources. In fact, the proportion of traditional peasants and peasants in land reform settlements (but not wage workers in agriculture) reporting that they regularly receive political information from various sources is larger than the proportion of individuals reporting so among industrial or commercial executives, owners and administrators of cattle ranches and agricultural enterprises, any middle socioeconomic status economic group, or urban low-status groups.

A closer look at the figures for each individual source indicates that peasants, more often than middle-class groups, report that friends or relatives and political parties are their regular sources of political information. Indeed, the only groups that report in a significantly larger proportion than the peasants that they regularly receive political information from political parties are high government officials, municipal councilmen, student leaders, and labor leaders; all of these are highly politicized groups. Is there a correlation between regularly receiving political information from various sources and having a high exposure to mass media and the amount of knowledge of political events?

The index of political information displayed in Table 4.11 tells us the proportion within each group that answered correctly or approximately correctly a question about the places President Betancourt had visited during an international trip he made, and a query about what the Corporation of Guayana was, and/or a request that the informant describe what happened to the ship *Anzoategui,* which had been recently hijacked. Two of the questions were relevant and widely publicized political events that happened shortly before the interviews were completed, and one referred to a very important and new governmental institution created for the development of a region that has been said to be the frontier of Venezuela. When we compare these three measures of communication (MASHI, 2SOURC, and NIVHI) across the sample groups, the Kendall tau coefficients show that the higher the exposure of a group to mass media, the higher is the likelihood of its being well-informed (tau = 0.82, $p < 0.00$). Nevertheless, neither of these two indicators correlates strongly with regularly receiving political information from more than one set of sources.[50]

As Table 4.12 shows, receiving political information regularly from two

TABLE 4.12   Social Location, Experience of Change, and Communication

Social Location and Experience of Change	Communication					
	MASHI		2SOURC		NIVI	
	Tau	p	Tau	p	Tau	p
HIRSES	0.72	0.00	0.18	0.23	0.76	0.00
CHANEX	0.56	0.00	−0.18	0.58	0.51	0.00
HORMOB	0.28	0.05	−0.21	0.15	0.28	0.05
FOREX	0.14	0.35	−0.46	0.00	0.16	0.28
VERTUP	0.16	0.29	0.00	0.98	0.19	0.19

or more sets of sources is not correlated with socioeconomic status; nor is it associated with any of the indexes of mobility, except with foreign experience, which shows a negative correlation. That is, the higher the proportion of persons in a group having lived or been born abroad, the less likely is this group to have several sources of political information. This is a conse-

[50] The tau coefficient between 2SOURC and MASHI is 0.26, $p < 0.08$ and with NIVHI is 0.28, which is significant at the 0.05 level.

quence of the low proportion of persons belonging to high- and middle-status economic groups (where the highest proportion of foreigners is found) who reported having at least two regular sources of political information, and of the high proportion of peasants (the groups that have received the least impact of change) who reported receiving information from two different sets of sources.

Table 4.12 also indicates that although socioeconomic status and global experience of change are quite strongly associated with both a high exposure to mass media and a high level of information, these last two variables are quite independent from variations in foreign experience, vertical mobility, and (less so) horizontal mobility.

Turning back to our expectations about the socioeconomic situation and the change experience of each particular group, we can say that they were largely confirmed.[51] However, some qualification has to be made for several groups. Executives in large commercial firms were found to be primarily foreigners, and their reported income was found to be on the mean less than, for instance, that of high government officials.

Primary school teaching and government employment were found to be the main mobility gates for the middle class, whereas for the lower-status groups the channels open were working positions in the emerging industries and small businesses, commercial or industrial.

Venezuelan experience of change, be it residential, vertical, or of other types, is striking. No group has escaped the impact of several factors leading to change. Even the traditional peasants are, in significant proportions, already moving from village to village and even crossing their state borders. But even if they do not move physically, they no doubt are reached through the radio and other means of communication. In spite of these massive movements and in spite of greater differentiation, not only has the social structure preserved the hierarchial order of approximately thirty years ago, but social inequalities, especially educational inequalities, have increased.

Along with this process, other and perhaps more specific but no less important changes are taking place in the social structure. If we focus again on Figure 1.1 and pay attention to the mobility arrows, supported by the data presented in this chapter, we can conclude that, although they are likely to continue in the same direction as long as the economy keeps growing at the present moderate rate, certain roles are no longer an ex-

[51] See Frank Bonilla and José A. Silva Michelena, "An Integrated Analytical Scheme for CONVEN, VENELITE, and VENUTOPIA I," *SRSP*, pp. 37–42.

panding source for mobility. Neither primary school jobs nor new government positions are likely to grow at a faster rate than the population. These were the doors open to the sons of the former rural and semiurban petite bourgeoisie, and these groups are now more urban, more educated, and have relatively higher prestige and income. They will probably aspire to executive positions either in government or in large commercial firms for their sons. This clearly means that there is going to be a continuous and expanding pressure on secondary schools and universities because in order to reach such positions a minimum of ten years of education is the empirical norm. However, no easy inferences about the psychological or political consequences of these processes should be drawn. The empirical evidence must be examined carefully first.

5 THE SOCIAL PSYCHOLOGY OF VENEZUELANS: NORMATIVE ORIENTATIONS

Introduction

The year 1845 was a turning point in Venezuela's history. The country was beginning to enter what is now known as the mid-century crisis. As Figure 3.1 indicates, not only did cacao exports, the country's main product, decline sharply, but the export market was disappearing as a primary source of income. This was due in part to a reduction of the world demand and in part to the critical conditions of the agricultural industry. Representatives of both parties then active in Venezuela, liberals and conservatives, acknowledged the existence of a crisis, although liberals claimed that it was a total crisis, whereas conservatives insisted that it was localized in the agricultural sector.

The Secretary of Finance at that time, Francisco Aranda, a liberal, submitted to Congress a bill proposing a remedy: the creation of a Land Credit Institute that would contract a loan internationally and then act as a financing agent to counter what he perceived to be the sole cause of the crisis — the high interest charged by profiteers. The debate that followed made clear the position of the conservatives. Although they recognized that there was a shortage of cash, they argued that the principal cause was the high cost of transport because of the critical condition of the roads. The president of the country, General Carlos Soublette, a conservative, argued in his message to Congress objecting to the bill that the proposed Institute was unjust:

The credit of the nation, being a property of all Venezuelans, cannot be used but in the benefit of all. . . . It should be preserved intact in case there is war (if such unfortunate circumstances should afflict us one day), for building roads or any other enterprises of general utility which are needed in an emerging and unschooled country such as Venezuela, and even for financial operations aimed to the conservation of the national credit itself.[1]

He went on to urge Congress to contract an international loan for a massive program of road construction. The bill was reconsidered and rejected, but no massive program of public works was undertaken. Then came a period of increasing conflicts that, years later, led the parties to a civil war known as the War of Federation, by far the bloodiest war in Venezuelan history.[2]

Why did these dedicated patriots who, on analyzing the situation of the country, came to similar conclusions propose and debate so heatedly such different solutions? One clue to the answer is that their attitudes toward the role of the state in national life were determined by different normative patterns. For the conservatives, the policy of laissez-faire was the norm. Liberals, on the contrary, conceived the role of the state as changing according to the stage of development of a country; in a new country like Venezuela, the state should actively intervene, guiding the economy. Both solutions, the establishment of a Land Credit Institute and the building of roads, were not technically incompatible, but because one of them collided with the normative orientations of at least one of the factions, no negotiations could be opened.

This episode illustrates the role of mediating dispositions, in this case, normative orientations in the establishment of social conflicts. Every judgment made involves some implicit or explicit comparison between a perceived phenomenon and a norm. Generally, whenever differences in perceptions correspond to incompatible normative orientations, solutions are likely to lie beyond the established rules of the game. This implies nothing about the causes of conflict; it does suggest that, whatever the causes, the way in which people perceive them influences the evolution of the conflict, at least in the short run.

But whether or not people engage in actual conflict also depends on many other factors, some of which have to do with psychological states. If people are confident that the future will be better and feel satisfied with

[1] Carlos Soublette, "Objecciones hechas por el poder ejecutivo al proyecto de ley sobre Instituto de Crédito Territorial," in Laureano Villanueva, *Ezequiel Zamora* (Caracas, n.d.), p.. 34.
[2] J. A. Silva Michelena, "Los diagnósticos de la crisis de 1845," mimeographed (Caracas: CENDES, 1970).

their current situation, they will act differently than they would if they are frustrated and pessimistic about the future.

Both normative orientations and psychological states are part of what we have called mediating dispositions, that is, "psychological prisms forming in determinate ways out of social experience and coloring perceptions and evaluations of the political universe."[3] Seen from a broader perspective, such normative styles may be considered, at any given moment, as a historical product. That is, the particular ways people have solved problems and dealt with issues contributes to the formation of the political culture of that country. In this heritage we also include the way people transmit history and see themselves. But, at the same time, the problems and issues that a country confronts at any given moment also are historically unique; this fact, in turn, generates a permanent pressure toward changing normative styles. The pace of change depends on the particular orientation but most probably is slow in any case. This, of course, does not preclude the possibility of sudden changes in styles as a result of social upheaval or revolution.

Normative styles are commonly induced through a set of socializing agencies. Some agencies are more efficient than others in forming specific orientations; for the kinds of mediating dispositions in which we are interested, however, occupation is probably the most important. Nevertheless, it should be made clear that this does not mean that people are socialized only in the occupation they hold, but it indicates that occupation probably summarizes a whole array of socializing contexts. Searing, using the data on which this study is based, found that current occupation was the variable, among 37 background factors, which had the greatest scope; it predicted more attitudes (58 altogether) than any other variable, that is, 84 percent of all attitudes predicted.[4] We know that development means more social differentiation, and, as Almond and Verba have noted,

The more complex political systems are characterized by specialized structures of roles — bureaucratic, military, political executive, party intergroup, media of communication. These centers of initiative and influence in the political system also produce cultural heterogeneity. The heterogeneity results from two sources. First, the elites who perform these roles may be recruited from particular political subcultures; and second, the process of induction and socialization into these roles produces different values, skills, loyalties, and cognitive maps. Since these elites are crucial in the formulation and execution of policy,

[3] Frank Bonilla and José A. Silva Michelena, "An Integrated Analytical Scheme for CONVEN, VENELITE, and VENUTOPIA I," chap. 2 in *SRSP*.
[4] Donald D. Searing, "Elite Socialization in Comparative Perspective," Table 1.1.

the kinds of cultural differences existing among them may seriously affect the performance of political systems.[5]

Complexity of a system, however, should refer not only to the process of differentiation but also, from a structural point of view, to the coexistence of different socioeconomic systems within the same nation. This dimension of complexity also interests us here because it further increases cultural heterogeneity by providing, within a single institutional sphere, different and frequently contrasting modes of socialization.

In this chapter we shall explore the political culture of Venezuelans, focusing on a selected set of normative orientations such as style of evaluation, nationalism, political efficacy, sanctioning style, and ideology. In the next chapter we shall study the distribution of certain psychological states such as the degree of satisfaction, optimism, frustration, and alienation, and how both normative orientations and psychological states vary according to socioeconomic status and experience of change.

Style of Evaluation

Ahumada's notion of cultural heterogeneity focused only on differences of styles of evaluation among individuals occupying similar power levels.[6] Evaluation is, indeed, a very important variable. There is some evidence that evaluation is a dominant and highly generalizable attribute of judgment,[7] and that evaluative judgments of political objects are acquired earliest.[8] Nevertheless, we have preferred both to expand Ahumada's concept of cultural heterogeneity so as to cover other normative orientations such as nationalism and to narrow his concept of style of evaluation. In his definition of style of evaluation Ahumada included the number of functions that a person was able to evaluate, that is, his opinion range, the amount of information possessed, the method used to evaluate ("magical" or "rational"), the ideological charge of the evaluation, and the degree of innovativeness.[9]

In this chapter, as noted, we shall restrict the notion of style of evalu-

[5] Gabriel A. Almond and Sidney Verba, *The Civic Culture,* pp. 29–30.
[6] Jorge Ahumada, "Hypothesis for Diagnosing Social Change," pp. 192–202.
[7] Charles E. Osgood, George J. Suci, and Percy H. Tannenbaum, *The Measurement of Meaning,* pp. 188 ff.
[8] Robert D. Hess and Judith Torney, "The Development of Basic Attitude Values toward Government and Citizenship during Elementary School Years," Part I.
[9] Ahumada, "Hypothesis for Diagnosing Social Change."

ation to include only opinion range, mass media exposure, level of information, sources of information, and innovative capacity of the individuals. Ideology will be treated separately because it is so complex a variable that it merits special attention. Finally, secularism, a variable closely related to rationality, will be treated in connection with nationalism. In this way we shall be able to tackle the problem of cultural heterogeneity, which is central in our hypothesis, from different angles. This broader approach will possibly increase our understanding of the political culture of Venezuelans and give us more clues for comprehending the nature of conflicts in this country.

Earlier we were able to classify Venezuelan groups in three types along a modern-traditional continuum of style of evaluation: sophisticated, cognizant, and confined. The more sophisticated a group, the more likely it was to have a greater opinion range and to be more exposed to mass media, better informed, and more secular and innovative.[10] One of the conclusions reached in that analysis was that the higher the socioeconomic status of a group, the more likely it was to have a greater proportion of persons with a sophisticated style of evaluation.

Furthermore, it was found that within each class status, the groups more likely to have a sophisticated style of evaluation were those who had a greater proportion of urban-born informants and a higher socioeconomic status of origin. It also was established that, both across the social structure and within each class status, cultural and political groups were more likely to have a more sophisticated style of evaluation than economic groups.

Finally, it was suggested that middle socioeconomic status groups tended to be more culturally heterogeneous, that is, to have a greater "mix" of styles of evaluation. The low-status groups showed greater homogeneity.

All these findings were retested for the present work for several reasons. First, at that time we had no good index of mobility and therefore did not really test for correlation between change experience and style of evaluation. Second, this time we have modified slightly the definition of style of evaluation. In fact, as was pointed out earlier, we restructured it by taking out the secularism dimension. This, of course, might have some effect on the conclusions. Finally, there was an operational reason, in that we are now using an entirely different method of index construction, which also might

[10] José A. Silva Michelena, "Desarrollo cultural y heterogeneidad cultural en Venezuela."

have some influence on the conclusions. This new index of style of evaluation will be described so that the reader may have a clearer picture of its implications.

We need here to explain only two of the five indexes used in the construction of the overall index of style of evaluation. The other three (exposure to mass media, number of sources of information used to obtain political information regularly, and level of information) were used and explained in the preceding chapter. The index of opinion range was constructed by tallying the number of problems mentioned by the informants when we asked them,

1. What do you consider to be the principal problems that confront families today in Venezuela?
2. What concerns you most about the current situation in Venezuela?
3. Who do you think should take the major responsibility for the solution of this situation?

It was assumed that the more problems a person mentioned, the greater was his opinion range.

The index of innovativeness also was formed from three questions:

1. What is your opinion of women working full time outside of the home? Do you think that it is acceptable, acceptable only in case of necessity, or unacceptable?
2. To prosper in your work or job, which one of the following things do you consider to be the *most* important thing that you must do? Make important friends; work hard; acquire new habits and skills; introduce new methods; be loyal to the organization or firm, or belong to the party of the boss.
3. Which do you think is better advice to give someone?
   a. A known evil is better than an unknown good, *or*
   b. New problems require new solutions.

The innovators were those who replied, to the second question, that to prosper in their work it was most important to acquire new habits and skills or introduce new methods, and who also answered that it was acceptable that a woman work full time outside of the home or would prefer to advise someone that new problems require new solutions.

Table 5.1 indicates that all variables used to form the index — mass media exposure (MASHI), level of information (NIVHI), regular sources of political information (2SOURC), opinion range (AWARE), and innovativeness (INVENT) — are interrelated. The weakest correlations, as was noted in the previous chapter, are found among sources of information and exposure to mass media and level of information. Nevertheless, that these

TABLE 5.1   Index of Style of Evaluation:
Kendall Tau Rank Correlation Coefficients

	SAVANT II	SAVANT	INVENT	AWARE	2SOURC	MASHI
SAVANT	0.87					
INVENT	0.55	0.45				
AWARE	0.76	0.81	0.39			
2SOURC	0.48	0.37	0.33	0.36		
MASHI	0.75	0.87	0.43	0.68	0.26*	
NIVHI	0.73	0.83	0.34	0.75	0.28	0.82

* The smallest coefficient (0.26) is significant at the 0.08 level.

variables combine nicely into an index of style of evaluation (SAVANT) is shown by the fact that the correlation of each component with the index is higher than the correlation between any given pair of them. A test of the reliability of SAVANT was made by correlating it with another index of style of evaluation (SAVANT II) built by following a different method.[11] The Kendall tau coefficient between these two indexes was highly significant (0.87; $p < 0.00$).

With this index in hand, a test of all previous conclusions was performed, and the results confirmed all of them. The higher the socioeconomic status of a group, the larger would be the proportion of persons having a sophisticated style of evaluation (tau = 0.45; $p < 0.00$). Political and cultural groups also were found to have a greater proportion of sophisticated persons than economic groups of similar status. The middle class was found to be the most heterogeneous and the lower classes the least. Moreover, the general hypothesis, not previously tested, that the higher the experience of change of a group, the greater the proportion of sophisticated persons in it, was confirmed (tau = 0.45; $p < 0.00$).

Nationalism

In 1958 Venezuelans, like their fellow citizens of more than a century ago, went through a national crisis. This was also a turning point in the history of the country. As in 1845, the main export product — oil, in this case — lost its role as the dynamic factor of the economy (see Figure 3.1). The rate of growth of oil exports fell to about 3 percent during the last decade, whereas it had been 9 percent a year for the previous 30 years.

[11] Ranking the sum of the ranks of the components.

The impact of such decline has been analyzed in *SRSP*.[12] Our main interest here is to point out that during this last period of national crisis (1958–1965) the degree to which people accepted state intervention in the economy was an important issue. Although government officials and top government elite this time conceived the role of the state as a guiding one, contrary positions were more radicalized along the liberal-socialist line. There is no point in pursuing this description further now. What has been said so far is sufficient to illustrate the point we want to make: One of the most important normative orientations is what has been called *national identification,* that is, the degree to which the state is perceived as a set of internalized social values.[13]

National identification is a multidimensional aspect of nationalism. Perhaps the most important of these dimensions is the degree to which the state is considered a supreme secular value, that is, the extent to which people accept "the expansion of state power into economic, occupational, and social areas." [14] Other dimensions are: (1) the sense of openness in the society, that is, the extent to which class barriers to mobility are perceived; (2) the degree to which a person has been able to internalize certain civic rights and duties, which will here be labeled citizen responsibility; (3) finally, secularism, which indicates the extent to which people are able to perceive natural objects and events as independent from supernatural or religious factors. In our earlier study (*SRSP*), it was shown that all of the dimensions except openness of society (which was not considered then) were closely related to having a strong sense of commitment and loyalties to the state which were above and beyond family, religious, or other types of loyalties. This analysis led to the construction of three categories of nationalists along a modern-traditional continuum.

These categories — modern, transitional, and traditional national identification — were shown to be related to still another aspect of nationalism: patriotism. Reformist individuals, those "who value the patriotic symbols

[12] Jorge Ahumada, *SRSP,* chap. 1.
[13] Nationalism is both theoretically and empirically discussed in the first volume of this study. Here we shall highlight only its main features. See José A. Silva Michelena, "Nationalism in Venezuela," *SRSP,* chap. 3. The theoretical framework and many of the questions used in this study lean heavily on the work of Kalman H. Silvert. See, for instance, "The Strategy of the Study of Nationalism," in Kalman H. Silvert, ed., *Expectant Peoples: Nationalism and Development* (New York: Random House, 1963); Kalman H. Silvert and Frank Bonilla, "Education and the Social Meaning of Development: A Preliminary Statement," mimeographed (New York: American Universities Field Staff, 1961).
[14] *SRSP,* p. 59.

of nationality but reinterpret them in terms of current pressing needs and the goals they have set for the country," [15] were more likely to be modern. Patriotistic individuals, those "who are aware of symbols of nationality but have an essentially ceremonial orientation toward them," [16] were more often classified as transitional. Finally, apathetic individuals, "who express no sentiment toward conspicuous and traditional symbols of nationality," [17] were classified mainly as traditional. However, no stratum was found to be homogeneous, not even when socioeconomic status was taken into account. In fact, as in the case of style of evaluation, the middle class emerged as the most heterogeneous. And, again, the least diversity was found among the lower stratum.

In the present study we shall retest these findings plus the following two hypotheses:

H1: The higher the experience of change of a group, the more likely it is that it will have a higher proportion of nationalists.

H2: The higher the style of evaluation of a group, the more likely it is that it will have a higher proportion of nationalists.

The definition of nationalism here will follow closely our previous one; however, because both method and questions used differ somewhat, we shall presently describe how each aspect and dimension was defined operationally.

The index of nationalism to be used here will combine only two aspects: patriotism and national identification. The politicoadministrative and juridical aspects of nationalism will be taken into account only as objects of orientation, that is, as they are reflected in the way people value the state. The ideological aspect of nationalism will be considered separately in a following section.

Patriotism, as a normative orientation, may be inferred from answers to a question about how people think symbols of nationality and patriotic days should be honored. As in *SRSP*, three types of patriotism are differentiated according to the replies given to the question "In your opinion what is the most appropriate way of celebrating the fifth of July?"

Defined as apathetic were those individuals who did not know that the

[15] Ibid., p. 60.
[16] Ibid.
[17] Ibid. We have elected, in this volume, to use the categories "reformist," "patriotistic," and "apathetic" rather than "modern," "transitional," and "traditional" to identify types of nationalism, for two reasons: first, because they are highly correlated, and, second, because the terminology chosen has more social meaning.

fifth of July is the anniversary of national independence from Spain; those who said that they would do nothing special; or those who would celebrate it by going to church, praying, or getting drunk. Individuals who replied that they would celebrate the fifth of July in a traditionally passive way, such as thinking about the heroes, or in a traditionally active way, such as going to see a parade, were considered to be patriotistic. Responses like the following served to identify the reformists: working, informational (or propagandistic) activities, popular meetings of a nationalist character. A few responses were quite revolutionary. For instance, one person said that he would promote the emancipation of the country from its new colonizers (meaning the United States). This type of answer was classified along with the reformists because there were too few to justify a separate category. The proportion of reformists (REFORM) in each group may be seen in Table 5.2.

No single index of national identification was constructed. Each of its dimensions was treated separately and then taken into account to build the general index of nationalism. How each of these dimensions was used will be described in the following paragraphs.

As was pointed out in *SRSP,* there are important historical reasons why Venezuelans typically do not see class barriers.[18] If directly asked they overwhelmingly (70 percent or more) reply that any person can become a general, an industrialist, or a lawyer. Nevertheless, any person who has lived long enough in Venezuela, and especially in the larger cities, notes certain subtle manifestations of racial or class discrimination or, as was illustrated vividly in the case of the revolutionary in *SRSP,* structural obstacles to social advancement which are difficult to overcome even by a motivated, intelligent person of low socioeconomic status.[19] Thus we attempted to get at this matter indirectly by asking, "There is a well-known popular saying that goes, "A monkey, although dressed in silk, remains a monkey." Do you completely agree, agree, disagree, or completely disagree with the idea that this saying tries to express?"

After the person chose one among the alternatives given, we asked, "Could you tell me why you think that?" In order to make the index very restrictive, we considered that a person did not perceive class barriers (NOBAR) when he said that he disagreed or completely disagreed with the saying because it is important to take into consideration a person's qualities, or explicitly stated that any person could move up in the social ladder,

TABLE 5.2   Indicators of Nationalism in Venezuela (percentages)

Groups	(N)	REFORM	NOBAR	CIVRES	STATVA	SECLR	NATION
High government officials	(100)	42	35	34	91	70	81
University professors	(190)	41	45	31	83	70	82
Oil industry executives	(224)	31	40	27	75	64	72
Industrial executives	(200)	18	27	24	68	54	56
Commercial executives	(176)	24	37	22	72	63	70
Owners of cattle ranches	(178)	12	31	17	69	51	57
Agricultural entrepreneurs	(174)	15	26	22	64	45	52
Staff in government	(162)	39	45	33	86	64	75
Secondary school teachers	(183)	49	53	39	77	54	77
Priests	(193)	37	30	35	54	1	37
Student leaders	(197)	51	34	34	88	55	77
Municipal council members	(152)	30	31	31	82	45	70
Owners of small industry	(200)	16	27	26	68	56	57
Small business owners	(179)	7	31	26	62	47	55
Primary school teachers	(202)	48	46	42	79	39	71
Government employees	(141)	13	32	40	77	53	70
Labor leaders	(220)	37	48	48	84	60	81
White-collar workers in commerce	(180)	11	38	26	74	51	63
Oil industry employees	(211)	10	36	18	74	48	59
Industrial workers	(666)	5	30	19	62	45	52
Rancho dwellers	(258)	2	33	7	61	46	49
Wage workers in agriculture	(168)	2	23	9	39	30	26
Traditional subsistence farmers	(182)	2	21	14	36	25	28
Farmers in land reform settlements	(191)	3	15	16	43	21	23

or said that personal changes could indeed facilitate upward mobility. In this group we also included those persons who did not perceive a class content in the saying; for example, a small industrialist said, "It is not a sin that a person wants to be something more," and a student leader

said, "Education makes it possible for a person to change." The *rancho*
dweller who said, "It is difficult for a monkey to get dressed in silk,"
obviously was unaware of the class content in the saying.

Citizen responsibility, in the sense taken here, is a set of norms about
what an individual should do to meet certain social and political responsibilities. In Latin America the lack of civic responsibility toward the
family is manifested by the large numbers of abandoned children. Although
this is a phenomenon closely related to economic deprivation, middle- and
upper-status groups are not exempt from it. Oscar Lewis has documented
this problem vividly in perhaps its most acute forms.[20] Again, the case of
the Venezuelan revolutionary provides us with an excellent and perhaps
more pertinent example.[21]

Civic responsibility has a profound political meaning. Almond and Verba
speak of the sense of civic competence in referring to what others have
called political efficacy, that is, the subjective feeling that one is capable
of influencing the government or authorities. In a later section of this
chapter we shall discuss this normative orientation separately. What is
of interest here is civic responsibility as it relates to social duties or as a
quality generally perceived by the people. Two questions were used to
build the index of civic responsibility:

1. What do you think should be done to a father who abandons his family?
2. Now I am going to read a list of qualities that can characterize an individual.
   Which of them do you consider *most* important? Being a good citizen, being
   a good father (or mother), performing well in your job or profession, being
   a good husband (or wife), or being a good friend.

The social dimension was directly identified in answers to the first
question, the global dimension was indirectly identified in the second
question. The responsible citizen (CIVRES) was defined as a person who
answered that a father who abandons his family should be reoriented
(reeducated) or that some legal sanction should be applied toward him,
and also said that the most important quality of character is being a
good citizen (see Table 5.2).

Changes in family relations and in social relations in general induced
by the emergence of capitalism have been taken into consideration since
Marx and Engels wrote the *Communist Manifesto*. However, a narrower
consideration of cultural changes reveals that the differentiation of social
structure from the cultural system created during the Reformation, Renais-

[20] Oscar Lewis, *La Vida* (New York: Knopf and Random House, 1968).
[21] Slote, "Case Analysis," p. 267.

sance, and Enlightenment opened the doors for the ramification and expansion of a secular culture. As Parsons pointed out, the establishment of an immediate relationship between man and God by the Reformation broke the Church's control of the family, school, and other social and political institutions. The secularization of the social structure was reinforced by the Renaissance; the developments in philosophy and science during the Enlightenment contributed definitely to the secularization of the cultural system.[22]

The process of secularization in most Latin American societies, however, has been very slow. Quite advanced nations, such as Argentina and Chile, have not yet institutionalized divorce. The influence of the Church in politics is surpassed only by its control of the educational system. As seen in Chapters 2 and 3, the Church, although important, has had less influence in Venezuela than in other countries; yet, as is so vividly documented in the elite interviews, its potential influence is still quite great.[23] Our index of secularism (SECLR) is a measure of the extent to which Venezuelan groups normatively accept the influence of the Church in their family lives in the sense of following Church proscriptions with respect to birth control and divorce; their tolerance of nonreligious behavior; and their concept of the appropriate role of the Church in politics. Each of these dimensions was tapped by a question; a secularly oriented individual was considered one who gave secular answers on at least three of the four dimensions mentioned.[24]

All variables of national identification discussed so far identify, in one

[22] Talcott Parsons, *Societies: Evolutionary and Comparative Perspectives* (Englewood Cliffs, N.J.: Prentice-Hall, 1966).

[23] Frank Bonilla, *The Failure of Elites,* chap. 7.

[24] The precise form of the questions is as follows:

1. Under what circumstances do you think a married couple have the right to avoid having children? In no case; only in cases when the Church permits it; * in some cases even when the Church does not permit it; or * whenever they want.

2. With which of the following phrases do you most agree? * Divorce should be granted to people seeking it; divorce should be granted only in special cases; or divorce should not be permitted in any case.

3. With respect to the relations between the Church and politics, which of the following phrases best expresses your thoughts? * The Church should never try to influence people's votes; the Church has the right to guide voters but not to impose parties or candidates on them; or the Church has the right to impose parties and candidates on voters.

4. What do you think should be done to people who never go to Church? (This was an open-ended question. Those who said that nothing should be done or who said that such behavior should be understood were considered to have a secular orientation.)

The index of secularism, then, was formed by grouping all those individuals who gave secular replies to at least three of the four questions. (Alternatives marked with an asterisk are those used to build the index.)

way or another, some aspect of the impact the state has had on the Venezuelan's normative orientation. The perception, or lack of it, of class barriers requires that the individual be able to conceive the nation or the society at large as an object of orientation. Civic responsibility is somewhat more directly connected with a general kind of political attitude emerging from the exigencies that the state and the society impose on individuals; secularism, as we just saw, compares the extent to which the nation and the Church compete for the loyalties of Venezuelans. Yet, in order to form an index of nationalism, we need to take more directly into consideration those aspects which, as may be inferred from the opening example in this chapter, are crucial: the degree to which individuals accept the extension of state power in other institutions, that is, the extent to which people attach more importance to national loyalties vis-à-vis other loyalties such as the family, religion, occupation, or political party.

The index of the extent to which people consider the state the supreme secular value was then formed by grouping those respondents who gave at least two nationalistic replies (those marked with an asterisk) to the following set of questions:

1. Which of the following types of loyalty do you think is most important for a person to have? Which is next in importance? Loyalty to his family; to the organization for which he works; to his profession or office; to his political party; to his church; or * to his country.

2. Which of the following phrases best expresses your thoughts regarding the role that the state should play in the economy?

   a. The economy should develop without any state intervention.

   b. The state should intervene in the economic sector only to orient the economy toward private enterprise.

   * *c.* The state should control only basic industries (for example, electricity, mines, petrochemicals, iron).

   * *d.* The state should assume total control of the economy.

3. As to worker-management relations, which of the following phrases best expresses your thoughts?

   a. The state should not intervene in worker-management relations.

   * *b.* The state should act only as mediator in worker-management relations.

   * *c.* The state should direct and control worker-management relations.

Results of the comparison of all these indexes with the general index of nationalism (NATION) may be seen in Table 5.3. In this table there is

TABLE 5.3   Interrelation of Nationalism and Its Components

Nationalism	NATION	PATROT	SECLR	STATVA	CIVRES
PATROT	0.66				
SECLR	0.63	0.36			
STATVA	0.81	0.35	0.52		
CIVRES	0.57	0.63	0.27	0.57	
NOBAR	0.67	0.58	0.39	0.63	0.49

NOTE: All coefficients are Kendall tau.

a high association among patriotism, perception of the society as open, a sense of civic responsibility, and valuing the state above both Church and any other social or economic institution. That all these aspects can be combined nicely to form a global index of nationalism is demonstrated not only by the high correlation between each item and the index (see Table 5.3) but also by their high concordance ($W = 0.77$, $x^2 = 89.3$, with 23 degrees of freedom).

A closer examination of the data in Table 5.2 reveals that cultural and political groups are more likely to have a greater proportion of nationalists than economic groups of comparable socioeconomic status. In effect, if we focus attention on the middle- and upper-status groups, we see that whereas the median percentage for the cultural groups is 75, for the economic groups it is 57. This distribution is explained in part by the fact that the higher the percentage of nationalists in a group, the more likely is that group to have a greater proportion of sophisticated individuals. This generalization is confirmed by the high Kendall tau (0.78) between our indexes of style of evaluation and of nationalism.

The higher the socioeconomic status of a group, the more likely is that group to have a high percentage of nationalists (tau $= 0.58$, $p < 0.00$); the experience of change also seems to work in that direction, although to a lesser degree (tau $= 0.28$; $p < 0.05$). Again, as was the case with respect to style of evaluation, middle-status groups seem to be the most heterogeneous of all and the low-status groups the most homogeneous.

Political Efficacy

A person may be highly sophisticated and nationalistic, yet if he lives privately, his influence on politics may be minimal. One can, of course, expect that those who try more frequently to influence government are those whose style of evaluation and national orientation are more advanced.

But because neither government nor sophisticated individuals generally make use of scientific instruments for finding out what the people really want, whenever they act, they will tend to do so on the basis of their own biased assessment of what should be done. However, those who are more likely to be influential are also more likely to belong to the upper-status groups, so it follows that pressure would more often be exercised in favor of those who need less. This tendency, of course, may be upset by the power of organizations. Strong unions or peasants' leagues can change that trend. Later we shall explore the political activism of the Venezuelan groups. Here, we focus on the normative aspect, namely, a person's belief that he can influence the government. As Almond and Verba have pointed out, in part the importance of having a subjective sense of competence is that "if an individual believes he has influence, he is more likely to attempt to use it." [25]

But the consequence for an individual of not having political efficacy is not only that he will be less likely to influence public policy, but also that he is more likely to be manipulated by others. This seems to be the case of the Venezuelan peasant, whose level of participation significantly surpasses his level of political efficacy.[26] Attempting to influence government through an organization or by mobilizing other individuals and protesting publicly by using mass media are specific styles of acting. It does, of course, make a difference for the political system whether the influential individuals prefer to exert pressure through organizations, prefer to stir up demonstrations, or choose still other ways of manifesting their desires or reactions to public policy. In Table 5.4 we can see both the level of political efficacy with respect to national government and the preferred means of influencing it. Percentages in Table 5.4 are figured on the basis of responses given to the following question: "Suppose that the national government were planning to do something that you considered harmful or unjust; what do you think you could do to stop it?"

As expected, persons sampled among lower-status groups more frequently said that they did not know what to do or that they could do nothing to alter such a situation. By the same token, the higher the socioeconomic status of persons belonging to a group, the more likely was it that the group would have a large proportion of subjective competents. This generalization also holds when the situation is phrased in terms of a

[25] Almond and Verba, *Civic Culture*, p. 182.
[26] John Mathiason, "The Venezuelan Campesino: Perspectives on Change," *SRSP*, p. 139.

TABLE 5.4   *What Individuals Would Do to Try to Influence National Government (percentages)*

Groups	Don't Know or Say Can Do Nothing	Seek Support of an Organization	Use Public Protest		Directly Influence Government	
			Mass Media	Demonstration, Rebel	Legally	More Radically
High government officials	22	13	37	5	10	4
University professors	30	6	24	17	26	6
Oil industry executives	47	4	21	12	11	4
Industrial executives	60	5	11	9	8	5
Commercial executives	56	6	15	8	11	4
Owners of cattle ranches	60	7	6	7	7	6
Owners of agriculture enterprises	61	5	14	5	8	6
Staff in government	36	8	29	8	11	4
Secondary school teachers	38	10	17	9	19	4
Priests	45	10	26	6	18	4
Student leaders	9	8	19	40	12	11
Councilmen	23	7	24	12	22	10
Owners of small industries	68	3	10	10	5	6
Owners of small shops	73	—	6	7	6	6
Primary school teachers	57	8	13	5	11	2
Government employees	59	1	11	5	10	9
Labor leaders	11	17	23	23	18	5
White-collar workers in commerce	70	2	7	7	6	8
Oil industry employees	66	3	12	3	10	5
Industrial workers	72	2	6	7	6	5
Rancho dwellers	77	—	2	4	9	5
Wage workers in agriculture	85	1	2	4	3	3
Traditional sub-sistence farmers	78	3	2	1	9	7
Farmers in land reform settlements	80	2	1	4	5	6

specific branch of government such as the police and/or when the prospective abuser of authority is the local government. The high correlation between the index of political efficacy (POLEFF) and socioeconomic status (HIRSES) supports this generalization (tau = 0.63, $p < 0.00$).[27]

We note, however, that some of the middle-status groups have a high level of political efficacy. In part this is due to their greater experience of change, because there is a positive and quite significant association between experience of change (CHANEX) and political efficacy (tau = 0.30, $p < 0.04$). Still another and more convincing reason is that political efficacy is related to other important normative orientations such as nationalism (NATION) and style of evaluation (SAVANT). This idea is strongly supported by their respective tau coefficients (tau = −0.66 and tau = 0.74, both significant at the 0.00 level).

The strategy typically preferred by most Venezuelan groups, regardless of their social position, is the use of mass media or some form of public communication to influence national government. This is particularly true of those working in the political sphere or of politicians themselves. For instance, whereas about half of the politically efficacious government decision makers and government staff said that they would use public communication to voice a protest, only 40 percent of the efficacious oil industry executives and about one-third of other high economic groups (except owners of cattle ranches) said that they would protest through the mass media. Cultural groups are much more diverse in their reactions. Thus, a sizable proportion of efficacious student leaders (44 percent) said that they would stir up demonstrations or some form of popular rally, but priests and primary school teachers would prefer mass media or some legal means, such as litigation. University professors and secondary school teachers reversed these choices: They preferred legal means first, although a little less than a third of them preferred to use mass communication.

A striking fact that emerges from a more detailed analysis of Table 5.4 is that about a third or more of most groups declared that they

---

[27] According to the index, a politically efficacious individual would be one who answered efficaciously to these two questions: (*a*) How interested are you in political affairs? Would you say that you are * very interested, * moderately interested, slightly interested, or not interested at all? (*b*) national efficacy (see question on p. 128). He also gave efficacious responses to at least one of the following questions: (*c*) If you felt unjustly treated by the police, what do you think you could do to stop it? (*d*) Suppose that the prefect or municipal council were planning to do something that you considered harmful or unjust. What could you do to stop it? Alternatives marked with an asterisk in question (*a*) are considered efficacious; all responses in columns 3 through 7 in Table 5.4 are considered efficacious replies to questions (*b*), (*c*), and (*d*).

would choose to stir up demonstrations or use some radical means to affect government. This tendency seems to be greater, the lower the socioeconomic status of the politically efficacious citizen. Thus, although between 35 and 55 percent of the subjectively competent low-status individuals favored the use of some radical means (demonstrating or directly influencing government), about one-third of most middle- or upper-status groups said that. In fact, only student leaders and the most typical representatives of the petite bourgeoisie (small industrialists or owners of small shops and white-collar workers in large commercial firms) matched the figure of politically efficacious low-status individuals. Why this should be so cannot easily be explained. A prominent Venezuelan leader, writing from jail, tells us that such reactions are typical of the petite bourgeoisie in time of revolutionary crisis:

> There are periods when the petite bourgeoisie overcome their own vacillations and are more intensively attracted toward revolutionary politics. . . .[28]

But he immediately warns us that in a different, nonrevolutionary situation the members of the petite bourgeoisie vacillate, and their opinions are fragmented and negate each other. Moreover, García Ponce continues,

> The petit bourgeois mind is not appropriate to maintain a long struggle, firmly and consistently, and to preserve lucidity in the face of affliction, when a setback shatters its ranks.[29]

He goes on to say that between 1958 and 1963, the situation in Venezuela was a revolutionary one, but that from 1963 onward it became one in which "the political panorama lacked precise definition and the manipulative game was substituted for the evident action of the masses." [30] Such hypotheses are, of course, difficult to test. However, data in Table 5.4, which were gathered in mid-1963, tell us that the lower the status of a group, the less efficacious that group will be, and especially so if it is a low economic group. Nevertheless, it is also evident from the data that the politically efficacious man with an economic occupation, and especially if he is of low status, is more prone to act radically than either political or cultural groups, with the exception of student leaders and possibly government clerks and labor leaders. In any case, these figures reveal that Venezuelans, in general, have a rather low propensity to act through organiza-

---

[28] Guillermo García Ponce, *Política y clase media* (Caracas: Editorial Muralla, 1966), p. 98.
[29] Ibid., p. 101.
[30] Ibid., p. 100.

tions. This is supported by the fact that among the subjectively competent individuals, no more than 21 percent chose to work through an organization as a strategy to influence government.

The data presented so far also suggest that, on the one hand, the higher the socioeconomic status of a group, the more inclined the politically efficacious members of that group are to use mass media to influence government. On the other hand, the lower the socioeconomic status of the subjectively competent person, the more likely it is that he will favor a radical way of influencing government. Moreover, when socioeconomic status is held constant, it seems that the politically efficacious economic men, if we except student and labor leaders, are more prone to choose radical ways of influencing government. Does this mean that these groups are, in general, more disposed to violence? We shall now turn to answer this question.

Propensity to Violence

Georges Sorel's *Reflections on Violence* is still the most provocative and complete treatise on the subject. He shocked his contemporaries by arguing that political violence was but a manifestation of the changing social order, a consequence of social struggles, and that violence is therefore to be regarded as ethically just when exercised in behalf of change. However, his view on the subject was far from simplistic. He explored different types of violence. Among the types he identified are: (1) struggle for life, which operates on the lowest level, meaning that it is closely related to the economic conditions of existence; (2) concentrated and organized violence, which in modern societies is the privilege of the state; and (3) violence properly so called which, according to him, is the principal object of history, namely, class struggle.[31] His brilliant analysis of the general strike as a political instrument of the working class is of great interest here. His insistence that an act such as a general strike is closely associated with men's images and belief systems and that this may be best revealed by questioning the political activist is directly and powerfully expressed in the following words:

> We have to question these men who take a very active part in the real revolutionary movement amidst the proletariat, men who do not aspire to climb into the middle class and whose minds are not dominated by corporative prejudices.
>
> . . . thanks to these men, we know that the general strike is indeed what I

[31] Georges Sorel, *Reflections on Violence* (New York: Free Press, 1950), p. 194.

have said: the *myth* in which Socialism is wholly comprised, i.e., a body of images capable of evoking instinctively all the sentiments which correspond to the different manifestations of the war undertaken by Socialism against modern society.[32]

He goes on to clarify the influence of strikes on the proletarian mind:

Strikes have engendered in the proletariat the noblest, deepest and most moving sentiments that they possess: the general strike groups them all in a coordinated picture, and, by bringing them together, gives to each one of them its maximum of intensity; appealing to their painful memories of particular conflicts, it colours with an intense life all the details of the composition presented to consciousness.[33]

General strikes continue to be a powerful weapon against governments, but they can no longer be considered exclusive to the proletariat. That nonrevolutionary but rebellious political movements may resort successfully to the use of general strikes is exemplified by the general strike that in the very dawn of 1958 did away with the ten-year dictatorship of Pérez Jiménez. In this case, even high socioeconomic status groups such as executives of oil industries, banks, and other large commercial firms solidly backed the general strike and participated massively in the general jubilee that followed after Pérez Jiménez fled in the early morning of January 23. Moreover, this group, represented by some of the most outstanding Venezuelan businessmen, also took part in the new government that was formed.

We asked no question referring directly to participation in the general strike; however, we attempted to tap this subject in a perhaps more general way by asking, "Under what circumstances do you think a violent protest against the government is justified?"

Responses to this question were coded and classified as shown in Table 5.5. Violent, in this sense, then, are persons who are inclined to justify a violent protest against the government in a variety of situations in which the government, as they perceive it, is not fulfilling its duties or benefiting the people. A typical reply of this sort was given by an industrial worker who said, "When there is hunger and nothing is being done," or the student leader who said, "Right now."

Those persons who answered that they would never protest violently against any government or who would do so only when the government was illegal were classified as LEGAL. In between were those persons who justified a violent protest specifically when the government was not dem-

---

[32] Ibid., p. 145.
[33] Ibid.

TABLE 5-5 *Operational Definitions of Styles of Sanctioning*

Question about	Violent	Mild	Legal
Violent protest against government is justified	When the government 1. Has not done what it offered 2. Is inefficient, incapable of solving the basic problems of the country or benefiting its citizens 3. Is antinational, lacks nationalism 4. Lacks representativeness or popular support 5. When there is a general state of chaos *or* 6. The situation is like the present one (1963)	When the government 1. Is not legal or unjust 2. Is the result of a coup d'état or revolution	1. Never 2. When the government is not legal or is unjust
Would justify the occupation of another person's land	1. When the land is not accomplishing a social function or rendering a service to the community 2. When it belongs to the rich 3. When people want it or when it is government land	1. When there is misery, extreme necessity, or calamity 2. When there is lack of vital space, overpopulation, etc. 3. Conditional answers	1. Under no circumstances 2. Only when it is prescribed by the law
What should be done to Unfaithful husband Unfaithful wife	1. Nothing or approve act 2. Nonviolent noninstitutional action 3. Moderate or extreme violence	1. Orient him (or her) 2. Nonviolent noninstitutional sanction 3. Conditional answer	1. Nonviolent noninstitutional action 2. Some form of legal or institutional sanction
A neighbor that upset public order	Same as above	Same as above	1. Some form of legal or institutional sanction
A son who is of working age and does not want to work	Same as above plus some form of legal or institutional sanction	Same as above	1. Orient him

ocratically elected, that is, if it were the result of a coup d'état or a revolution. As may be noted, these last two types are not mutually exclusive. This is justified because preliminary tests looking for consistency among the different replies to all questions displayed in Table 5.5 revealed that people who were coded as saying that they would condone a violent protest against a government that was illegal or unjust behave very much like those who were coded in the other two alternatives ("coup d'état or revolution" or "never"), but people coded in these last two categories could not be grouped together. This technique was also followed in the case of the other questions.[34]

Table 5.5 makes clear that a set of other situations was taken into consideration in defining the types of sanctioning styles. Invasion of lands, either private or government, may be taken as a manifestation of protest against an unjust situation. In rural areas, after 1958, peasants began to invade farms as a means of accelerating the process of land reform. These movements were kept in check by the effective intervention of the Venezuelan Federation of Peasants, which at that time was massively supporting the government. We have mentioned already how underprivileged people invaded unoccupied city lands, building *ranchos* and forming marginal communities. Types were formed according to the reply given to the question (see Table 5.5) "In what circumstances would you justify the occupation of another person's land?"

So far we have examined all forms of violence that would fit Sorel's classification. However, there is still a large area of behavior that Sorel ignored, that is, violence in private life. He was, of course, concerned only with political violence, but because the most common form of deviant behavior in the rural areas and the second most common in the urban areas of Venezuela are crimes committed against persons for private, often family, reasons, we felt that in order to tap a general propensity to violence, we should consider some of the private situations that might lead a person to exercise personal violence against others. Thus, we asked the following set of questions:

Now I'm going to ask you some questions about what you would do in certain

[34] The operation performed is as follows: Every alternative of a particular question is intersected with every alternative of all other questions. Empirical consistency is found when the number of people in each intersection (for example, cells of a table) has a probability of 90 percent or more of not being due to chance. The statistic used is what in ADMINS language is called the sig test, which is similar to a Fisher exact test. This operation is repeated, rotating the question until a satisfactory way of grouping alternatives is found.

family situations. What do you think should be done:
to a man who deceives (is unfaithful to) his wife?
to a son who is of working age and does not want to work?
to a wife who deceives (is unfaithful to) her husband?
to a neighbor who disturbs the public order?

Answers to these questions were coded according to the same scheme, yet a person saying that he would send his lazy child to a government reformatory or, for that matter, that he would use other legal means to punish him, denotes a more violent attitude than a person who would try to orient (educate) the child. However, the intention to use a legal or institutional means to solve a situation provoked by an unfaithful husband or wife denotes a less violent attitude than the intention to do nothing about such deviant acts.

This last example points to the fact that propensity to violence may be a U- or J-shaped curve. On one end we find the passive people, those who would not respond to any social misdemeanors. Because of their passivity they contribute to creating an environment where violent acts, the other end of the continuum, can more easily be committed. In the middle we find (MILD) people, who would be more inclined to handle such situations by using some persuasive or other nonviolent but noninstitutional action and, finally, those who in any event would prefer to resort to whatever legal institutional action is available to solve the situation. Sometimes, however, an institutional sanction reveals a greater propensity to violence, as in the case of sanctions to be applied to the lazy son. These overlaps in the operational definition of each style of sanctioning reflect not only a theoretical ambiguity but also an empirical reality.

Three indexes were then constructed from these six questions. In Table 5.6 we can see the distribution of the population of each group along the three basic types discussed here.[35] In Table 5.6, as in all tables of this same format, groups are ordered according to class status. It is easy to see from this table that the lower the status of a group, the more likely we are to find violent (BLOODY) respondents and, conversely, the higher the status of a group, the more likely we are to find respondents with a LEGAL orientation. People with a MILD orientation are as likely to be found in high-status as in low-status groups. These generalizations are confirmed by the rank correlation between socioeconomic status and all three types

[35] An individual was classified as BLOODY when he gave a violent answer to at least four of the six questions; MILD when he gave a mild type of response to at least three of the six questions; and LEGAL when he gave such answers to at least four of the six questions.

TABLE 5.6   Ideology and Style of Sanctioning

Groups	LEFT	CENTER	RIGHT	LEGAL	MILD	BLOODY
High government officials	11	11	55	37	56	39
University professors	23	15	43	34	60	36
Oil industry executives	3	12	71	43	50	42
Industrial executives	12	19	57	32	56	47
Commercial executives	6	13	70	38	51	48
Owners of cattle ranches	28	16	43	29	42	72
Agricultural entrepreneurs	23	16	48	37	47	59
Staff in government	15	7	51	39	52	43
Secondary school teachers	30	24	31	33	68	32
Priests	8	11	66	37	67	32
Student leaders	51	21	17	24	61	40
Municipal council members	26	31	29	45	43	53
Owners of small industry	24	20	40	25	51	63
Small business owners	25	20	29	25	44	75
Primary school teachers	31	34	25	28	61	43
Government employees	22	39	26	26	55	54
Labor leaders	40	24	20	39	49	37
White-collar workers in commerce	21	29	39	23	52	65
Oil industry employees	19	23	40	33	50	55
Industrial workers	31	22	23	22	54	70
Rancho dwellers	41	10	12	14	62	84
Wage workers in agriculture	37	18	10	15	51	86
Traditional subsistence farmers	34	10	8	10	53	89
Farmers in land reform settlements	32	12	8	14	48	85

of sanctioning styles.[36] This trend seems to be reinforced by the experience of change. Thus, in general, the higher the proportion of people in a group that has had a high experience of change, the higher will be the proportion of persons with a LEGAL orientation in that group (tau = 0.50; $p < 0.00$), and the lower the proportion of those with a BLOODY orientation (tau = −0.43; $p < 0.00$). The MILD ones are equally likely to have a high as a low experience of change.

A more detailed analysis of Table 5.6 reveals other and quite interesting facts. If we take the modal response as a figure indicating the typical member of a group, we see that in *no* group does the typical member have a LEGAL orientation; roughly half of the groups are typically MILD, whereas

[36] Tau coefficients between HIRSES and LEGAL, MILD, and BLOODY types are, respectively, 0.58, 0.20, and −0.71. All of them are highly significant ($p < 0.00$).

the other half are BLOODY according to the mode criterion. Groups with a MILD orientation are all the cultural groups, all the upper-status urbanites, plus staff in government and labor leaders.

The upper-status rural groups, on the contrary, are typically BLOODY, as are all low-status groups, whether urban or rural. The economic petite bourgeoisie is also BLOODY, as are the members of the municipal councils and government clerks. However, this classification should be accepted with some reservations, not only because the mode is a weak measure but also because, in this case, the indexes are not mutually exclusive. Yet the findings reported seem to confirm the general hypothesis that Venezuelans are more prone to use violence than to use available legal means.

At this point, it is useful to seek the relationship between propensity to violence and other normative orientations. The answer is supplied by data in Table 5.7. The high coefficients of correlation show that the higher the

TABLE 5.7   Relationship between Sanctioning Styles and Other Normative Orientations of Venezuelans

Normative Orientations	Legal Orientation Tau	(p)
SAVANT	0.57	(0.00)
NATION	0.41	(0.00)
POLEFF	0.64	(0.00)

proportion of LEGAL persons in a group, the higher the likelihood that we shall find a larger proportion of politically efficacious, sophisticated nationalists.

Ideological Orientations

We can see even from the brief quotation from Sorel that he considered political violence to be linked closely to socialism. Indeed, political protest against governments is usually associated with an ideology that gives coherence and emotional substance to such acts of violence. Marx made this point so powerfully clear in his writings that it led to the foundation and spread of what has been aptly called the interest theory of ideology:

The fundamentals of the interest theory are too well known to need review: developed to perfection of a sort by the Marxist tradition, they are now standard intellectual equipment of the man-in-the-street, who is only too aware that in political argumentation it all comes down to whose ox is gored.[37]

Because this conception of ideology so overemphasizes the power struggle and almost totally neglects motivations and other psychological processes — and, of course, because of the primary role of ideology in the early stages of both socialist and other new nations — some Western intellectuals have come to despise ideology or, at least, to assign the concept a pejorative connotation.[38] Efforts to overcome the empirical difficulties that arise out of the application of interest theory led to the formulation of a strain theory of the social determinants of ideology.[39] This theory focuses on the impact of social or psychological incongruencies on the systems of belief and of value orientation. "Furthermore, of course, the general strain to consistency in a cultural tradition . . . means that in general the value-orientations tend to be relatively consistent with the belief system. . . . Ideology thus serves as one of the primary bases of the cognitive legitimation of patterns of value orientations." [40] It follows then that social inconsistencies, deviant behavior, and other forms of strain have an ideological concomitant that may be a "counterideology," as in the case of total rejection of the cultural tradition or a reformulation in a radical ideology.

Numerous studies document both of these theories,[41] yet

[37] Clifford Geertz, "Ideology as a Cultural System," in David E. Apter, ed., *Ideology and Discontent* (New York: Free Press, 1964), p. 52.
[38] Ibid., pp. 49–52. See also Benjamin Akzin, *States and Nations* (Garden City, N.Y.: Doubleday, 1966), pp. 72–74.
[39] Geertz, "Ideology," p. 52.
[40] Talcott Parsons, *The Social System* (Glencoe, Ill.: Free Press, 1951), pp. 350–351.
[41] See, for instance, F. X. Sutton, S. E. Harris, C. Kaysen, and J. Tobin, *The American Business Creed* (Cambridge: Harvard University Press, 1956); S. M. Lipset, P. F. Lazarsfeld, A. Baron, and J. Linz, "The Psychology of Voting: An Analysis of Political Behavior," in Gardner Lindzey, ed., *Handbook of Social Psychology*, vol. 2 (Cambridge, Mass.: Addison-Wesley, 1954), pp. 124–170. Some of the studies documenting these theories for the case of Latin America are Maurice Zeitlin, *Revolutionary Politics and the Cuban Working Class* (Princeton, N.J.: Princeton University Press, 1967), chap. 8; Glaucio A. Dillon Soares, "Intellectual Identity and Political Ideology among University Students," in S. M. Lipset and Aldo Solari, eds., *Elites in Latin America*, pp. 431–455; Joseph Kahl, "Desarrollo económico y radicalismo político," in Joseph Kahl, ed., *La industrializacion en América Latina* (Mexico: Fondo de Cultura Económica, 1965); and Glaucio Soares and Robert L. Hamblin, "Socioeconomic Variables and Voting for the Radical Left: Chile, 1952," *American Political Science Review*, vol. 61, no. 4 (December 1967).

The problem of how, after all, ideologies transform sentiment into significance and so make it socially available is short-circuited by the crude device of placing particular symbols and particular strains (or interests) side by side in such a way that the fact that the first are derivatives of the second seems more common sense — or at least post-Freudian, post-Marxian common sense.[42]

In the next chapter, we shall test the relationship between ideological orientation and certain psychic states; in this section the main interest is to explore the relationship that may exist between certain ideological leanings and other normative orientations such as nationalism, style of evaluation, political efficacy, and style of sanctioning.

Ideology may be conceived as a set of evaluative statements about empirical reality which, at the same time, carry some commitment to action.[43] In *SRSP* we had the occasion to argue that within the present context of Venezuelan politics, it is fruitful to study ideology along a left-right continuum.[44] In that analysis it was shown that the distribution of Venezuelan groups along such a continuum is quite complex. Some groups had an essentially antileft-antiright orientation; these were classified as "unstable center." Others were "permeable" in the sense that they were both proright and proleft, and still other groups showed a definite orientation toward the left and others toward the right. It was shown also that high-status groups tended to be either rightist or unstable centrist; middle-status groups were either stable centrists or leftists, and low-status groups were primarily permeable. However, no evident relationship could be established between nationalism and ideological orientation. Presently, we shall attempt to make a more refined test of these conclusions along with the consideration of a new hypothesis.

Data in Table 5.6 show, for each group, the proportion of leftists, centrists, and rightists. But before we make any analysis of these particular distributions, it is important to understand fully how these types were built.

In the questionnaire we included a set of ten questions specifically designed to extract the ideological orientation of the respondents. All of these questions confronted the respondent with some prospective policy, mostly of an economic nature, that a government might take. All of these policies were, and still are, important issues in Venezuela. We asked the interviewers to note whether they were in complete agreement, in agree-

[42] Geertz, "Ideology," pp. 56–57.
[43] Frank Bonilla, "Cultural Elites," in Lipset and Solari, eds., *Elites in Latin America,* pp. 237–242.
[44] Silva Michelena, "Nationalism in Venezuela," in *SRSP,* pp. 75–77.

ment, indifferent, opposed, or definitely opposed to each of the following phrases:

Leftist

The state should immediately nationalize the oil firms.
Foreign companies should become the property of the Venezuelan state.
The state should be the owner of all industries.
The state should control the price of land and the value of dwellings.

Rightist

The state should give less money for agrarian reform.
The state should not regulate wages.
Venezuela should trade only with Western (nonsocialist) countries.
Agrarian reform should be carried out only on state lands.
The influence of political parties in unions should be eliminated.
The administration of all industries including those of the state should remain in private hands.

Each alternative answer was given a value that ranged from one to five. (The higher the value, the greater the leftist orientation.) Then the mean values of the responses given by every individual to the rightist and leftist questions were computed separately. After that, six partial indexes of ideological orientation were computed: proright, center-right, antiright, proleft, center-left, and antileft. These indexes were intersected to form three basic types: left, center, and right. This operation may be best communicated to the reader in tabular form (see Table 5.8).

TABLE 5.8   Building Types of Ideological Orientation

Based on Answers to Rightist Questions	Based on Answers to Leftist Questions						Totals
	Proleft (4 and 5)		Center-Left (3)		Antileft (1 and 2)		
	N	sig	N	sig	N	sig	
Proright (1 and 2)	330	(1.00)	A 348	(0.65)	B 405	(0.99)	1,083
Center-right (3)	D 652	(0.00)	1,066	(1.00)	C 1,137	(1.00)	1,855
Antiright (4 and 5)	E 475	(1.00)	F 325	(0.00)	357	(0.00)	1,157
Totals	1,457		1,739		1,899		4,095

NOTE: Sig is a measure of the probability that the figure in the cell, given the three totals, might not be due to randomness. This test is similar to the Fisher exact test.

Table 5.8 is only indicative because our samples cannot be aggregated.[45] Therefore, we cannot derive conclusions from it. Nevertheless, Table 5.8 gives some clues for analysis. They suggest, for instance, that center-rightists are likely to be either center-leftists or antileftists. The types were built in the following way.

Rightists: Those respondents who were prorightist and either center-leftist (cell A) or antileftist (cell B), plus those who were center-rightist and antileftist (cell C).

Centrists: Those who were center-rightist and center-leftist.

Leftists: Those who were proleftist and either center-rightist (cell D) or antirightist (cell E), plus those who were center-leftist and antirightist (cell F).

As may be noted, 330 "permeables" (proleft and proright) and 357 "unstable centrists" were left out of the ideological types established. The main reason for so doing is that these individuals, though in a sense "centrists," are likely to have entirely different attitudes and opinions as well as background characteristics; thus empirically they cannot be grouped together without running a great risk of obscuring the meaning of the types. In *SRSP* we showed that "unstable centrists" are likely to be high government officials, university professors, oil industry executives, and staff in government, whereas "permeables" are likely to be wage workers in agriculture or low-status urban groups (*rancho* dwellers and industrial workers).[46] Having thus defined operationally the ideological types, we can proceed with the analysis.

Focusing on Table 5.7, we see that, as expected, the higher the class status of a group, the more likely it is to have a larger proportion of rightists and a smaller proportion of leftists. Thus, all high-status groups, regardless of their institutional locus, are typically rightists, although university professors, high government officials, and the upper-status rural groups have a greater internal heterogeneity. All low-status groups, on the contrary, regardless of their residential environment (rural or urban), are typically leftists. Nevertheless, the proportion of leftists is only about one-third. Such a low figure is due to the fact that, on the one hand, a high proportion of the rural groups (between one-half and one-third) gave signs of not being ideologically aware when they answered that they did

---

[45] Basically there are two deterrents: (1) Samples were independently derived using different sampling models (see *SRSP*, pp. 46–50), and (2) even if sampling errors were assumed to be comparable, still the groups would have to be weighted by the size of each population if the figures were to have any substantive meaning.

[46] *SRSP*, p. 78.

not know what alternative to choose. On the other hand, a sizable proportion of the *rancho* dwellers and industrial workers were "permeables";
that is, they accepted both proleftist and prorightist statements. This, of
course, suggests that the leftist commitment of the low-status individual
may grow as much from a paternalistic acceptance of the state as from the
realization that drastic economic measures may improve their lot.

The ideological orientation of the middle-status groups is less clear-cut;
all groups, except student leaders and labor leaders (who are predominantly leftists), gave signs of being quite heterogeneous internally. The
extreme case is that of the owners of small shops, who are leftist, centrist,
rightist, and not ideologically aware in approximately equal proportions
(about one-fourth of each). Owners of small industries, on the contrary,
clearly leaned more to the right, and both white-collar workers in large
commercial firms and oil industry employees are split between center and
right, whereas middle- and low-status educators (secondary and primary
school teachers) divide between center and left.

That the objective conditions of life influence the ideological leanings
of Venezuelans in the direction expected by interest theorists is supported
by the high positive Kendall tau correlation coefficient between socioeconomic status and rightism, as well as the significant negative, but less
strong, correlation between leftism and socioeconomic status (see Table
5.9). Venezuelans' tremendous experience of change has made them more

TABLE 5.9   Correlates of Ideology

	Ideological Orientation					
	Left		Center		Right	
	Tau	(*p*)	Tau	(*p*)	Tau	(*p*)
HIRSES	−0.36	(0.01)	−0.11	(0.44)	0.53	(0.01)
CHANEX	−0.62	(0.00)	−0.14	(0.32)	0.64	(0.00)
SAVANT	−0.36	(0.01)	0.06	(0.70)	0.38	(0.01)
NATION	−0.17	(0.25)	0.22	(0.13)	0.17	(0.24)
POLEFF	−0.25	(0.09)	0.09	(0.56)	0.30	(0.04)
LEGAL	−0.47	(0.00)	−0.02	(0.88)	0.58	(0.00)
BLOODY	0.33	(0.03)	−0.08	(0.58)	−0.38	(0.01)
MILD	−0.01	(0.96)	−0.05	(0.72)	−0.01	(0.92)

rightist and less leftist. This process, as suggested in the previous discussion, seems to operate differently according to the status level of the
mobilized individual. Our hypothesis is that the low-status individual who

has experienced a great deal of change is more likely to accept rightist statements, but at the same time he is as likely to preserve his inclination to accept drastic state intervention in the economy.

Middle- and upper-status individuals who have experienced change more intensively, because — as was seen in Chapter 4 — they are more likely to come from families of a higher status, are also more likely to preserve their rightist orientation.

Class status and experience of change, important as they are, are not the only variables associated with ideological orientation. Later we shall test whether various psychological states are associated with ideological orientation. Here we limit ourselves to establishing the relationship between ideology and other normative orientations. Referring to Table 5.9, we see that rightists are more likely to have a more sophisticated style of evaluation (SAVANT), to have a LEGAL style of sanctioning, and to be politically efficacious. Leftists, on the contrary, tend to be less sophisticated, more prone to violence, though not necessarily politically inefficacious. Finally, we observe that both leftists and rightists are equally likely to be nationalistic.

In the previous discussion of ideology, we referred to commitment as an important ingredient of ideology. This commitment dimension should be taken into account if one is interested, as we are here, in the relevance of ideology and other normative orientations for explaining antagonism among groups. However, so far, we have not really analyzed this dimension of the normative orientations of Venezuelan groups. It is to this task that we now turn.

Capacity to Defer Gratification and Familism

The developmental ideology that has been grasped so thoroughly by Latin Americans is not new only to this part of the world. The Protestant ethic as a set of values that has impelled the development of capitalism did not involve any conception of development or of the welfare state as we know these ideas today. Max Weber made this point very clear in the following passage:

> In fact, the *summum bonum* of this ethic, the earning of more and more money, combined with the strict avoidance of all spontaneous enjoyment of life, is above all completely devoid of any eudaemonistic, not to say hedonistic, admixture. It is thought of so purely as an end in itself, that from the point of

view of the happiness of, or utility to, the single individual, it appears entirely transcendental and absolutely irrational.[47]

Weber himself demonstrated that this ethic was not exclusive to either Protestantism or capitalism. However, it was McClelland who, after careful research, transformed this concept into his more general motive, n-achievement, and related it to economic development.[48] As we now know, Catholicism does not precisely foster n-achievement, a fact that, because of certain structural characteristics, can in effect hinder development.

Lipset has reviewed recently almost everything that has been written on the subject with respect to Latin America and specifically the value orientation of entrepreneurs. The impressive mass of evidence reported in his work points to the fact that

Almost everywhere in Latin America, the original upper class was composed of the owners of *latifundia,* and these set the model for elite behavior to which lesser classes, including the businessmen of the towns, sought to adapt.[49]

The model to which this author refers is one impregnated with familism, personalism, and aristocratism. Lipset argues that in the modern business elite these values are less evident, though still of comparatively high incidence. He quotes Cochran, who summarized the influence of such orientations on entrepreneurial behavior:

Comparatively the Latin American complex: (1) sacrifices rigorous economically directed effort, or profit maximization, to family interests; (2) places social and personal emotional interests ahead of business obligations; (3) impedes mergers and other changes in ownership desirable for higher levels of technological efficiency and better adjustments to markets; (4) fosters nepotism to a degree harmful to continuously able top-management; (5) hinders the building up of a supply of competent and cooperative middle managers; (6) makes managers and workers less amenable to constructive criticism; (7) creates barriers of disinterest in the flow of technological communication; and (8) lessens the urge for expansion and risk-taking.[50]

Our interest here, however, is not so much to concentrate on values specifically facilitating successful entrepreneurial behavior, but to focus on

[47] Max Weber, *The Protestant Ethic and the Spirit of Capitalism* (New York: Scribner's, 1958), p. 53.
[48] David C. McClelland, *The Achieving Society.* See especially chaps. 2, 6, and 7.
[49] Lipset and Solari, eds., *Elites in Latin America,* p. 8.
[50] Cochran, "Cultural Factors in Economic Growth," as cited by Lipset and Solari, eds., *Elites in Latin America,* p. 16.

the more general orientations that may be called capacity to defer gratification and familism.

The interest in familism is, of course, deeply rooted in the desire to test how this particularistic orientation, which is said to be so common in Latin America, is related to style of evaluation, political efficacy, nationalism, and propensity to violence. Also we wish to explore how socioeconomic status and the experience of change influence this value of familism. If the findings reported by Cochran hold for Venezuela, we shall find less familism among upper-status groups, and especially among businessmen; yet we expect the general level of familism to be high. This orientation, of course, will run contrary to nationalism, sophistication, political efficacy, legalism, and the capacity to defer gratification.

The capacity to defer gratification adds still another dimension to those already mentioned. As Ahumada's hypotheses stated, the peculiar way in which Venezuela developed, "initiated by foreigners, with imported techniques, capital, and organization," [51] made it possible to grow economically without having the technical and attitudinal capacity for it. On the contrary, because there was an abundance of foreign currency, the country could import in massive quantities the most sophisticated goods produced by the developed economies, thus inflating the pattern of consumption and making more difficult the emergence of the appropriate normative orientations that stimulate thrift and the willingness to make the necessary sacrifices that development imposes on any backward society.

Perhaps the most evident landmarks of the easy-spending Venezuelan are the luxurious hotels, cable cars, turnpikes, and monuments that, for about ten years, as they were being built, were praised in each annual message to Congress by the president of the country at the time, dictator Marcos Pérez Jiménez. "The biggest or the most expensive in the world" was the slogan of the day. With respect to the standard of living, the middle-class Venezuelan has no reason to envy his European or even North American counterpart. All the gadgetry produced in these countries was and still is — although to a lesser extent — readily acquired by this conspicuously consuming middle-class man whose alleged passion for comfort is checked only by the regularity with which the bill collector rings the doorbell.

An indicator of the normative capacity of Venezuelans to defer gratification was obtained by computing the mean value of response given to the following set of questions:

[51] Ahumada, "Hypothesis for Diagnosing Social Change," *SRSP*, pp. 9–10.

Now I am going to mention some of the sacrifices that may be necessary for Venezuela to be able to advance economically most rapidly in the next ten years. Of course, some may not apply to certain groups. Which of the following sacrifices do you think should not be required of you?

1. Renounce individual pay raises.
2. Pay higher taxes.
3. Renounce having (or give up) an automobile or television set.
4. Spend less on amusements, vacation, or luxuries.

Responses indicating that the individual felt that a particular sacrifice should be required of him were given a value of three; if the individual felt that a particular sacrifice should not be required of him, a value of one was assigned to that response. The index of capacity to defer gratification was then built by averaging the responses given by each individual. In Table 5.10 we can see the proportion of individuals within each group who said that at least two such sacrifices should be required of them. The high

TABLE 5.10 *Capacity to Defer Gratification and Familism* (*percentages*)

Groups	DEFER I	FAMOR
High government officials	87	38
University professors	83	36
Oil industry executives	69	46
Industrial executives	69	51
Commercial executives	72	44
Owners of cattle ranches	66	52
Agricultural entrepreneurs	64	47
Staff in government	80	30
Secondary school teachers	73	37
Priests	66	21
Student leaders	83	35
Municipal council members	70	39
Owners of small industry	67	36
Small business owners	57	40
Primary school teachers	59	22
Government employees	52	31
Labor leaders	76	25
White-collar workers in commerce	50	48
Oil industry employees	56	53
Industrial workers	44	50
Rancho dwellers	28	48
Wage workers in agriculture	35	46
Traditional subsistence farmers	30	49
Farmers in land reform settlements	38	39

proportion of Venezuelans who, at least on a normative level, are willing to
sacrifice something for the development of the country leaves groundless
the expectations set forth in previous paragraphs. Even one-third of the
peasants, who live on a subsistence level, were ready to give up something.
Of course, it may be that pay raises, taxes, automobiles, television sets,
amusements, vacations, and luxuries are so remote from their lives that they
lose nothing by saying that they will indeed accept the sacrifice of giving
them up for the development of the country. However, we have no evidence
indicating that this was the psychological mechanism that compelled them,
or the *rancho* dwellers and the industrial workers, to answer as they did.

Capacity to defer gratification tends to be greater, the higher the socioeconomic status of a group. It is also strongly associated with the other
normative orientations previously explored (see Table 5.11). The more

TABLE 5.11   Correlates of Capacity to Defer Gratification and Familism

	Capacity to Defer Gratification (DEFER I)		Familistic Orientation (FAMOR)	
	Tau	*p*	Tau	*p*
HIRSES	0.69	(0.00)	−0.34	(0.02)
CHANEX	0.43	(0.00)	−0.09	(0.55)
SAVANT	0.72	(0.00)	−0.30	(0.04)
NATION	0.63	(0.00)	−0.31	(0.03)
POLEFF	0.71	(0.00)	−0.38	(0.01)
LEGAL	0.57	(0.00)	−0.22	(0.12)
RIGHT	0.38	(0.01)	−0.01	(0.96)
LEFT	−0.26	(0.07)	0.00	(1.00)

sophisticated, nationalist, politically efficacious, legally oriented a group is,
the more likely is it that we shall find there a greater proportion of people
willing to make sacrifices for the sake of the economic development of the
country. It is more probable that these groups will have a greater proportion of rightists, although leftists are also likely to be found but perhaps
less frequently. In fact, middle-class leftists are as likely to make sacrifices
as are the executives of large firms. However, in general, it is less probable
that economic groups will accept sacrifices than cultural or political groups
of a similar status. Finally, it should be pointed out that the experience
of change is also associated with the capacity to defer gratification. In
general, the higher the experience of change, the greater will be the capacity

to make sacrifices for the development of the country. This rather optimistic view of the social psychology of Venezuelans is not completely blurred by the alleged familism which is generally attributed to Latin Americans.

This index was built from responses to two questions that were used previously for the construction of the index of nationalism. However, the number of alternative answers that each of these questions offered had prevented the index of familism from being anything more than a complement of the index of nationalism. One question required the respondent to name which of a set of five qualities he considered to be the most important personal characteristics.[52] The other question asked the respondent to rank a set of six loyalties.[53] Those persons who said the most important qualities that can characterize an individual are being a good husband (or wife), a good father (or mother), and a good friend also said that the first or second most important loyalty was loyalty to his family.

Kendall tau coefficients cited in Table 5.11 show that there is a rather weak negative association between familism (FAMOR) and style of evaluation, nationalism, and political efficacy. That is, the larger the proportion of sophisticated, nationalist, and politically efficacious persons in a group, the more likely are we to find there a smaller proportion of individuals with a familistic orientation. However, leftists, rightists, and those who have a legally oriented sanctioning style are as likely to be familistically oriented as those who do not possess such characteristics. Nor does the experience of change seem to disrupt the familism of Venezuelans.

Finally, we can expect that the higher the socioeconomic status of a group, the smaller will be the proportion of familistic individuals found in that group (see Table 5.11). However, if the sphere of activity is considered, an interesting fact is revealed: Cultural and political groups are less likely to have familistically oriented individuals than economic groups, regardless of their class status. That is, the difference in familism between low-status groups and those of middle and upper status occupied in economic activities is meager. Thus, whereas the range of the proportion of familistic individuals that is to be found among executives of large firms or rural entrepreneurs is between 44 and 52 percent, the range for the petite bourgeoisie is between 36 and 53 percent, and for the low-status groups it is between 39 and 50 percent. The highest proportion of familists

---

[52] These qualities were as follows: being a good citizen, being a good parent, performing well at work, being a good husband or wife, and being a good friend.

[53] The six loyalties were as follows: to one's family, to the organization where one works, to one's profession or office, to a political party, to one's church, and to one's country.

among the upper-status groups is to be found among the industrial executives (51 percent) and the owners of cattle ranches (52 percent). Oil industry employees stand out as the middle-class group where familistically
oriented individuals are more frequently found. Industrial workers are the
most familistically oriented among the low-status groups and in a proportion that matches that of their bosses (industrial executives).

The Political Ethos of Venezuelans

Anthropologists pioneered the study of what has been called national
character, national ethos, or the fundamental values of a people. But
because they worked mostly with small communities, they felt no need to
differentiate the extent to which various members of the community
shared those values.[54] Other authors, notably Gorer, applied these concepts to national societies in what are known to be highly contradictory
studies.[55] The study of personality and politics has also been at the center
of attention of political scientists for some time.[56] Yet only recently have
attempts been made both to relate personality characteristics and development and to measure the distribution of certain psychological orientations
in the population.

After reviewing the literature on the subject, we said in Chapter 1 that
the process of political development is conceived usually as framed by
certain institutional processes that lead to crises of identity, authority, and
equality. These crises are usually accompanied by a generalized tendency
toward greater social differentiation. It was noted also that unless these
institutional processes crystallized in an integrative set of normative orientations, such as nationalism, the crises were likely to be quite disruptive and
societal achievements to be timid. Thus, on the basis of current theory,
one can say that wherever such integrative elements in political culture are
found, the process of development may be facilitated. In this sense one can
speak of normative orientations compatible with development.

Almond and Verba made the first systematic attempt to gather data
that seek to establish the degree to which different sectors of a nation

---

[54] The following studies have already become classics on this subject: Ruth Benedict,
Patterns of Culture (Boston: Houghton Mifflin, 1934); Margaret Mead, "National
Character," *International Symposium on Anthropology* (New York, 1953), pp. 642–
667.

[55] Geoffrey Gorer, *The American People: A Study in National Character* (New York:
Norton, 1948); and *Exploring English Character* (New York: Criterion, 1955).

[56] Harold D. Lasswell, *Psychopathology and Politics* (New York: Viking, 1930),
and *Power and Personality* (New York: Norton, 1948).

share some particular normative orientation.[57] They did this for five nations: the United States, England, Germany, Italy, and Mexico. However, because their work was based on national samples, they were able to explore only to a limited extent intranational differences, that is, broad aggregates of population such as educational levels or occupations. This limitation, of course, cannot be blamed on the authors, because their aim was to make international comparisons rather than to dig into the political culture of each nation.

In the present study we have simultaneously taken a developmental approach and sought to establish intranational differences in a systematic way. In our exploration of the normative orientations of Venezuelans we have been able to establish that the higher the socioeconomic status of a group and the more intense its experience of change, the more likely it is that we shall find in that group a large proportion of sophisticated, politically efficacious nationalists. These persons will tend to be legal-minded in the event that some social misdemeanor is committed or when it comes to protesting against the government. The deep-rooted familism of Latin Americans is likely to be absent in such a group; they are more likely to choose to make sacrifices such as giving up pay raises or paying higher taxes. Although such relationships were shown to be quite strong, individual groups do not necessarily rank in equivalent slots along so many dimensions. Thus the question of making a general assessment of the normative orientation of each group arises.

Fortunately, this task can be easily accomplished with the analytic tool we have been using. In fact, a general index of the normative orientations of Venezuelans was built by counting for each individual the normative characteristics he possessed. A person having a majority (four or more) of such characteristics was considered to have a positive ethos in the sense that such psychological characteristics are considered congenial with development. In Table 5.12 we can see almost graphically how each group may be classified according to each of its characteristics and in the general index (ETHOS). Three sets of orientations may be distinguished. At the top, having the most modern ethos (plus [+] signs), we find all political groups except municipal councilmen, all cultural groups, and executives of the oil industry and large commercial firms. Industrial executives, together with agricultural entrepreneurs and government and oil industry employees, are in the middle (zeros[o]); between the groups just defined are all other groups (minus [−] signs).

[57] Almond and Verba, *The Civic Culture*.

TABLE 5.12 The Normative Orientations of Venezuelans

Groups	HIRSES	CHANEX	POLEFF	SAVANT	LEGAL	DEFERI	FAMOR	LEFT	RIGHT	NATION	ETHOS
DMAKER	+	+	+	+	+	+	o	−	+	+	+
UNPROF	+	+	+	+	o	+	o	o	+	+	+
OILEXE	+	+	o	+	+	+	o	−	+	+	+
INDEXE	+	+	o	+	o	+	+	−	+	o	o
COMEXE	+	+	o	+	+	+	o	−	+	+	+
CATLER	+	−	o	−	o	o	+	o	+	o	−
FARMER	−	−	o	−	+	o	o	o	+	−	o
GSTAFF	+	+	+	+	+	+	−	−	+	+	+
LICEOS	+	+	+	+	o	+	o	o	o	+	+
PRIEST	+	+	+	+	+	o	−	−	+	−	+
STUDEN	+	−	+	+	o	+	o	+	−	+	+
COUNCL	o	o	+	+	+	+	o	o	o	+	+
PEQIND	o	+	o	−	o	o	o	o	o	o	−
SHOPOW	−	+	−	−	o	o	o	o	o	o	−
SCHOOL	+	o	o	o	o	o	−	o	−	+	+
CLERKS	o	−	o	+	o	−	−	o	−	+	o
LABORL	o	o	+	+	+	+	−	+	−	+	+
COLLAR	−	o	−	o	o	−	+	o	o	o	−
MPLOIL	−	o	o	o	o	o	+	o	o	o	o
WORKER	−	o	−	−	−	−	+	o	−	−	−
RANCHO	−	−	−	−	−	−	+	+	−	−	−
AGWORK	−	−	−	−	−	−	o	+	−	−	−
PEASAN	−	−	−	−	−	−	+	+	−	−	−
LANREF	−	−	−	−	−	−	o	+	−	−	−
Mean	0.63	0.53	0.60	0.48	0.29	0.61	0.40	0.25	0.36	0.60	0.44

Of special relevance here is the fact that the middle class is the most heterogeneous. There we find groups in which all three types of ethos are found. The lower-status groups, on the contrary, are solidly classified at the bottom.

As analysis proceeds in the chapters that follow, we shall establish the relationship between a positive ethos and psychological states, evaluations, and political capacity. At the end, we shall explore the consequences that such interrelations may have for the establishment of antagonisms.

6   PSYCHOLOGICAL STATES

Introduction

Chapter 4 documents the fact that, although Venezuelans of all social positions have experienced a great deal of change in their lives, Venezuelan social structure has changed little. Venezuelans have moved not only horizontally but also upward with respect to their parents. Every group has a sizable proportion of persons who have gone through some positive kind of change.[1] Yet social inequalities among groups seem to have increased. What are the psychological effects of these experiences?

As Chapter 5 points out, both higher socioeconomic status and experience of change, in general, are associated with the formation of a political culture that is likely to foster development. Thus, sophistication, nationalism, political efficacy, capacity to defer gratification, and a propensity to use legal sanctions to solve deviant situations are all associated with socioeconomic status and experience of change. Yet within no group were all such normative orientations to be found. Sizable portions of each population group still have a less functional ethos — less functional in the sense that these individuals are familistic, have a low capacity to defer gratification, are not nationalistic, are rigid and politically inefficacious. The fact that they also are more prone to violence and leftism cannot, however, be considered dysfunctional for development, because such attitudes may facilitate socialist change, which is a form of development. In any case, we find in Venezuela a form of psychological incongruence that has been called, in this study, cultural heterogeneity.

---

[1] A positive kind of change in this context means migration from rural to urban areas, some international experience, and upward occupational and educational mobility. See Chapter 4 for a fuller exposition of these concepts.

Marx and a host of post-Marxist thinkers have theorized that the objective conditions of life determine a person's feelings of dissatisfaction and personal adjustment. Yet even Marx,[2] and others to a greater extent, recognized that feelings of dissatisfaction and personality incongruences may be, in certain circumstances, more truly significant variables for determining a person's or group's state of mind.[3] Social scientists have debated, sometimes heatedly, about which of these two approaches is more useful in understanding social conflicts. But when hard data are used in examining this issue, neither faction wins a clear victory. In a preliminary test that we made of these hypotheses, we came to the following conclusions:

> . . . we have shown that both the socioeconomic status level and the ratio of aspirations to achievements largely account for [variations in the levels of satisfaction].
>
> Manifestations of personal disadjustments (lack of social adjustment, paranoid states, and powerlessness) at any class level are better explained by variations in socioeconomic status than by any other factor. Feelings of satisfaction in the middle- and upper-status groups are more likely to vary with incongruencies between objective position in the social hierarchy and subjective class identification criteria only when incongruencies among the latter are taken into account. Imbalances among income, prestige, and educational levels seem to be independent of either satisfaction or personal adjustment levels.[4]

In this chapter we again explore such states of mind in the Venezuelan sample groups, this time, however, in a search for wider relations between social location, experience of change, normative orientations, and the following characteristics: personal adjustment, the balance between wants and achievement, and levels of satisfaction.

Personal Adjustment

The presence of personal adjustment, like any healthy state in man, is hard to define except in terms of its absence. One knows that a man is *not* healthy only when some disease is diagnosed.[5] In the psychological

---

[2] See Chapter 4, p. 80.

[3] The notion that troubles deepen whenever any set of parts of man or society is not in accord is an ancient one. Aristotle was among the first to note the effect of incongruences in a wide range of subjects, for example, the influence of the moral character of a speaker on his audience's opinions, or his observation on the likelihood of emergence of class conflicts.

[4] José A. Silva Michelena, "Satisfaction, Personal Adjustment, and Incongruencies in Venezuelan Society."

[5] In fact, the definition of health given by the World Health Organization is phrased in terms of lack of any kind of disease, including mental disorders.

realm such diagnosis, especially on the level of groups, is more difficult still, not only because we have no more than rudimentary tools to apply to a complex task but also because "deviant" behavior or psychological deviations are, at least in part, inevitably defined in terms of a set of social norms that are not necessarily healthy in themselves. The social and cultural situation may be such that it impedes the full realization of man as well as inflicting on him deprivations that sometimes, as in the case of Nazi Germany, are excessively cruel. The study of personal adjustment, therefore, is carried out better by means of prolonged open-ended interviews than within the fixed, impersonal frame of a questionnaire. The study of the case of a revolutionary reported in *SRSP* gives us a sample of how complex and subtle the mind of a man can be. The variety of situations, the diversity of family influences, and the role they play in the life of the elite are vividly illuminated by Bonilla's analysis in *The Failure of Elites*.[6] Here, we can hope only to establish some patterns from responses quickly given to an interviewer. However, as indicated in *SRSP*, these responses can be used to identify certain psychic states that may significantly affect even as large an organization as a government bureaucracy.[7]

There are, as just implied, many aspects that may be studied with respect to personal adjustment, but we have chosen here to focus only on five: (1) interpersonal adjustment, (2) paranoid reactions, (3) powerlessness, (4) want-get balance, and (5) level of satisfaction. The first three dimensions were used to form a general index of personal disadjustment. For the sake of clarity, however, let us begin by defining each of them separately.

Interpersonal Adjustment

Psychoanalytic theories of interpersonal relations have emphasized the role of intimate family and friendship relations in personality integration.[8] Because this frame of reference was used almost exclusively in the case study of a revolutionary in *SRSP* and to a lesser extent in the study of the Venezuelan bureaucrat, here we shall simply explain how we defined this dimension of personal adjustment operationally.

[6] Frank Bonilla, *The Failure of Elites,* chap. 5.
[7] *SRSP,* chap. 4, pp. 86–119.
[8] The founder of this school of thought is Harry Stack Sullivan. See, for instance, Harry Stack Sullivan, *The Interpersonal Theory of Psychiatry,* Helen Swick Perry, Mary Ladd Gowel, and Martha Gibbon, eds. (New York: Norton, 1954).

Two questions were designed specifically to grasp the extent to which each of the interviewees had positive (or negative) interpersonal relations:

1. Apart from your immediate family, is there anyone to whom you confide your most intimate problems?
2. Could you tell me if you *ever* belonged to any group in which all were truly good friends and from which you received full satisfaction?

Paranoid States

The opening statement of Ahumada's "Hypothesis for Diagnosing Social Change" conveys a striking picture of Venezuela:

> No major research is required to support the conclusion that something is wrong with Venezuelan society, for in every aspect the observer is immediately struck by the pervading tone of violence and insecurity.[9]

Such existential conditions are assumed to be rooted deeply in the Venezuelan character. Bonilla, for example, describes how the country's most important leaders were popularly designated as some type of fierce animal.[10] The first two chapters of this volume reviewed the many internal struggles, skirmishes, and wars that characterized political life in Venezuela during the nineteenth century. Today we often hear the Venezuelan described as aggressive, tending to flare up easily. A perceptive Venezuelan novelist likes to tell foreigners an anecdote, supposedly descriptive of the Venezuelan character, about a man who enters a bar, sits down, and looks to the left and right. Immediately, almost without an intervening word, one of the others in the bar stands up and shoots the newcomer. When the police arrive and ask the killer his motive for the act, he answers calmly, "He gave me a dirty look."

The story is obviously an exaggeration, but no one acquainted with Venezuelan life would be willing to say that it could never have happened. Attitudes such as this point to the general hypothesis that Venezuelan political culture is colored by a pervasive sense of mistrust, suspicion, and vindictiveness that gives it a paranoid quality. Zamansky describes a paranoid person as one who

> . . . is especially sensitive to attitudes and tendencies of others which coincide with his own impulses and conflicts. His perception of his environment reflects

[9] *SRSP*, p. 3.
[10] Bonilla, *Failure of Elites,* chap. 2.

the fact that the paranoid person is almost invariably an intensely hostile person. He is characteristically suspicious and vigilant, living in a world teeming with potential dangers and implied threats.[11]

In order to search for this alleged paranoid quality among Venezuelans, we asked the following set of questions:

Now I am going to ask you some questions of another type that are quite interesting. I am going to read you several pairs of proverbs. After reading each pair, I would like you to tell me which of the proverbs you think is better advice to give someone:
a. Trust in people and you'll go a long way. *Or*
   *Never hurt anyone but yourself.
b. *An eye for an eye and a tooth for a tooth. *Or*
   To forgive is better than to condemn.
c. *In this world those who are not your friends are probably your enemies. *Or*
   Think well of strangers and things will go better for you.

From these questions we constructed indexes of mistrust, vindictiveness, and suspiciousness; those informants who selected the asterisked alternatives were so classified.

In its extreme forms, paranoia may include delusions of grandeur and megalomania, but, more commonly, paranoid reactions

. . . appear to be more prevalent among groups who are to some extent isolated from the larger societal setting. Relatively higher rates of disorder have been reported for displaced persons and refugees and for migratory and minority groups.[12]

Such persons are apt to feel like "outsiders" whose political opinions carry no weight. This feeling of lack of self-importance is probably part of a more general syndrome that sometimes has been, at least partially, identified with alienation.[13] One of the characteristics of the alienated man is his utter sense of powerlessness to command his immediate world.

Powerlessness

When a person feels unimportant and powerless, he will probably feel also that the political process is something to which he has no access or

[11] Harold S. Zamansky, "Paranoid Reactions," in *International Encyclopedia of the Social Sciences,* vol. 11 (New York: Macmillan and Free Press, 1968), p. 382.
[12] Ibid.
[13] E. H. Mizruchi, "Alienation and Avarice: Theoretical and Empirical Perspectives" in Irving L. Horowitz, ed., *The New Sociology: Essays in Social Science and Social Theory in Honor of C. Wright Mills* (New York: Oxford University Press, 1964).

which he cannot really influence. Hence this person will tend to regard politics as an activity both evil and removed from himself.

These three psychological states — powerlessness, lack of self-importance, and political cynicism — were identified in our survey by means of the following questions:

1. How often do you feel that your problems or difficulties are more than you can bear? *Frequently, *occasionally, very rarely, or never?
2. In general, how much importance do you think the opinions and political activities of a person like yourself have? A lot, enough, *little, or *none?
3. People often say that politics is pure fraud, or at best they say it is a necessary evil. What do you think of this? Do you *completely agree, *agree, disagree, or completely disagree?

Those persons who chose at least two of the asterisked alternatives were considered to have signs of political alienation. Because in the preliminary analysis of *SRSP* we found that all these characteristics were closely interrelated,[14] we deemed it advisable to take a more general approach and build an index summarizing all these manifestations of personal maladjustment: lack of appropriate interpersonal relations, paranoid state, and alienation.

Index of Personal Maladjustment

The *proportion* of individuals showing at least two of these conditions is indicated in Table 6.2, but Table 6.1 is more explanatory of why some people are less well adjusted than others. In this table we see that the upper-status groups are less likely to have personally maladjusted individuals (NEURA) within their ranks. Apparently, the basic hypothesis of the so-called interest theory is thus confirmed. Objective life conditions do significantly influence states of mind. The better off a person is, the less likely is he to be paranoid, to lack good group or personal relationships, and to feel alienated.

Yet such upper-status groups as the owners of cattle ranches and especially agricultural entrepreneurs have as large a proportion of maladjusted individuals as do some of the middle-status groups. One possible explanation is that these groups have experienced fewer positive changes. In Venezuela (see Table 6.1), the greater the proportion of persons in a group who have had an intense experience of change, the more likely it is that the group will have a smaller proportion of personally maladjusted individuals.

[14] *SRSP*, pp. 94–102.

TABLE 6.1   Correlates of Personal Maladjustment

	NEURA	
	Tau	p
HIRSES	−0.64	(0.00)
CHANEX	−0.46	(0.00)
SAVANT	−0.67	(0.00)
POLEFF	−0.70	(0.00)
NATION	−0.54	(0.00)
LEGAL	−0.64	(0.00)
ETHOS	−0.66	(0.00)
RIGHT	−0.47	(0.00)
LEFT	0.38	(0.00)

That positive change works toward personality integration should not surprise us greatly, although it is true that change tends to produce some insecurity. The insecurity will affect a person adversely only if he experiences some subjective or objective deprivation.

Table 6.1 indicates that there is a very high correlation between the normative orientation of Venezuelans and their psychic state. The ETHOS, when it is in the direction of greater nationalism, political efficacy, sophistication, propensity to use legal means, and capacity to defer gratifications, is likely to help the integration of personality. On the other hand, it is evident that radically oriented persons (LEFT) — that is, those who will back measures that will significantly transform the status quo — are more likely to feel socially unrelated, to experience certain paranoid symptoms and a fair amount of alienation. This finding also holds, somewhat more strongly, when the ideological direction of a group is toward the right. However, a close inspection of the groups reveals that these relations are not entirely monotonic.

For instance, the two groups in which leftism is more widespread, student and labor leaders, are also the groups with minimal frequencies of personal maladjustment. Moreover, contrary to some popular assumptions, activity in the political or cultural spheres apparently is a negative indicator of personal maladjustment. Thus, as Table 6.2 indicates, if we except low-level government employees and primary school teachers, who have a rather high incidence of personality maladjustments, and executives of oil industries who, unlike their high-status colleagues, have a low incidence, we see that whereas in the political and cultural spheres incidence ranges from 20 percent (priests) to 37 percent (secondary school teachers),

TABLE 6.2 Percentage Distribution of Personally Maladjusted
Individuals (NEURA) by Functional Sphere and by Status

Status	Political	NEURA	Cultural	NEURA	Economic	NEURA
				Functional Sphere		
High	High government officials	25	University professors	33	Oil industry executives	29
					Industrial executives	47
					Commercial executives	40
					Owners of cattle ranches	47
					Agricultural entrepreneurs	53
Middle	Government staff	28	Secondary school teachers	37	Owners of small industries	51
	Municipal council members	31	Priests	20	Owners of small shops	52
	Government employees	59	Student leaders	32	White-collar workers in commerce	54
	Labor leaders	28	Primary school teachers	54	Oil industry employees	46
Low					Industrial workers	56
					Rancho dwellers	65
					Wage workers in agriculture	63
					Subsistence farmers	62
					Land reform peasants	65

among the middle- and upper-status economic groups it ranges from 40 to
54 percent, oddly enough corresponding respectively to executives and
white-collar workers in commerce.

Why should the upper and middle bourgeoisie feel so distressed in comparison with people who work in such conflictual political settings as the
educational or the bureaucratic? This is astonishing in view of Bonilla's
findings that the economic elite is, among all the top elites, the most secure
and the least subject to unexpected changes. One possible explanation could
be that the middle and upper bourgeoisie, as noted in Chapter 4, are popu-

lated largely by immigrants from foreign countries; they may consequently
experience special psychological pressures and stress. But the data do not
confirm this hypothesis. The foreign-born businessman is no more likely to
be personally maladjusted than are his Venezuelan colleagues. Table 6.3

TABLE 6.3   Variables Associated with Paranoid State (NEURA)

Group Showing a Significant Relationship between NEURA and Some Other Variable	Variables Associated with NEURA (Probability of Association) Sig	
High government officials	RIGHT	(0.99)
	BORNEX	(0.90)
University professors	BORNEX	(0.96)
Industrial executives	HIRSES	(0.96)
Priests	LEGAL	(0.91)
Student leaders	LEFT	(0.94)
Owners of small industries	LEFT	(0.94)
Government employees	HIRSES	(1.00)
	RIGHT	(0.98)
Wage workers in agriculture	LEFT	(1.00)

shows no single variable that seems to account for the paranoid tendencies
of businessmen, although ideological orientation seems to be the only
variable that, at a group level, is more frequently associated with paranoid
attitudes.

The case of lower-status groups is different. They also, like the bourgeoisie, feel isolated, exhibit paranoid symptoms, and often feel alienated.
However, these states of mind are explained in terms of their income, education, and occupational prestige, all of which are low; their lower experience of positive change; their lesser sophistication, political efficacy, and
nationalism; and their greater propensity to violence — in short, to the
particular ETHOS that places them at the bottom of the major lines and
benefits of development. Yet if these characteristics tell a great deal about
the psychological mood of Venezuelans of all walks of life, which makes
the novelist's anecdote sound frighteningly true at the personal level, they
are not sufficient to explain conflicts and violence at the societal level. The
relevant literature on the subject indicates that persons with paranoid

reactions can "control the more blatant, socially disruptive manifestations of their delusions." [15] Moreover, we must take into account the counteracting effects of the greater incorporation of all Venezuelans into the stream of change. Even the usually isolated subsistence farmers are moving from one place to another in sizable proportions; they are now more in touch with educational institutions and especially with the larger society through their extensive exposure to mass communications.

Nevertheless, the prognosis for the prospective migrant to the city is not encouraging with respect to reducing the incidence of NEURA; even those migrants who get jobs in manufacturing industry are vulnerable, in about 50–50 proportions, to the development of personal maladjustment as defined here (see Table 6.4). It may well be that other forces are at work that, as in the case of the foreign origin of the bourgeoisie, are affecting the psychological state of the low-status urban population in a particular way. One possible additional explanation may be that the largely positive experience of change among these groups has induced a disproportionate growth of expectations compared to what they have actually received. We now turn to the consideration of this hypothesis.

Want-Get Ratio Equals Satisfaction?

Sixteen years ago Eugene Staley wrote that "a 'revolution of rising expectations,' as it has been called, is sweeping the underdeveloped nations of the world." [16] Ten years later Daniel Lerner wrote, "There is a new concern that the 1960's may witness a radical counterformation; a revolution of rising frustrations." [17] The core of this theory may be subsumed in the following propositions:

1. Mass media bring new aspirations to people — and then, since the empathic individual imagination quickly (logarithmically, it appears) outruns societal achievements, it brings dissatisfaction conceived as frustration of aspirations.[18]
2. Such imbalances tend to become circular and to accelerate social disorganization rather than self-sustaining growth.[19]

[15] Zamansky, "Paranoid Reactions," p. 382.
[16] Eugene Staley, *The Future of Underdeveloped Countries* (New York: Harper, 1954), p. 20.
[17] Daniel Lerner, "Toward a Communication Theory of Modernization: A Set of Considerations," in Lucian Pye, ed., *Communications and Political Development*, p. 331.
[18] Ibid., p. 335.
[19] Daniel Lerner, *The Passing of Traditional Society*, p. 88.

3. A corollary would be "that an individual's level of satisfaction is always, at any moment of his life, a ratio between what he wants and what he gets, i.e., between his aspirations and achievements." [20]

To test this hypothesis we need, of course, longitudinal data. However, as we stated in a preliminary report,

Lacking these kinds of data, and encouraged by the implications of the corollary, we shall use our survey results to assess, if not the theory as a whole, at least its core proposition, which expressed in a canonical manner may read as follows:
The higher an individal's want-get ratio, the more likely it is that he will manifest satisfaction and personal adjustment.[21]

After building rank order indexes that tapped several institutional settings (family, economic, education, general) for the 28 sample groups on which this study is based, the general conclusions we reached were:

1. The personal level of satisfaction of the middle and upper status groups, as measured by the Want-Get Index, seems to be more strongly associated with the balance of aspirations and achievements than with the level of achievement considered alone.
2. Contrariwise, low status groups' variations in levels of satisfaction are better explained by achievements alone.
3. Regardless of class status, variations in personal adjustment levels seem to be better explained by achievements than by the Want-Get ratio.[22]

In this study we test these propositions again, using more sophisticated analytic tools, but building on the experience gained in the previous work. Moreover, we shall now have a chance to expand the scope of the generalizations, for we shall consider the other characteristics with which we have worked up to now.

Previous analysis of a set of questions showed that respondents could be classified according to three basic levels of "wants" and three levels of "got." In order to clarify the exact meaning of these categories, it is necessary to proceed step by step.

Responses to the following three questions were used to construct the achievement types:

1. Would you say that in the last five years your economic situation has improved, gotten worse, or remained the same?
2. During your childhood were you very happy, rather happy, rather unhappy, or very unhappy?

[20] Lerner, "Toward a Communication Theory," p. 8.
[21] Silva Michelena, "Satisfaction, Personal Adjustment," p. 8.
[22] Ibid., p. 23.

3. If you were to try to borrow a sizable amount of money, would this be easy, somewhat difficult, or impossible?

Achievements were measured by the positive responses (improved economic situation, rather happy or very happy childhood, and opportunity to borrow a sizable amount of money). A GOT person was defined as a respondent who gave at least two such positive answers. On the contrary, a NOTGOT individual was defined as one answering that his economic situation has worsened in the last five years, that his was a rather unhappy or very unhappy childhood, and that it would be impossible for him to borrow a sizable amount of money. In the middle were a certain number of individuals who were ambiguous with respect to their achievement (GOTAMB); here we find those who said that their economic situation had remained the same for the past five years, that they had a rather happy or rather unhappy childhood, and that it would be somewhat difficult for them to borrow a large amount of money.

Aspirations are more difficult than achievements to measure with a survey questionnaire. "Gots" either refer to the past or, as in the case of borrowing money, can be expressed with respect to concrete actions. "Wants" are realized only in the future. Thus, questions about aspirations require that the respondent be able to project himself or a situation into the future, because aspirations reflect a state of mind in which the individual is in some sense looking ahead. Thus, in an interview situation people are more likely to articulate their gots than their wants. We tried to measure wants by asking as concrete questions as we could:

1. Where would you like to be living now?
2. How much more would you need to make your income satisfactory?
3. Is there anything that you or your family need but do not expect to obtain, let's say, in the next five years?
4. Approximately, how much education do you think is the minimum necessary for youth today to prepare them well for life?

A person with a high level of aspirations (HIWANT) was considered one who wanted to move away from the place he was living in currently, who said that he would need 700 or more bolivares monthly in order to make his income satisfactory,[23] or who said that he had needs for his family which he did not expect to obtain in the next five years and that the minimum necessary education to get ahead in life was secondary school or university education. On the contrary, a person with a low level of want

[23] One bolivar is equal to approximately 22 U.S. cents.

(LOWANT) was one who said that he would like to continue living in his current place and whose additional monthly income needs were less than 700 bolivares; or a person who answered that there was nothing his family needed that they could not get in the next five years, and who also said the minimum necessary education for a youth was primary school or less. Those who had neither high wants nor low wants were put in the middle (MEWANT).

By grouping the significant intersections of these basic types of achievements and aspirations, we were finally able to identify three types of individuals: (1) those who were middle or high in gots and whose needs were middle or low (PLACID), (2) those who had ambiguous or no gots and who had high wants (FRUST), and (3) those who had no gots and had low wants (AUTIST). The operation is conveyed perhaps more clearly if expressed in conventional tabular form (see Table 6.4).

TABLE 6.4   Definition of Three Basic Types According to the Relationship of Their Level of Aspiration and of Achievement

Level of Wants	Level of Achievement		
	GOT	GOTAMB	NOTGOT
LOWANT	PLACID = 2,582		AUTIST = 663
MEWANT			
HIWANT		FRUST = 1,020	

NOTE: Figures are the total number of individuals in each category.

We might expect that in those groups where we find a large proportion of PLACID people, we would also find a small proportion of frustrated individuals. However, this expectation is not supported by the data (tau = 0.02). By the same token, in general, we are almost as likely to find, in a group, as "large" a proportion (large in relative terms) of AUTIST as of either PLACID or frustrated persons (respective taus are −0.16 and −0.12). A closer examination of the data presented in Table 6.5 reveals some interesting facts, however.

First of all, except for the owners of cattle ranches, rural groups tend to have a large proportion of both PLACID and AUTIST, although the largest proportion of AUTIST is to be found among the low-status rural groups. Second, upper-status groups (except, of course, owners of agricultural enterprises) tend to have a large proportion of PLACID and a low incidence of AUTIST. However, in general, a relatively high incidence of frustrated individuals is to be found throughout the social structure. Finally, it seems that no definite pattern emerges in the middle class; but at least four of the twelve middle-class groups, though different ones in each case, can be considered as having a relatively high proportion of either PLACID, AUTIST, or FRUST individuals. Worth noting are the educators and bureaucrats, who are among the groups whose aspirations most clearly exceed their achievements. Having thus specified both the definition and the distribution of the types of balances (or imbalances) between aspiration and achievement, we can proceed with the analysis.

In order to test the hypothesis proposed at the beginning of this subsection, we also need to measure the level of satisfaction among the Venezuelan groups in the sample. Four questions were used to build an index of satisfaction:

1. In general, do you experience this satisfaction [the principal in family life] in your own family life? *yes, sometimes, no.
2. Do you think your present income compensates you *well for the work you do, more or less adequately, or badly?
3. In general, how would you describe your life: *very happy, *happy, not very happy, or unhappy?
4. Are you satisfied with the education you received? *yes or no.

A satisfied individual was considered one who chose at least three of the asterisked alternatives. The percentage distribution of satisfied persons (SATISF) may be appreciated by looking at Table 6.5. Perhaps the most striking fact that emerges at first glance is the relatively high level of satisfaction of middle- and upper-status groups, and especially of those who work in the cultural or political spheres. In contrast, the lower-status groups show a very low incidence of satisfied individuals. Thus, the exceptionally dissatisfied (when compared with groups of similar status) owners of small industries (38 percent) and labor leaders (36 per cent), respectively, top and equal the exceptionally satisfied industrial workers (36 percent).

Table 6.6 gives some clues about the general trend just noted. First, it seems that the variance in levels of satisfaction is better explained by either low levels of wants or high levels of gots alone than by the combined effect of these two variables (tau between SATISF and PLACID is equal to 0.49). The fact that across the social hierarchy achievements are largely responsible for inducing satisfaction is further corroborated by the high correlation between socioeconomic status and positive experience of change,

TABLE 6.5 Psychological States of Venezuelan Groups (percentages)

Sample Groups	Psychological States						
	GOT	AUTIST	PLACID	FRUST	NEURA	SATISF	A.MOOD
DMAKER	73	02	63	12	25	85	81
UNPROF	67	01	51	26	33	75	67
OILEXE	84	02	64	13	29	76	68
INDEXE	63	06	55	20	47	61	43
COMEXE	64	05	53	19	40	65	53
CATLER	54	04	49	15	47	58	45
FARMER	49	14	53	12	53	47	36
GSTAFF	62	04	54	25	28	60	65
LICEOS	67	05	54	28	37	67	55
PRIEST	27	00	24	06	20	56	65
STUDEN	35	00	24	30	32	42	68
COUNCL	48	13	49	18	31	41	63
SMALIN	41	13	38	22	51	38	38
SHOPOW	34	15	40	13	52	40	32
SCHOOL	61	15	64	15	54	50	43
CLERKS	42	16	45	29	59	43	33
LABORL	44	15	44	20	28	36	69
COLLAR	49	11	52	21	54	48	38
MPLOIL	73	03	59	16	46	54	45
WORKER	43	23	52	20	56	36	35
RANCHO	21	08	24	19	65	17	24
AGWORK	20	35	43	11	63	24	21
PEASAN	23	29	43	13	62	12	25
LANREF	24	38	45	13	65	12	22

on the one hand, and satisfaction, on the other. Yet they are far from being the only influences on such levels.

In Table 6.6 we also see that levels of satisfaction are highly and positively associated with an important set of normative orientations. The higher the percentage of sophisticated, nationalistic, efficacious, and legalistically oriented individuals in a group, the more likely are we to find a large proportion of PLACID and satisfied individuals. In short, the more positive the ETHOS of a group, the more likely is it that this group will have a high proportion of personally adjusted and satisfied individuals.

The same relationship, however, is not found among those individuals whose levels of achievement are equal to or greater than their levels of wants (PLACID).

Although the PLACID person is likely to have a positive ETHOS, this is more a consequence of his tendency to prefer legal sanctions than of other

TABLE 6.6 Correlates of Levels of Satisfaction and Placidness

	Levels of			
	SATISF		PLACID	
	Tau	p	Tau	p
HIRSES	0.53	(0.00)	0.27	(0.06)
CHANEX	0.67	(0.00)	0.36	(0.01)
SAVANT	0.59	(0.00)	0.28	(0.06)
NATION	0.46	(0.00)	0.28	(0.05)
POLEFF	0.46	(0.00)	0.22	(0.14)
LEGAL	0.55	(0.00)	0.34	(0.02)
ETHOS	0.52	(0.00)	−0.50	(0.00)
RIGHT	0.67	(0.00)	0.38	(0.01)
LEFT	−0.57	(0.00)	−0.42	(0.00)
NEURA	−0.50	(0.00)	−0.17	(0.23)
LOWANT	−0.53	(0.00)	—	—
HIWANT	−0.26*	(0.08)	—	—
GOT	0.72	(0.00)	—	—
NOTGOT	−0.79*	(0.00)	—	—

* These are correlations with dissatisfaction, an index that may be thought of as a complement of the index of satisfaction.

normative orientations. Nevertheless, in no case is the general tendency just outlined reversed. On the contrary, it seems to be reinforced. The fact that there is a low level of association between socioeconomic status and PLACID, and at the same time a rather high level of association between PLACID and experience of change, suggests that GOTS (other than those from whom the index PLACID was derived) derive more from a positive change experience than from actual status level.

Again, if we focus on the relationship between ideological orientation and psychic states, we can conclude that, in general, those who agree with certain prospective radical policies open to the government are likely to be less PLACID and satisfied than those who disagree with such policies. However, this seems to be connected more with status than with the effects of ideology itself: Upper-status groups whose ethos is more positive for development and lower-status groups whose ethos is less congruent with change tend to be rightist, but the most leftist of the groups, student and labor leaders, are less likely than the rightists to be PLACID. Secondary and primary school teachers are among the more personally adjusted, PLACID, and, with the exception of secondary school teachers who are *very* satisfied, show an acceptable level of satisfaction.

The Mood of Venezuelans

Socioeconomic status and experience of change are generally and positively associated with a state of personal adjustment, placidness, and satisfaction. Also, personal adjustment and satisfaction are usually associated
with a normative orientation that is believed to be congenial with national
development; that is, these characteristics probably enhance the cultural
capacity of the country. Moreover, the larger the proportion of personally
adjusted individuals in a group, the more likely it is that we shall also find
a large proportion of satisfied persons. From now on we shall refer to the
personally adjusted or satisfied individual as one having a feeling of
autonomy. An autonomous state of mind is then characterized by a feeling
of positive relatedness, the absence of paranoid symptoms, the absence of
a generalized feeling of powerlessness or of political cynicism, and a sense
of self-importance, that is, the belief that one is capable of influencing
others. The autonomous man probably will also experience a general sense
of satisfaction. The percentage of such persons in each group may be
noted in Table 6.5 (A.MOOD).

A state of PLACIDness, that is, a balanced state of mind characterized
by a medium or low level of WANTS and a medium or high level of GOTS,
was also found to be associated, though to a lesser extent, with high levels
of satisfaction and a positive ETHOS, although it proved to be unrelated
to levels of personal adjustment.

Some variations in these patterns of relationship were also found when
other characteristics were brought to the fore in the analysis. Thus, whereas
cultural and political groups were found to have low levels of incidence of
personal maladjustment, the economic bourgeoisie, whether upper or petite,
had more individuals who felt personally maladjusted than could be predicted from their socioeconomic status, general experience of change,
normative orientation, or PLACIDness. This unusual sign of distress in men
who are among the most economically or otherwise favored and who share
an ideological orientation that is less apt to be associated with such signs
of strain could not be attributed to the fact that most of the industrial and
commercial executives and a large proportion of the small industrialists and
shopowners are foreign immigrants. It may be hypothesized that such signs
of distress show an objective alienation stemming from their economic
activity.

Groups in which the percentage of persons adhering to a rightist ideology is larger were also found to be more likely to be personally adjusted, placid, and satisfied. Leftism in general was found to be negatively associated with such states of mind. However, neither ideology necessarily reflects a non-autonomous state of mind. It is true that the leftist student leaders, owners of small industries, and wage workers in agriculture were more likely to be personally maladjusted than their colleagues with a nonleftist orientation; but it is also true that the more rightist of the government officials were also more likely to feel personally maladjusted.

Satisfaction, on the other hand, as the data in Table 6.7 show, may be

TABLE 6.7   *Four Best Predictors of Level of Satisfaction by Status Aggregates*

High Status		Middle Status		Low Status	
Urban	Rural	Urban	Lower	Urban	Rural
FAMILY	FAMILY	FAMILY	FAMILY	FAMILY	FAMILY
(0.29)	(0.30)	(0.33)	(0.28)	(0.33)	(0.33)
POLITY	POLITY	ECNOMY	ECNOMY	POLITY	EDUCAT
(−0.10)	(−0.10)	(0.14)	(0.13)	(−0.11)	(0.16)
EDUCAT	EDUCAT	EDUCAT	EDUCAT	EDUCAT	EDUCAT
(0.10)	(0.17)	(−0.10)	(−0.11)	(0.09)	(0.14)
WANTS	WANTS	WANTS	WANTS	WANTS	WANTS
(−0.29)	(−0.16)	(−0.21)	(−0.21)	(−0.20)	(−0.14)

more a function of the evaluations that a person makes of certain social systems and of his bare level of wants than from a whole set of other variables that are conceptually similar to those considered up to now.

The data in Table 6.7 are the beta weights of a multiple linear regression equation that picked the four best predictors, among 47 variables, of the level of satisfaction.[24] This operation was performed independently for each of the six class aggregates shown in the table. From these data it can be inferred that high evaluation of the family, political, and educational systems is quite influential in inducing a state of satisfaction, although for all groups the level of wants also has some significance. Stimulated by this finding then, we shall next examine the evaluations that Venezuelans make of systems, roles, and the society in general.

[24] See Appendix A.

7   EVALUATIONS: PRIORITIES, MEASURES, AND AGENTS

Introduction

In the preceding chapters we postulated close, positive inter-relationships among status, experience of change, a positive ethos, and psychological autonomy. That is, the larger the proportion of persons in a high socioeconomic group, the more likely it is that the group will contain a large proportion of individuals whose normative orientations are congenial with development and whose psychological state is unlikely to hinder positive social relations. Studies of the relationship between such characteristics and outlook on life, whether at the individual or the social level, almost invariably point out that they are associated with a positive view of the human environment surrounding them. According to Rokeach, in his study of the open and closed mind — a concept similar to the concept of style of evaluation here —

At the individual level, threat may arise out of adverse experiences, temporary or enduring, which are shaped by and which, in turn, shape broader human conditions. To varying degrees, individuals may become disposed to accept or to form closed systems of thinking and believing in proportion to the degree to which they are made to feel alone, isolated, and helpless in the world in which they live and thus anxious of what the future holds in store for them. Attempts may be made to overcome such feelings by becoming excessively concerned with needs for power and status. Along with such an overconcern follow compensatory attitudes of egotism on the one hand and misanthropy on the other. These, in turn, should lead to feelings of guilt and, by rationalization and projection, to a generally disaffected outlook on life.[1]

[1] Milton Rokeach, *The Open and Closed Mind* (New York: Basic Books, 1960), p. 69.

172

Almond and Verba's statement, which covers research on five nations, would seem definitive:

> In many ways, then, the belief in one's competence is a key political attitude. The self-confident citizen appears to be the democratic citizen. Not only does he think he can participate, he thinks that others ought to participate as well. Furthermore, he does not merely think he can take part in politics: he is likely to *be* more active. And, perhaps most significant of all, the self-confident citizen is also likely to be the most satisfied and loyal citizen.[2]

Yet these findings do not square with the Venezuelan data. Indeed, the following statement points to the contrary conclusion that

> . . . the higher the income, political efficacy, political participation, and newspaper exposure and the more modern the internalized values of nationalism of a given group, the greater the likelihood is that the group will be a highly critical one.[3]

The groups were critical in the sense that they felt there was no national unity and too much foreign influence; they reported being frequently irritated with government because of actions the government did or did not take. Why is this trend reversed?

The subject is too controversial to permit definitive answers. However, as Chapter 3 documented, Venezuela is confronting several intra- and intersystemic maladjustments that make the general situation a highly critical one. Splits in the major political parties had just occurred when these interviews were in progress, and the economic consequences of the slowing down of the rate of increase in oil exports were still vivid in the minds of almost every sophisticated Venezuelan.

Further, the forebodings voiced by government as well as by privately owned mass media concerning international communism, and especially socialist Cuba, as the invisible evil manipulators behind the country's acute political problems made those who were more psychologically accessible most aware of such international influences. The saliency of these issues obscured the fact that the economy, as a whole, was already growing again and that the truly critical aspects of the 1958 crises were already over. But economic prosperity is not, of course, the only determinant of a positive evaluation of society. If these interviews had been done in 1954, or earlier, when the country was growing at 9 percent per year, we doubt that, in general, different results would have been obtained.

---

[2] Gabriel A. Almond and Sidney Verba, *The Civic Culture*, p. 257.
[3] *SRSP*, p. 82.

Implicit in both the Rokeach and the Almond and Verba statements is the belief that the "state of the world" is such that it *should* be positively evaluated by the open-minded, participant individual. But suppose that the current system, by some objective measure, is indeed one that inflicts deprivation on large sectors of the population or that hampers further development of the country? Chapter 3 described the system incongruences as well as the social inequalities prevailing in Venezuela. Chapter 4 documents the fact that inequalities of socioeconomic status (especially of educational levels) among key groups of the population have been widened rather than reduced, even though among all groups their absolute social position has improved. But such incongruences need not affect the outlook that people have of the present or future.

Moreover, the historically rooted character of the Venezuelan population (see Chapter 2) is such that no matter how badly the present is evaluated, the future is perceived as *el dorado*. For instance, in spite of the critical situation in the country at the time these interviews were being held, of the 24 groups interviewed — from peasants to student leaders and government officials — not a single one showed less than 70 percent who believed that in the next five years their economic situation would improve, that children of today have more or many more opportunities to improve, and that in the next twenty years Venezuela would improve its situation rather than remain more or less the same or get worse.

In the pages following we shall make a more exhaustive examination of Venezuelan images of the social systems, roles, priorities, and recommendations for solving the country's problems. Our aim is to establish patterns of relationship among the people's view of their world and their other characteristics. These patterns should help us to understand the bases of antagonisms that are believed to rest on conflicting or contrasting evaluations.

Differences of evaluation can, of course, occur in a great variety of areas. The historical digression that opens Chapter 4 is an excellent example of how deadlocks may occur on measures to be taken to correct a situation that both factions perceive as problematic. Furthermore, not infrequently substantial agreement on what is wrong can coexist with disagreement about what should be done first. Finally, who should carry out the proposed policies is also an area of frequent disagreement. To summarize our approach to the question of evaluations, we shall attempt to establish how Venezuelans of different walks of life answer these general questions: What is wrong? What is to be done? Who should do it?

Evaluation of Systems

The evaluation a person makes of a social system is likely to vary with the frame of reference he adopts (focus of evaluations) and with the saliency of the problem. For instance, a person whose children are confronting serious problems in the neighborhood school may blame the school system for causing such problems. Yet when this person is questioned about the most important problems of the country, he will not necessarily refer to the educational system. Focus and saliency are closely interconnected.

To obtain the interviewee's evaluation of several social systems, four questions, each bringing to the fore a different focus, were formulated:

1. What *personal* problem most preoccupies you now?
2. What do you consider to be the principal problems that confront *families* today in Venezuela?
3. What do you like least about the *place* where you live now?
4. What concerns you most about the current situation in *Venezuela?*

Responses to each of these questions were coded so that it was possible to obtain a global evaluation of each of the following systems: FAMILY, BARRIO (community), EDUCAT (education), POLITY, ECNOMY (economy), and BEHAVE (social behavior or social disorganization). The evaluation of the CHURCH was obtained by coding the positive responses to the following question: In your opinion, what do you think is the present role of the church? (1) It is a positive factor in the development of our country; (2) it plays no role in the development of the country; or (3) it makes full national development more difficult.

The examples of responses coded in each category given in Table 7.1 illustrate clearly that an individual may give the same substantive response. Ordinarily, what is grasped with the survey technique are the problems most salient to a person; if they are salient enough, we would expect the problem to be mentioned repeatedly even when the focus of the question is changed. Recurrence of an answer may also, however, be the effect of other factors. One such factor is what Converse calls "constraint," that is,

. . . the success we would have in predicting, given initial knowledge that an individual holds a specified attitude, that he holds certain further ideas and attitudes.[4]

[4] Philip E. Converse, "The Nature of Belief Systems in Mass Publics" in Norman R. Luttenberg, ed., *Public Opinion and Public Policy: Models of Political Linkage* (Homewood, Ill.: Dorsey Press, 1968), p. 248.

TABLE 7.1   Foci of the Problems

System	Personal	Family	Community	Nation
FAMILY	"I don't see my children" "Home quarrels" "To get married" "The disintegration of my family"	"Negligence of parents" "Lack of authority" "Lack of family unity" "Lack of love"	"My family lives there" "I don't have friends here" "Because I have my girlfriend there"	"To unite the Venezuelan family" "There are too many illegitimate families"
BARRIO	"I don't have a house" "The place where I live"	"Lack of appropriate housing" "Deficiency of the water supply system"	"There are too many *ranchos*" "Streets are in very bad condition" "There are no recreational facilities"	"There are no basic community services" "The regional crisis of Zulia State"
EDUCAT	"I have not been able to study" "To improve my skills"	"Lack of good education" "Lack of marriage education"	"There are no schools for the children" "The cultural apathy of this city"	"Politics that have invaded the educational sector" "Bad quality of education"
POLITY	"The future of the country" "Social insecurity" "Lack of government" "Lack of vigilance"	"Insecurity due to the *bochinche* in the country" "You can live in peace"	"Political agitation" "Terrorism; there is no vigilance" "There is no opportunity for political activity"	"Government is corrupt" "Parties are deficient" "Lawlessness, lack of political honesty"
ECNOMY	"To find a job" "Low salary" "I feel unstable in my job" "Debts I have"	"Lack of employment sources" "The misery" "A few produce and many consume"	"Lack of comfort" "There is no land for farming" "The high cost of living" "It is difficult to find a job"	"Low salaries" "National economic crisis" "Unemployment"
BEHAVE	"Solitude" "To be happy" "My lack of will or perseverance" "I don't have spiritual relaxation" "The world is far from God"	"The hooligans" "The presence of street gangs"	"There are too many prostitutes" "People are not well educated" "There are too many drunkards"	"Moral abandonment" "Lack of religiosity" "People do not obey the law" "Lack of conscience"

The salient aspect of the evaluation of systemic areas may be appreciated by looking at Table 7.2, which establishes that economic problems were at the center of attention for all groups, whereas educational problems (except for the educators of all levels, student leaders, and oil industry executives) were elicited by the queries in less than one-third of each group of re-

TABLE 7.2   Perception of Problems in Systemic Areas (percentages)

Groups	FAMILY	BARRIO	EDUCAT	POLITY	ECNOMY	BEHAVE	CHURCH
DMAKER	46	34	24	61	55	61	69
UNPROF	53	46	35	43	61	53	58
OILEXE	44	40	40	63	48	46	68
INDEXE	46	36	16	61	63	44	65
COMEXE	47	40	22	61	57	45	65
CATLER	31	44	24	38	65	39	73
FARMER	36	32	29	38	75	43	67
GSTAFF	50	35	21	66	46	49	64
LICEOS	51	39	42	33	66	50	66
PRIEST	55	27	26	44	44	73	90
STUDEN	41	36	49	45	74	53	46
COUNCL	35	43	29	49	78	39	68
SMALIN	35	39	20	36	79	43	58
SHOPOW	40	32	17	39	72	41	53
SCHOOL	44	39	30	22	80	38	75
CLERKS	40	29	16	61	75	48	61
LABORL	40	50	19	60	73	38	57
COLLAR	37	36	17	44	79	43	62
MPLOIL	39	49	28	46	65	36	69
WORKER	34	39	14	38	79	37	54
RANCHO	37	52	7	20	84	33	52
AGWORK	14	32	14	13	74	18	46
PEASAN	13	45	12	13	80	20	50
LANREF	20	50	11	17	77	19	47

spondents. More interesting to note in Table 7.2 is the finding that there are two definite patterns of system evaluation. On the one hand, those groups that more frequently mention family problems also are likely to mention problems in all other systems, except with respect to the Church (which they tend to evaluate rather positively), the community, and the economy.

On the other hand, those groups which mention economic problems are more likely to perceive community problems, although this is a weaker tendency. The typical representatives of this last pattern are the *rancho* dwellers and the land reform peasants. These two tendencies perhaps may

TABLE 7.3   Systems Constraint: Kendall Tau Rank Correlation Matrix

	SYSTEM		CHURCH		BEHAVE		ECNOMY		POLITY		EDUCAT		BARRIO	
	Tau	p	Tau	p	Tau	p	Tau	p	Tau	p	Tau	p	Tau	p
CHURCH	0.51	(0.00)												
BEHAVE	0.53	(0.00)	0.28	(0.05)										
ECNOMY	−0.41	(0.00)	−0.28	(0.05)	−0.45	(0.00)								
POLITY	0.43	(0.00)	0.29	(0.05)	0.46	(0.00)	−0.50	(0.00)						
EDUCAT	0.63	(0.00)	0.42	(0.00)	0.41	(0.01)	−0.29	(0.05)	0.17	(0.20)				
BARRIO	−0.03	(0.82)	−0.11	(0.45)	−0.38	(0.01)	0.16	(0.28)	−0.15	(0.29)	−0.10	(0.48)		
FAMILY	0.60	(0.00)	0.27	(0.06)	0.64	(0.00)	−0.47	(0.00)	0.44	(0.00)	0.35	(0.02)	−0.19	(0.19)

be best appreciated by looking at Table 7.3, where, if we except the evaluation of the community, we see generally only a small probability that the association might be due to chance. The two sets of evaluations are more clearly depicted if we average the tau coefficients within and between each set of evaluations (see Figure 7.1). How do these evaluations relate to other characteristics?

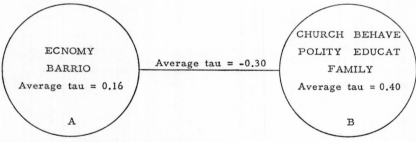

Figure 7.1   Sets of System Evaluations

Table 7.4 indicates that, although groups that more frequently perceive economic problems are also more likely to be of low socioeconomic status, have little experience of change, have a backward normative orientation, and feel little psychological autonomy, the same tendencies are present among those who evaluate the community problems. Here, however, the relationship is so weak that it might be due to chance. On the contrary, those who are more prone to perceive problems of Set B (family, community, educational, political, social behavior, and religious) tend to be of high socioeconomic status, to have experienced a great deal of change, to have a modern normative orientation, and to feel psychologically autonomous.

The use of the ideological continuum left-right (or progressive-conserv-

TABLE 7.4 Correlates of System Evaluations

System Evaluated	HIRSES Tau	p	CHANEX Tau	p	ETHOS Tau	p	A.MOOD Tau	p	LEFT Tau	p	RIGHT Tau	p
Set A:												
BARRIO	−0.19	(0.20)	−0.09	(0.55)	−0.04	(0.80)	−0.12	(0.00)	0.23	(0.11)	−0.20	(0.16)
ECNOMY	−0.56	(0.00)	−0.46	(0.00)	−0.36	(0.01)	−0.65	(0.00)	0.49	(0.00)	−0.57	(0.00)
Set B:												
FAMILY	0.68	(0.00)	0.55	(0.00)	0.53	(0.00)	0.61	(0.00)	−0.48	(0.00)	0.43	(0.00)
EDUCAT	0.48	(0.00)	0 19	(0.20)	0.53	(0.00)	0.52	(0.00)	−0.26	(0.07)	0.30	(0.04)
POLITY	0.48	(0.00)	0.49	(0.00)	0.54	(0.00)	0.50	(0.00)	−0.57	(0.00)	0.50	(0.00)
BEHAVE	0.68	(0.00)	0.43	(0.00)	0.56	(0.00)	0.58	(0.00)	−0.55	(0.00)	0.52	(0.00)
CHURCH	0.40	(0.01)	0.33	(0.03)	0.29	(0.05)	0.46	(0.00)	−0.50	(0.00)	0.51	(0.00)

ative) has been questioned on several grounds. However, sociological literature is full of examples of how ideology increases constraints on belief
systems. A recent study makes this point very clearly:

> One judgmental dimension or "yardstick" that has been highly serviceable for
> simplifying and organizing events in most Western politics for the past century
> has been the liberal-conservative continuum, on which parties, political leaders,
> legislation, court decisions, and a number of other primary objects of politics
> could be more-or-less-adequately located.[5]

The tau coefficients in Table 7.4 seem to confirm that ideology is highly
associated with evaluations. Thus, we see that the more rightist individuals
tend more often to perceive problems in systemic areas other than the
Church, the economy, or the community; leftists are more prone to mention problems in precisely those areas (economy and community) which
are less salient for the rightist individuals.

We have found that social class, experience of change, and the social
psychology of individuals (normative orientations and psychological states)
are associated with patterns of evaluation of social systems and also that
among these patterns there is a certain degree of constraint. Yet we are
not sure which of these two sets (characteristics and evaluations) is more
important for predicting a given "view of the world." In Chapter 1 we
argued that evaluations are part of a system in the sense that they relate
more closely to each other than to other clusters of variables. Figure 1.4
graphically depicts this idea for low-status urban groups. Table 7.5 suggests
that this is the case for other social strata as well. Indeed, between 30 and
53 percent of the four most predictive variables (out of a total of 47)
turned out to be evaluations either of systems or of roles. All of these
figures are too high to be due to chance.

[5] Ibid., p. 254.

TABLE 7.5   Evaluations and Best Predictors of Evaluations

	Predictors of System Evaluations (N = 28*)		Predictors of Role Evaluations (N = 62*)	
	Number	%	Number	%
High				
Urban	15	53	50	80
Rural	14	50	44	70
Middle				
Upper	12	43	46	74
Lower	11	39	40	65
Low				
Urban	10	35	49	79
Rural	8	30	47	76

* Four predictors for each of seven systems and for each of thirteen roles

The meaning of these findings is that although a person's evaluations are influenced by objective characteristics (such as socioeconomic status and experience of change) or mediating dispositions (such as ETHOS or A.MOOD), these evaluations are largely self-contained systems in the sense that they best can be predicted from other evaluations. This same generalization, as is evident from Table 7.5, seems to hold for the evaluation of roles, but to an even greater extent. Indeed, between 70 to 80 percent of the evaluations of a given role can best be predicted from other such evaluations.

Evaluation of Roles

Most commonly, the "diagnosis" each person makes of his environment seems to be unsystematic; yet, no matter how unsophisticated, it is a very complex operation. If we leave aside the case of those persons who say simply "don't know" to a given query, we can postulate that any evaluation involves a certain level of differentiation of the environment, a comparison between a norm and an appreciation of "reality" (as the person sees it), and a decision as to whether the present state of the object being evaluated is good or bad. We have unraveled certain characteristics of the way Venezuelans of different status evaluate some social systems, but this is just one part of the picture.

Although roles are part of systems, they are distinguishable enough to be treated independently by individuals. In fact, a person may have a very positive evaluation of a system and yet recognize that the people working in the system are not fulfilling their duties properly. An electoral change, for instance, may be interpreted as an instance where people attempt to influence a change in roles, but not in the political system itself. Thus, to complete our exploration of the view that Venezuelans have of their society, we need to examine how they think certain roles are being fulfilled.

The evaluation of a role can be made, as is the case of systems, having different foci of reference. In this study we were interested mainly in evaluation of certain roles with respect to their contribution to the nation. Thus we asked the following question:

> Now I am going to read a list of groups. I would like you to indicate if you consider that what each of these groups is doing for the country is positive, negative, or neither of the two.

The responses to this question are displayed in Table 7.6, which shows patterns of answers based on the percentages of individuals within each group who gave positive evaluations of various groups listed in this question. The most striking finding here is that those in political roles, especially government officials and politicians, are the least positively evaluated. The role of the government official, however, as can be seen by the frequencies of plus and minus signs, was the one that elicited the most polarization of opinion. In contrast, teachers and peasants were perceived almost idealistically by all groups (across-group mean above 80 percent). Evaluation of other roles, although generally positive, was rather ambiguous. If we examine Table 7.6 from the point of view of the evaluator, student leaders stand out as the most, and perhaps only, angry group. They gave relatively negative evaluations (minus signs) to eight out of twelve roles being evaluated. They perceive as positive for the country only that which labor leaders, politicians, and themselves were doing.

Focusing now on Table 7.7, we begin to see that the foregoing description gives us but a lead toward the identification of more defined patterns. First, across the social structure there are two role groups that are evaluated in opposite directions by most other groups, yet the same evaluating groups share a negative evaluation of several other specific groups. The larger the proportion of persons evaluating the role of student leaders positively, the smaller is the proportion of persons within that group

TABLE 7.6 Evaluation of Roles

Groups	TEACHR	PRIEST	TALKER	STUDEN	CULROL	GOVOFF	JUDGES
DMAKER	+	+	o	o	o	+	o
UNPROF	o	−	−	o	o	−	−
OILEXE	o	o	o	−	−	o	o
INDEXE	o	o	o	o	o	−	o
COMEXE	o	o	o	o	o	−	o
CATLER	−	+	o	o	o	o	o
FARMER	o	+	o	o	o	−	o
GSTAFF	o	−	o	−	o	+	+
LICEOS	o	−	o	o	o	o	o
PRIEST	o	+	o	o	o	+	+
STUDEN	o	−	−	+	−	−	−
COUNCL	o	o	o	o	+	o	o
SMALIN	o	o	+	o	+	o	o
SHOPOW	o	o	o	−	o	o	o
TEACHR	+	+	+	+	+	+	o
CLERKS	o	o	o	o	o	+	o
LABORL	+	−	o	o	−	+	o
COLLAR	o	o	o	o	o	−	o
MPLOIL	o	o	+	o	+	+	+
WORKER	o	o	+	o	o	o	o
RANCHO	−	o	o	o	o	−	o
AGWORK	−	+	o	o	+	+	+
PEASAN	o	o	−	−	o	+	o
LANREF	−	−	−	−	−	o	−
Across-group mean	0.89	0.73	0.69	0.71	0.44	0.54	0.65

NOTE: A plus sign means that the percentage is 1.96 standard errors or more above the across-group mean, and a minus sign is 1.96 standard errors below.

positively evaluating businessmen, government officials, judges, police, and the armed forces in general. Those groups in which a large proportion of persons evaluate businessmen positively are also those likely to have a smaller proportion of persons saying that what the political roles in general, and politicians and government officials in particular, have contributed to the country is positive.

Another pattern that emerges from Table 7.7 is that each set of roles, with the possible exception of the economic ones, "hang together" in the sense that the relationship among them is quite significant. Thus the cultural, political, armed, and (less so) economic roles seem to form units

POLTCO	POLROL	MILITR	POLICE	ARMROL	BUSNES	LABORL	PEASAN	ECOROL
+	+	o	o	o	+	+	o	+
o	o	o	−	−	o	o	o	o
−	−	o	o	o	o	o	o	o
−	−	o	o	o	+	o	o	o
−	−	o	o	o	+	−	o	o
o	o	+	+	+	o	o	o	o
o	o	o	o	o	o	o	o	o
o	+	−	o	o	o	o	−	o
o	o	o	−	o	o	o	−	o
o	o	+	+	+	+	o	o	o
+	o	−	−	−	−	+	−	o
+	+	+	+	+	o	+	o	+
o	o	o	o	o	o	−	o	o
−	−	o	−	o	o	−	−	−
o	o	o	o	o	o	o	o	o
−	o	o	o	o	o	o	−	o
+	+	o	o	+	o	+	+	+
−	−	−	o	−	o	−	o	−
o	o	+	+	+	o	+	+	+
o	o	o	o	o	o	o	o	o
−	o	−	o	o	−	−	o	o
o	+	o	+	+	o	o	o	o
o	o	o	o	o	−	o	+	o
o	o	o	o	o	−	o	+	o
0.39	0.26	0.64	0.58	0.49	0.70	0.60	0.81	0.43

of evaluation. Among these, however, it is remarkable that the evaluation of the armed forces role follows nicely and quite strongly the same direction as evaluation of political and economic roles.

These patterns can best be appreciated by looking at Figure 7.2. For the sake of brevity, but also based on previous findings that highlight the importance of considering institutional settings as analytical frames (and encouraged by the more or less high degree of constraint that exists within such institutional settings), we decided to group individual role evaluations into four wider categories: cultural (CULROL), political (POLROL), economic (ECOROL), and armed roles (ARMROL). A person evaluating cultural roles

TABLE 7.7 *Constraint among Role Evaluations*

Group	TEACHR	PRIEST	TALKER	STUDEN	CULROL	GOVOFF	JUDGES	POLTCO	POLROL	MILITR	POLICE	ARMROL	BUSNES	LABORL	PEASAN
PRIEST	—0.12														
TALKER	0.24	0.29													
STUDEN	0.25	0.03	0.12												
CULROL	—0.05	0.57	0.51	0.28											
GOVOFF	0.13	0.19	0.26	—0.06	0.25										
JUDGES	0.17	0.56	0.39	—0.01	0.44	0.26									
POLTCO	0.23	—0.06	—0.04	0.33	0.02	0.33	0.03								
POLROL	0.13	0.19	0.16	0.12	0.22	0.62	0.25	0.67							
MILITR	0.13	0.42	0.20	0.17	0.31	0.28	0.36	0.22	0.38						
POLICE	0.06	0.48	0.24	—0.04	0.28	0.44	0.41	0.22	0.46	0.59					
ARMROL	—0.05	0.53	0.19	—0.04	0.30	0.37	0.37	0.17	0.40	0.64	0.82				
BUSNES	0.20	0.29	0.26	—0.06	0.20	—0.09	0.41	—0.25	—0.13	0.22	0.09	0.07			
LABORL	0.35	—0.06	0.07	0.22	—0.07	0.28	0.09	0.64	0.44	0.34	0.26	0.25	—0.12		
PEASAN	0.05	0.31	0.07	0.01	0.19	0.24	0.21	0.18	0.28	0.36	0.54	0.58	—0.01	0.22	
ECOROL	0.28	0.27	0.25	0.24	0.26	0.37	0.36	0.40	0.46	0.60	0.42	0.40	—0.24	0.55	0.30

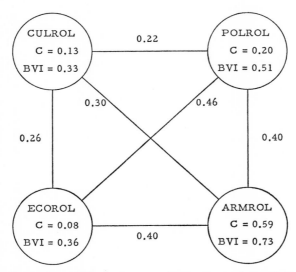

Figure 7.2 Constraint within and among Evaluations of Institutional Sets of Roles

NOTE: C = within-set constraint (average tau),
BVI = tau average between set variables and index.

positively turned out to be one who evaluated positively all of the following roles: primary school teachers, university students, priests, and communicators. A positive evaluation of the roles of politicians, government officials, and judges is an indicator of a positive evaluation of political roles. The military and the police were taken as representative roles of the armed institutions; therefore, a positive evaluation of both such roles was considered an indicator of a positive evaluation of the armed roles. Finally, a person who said that businessmen, labor leaders, and peasants were making a positive contribution to the country was considered a person who evaluated economic roles positively.

Perhaps a less precise but certainly a clearer way of conveying the patterns of relationship within and among such evaluations of institutional roles is to average the pertinent tau coefficients. Thus in Figure 7.2 the armed roles not only have the greatest degree of constraint (C and BVI) but, except for the relationship between economic and political roles, also have the higher degree of relationship with other sets as well. As noted before, it is within the economic roles that the weakest relationships are found (C = 0.08); however, the relationship between the evaluation of individual economic roles and evaluation of economic roles in general (as defined here) has a very small probability of being due to chance.[6] This means that each role evaluation had something to contribute to the more general index.

Evaluations are largely self-explained, in the sense that they can be explained more frequently in terms of other evaluations than in terms of a set of characteristics such as socioeconomic status, experience of change, normative orientations, and psychological states. However, the saliency with which people perceive problem areas was found to be dependent largely on such characteristics. Table 7.8 reveals that evaluation of institutional

TABLE 7.8   Correlates of Role Evaluation

	CULROL		POLROL		ARMROL		ECOROL	
Correlates	Tau	*p*	Tau	*p*	Tau	*p*	Tau	*p*
HIRSES	−0.18	(0.22)	0.08	(0.61)	−0.19	(0.21)	0.19	(0.21)
CHANEX	−0.06	(0.69)	−0.05	(0.77)	−0.14	(0.33)	0.16	(0.28)
ETHOS	−0.25	(0.08)	−0.19	(0.20)	−0.27	(0.16)	0.25	(0.08)
A.MOOD	−0.14	(0.32)	0.04	(0.81)	−0.08	(0.56)	0.22	(0.14)
LEFT	0.04	(0.77)	0.08	(0.59)	0.07	(0.64)	−0.12	(0.42)
RIGHT	−0.04	(0.76)	−0.11	(0.45)	−0.04	(0.78)	0.13	(0.42)
EVSETA	0.19	(0.20)	0.11	(0.46)	0.16	(0.29)	−0.03	(0.84)
EVSETB	−0.28	(0.05)	0.04	(0.77)	−0.19	(0.19)	0.20	(0.18)

sets of roles cannot be explained by any of those characteristics. Furthermore, perception of problems in system areas apparently is not unrelated to evaluation of roles.[7]

In other words, if we want to predict across the social structure the evaluation that people of a specific group make of a certain role (for instance, armed role), it will help little if we know the group members' socioeconomic status, experience of change, normative orientation, psychological state, or the way these individuals perceive problems. To make such a prediction, we should look at how these people evaluate the contribution of other roles (economic, cultural, and political) to the country.

Nevertheless, if we look to each group individually, a few notable consistencies appear. Thus, when specific occupational categories such as

---

[6] The highest probability of error is given by the relationship between the evaluation of peasants and of ECOROL, which is 4 percent.

[7] Note that EVSETA is an index of evaluation of BARRIO and of ECNOMY and EVSETB is an index of the number of people evaluating at least three of the other systems (EDUCAT, FAMILY, POLITY, CHURCH, BEHAVE).

student leaders, government officials, or peasants are taken into account, a variety of patterns can be discovered. First, as pointed out before, student leaders were the most critical of all groups, and they were especially critical of the political and armed roles, except that of judges. Members of the municipal councils, on the contrary, consistently tended to evaluate all roles somewhat positively. Second, as was also noted in *SRSP*,[8] an individual's evaluation of his own role tends to be higher than his evaluation of other roles; yet this is not true of institutional spheres. Table 7.9

TABLE 7.9   Role   Evaluation   by   Institutional   Sphere   (percentages)

Institutional Sphere	Mean Evaluation of Roles			
	CULROL	POLROL	ARMROL	ECOROL
Political groups	48.2	36.6	50.2	50.0
Cultural groups	42.6	25.0	42.6	42.0
Economic groups				
High-status	41.0	19.6	50.0	41.8
Middle-status	48.3	22.3	49.3	36.8
Low-status	45.6	25.2	52.4	41.2

shows that although political groups, on the mean, tend to evaluate political roles more positively than groups belonging to any other sphere, neither cultural nor economic groups more frequently evaluate their own spheres positively.

Evaluation of the Polity

So far we have been concerned with evaluation of systems or roles without probing very deeply into any of those areas. Such evaluations are important because they constitute a framework within which people may, given certain circumstances, become antagonistic to each other. In the next chapter we shall pursue this matter further. Suffice it to say here that social conflicts very often are established also on the basis of differences of opinion about particular matters or sectors within each of those systems. The fact that people perceive pressing needs stemming from the political or educational system does not mean that if we probe more deeply we shall find consistently negative evaluations of every part of these systems. We cannot

[8] *SRSP*, p. 108.

examine in detail here all such SYSTEM areas — an encyclopedic task well
beyond the scope of this study. Nevertheless, we did probe into the political
area, asking some questions we felt were of prime relevance.

One of these questions touches on the subject of national unity. As
pointed out in Chapter 1, perhaps the most salient characteristic of Venezuelan politics now is the pervasive instability of political institutions and
of interest groups. This phenomenon is expressed not only in the recurrent
divisions and subdivisions of the political parties, the delicate balance of
interest organizations such as the Venezuelan Confederation of Workers
but also in the relationships among broader groups. Evident signs of such
lack of unity are found also at the individual level, where personal loyalties
have been shattered by the political stasis. In order to discover how people
perceived these ongoing processes, we asked, "Do you consider that in
Venezuela there exists much, enough, little, or no national unity?" Answers
to this question were examined in *SRSP* in relation to nationalism.[9] The
focus here on these responses is as an indicator of how people perceive
the general political state of the country. For this reason we combined
such responses with those given to the question: "What do you think of
the Venezuelan constitution? Do you consider that the political system
it creates is basically very good, good, average, bad, or very bad?"

This question refers to an issue relevant in any country, but especially
so in the specific situation of Venezuela. In 1963, when we were doing the
survey on which this study is based, Venezuelans were beginning to live
under a constitution that had just been approved by Congress (1960)
after having experienced a new constitution every six years since 1830.
When the first republican constitution was drafted, one could say, of course,
that a question about a constitution that was only three years old was
premature. People could not have realistic bases on which to form opinions
about so new a political event. Yet there are valid reasons to argue the
contrary. In the first place, the fact that it was a new, widely and continuously publicized event should have made people more aware of it.
Second, if we judge by the mean length of life of Venezuelan constitutions
(although perhaps it is not fair to say this), at the time we were conducting
the interviews, the Venezuelan constitution was middle-aged!

In any case, it is theoretically a sound idea to assess what people were
thinking about the political system. Those people who answered that there
was little or no national unity in Venezuela and who also said that the
political system that the new constitution created was basically bad or

[9] Ibid., pp. 80–82.

TABLE 7.10   *Evaluation of the Political System (percentages)*

Groups	BADPAI	IRRITG	CIVICS	INTERV	WPARTY
DMAKER	68	70	82	16	86
UNPROF	58	67	65	31	74
OILEXE	64	63	70	29	69
INDEXE	63	39	54	39	54
COMEXE	55	44	52	43	64
CATLER	40	39	49	43	54
FARMER	52	36	44	43	52
GSTAFF	54	60	71	25	77
LICEOS	61	56	53	44	62
PRIEST	53	44	46	47	76
STUDEN	78	87	37	62	56
COUNCL	50	45	60	37	45
SMALIN	49	33	44	50	58
SHOPOW	39	27	42	40	36
TEACHR	65	28	37	59	57
CLERKS	61	40	52	43	46
LABORL	60	60	68	29	52
COLLAR	62	42	31	66	48
MPLOIL	45	27	60	30	38
WORKER	51	28	37	52	40
RANCHO	46	39	31	45	35
AGWORK	30	12	38	27	24
PEASAN	28	10	38	24	18
LANREF	27	14	41	23	15

very bad were considered to be evaluating the political system negatively (BADPAI). Table 7.10 shows the distribution of such responses. Two facts are worth noting here. The first is the large percentage of individuals who negatively perceived the political system in which they were living—for almost one-third [10] of the low-status rural groups did so. Second, regardless of institutional locus, groups of similar status tended to evaluate the political climate equally negatively. For instance, about the same proportion of high government officials, business executives, and university professors said that there was no national unity and that the political system created by the constitution was basically bad.

Government

Although the political system generally was undervalued and government officials were scorned by most of the people we interviewed, these

[10] Or about half the campesinos who answered this question.

attitudes may very well represent stereotypes, ungrounded views, and people may in fact rarely feel genuine anger at the government. But responses to our query confirm that in the year previous to the interview people indeed had been irritated by some government action, or lack of it, a few times or frequently. As a matter of fact, a large proportion of individuals within each group readily indicated that they had been irritated by the government. However, this time only one-tenth of the campesinos dared to say so.

Such pervasive negative evaluation of politics and government may indicate that the stage is set for an uprising or a coup d'état, for a substantial proportion of Venezuelans are prone to violent protest as a means of combating government inefficiency or a state of chaos. Yet many of them showed a marked inclination toward the use of legal means. More typical, however, was the finding of great heterogeneity in such normative orientation, especially among middle-class groups. Does this mean that either of the two alternatives mentioned here is equally likely to happen?

The question we asked was: "Has anything that the government has done or has failed to do irritated you during the last year? Has this occurred frequently, a few times, or very few times?" Which alternative people will pick depends, of course, on many factors that cannot be measured or grasped by the questionnaire technique. Nor can one expect that evaluations will automatically lead to action. However, if people believe that something radical should be done when politics and the government are perceived as doing evil (and in fact people do perceive the present political system and government as basically bad), it is evident that the situation is ripe for a political change. Indeed, the years 1960–1964 were full of political turbulence. Elections at the end of 1964 revealed that the government party, Acción Democrática, had lost some support but that it still had enough to allow party members to win the elections. In the next chapter we shall have more to say about the relationship between political participation and evaluations. Here we prefer to keep the exploration within the limits set by the Venezuelan images of politics.

Political Role of the Army

One such image, and a very important one, is what people believe should be the participation of the armed forces in politics. In the 139 years of its republican history, Venezuela has had transference of power from one elected civilian president to another only in 1964 and 1969. Previously, it was primarily military intervention in politics that led to presidential successions.

What is the likelihood that the military will intervene? To answer that question authoritatively would require the social scientist to probe deeply into the attitudes of the population toward military intervention in politics and to study the military themselves. Moreover, many case studies in depth should be done in order to search for patterns and motivations. If the focus was on this century, it would also be necessary to study the role of the United States Defense and State Departments in Latin American military coups. Some studies have been made recently on the subject, but none examines empirically the attitudes of populations toward military intervention in politics.[11] Admittedly, this is just one variable, and we do not know how important it is. The assumption here is that the more people accept the right of the military to play a role in national politics, the easier it will be for the military to do so. We treat this propensity to accept military intervention in political matters in this chapter on evaluations in spite of the fact that, in a strict sense, it would be defined as a normative orientation. The rationale for this decision arises out of the reality that the propensity itself stems from strong evaluative judgments. The following question was designed to probe into the matter:

> As to the role that the armed forces should play in national life, do you think:
> 1. The armed forces should always respect constitutional government.
> 2. The armed forces should act politically only when they think the constitution is not being complied with.
> 3. The armed forces should enforce the popular will when the regime is not responding to the aspirations of the people.
> 4. The armed forces should intervene in politics whenever they feel it is necessary.

Responses to the first alternative (CIVICS) as well as the proportion of people within each group favoring some kind of military intervention in politics (INTERV) may be seen in Table 7.10. A careful examination of these two figures leads us to classify sample groups into four categories. The first one clusters those groups which show a predominantly civilian orientation toward politics (CIVICS ≥ 60 percent). This aggregate is com-

---

[11] L. N. McAlister compiled a recent summary of the literature on the subject. See "Recent Research and Writings on the Role of the Military in Latin America," *Latin American Research Review*, vol. 2, no. 1 (1966), pp. 5–36.

posed of high and middle government officials, university professors, oil industry executives and employees, labor leaders, and municipal council members.

The second category clusters those groups where the greatest proportion of individuals assign the armed forces an active role in politics. Within this group we find student leaders, primary school teachers, white-collar workers in commerce, and the low-status urban groups.

The low-status rural groups make up the third category. Individuals within this category reject military intervention in politics in more or less equal proportions (between 23 and 27 percent) or have no opinion.

Finally, we find a cluster of groups that are more or less evenly split between intervention and nonintervention. In this category we find upper- or middle-status economic groups (executives of industrial and commercial firms, upper-status rural groups, and the petite bourgeoisie), middle-status cultural groups (secondary school teachers and priests), but none of the political groups.

Status and institutional loci, then, seem to be important determinants of attitude toward military intervention in politics. But some care must be exercised in interpreting these findings. The categories do not necessarily imply homogeneity of evaluation. Although this seems to hold true in those groups where consensus on nonintervention is found, it does not in the groups where an almost equally high consensus on the alternative of military intervention in politics exists. For instance, the student leaders who overwhelmingly favor intervention (75 percent) say that the army should intervene when the regime is not responding to the aspirations of the people. Only about half of the intervention-minded industrial workers or *rancho* inhabitants favor that alternative. These low-status urban groups, together with industrial executives, owners of cattle ranches, white-collar workers in commerce, and schoolteachers, are the groups in which the highest proportion (between one-fifth and one-fourth) of individuals favor unrestricted military intervention in politics.

In any case, it is evident that the majority of the population (the majority is of low status) either favors military intervention in politics or has no opinion on the subject. But if a military coup is staged in Venezuela in the near future, and we were to predict on the basis of this limited amount of knowledge the probable attitude of the different groups of the population, we might venture to say that most government officials (high and middle level), university professors, municipal councilmen, labor leaders, executives, and employees of oil industry would be in opposition to it, and that industrial and commercial executives, upper-status rural groups, and all other middle-status groups would be either in favor of or in opposition to the intervention depending on the ideological leanings of the rebels. If the leaders of the intervention were traditional Latin American dictators, they would encounter opposition from the majority of educators and student leaders, whereas the rest of the population would remain paralyzed by their own ambivalence or would overtly favor such intervention.

Political Parties

Reactions such as the one described in the preceding section are rarely articulated through occupational roles. Conglomerates such as industrial executives, farmers, campesinos, and educators usually articulate their demands through their respective organizations; however, such demands are more likely to be of an "interest" type, that is, professional or ameliorative. More commonly, demands are aggregated through political parties. Venezuelan professional organizations (from labor unions to schoolteacher associations) were fostered initially by political party agents, with the result that there has been some important overlapping between political party functions and organizational activities. Some obvious examples are the Venezuelan Campesino Federation, the Venezuelan Confederation of Workers, the Venezuelan Federation of Teachers, or the Federation of University Centers. Thus it was interesting to find out what people felt the function of political parties should be. The following question was designed to illuminate this matter:

> As to the responsibilities of a political party, could you tell which of the following phrases most faithfully reflects your opinion?
>   1. The political party should represent the interests of definite sectors of the country (for example, workers, employees, merchants).
>   2. The political party should represent the interests of broad groups (for example, the middle class, the lower class, the upper class).
>   3. The political party should represent points of view that are above the interests of any particular group.

The percentage of people in each group choosing the third alternative is shown in Table 7.10. Although there is some degree of coincidence between what people think should be the role of the military in politics and their conception about the constituency of a political party, it is possible to distinguish only three broad categories of response. First we have those people who conceive political parties as aggregating wide sectoral interests rather than those of any particular group. This, of course, may represent a desire to look for a way out of the perceived national chaos rather than ungrounded idealism. This seems to be confirmed by the high tau coefficients between negative evaluation of the political system (BADPAI), being irritated with government (IRRITG), and a noninterest conception of the role of political parties (WPARTY).[12] These three characteristics also seem to hang together with a desire for civilian rather than military control of politics.

Evaluation of aspects of the political system also seems to be closely associated with the way people evaluate SYSTEMS in general, but not with their evaluation of roles. The data in Table 7.11 reveal that the irritated

TABLE 7.11   Degree of Constraint of Evaluation of Systems, Roles, and Politics

Evaluation of Systems and Roles	Evaluation of Politics							
	BADPAI		IRRITG		CIVICS		WPARTY	
	Tau	p	Tau	p	Tau	p	Tau	p
EVSETA	−0.33	(0.02)	−0.35	(0.02)	−0.37	(0.01)	−0.51	(0.00)
EVSETB	0.51	(0.00)	0.69	(0.00)	0.40	(0.01)	0.67	(0.00)
CULROL	−0.25	(0.09)	−0.36	(0.01)	−0.22	(0.13)	−0.12	(0.12)
POLROL	−0.07	(0.65)	0.02	(0.89)	−0.07	(0.65)	0.08	(0.59)
ARMROL	−0.32	(0.03)	−0.36	(0.01)	−0.51	(0.00)	−0.19	(0.20)
ECOROL	0.10	(0.49)	0.09	(0.56)	0.09	(0.56)	0.13	(0.38)

citizens (IRRITG) who are highly critical of the political system (BADPAI) but who conceive the role of the military as foreign to politics (CIVICS) and believe that the responsibilities of the political parties should transcend group interests (WPARTY) are more likely to perceive problems in the family, political, religious, and educational systems along with problems of misconduct or deviant behavior (EVSETB) than to perceive problems as stemming from the community or the economy (EVSETA). These same

[12] Tau coefficients among political SYSTEM variables:

	BADPAI		IRRITG		CIVICS	
IRRITG	0.57	(0.00)				
CIVICS	0.22	(0.13)	0.43	(0.00)		
WPARTY	0.51	(0.00)	0.57	(0.00)	0.35	(0.02)

citizens, though to a lesser extent, are also likely to evaluate less positively both cultural and armed roles.

In Table 7.12 we can see that such evaluations are, across the social structure, largely dependent on the group's characteristics. Thus, in any group, the larger the percentage of individuals of high socioeconomic status with an intensive experience of change, of positive ETHOS, and in an

TABLE 7.12 Evaluation of the Political System and Some Characteristics

	BADPAI		IRRITG		DEMCRA		WPARTY	
Characteristics	Tau	p	Tau	p	Tau	p	Tau	p
HIRSES	0.49	(0.00)	0.62	(0.00)	0.47	(0.00)	0.70	(0.00)
CHANEX	0.30	(0.00)	0.35	(0.00)	0.49	(0.00)	0.45	(0.00)
ETHOS	0.51	(0.00)	0.70	(0.00)	0.49	(0.00)	0.52	(0.00)
A.MOOD	0.49	(0.00)	0.68	(0.00)	0.53	(0.00)	0.57	(0.00)

autonomous mood (A.MOOD), the more likely it is that we shall find a large proportion of individuals who perceive national politics as chaotic (BADPAI and IRRITG) but who at the same time tend to oppose military intervention and are likely to conceive of the responsibilities of a political party as not linked to any group in particular. However, this is only a general trend, and there are groups, such as student leaders, to which this trend does not apply.

Foreign Influence

The question of foreign influence in Venezuelan politics has been a hot issue for the past forty years. It is possible, of course, to find in the republican history of the country earlier episodes in which the question of foreign intervention in internal affairs caught the attention of Venezuelans. In Chapter 2 we mentioned a few instances, such as the blockade of Puerto Cabello (a port to the west of Caracas, third in importance in the country) at the turn of this century. But although some inflammatory speeches were made, especially by former president Cipriano Castro, and some popular agitation was stirred up, the issue faded quickly. It was only when the young activists of the generation of 1928 began to speak of anti-imperialism that evaluation of foreign influence was recurrently and systematically brought to the wider public. In this sense it can be said that with the emergence of popular politics after 1936, discussion of foreign intervention in national life flourished. This should surprise no one, because by that time the oil business already had deeply affected the lives of most Venezuelans. So central was the anti-imperialist banner to these emerging political groups that when the government repressed these new groups by jailing or exiling them, anti-Communist slogans were diffused widely to provide justification for the repressive acts. Central to the government arguments was that communism was an international (meaning foreign) doctrine.

Both attitudes, anti-imperialism and anticommunism, were to be encountered again and again up to the present. When the interviews were being conducted, such evaluative statements were perhaps more than ever at the center of political conflicts. In a variety of ways television and radio constantly hammered at the "Communists," meaning the urban and rural guerrillas as well as the political parties of the left. Yet very little is known about the people's evaluation of foreign influence. Precisely in order to get at this, we asked our informants,

> Would you mention, in order of importance, two of the most important foreign influences that you consider to have been prejudicial to the country? And the two that you consider to have been most beneficial?

Responses to these questions may be seen in Table 7.13. The first significant result is that the question about prejudicial influences on the whole elicited more responses than the question about beneficial foreign influences.[13] This negative saliency may be a product of the conflictual context in which the question of foreign influences, and especially the ideological issues of "communism" and "capitalism," has been debated. Yet if we are to judge by the low saliency that the foreign influence issue has for the low-status groups (19 percent at most), we have to conclude that this is an issue mostly for the upper-status groups and for the educated middle class. A reflection of this tendency is the high degree of correlation that exists among all responses about foreign influences. Table 7.14 affirms that in those groups where a high level of response of one kind was given, it is likely that a high level of response of another kind was given also. Because the kinds of responses are contradictory, these figures may be interpreted also as an indication of heterogeneity-homogeneity. We shall consider this question more qualitatively.

Examining the data more closely, we see that, except for the student

---

[13] Percentages shown do not necessarily add to 100 because they are the percentage of people who gave a particular response as first or second most prejudicial (beneficial).

TABLE 7.13   Most Beneficial and Most Prejudicial Foreign Influences (percentages)

Groups	Most Beneficial		Most Prejudicial		
	OTHRGD	CAPGD	COMBAD	BADCAP	OTHRBD
DMAKER	36	31	52	32	22
UNPROF	54	31	41	47	25
OILEXE	45	34	55	20	12
INDEXE	30	19	40	20	12
COMEXE	23	24	40	17	11
CATLER	12	29	31	16	10
FARMER	20	21	37	18	7
GSTAFF	41	28	44	20	28
LICEOS	36	34	47	36	19
PRIEST	38	31	59	21	11
STUDEN	55	15	27	63	20
COUNCL	24	25	43	24	16
SMALIN	14	27	33	13	10
SHOPOW	11	11	21	11	5
TEACHR	20	29	34	15	11
CLERKS	16	30	30	23	11
LABORL	30	35	51	35	15
COLLAR	21	19	27	21	15
MPLOIL	19	26	31	9	10
WORKER	11	14	19	13	12
RANCHO	6	8	14	8	9
AGWORK	2	7	10	6	6
PEASAN	3	6	6	3	8
LANREF	3	7	7	3	10

leaders and the university professors, all groups show a higher proportion of persons naming Communist influences as most prejudicial. A typical example of this kind of response was the one given by a high government official who emphatically said "Castro-communism." But high government officials are a heterogeneous group in this respect. In spite of the high incidence of anti-Communist responses, they rank fifth among those who scorned the "capitalist," that is, among those who ranked as the first or second most prejudicial foreign influence "U.S. imperialism," "General Motors," the Alliance for Progress, or some other influence coming from capitalist nations. Worth noting at this point is the difference of opinion between student and labor leaders. The former quite overwhelmingly (63 percent) blamed capitalism, and the latter primarily mentioned negative Communist influences.

*TABLE 7.14 Interrelation among Different Evaluations
of Foreign Influence*

Kinds of Foreign Influence	OTHRBD		BADCAP		CAPGD		OTHRGD	
	Tau	*p*	Tau	*p*	Tau	*p*	Tau	*p*
BADCAP	0.62	(0.00)						
CAPGD	0.41	(0.01)	0.51	(0.00)				
OTHRGD	0.64	(0.00)	0.70	(0.00)	0.48	(0.00)		
COMBAD	0.43	(0.00)	0.54	(0.00)	0.69	(0.00)	0.66	(0.00)

Turning now to evaluation of good influences, we see that approximately the same percentage of people mentioned capitalism and influences such as international organizations, immigrants, and technological or cultural influences. Almost no one said that there were positive Communist influences. But this fact should not be taken at face value. In the first place, Venezuela has not had diplomatic or commercial relations with socialist countries for about twenty years; therefore, people have not experienced the broader sorts of economic or technological influences that could come from socialist nations as they do now from capitalist countries. And second, at the time we were making the interviews, the "extremists" were being persecuted by the police or fired from their jobs. In such a situation it is almost natural that positive statements about communism be self-censored.

If we focus on the interrelations among evaluation of foreign influences and other evaluations, it becomes evident that there is no difference between what people think are the most prejudicial or beneficial influences and the way they evaluate other systems or roles. Table 7.15 reveals that the larger the percentage of persons in a group saying that some kind of foreign influence is beneficial or prejudicial, the larger the percentage of people perceiving problems in the family, education, polity, church, and social behavior (EVSETB) and the smaller the proportion of people mentioning community or economic problems. Moreover, their evaluation of roles tends to be equally unpredictable.

Table 7.15 also suggests that those groups which had a larger proportion of people evaluating foreign influences, no matter what the particular judgments, tended to have a larger proportion of upper-status persons who have experienced a great deal of change, whose normative orientation is congenial with development, and whose psychological state is autonomous.

Thus, these questions seem to identify above all the capacity to *perceive*

TABLE 7.15 Correlates of Evaluation of Foreign Influence

Groups	CAPGD		OTHRGD		CAPBAD		COMBAD	
	Tau	p	Tau	p	Tau	p	Tau	p
EVSETA	−0.30	(0.04)	−0.42	(0.00)	−0.37	(0.01)	−0.40	(0.00)
EVSETB	0.56	(0.00)	0.78	(0.00)	0.64	(0.00)	0.72	(0.00)
CULROL	−0.07	(0.62)	−0.29	(0.00)	−0.30	(0.04)	−0.09	(0.00)
POLROL	0.20	(0.18)	0.02	(0.89)	0.04	(0.77)	0.20	(0.17)
ARMROL	−0.01	(0.94)	−0.26	(0.08)	−0.31	(0.03)	0.00	(0.98)
ECOROL	0.29	(0.05)	0.12	(0.43)	0.12	(0.40)	0.37	(0.01)
HIRSES	0.56	(0.00)	0.70	(0.00)	0.59	(0.00)	0.70	(0.00)
CHANEX	0.39	(0.01)	0.45	(0.00)	0.25	(0.08)	0.54	(0.00)
ETHOS	0.53	(0.00)	0.76	(0.00)	0.68	(0.00)	0.70	(0.00)
A.MOOD	0.57	(0.00)	0.77	(0.00)	0.69	(0.00)	0.69	(0.00)

foreign influences. And indeed, those groups which saw no beneficial foreign influences saw no negative influences either (tau = 0.83, $p <$ 0.00). A more detailed analysis searching for differences of opinion has to be done group by group, for these differences (COMBAD, CAPBAD, OTHRBD, CAPGD, OTHRGD) are maintained across groups even when status is controlled. Such detailed analysis is beyond the scope of this work, yet we do not wish to close this section without suggesting that the most commonsense explanation seems to be that such differences might be accounted for by variations in ideological orientation. An almost perfect example of this tendency is afforded by the comparison of student leaders, who are mostly leftist (51 percent), with the rightist-oriented priests (66 percent). Whereas 27 percent of student leaders mention Communist influences as prejudicial, a *majority* of the priests (59 percent) hold this opinion. On the other hand, whereas 63 percent of student leaders scorn capitalism, only one of every five priests does so.

With this observation, we conclude the exploration of the Venezuelan images of what is wrong with their society, systems, and roles. It now remains to examine what they recommend as solutions.

What Is to Be Done?

A given group's evaluation of societal systems is a sound predictor of its evaluation of the political system. Thus, groups most critical of the political system, irritated with the government, civic minded about the role of the military in politics, and holding the belief that party interests should be above those of any specific group tend to perceive problems in areas other than economic or community. These groups are also more likely to have high socioeconomic status, a high experience of change, a positive ethos, and to feel autonomous. Do these differences in evaluation also correspond to differences in recommended measures?

A recommended measure is the logical consequence of a diagnosis. The way people perceive problems obviously is correlated with the measures that they recommend. Thus, we would expect those perceiving economic problems to recommend some kind of economic measure. But this intuitive reasoning proved to be too simplistic. If a functional criterion such as the one just mentioned were readily applicable, the problem of rationality would be solved, and the potential for conflict stemming from differences of opinion about what should be done would be minimal. The fact is that almost no problem that people are likely to identify has, even from a technical point of view, a single solution. Unemployment, for instance, may be tackled in a variety of ways, some of which denote basic differences in normative orientations and even psychic states. Moreover, agreement about what is wrong is generally easier to reach than agreement about what measures should be implemented. Thus, if we are to assess the political views of Venezuelans, we must take into consideration the solutions they prefer and their priorities.

After we asked people which problems they saw in the occupational and national areas, we immediately sought to learn what they thought were the appropriate measures to be taken. Table 7.16 shows examples of the responses we received. As the table indicates, the measures recommended can be differentiated into three types: economic, political, and social. Looking now at Table 7.17, we see that those groups which recommend political measures also tend to prefer social solutions (tau = 0.28; $p < 0.05$) and to avoid economic measures.[14] Such patterns, as we have postulated, should correlate with the particular "diagnosis" each group favors. Indeed, Table 7.18 confirms that groups that more frequently pick political (DOPOLI) and social (DOSOC) measures are those that more frequently perceive problems in the following set of areas: family, education, behavior, polity, and religion. Those who prefer economic measures were those who more frequently perceived either economic or community prob-

---

[14] Tau between economic and political measures is —0.14; with social measures it is still more differentiating (—0.18), although not large enough to say that it is a firm tendency.

TABLE 7.16 *Preferred Instruments for Solving National and Work Problems: Examples of Typical Answers*

Type of Measure	National Problems	Occupational Problems
	What can be done to better this situation?	In your opinion, what are the most adequate means to solve this problem?
Economic (DOECON)	Create new industries; open up job sources; more economic development.	Increase salaries; find a job; lower the prices; more budget; open up jobs.
Political (DOPOL)	*Revolutionary:* Change government in any possible way; a profound structural transformation of the country. *Peaceful change of government or institutional measures:* A new government; a new ministry; give constitutional freedoms.	*Administrative:* Reduce bureaucracy; ask for a transfer; director should socialize more with employees. *Governmental:* Government should mediate; government should help private enterprise; new laws. *Political:* Fire the extremists from their jobs; a strong political hand; change of government.
Social (DOSOC)	*Cooperation:* Foster a spirit of mutual understanding among all Venezuelans. *Educational and research:* A study of the causes of this insecurity should be made to orient the population; give more education. *Moral-religious:* Preach the Gospel to all so that they may return to God; improve the conscience of the people.	*Educational:* Improve the school curriculum; create centers of popular culture. *Services:* Give housing; promote clubs or sports organizations. *General:* Search for a consensus; better understanding among one another. *Activities:* Talk problems over with the firm's owners; make more propaganda; work harder.

lems. Again, what type of measure a person prefers apparently has nothing to do with his evaluation of role performance.

Table 7.18 documents that those groups with a larger proportion of persons choosing social or political measures tend also to have a larger proportion of persons saying that there was no national unity in the

TABLE 7.17   Type of Measures Preferred by Sample Groups
(*percentages*)

Groups	DOECON	DOPOLI	DOSOC	LONRUN
DMAKER	27	55	50	48
UNPROF	39	49	66	43
OILEXE	21	58	42	61
INDEXE	38	58	32	47
COMEXE	45	57	32	45
CATLER	46	62	34	42
FARMER	50	56	21	36
GSTAFF	20	60	47	53
LICEOS	34	38	72	39
PRIEST	31	52	69	40
STUDEN	38	70	49	18
COUNCL	53	51	34	34
SMALIN	65	55	20	36
SHOPOW	59	37	12	30
TEACHR	50	34	58	25
CLERKS	39	53	22	34
LABORL	45	63	40	35
COLLAR	44	48	19	37
MPLOIL	32	45	20	38
WORKER	39	44	19	21
RANCHO	31	40	10	10
AGWORK	36	24	13	11
PEASAN	47	24	21	7
LANREF	45	32	23	3

country, that the political system created by the constitution was a bad one, and that they frequently had been irritated with the government. Finally, groups having a larger proportion of social- or political-minded individuals were also more likely to be in favor of the exclusion of the military from politics and to believe that the political parties should strive for socially transcendent interests, that is, interests beyond and above those of any particular group.

To complete this picture of Venezuelan policy recommendations, those groups having a larger proportion of individuals perceiving some kind of foreign influence, whether capitalist, Communist, or any other kind, prejudicial or beneficial, also tend to recommend social and political measures, whereas those whose evaluations focus on economic problems or who recommend local or economic types of solutions generally do not perceive any foreign influence at all.

Searching Table 7.17 for group patterns of response, we see that one

TABLE 7.18 Characteristics of Measures to Solve System and Role Problems

System and Role	DOECON		DOPOLI		DOSOC		LONRUN	
	Tau	p	Tau	p	Tau	p	Tau	p
EVSETA	−0.28	(0.06)	−0.33	(0.02)	−0.25	(0.08)	−0.54	(0.00)
EVSETB	−0.37	(0.01)	0.50	(0.00)	0.57	(0.00)	0.59	(0.00)
BADPAI	−0.26	(0.08)	0.38	(0.01)	0.40	(0.00)	0.35	(0.02)
IRRITG	−0.30	(0.04)	0.51	(0.00)	0.49	(0.00)	0.43	(0.00)
CIVICS	−0.25	(0.09)	0.38	(0.01)	0.37	(0.01)	0.50	(0.00)
WPARTY	−0.25	(0.09)	0.45	(0.00)	0.56	(0.00)	0.65	(0.00)
CULROL	0.13	(0.39)	−0.35	(0.02)	−0.22	(0.12)	−0.13	(0.37)
POLROL	−0.06	(0.67)	−0.04	(0.80)	0.22	(0.14)	−0.01	(0.96)
ARMROL	0.06	(0.70)	−0.11	(0.47)	−0.05	(0.74)	−0.08	(0.56)
ECOROL	−0.13	(0.38)	0.14	(0.32)	0.22	(0.13)	0.16	(0.28)

is immediately evident: Both cultural and political groups focus more of their attention on social or political measures. However, there are important deviations. For instance, oil and industrial executives only infrequently recommended what we have defined as economic measures. Of course, for people working in these institutions and at these levels, an administrative measure such as building houses for the workers or establishing more cordial relations with them may in fact have direct economic significance, namely, increasing profits. Nevertheless, the fact that a large proportion of industrial managers are worried by what we have defined as social problems and not about salaries, budgets, investment opportunities, and the like is significant in itself.

Our awareness that in real life many decisions are not so unambiguously economic, social, or political but involve all of those areas at once led us to confront the interviewees with a set of forced choices where many such aspects of the problem were highlighted. More concretely, we presented sets of choices that were either mutually exclusive or geared to different problems. But they involved issues that at the time of the interviewing were key (and still are) in Venezuela:

Now I am going to present you with three pairs of alternatives. I want you to select *one* from each pair. Some of the alternatives are not mutually exclusive. In such cases please select the one that you consider more important (or less bad) for Venezuela today:

    A. 1. Immediately to improve the living standard of the poor *or*

    *2. Invest capital in new industries.

B. 1. Nationalize the productive resources of the country *or*
   *2. Avoid interruptions or decline in economic productivity.
C. 1. Raise the taxes on company profits *or*
   *2. Stimulate free enterprise to make new investments.

The alternatives marked with an asterisk clearly have a conservative tint, but they also invoke long-run solutions rather than immediate actions. Indeed, rightists were more likely to pick these asterisked alternatives, whereas leftists were more likely to favor the others (minimum tau = 0.40; $p < 0.00$). In Table 7.17 we can see the percentage distribution of people leaning toward the long-run, conservative alternatives (LONRUN).[15] These responses seem to follow the general pattern established for the types of measures; however, there are two important differences. First, low-status groups, either urban or rural, generally favor these LONRUN alternatives much less than they favor, for instance, political or social measures. Second, the difference between economic groups, on the one side, and cultural and political groups on the other seems to be less pronounced; in fact, if we focus on student leaders and secondary and primary school teachers, the trend reverses. This might be an effect of the ideological implications hidden in these choices which probably made the politically aware educators and student leaders reject the conservative alternatives.

A more general indication as to which alternative measure is most often preferred is presented in Table 7.19, where it is evident that the higher

TABLE 7.19   Type of Measures Recommended and Social Characteristics

Characteristics	DOECON	DOPOLI	DOSOC	LONRUN
HIRSES	−0.28	0.43	0.62	0.59
CHANEX	−0.19	0.28	0.21	0.64
ETHOS	−0.19	0.47	0.51	0.40
A.MOOD	−0.24	0.49	0.54	0.54

the socioeconomic status and experience of change of a group, the more likely it is that a larger proportion of persons will choose social, political, or long-run, conservative alternatives. Moreover, looking across the social structure, we find that the more persons in a group having a positive ethos and an autonomous mood, the more likely is it that we shall find social

[15] The LONRUN index was built giving a value of one to the nonasterisked alternatives, and a value of three to the asterisked ones. Then for each respondent an average value was computed based on his replies to these two sets of alternatives. *Don't know* or *no reply* was not taken into consideration for computing the average.

and political measures recommended or solutions preferred that produce no immediate effects but that, compared with other alternatives, are somewhat conservative.

Priorities

So far we have established some definite patterns of association between the type of problem a group perceives and the type of measures the members of that group chose to solve the identified problem. Both problems and measures were established having as their frame of reference more than a personal, occupational, community, or national area of interest. But to complete the description of the Venezuelan view of the political world we have to consider the question of priorities.

What should be done first? This is a question that seems difficult to answer, especially because people usually are poorly informed about political events.[16] Yet community development manuals advise practitioners that when starting a new program in any community, they should satisfy the "felt need" of the population. The underlying assumption is, of course, that people perceive certain needs and, when asked, are able to rank them. This perceived need may or may not square with the technicians' priorities, yet the idea of focusing on needs first is that people will be more willing to cooperate.

The implication of this argument is that even those people whose style of evaluation is more confined have a certain idea about what should be done first, and that the priority chosen is an important element in their world view. We attempted to differentiate among certain highly relevant priorities by giving the interviewees a list of policies and asking them to rank those policies according to the degree of importance they attached to them. The first such set refers to broad issues that were at the center of attention of national politics:

> To conclude this section, could you tell me which of the following three types of measures you consider *most important* for Venezuela today and, by your criteria, which is next in importance?
> 1. Improve the distribution of wealth.
> 2. Maintain democracy.
> 3. Accelerate economic growth.

All three measures were and still are important issues. One of the most

---

[16] See, for instance, Richard R. Fagen, *Politics and Communication* (Boston: Little, Brown, 1966), p. 83.

salient structural maladjustments of the country is its extreme concentration of wealth. Even at the personal income level, the interviews reveal,
for instance, that the difference in income between a university professor
and a peasant is on the order of one to twenty. Economic growth, though
a conceptually more complicated concept, became an acute issue for
Venezuelans of the 1960s. As mentioned, during this year not only was
the country hit by an economic crisis, but there was also an increasing
concern that the sources of growth had already been exhausted. Finally,
in 1963, when these interviews were in progress, efforts were being made
to overthrow the government. Thus, the question of maintaining democracy
was of utmost importance for certain people. There is evidence that the
president of the country induced his *compañero* leaders of the Venezuelan
Confederation of Workers and of the Venezuelan Campesino Federation to
postpone popular demands in order to maintain political stability.[17] Was
this a sound strategy?

Holding down the aspirations of the workers and peasants for the sake
of political stability was but one of a set of policies that allowed President
Betancourt to finish his term of office. Thus, it is almost impossible, given
the data we have, to know whether the strategy was sound. However, if
we look at the average answer given by individuals of each group to the
question just posed (see Table 7.20), we see that low-status rural groups,
members of municipal councils, and labor leaders gave first priority to
maintaining democracy. Whether this is the consequence rather than the
cause of the success of Betancourt's policy is difficult to tell, and there is
no point in speculating about it.

It is significant, however, that those groups that were most critical of
the government ranked the maintenance of democracy last. University
professors, secondary school teachers, and student leaders, along with
priests and owners of small shops, elected the acceleration of economic
growth as their first choice. In this they differed from *rancho* inhabitants,
who, with the low-status rural groups, gave first priority to redistribution
of wealth. High government officials also gave first priority to the redistribution of wealth, but they gave equal importance to maintaining
democracy and accelerating economic growth. In fact, the small differences
in the averages suggest that government officials were split quite evenly
among the three choices.

The rest of the groups — staff in government, schoolteachers, the upper

[17] VENELITE interview 138163. See also John R. Mathiason, in *SRSP*, chap. 5,
pp. 120–155.

TABLE 7.20 *Priority of Goals (average ranks)*

Groups	Redistribute Wealth	Maintain Democracy	Accelerate Growth
DMAKER	1.93	2.01	2.01
UNPROF	1.94	2.22	1.79
OILEXE	2.32	2.16	1.50
COMEXE	2.31	2.13	1.49
INDEXE	2.27	1.94	1.69
CATLER	2.13	1.96	1.87
FARMER	2.14	2.06	1.73
GSTAFF	2.11	2.04	1.76
LICEOS	2.08	2.15	1.77
PRIEST	1.78	2.48	1.72
STUDEN	1.86	2.35	1.80
COUNCL	2.39	1.64	1.97
LABORL	2.23	1.60	2.13
PEQIND	2.15	2.06	1.67
SHOPOW	1.93	2.02	1.85
TEACHR	2.17	1.95	1.88
CLERKS	2.23	1.93	1.84
COLLAR	2.27	2.19	1.56
MPLOIL	2.31	1.96	1.68
WORKER	2.10	2.05	1.80
RANCHO	1.82	2.18	1.90
AGWORK	1.86	1.70	2.26
PEASAN	1.80	1.49	2.58
LANREF	1.63	1.33	3.03

and middle bourgeoisie, and industrial workers — chose the same pattern: first, accelerate economic growth; second, maintain democracy; and last, redistribute wealth.

The maintenance of democracy, redistribution of wealth, and acceleration of economic growth certainly are believed to be instruments for achieving happiness. But they are so general in nature that they are conceived more often as goals in themselves than as instruments. Therefore, these issues can hardly be used to identify Venezuelan priorities on what is to be done. The following question, however, although also referring to general policies, is much more specific and offers a wider variety of alternatives:

Now I am going to read some of the things people say Venezuela needs most urgently. Please rank them according to the importance you give to each one: create new industries, accelerate agrarian reform, improve the quality of education, establish the electoral system, protect all citizens from violence, construct more dwellings for poor people, and eliminate unemployment.

People were asked to give a rank of one to the alternative they considered the most important, two to the next, and so on up to seven, the least important. In Table 7.21 we can see the average ranks of all alternatives for each group. The first finding to note is that increasing the number of alternatives obviously diminishes the possibility of finding common patterns.

The first such pattern includes three groups: owners and administrators of agricultural enterprises, staff in government, and high government officials. They, like the middle and upper bourgeoisie, assign first priority to the creation of new industries and, like *every* group, the least priority to the consolidation of the electoral system. Second and third priorities are given to the elimination of unemployment or to improvement in the quality of education. The acceleration of agrarian reform is ranked fourth, before either construction of more dwellings for the poor or protection against violence.

The second pattern follows closely the one just described, the main difference being that protection against violence is ranked fourth, whereas acceleration of agrarian reform is pushed back to next to last place. We find those groups which had something to lose from violence and nothing obvious to gain from acceleration of agrarian reform favoring this pattern, that is, the upper and middle bourgeoisie (executives in general, owners of small business, and white-collar workers, including those in government). Priests could also fit into this pattern, although they assign more importance to the improvement in the quality of education.

The third pattern has one main difference from the pattern just described. Acceleration of agrarian reform is ranked second and protection against violence is moved to sixth place. In this group we find owners of cattle ranches together with student leaders. Except for the lower priority that they assign to the creation of new industries and to the improvement in the quality of education, the rural low-status groups also could be incorporated into this pattern of preferences.

A fourth pattern may be formed by workers and *rancho* inhabitants, who push agrarian reform, protection against violence, and consolidation of the electoral system to the last three places. However, although *rancho* inhabitants' first priority is the elimination of unemployment, industrial workers put this alternative in fourth place and move forward the creation of new industries.

Finally, we note a fifth pattern of priorities that is markedly different from the other four. Educators of all levels almost monotonously rank the

TABLE 7.21 *Patterns of Policy Priorities for Venezuela (by rank)*

Group Patterns	Create New Industries	Eliminate Unemployment	Improve Quality of Education	More Dwellings for the Poor	Accelerate Land Reform	Protect against Violence	Consolidate Electoral System
Pattern I							
DMAKER	1	3.5	2	6	3.5	5	7
GSTAFF	1	2	3	5	4	6	7
FARMER	1	2	6	2	4	5	7
Pattern II							
OILEXE	1	2	3	6	5	4	7
COMEXE	1	2	3	5	6	4	7
INDEXE	1	4	2	5	6	3	7
SMALIN	1	2	3	5	6	4	7
COLLAR	1	2	3	5	6	4	7
CLERKS	1	2	3	5	6	5	7
PRIEST	1	3	2	4.5	6	4.5	7
MPLOIL	1	2	3	4	6	5	7
SHOPOW	1	2	5	3	6	4	7
Pattern III							
CATLER	1	3	4	5	2	6	7
STUDEN	1	3	4	5	2	6	7
COUNCL	1	4	3	5	2	6	7
LABORL	1	3	5	4	2	6	7
Pattern IV							
WORKER	1	4	3	2	6	5	7
RANCHO	4	1	3	2	6	5	7
Pattern V							
UNPROF	2	3	1	5	4	6	7
LICEOS	2	3	1	5	4	6	7
TEACHR	2	3	1	4	5	6	7

improvement in the quality of education first, the creation of new industries second, the elimination of unemployment third, acceleration of agrarian reform fourth, construction of dwellings for the poor people fifth. The
political alternatives they assign to the last two places.

The distribution of groups in the five patterns of priorities is, in many
ways, suggestive. First, it seems that the institutional focus is quite important in inducing certain priorities. The most obvious examples are business
and education, which, incidentally, are perhaps the two that differ most
in their patterns of priorities. Second, economic measures geared to urban
areas are given far more importance than land reform policy. Even government officials give the latter only a middle priority.

Finally, there is quite a high degree of consistency in ranking of goals
(democracy, wealth, and growth) and ranking of specific policies. The
only apparent inconsistency is found among those groups which ranked
the maintenance of democracy first but, when confronted with specific
policies aimed at this goal (consolidation of the electoral system and
protection against violence), ranked them last. One could argue, of
course, that these people (councilmen, labor leaders, and campesinos)
think that the best way to maintain democracy is through economic
development policies; yet such an argument seems to be a little too
sophisticated. What if, as in the case of the peasant, the word democracy
still was inexorably linked to the Acción Democrática party? In fact, it is
known that peasants identify the word democracy with the party. When
asked, they would say that they voted for *la democracia,* meaning AD.
Whether this is also the case among municipal councilmen and labor
leaders we do not know. Yet it is significant that AD was significantly
represented in both organizations. However, because we did not ask party
affiliation, this hypothesis cannot be tested.

Who Should Implement the Policies?

In the preceding sections we examined what different Venezuelan groups
perceive as being wrong and what policies they recommend. We shall now
consider responses to the question "Who do you think should have the
principal responsibility for solving this problem?"

This query was made immediately after the respondent had identified
a problem and the means to solve it in relation to national and occupational
areas. The bulk of responses singled out two responsible sectors. The
majority of the people felt that the government should take the principal

responsibility. They mentioned the government more often in connection with national problems, yet a preliminary test revealed that people who singled out the government as principally responsible in the national sphere were very likely to assign it a similar responsibility in the occupational sphere.[18]

The second sector held responsible for solving the problem was *all* the people. Responses such as "all Venezuelans," "all the nation," "the people themselves," "all the families," "a great social movement" perhaps indicated bewilderment in face of the magnitude of the problem, or possibly a desire for national unity. Both interpretations seem equally reasonable, especially if we take into consideration that most people within each group felt both that the government was inefficient and that there was no national unity. Be it bewilderment or hope, the fact that (as may be seen in Table 7.22) only between one-fourth and one-third of the middle- and upper-status individuals (except white-collar workers and oil industry employees) said that a large aggregate of people should be responsible, whereas about two-thirds of the members of each group (except agricultural workers) mentioned that the government or a particular government agency should be held responsible for solving the perceived problem, is indicative of the pervasive role that most people expect government to play in national life.

Interestingly, holding government responsible for solving problems is not related to any particular way of perceiving problems. That is, the percentage of people who assign government an active role is so uniform that it cannot be explained by any variable examined so far. In this sense it may be considered a national character trait, perhaps deeply rooted in the psychology created by the traditional paternalistic attitude of the conquistadores and later reinforced by the succession of strong caudillos who governed the country so tightly for most of its history. Thus government is likely to be always at the *picota* (pillory), for even a substantive proportion of the conservative, foreign-born businessmen expect the government to have the principal responsibility for solving the problems they perceive and for implementing the policies they recommend.

There are indications that this attitude may be changing: One is the high degree of association that exists between certain background characteristics and the desire for wider participation in problem solving. This new attitude will be found more frequently in those groups containing a

[18] The sig test for the majority of the group was over 0.90, that is, a high probability that the event was not due to chance.

*TABLE 7.22   Principal Responsibility for Implementing
the Recommended Action (percentages)*

Groups	Principal Responsible Should Be	
	Government	All
DMAKER	76	34
UNPROF	67	31
OILEXE	61	26
INDEXE	66	26
COMEXE	70	23
CATLER	83	19
FARMER	81	20
GSTAFF	64	30
LICEOS	81	32
PRIEST	71	34
STUDEN	56	19
COUNCL	86	22
SMALIN	76	30
SHOPOW	69	26
TEACHR	83	26
CLERKS	62	24
LABORL	61	33
COLLAR	74	16
MPLOIL	64	14
WORKER	64	17
RANCHO	64	12
AGWORK	44	12
PEASAN	62	10
LANREF	72	10

larger proportion of upper socioeconomic status individuals who have experienced a great deal of change. Also, having a positive ethos and feeling psychologically autonomous are associated with such an attitude.[19]

Evaluations

In this chapter we have attempted to answer these questions: What do people perceive as wrong? What should be done? And by whom? All three questions are basic for making a "diagnosis" of a situation.

In the course of the analysis we were able to establish two definite patterns. On the one hand, people who are high in socioeconomic status

---

[19] Tau coefficients between ALL and these variables are HIRSES (0.66), CHANEX (0.51), ETHOS (0.54), and A.MOOD (0.51), all significant at the 0.00 level.

and experience of change, who have a positive ethos and feel psychologically autonomous, more often tend to perceive political, behavioral, family, educational, or religious problems, to recommend social or political measures to solve them, and they also more frequently tend to hold the wider community or broad social aggregates principally responsible for their solution. On the other hand, the lower the socioeconomic status of a group, the smaller its experience of change, the less positive its ethos, and the less autonomous, the more likely it is that its members will identify community or economic problems and recommend economic measures to solve them. It is also likely that very few individuals among them would say that all should be responsible for the solution of the problems. However, regardless of their characteristics, an overwhelming proportion of individuals is likely to single out the government as having the principal responsibility for solving all kinds of problems.

Evaluations of roles, on the contrary, were found to be quite self-contained. We could not identify definite group patterns, nor could we find an association among characteristics such as experience of change, ethos, psychological state, and role evaluation. However, some important differences were noted among specific groups.

In the main, we have emphasized differences in this chapter. Thus, the principal thrust of the analysis was geared to finding patterns that enhanced differences among groups. Now, by way of summary, we want to change the focus of analysis and concentrate on similarities. One way of doing it is to compute a rank order correlation coefficient (tau) for the evaluation of both systems and roles. The rank order could be established on the basis of the percentage of people within each group identifying problems in all seven system areas and the percentage evaluating positively each of the twelve roles. This measure will give us the degree of agreement between any pair of groups. Yet, it is difficult to see interconnections in a 28-by-27 matrix of correlation coefficients. For that reason we used both of these matrices as input to the cluster program described in Chapter 1.

This program cluster group is based on a measure of association minimizing redundancy of information, that is, minimizing the links *among* clusters but maximizing links *within* clusters. Figure 7.3 shows the clusters based on system evaluations. Most of these clusters are quite mixed, in the sense that they are formed by groups that have different characteristics and patterns of evaluation. Most notable is the case of high government officials (DMAKER) and land reform farmers (LANREF). Also quite mixed

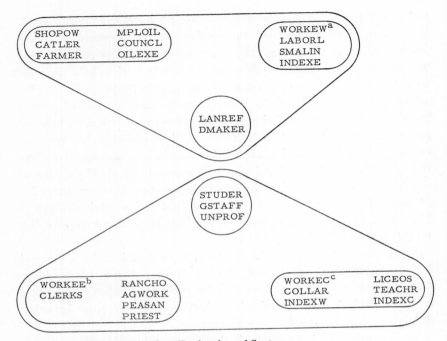

Figure 7.3   Clusters Based on Evaluation of Systems

[a] Workers of the western region.
[b] Workers of the eastern region.
[c] Workers of the central region.

is the cluster of industrial executives of the central (INDEXC) and western (INDEXW) regions, workers of the central region (WORKEC), white-collar workers (COLLAR), and middle-level educators (LICEOS, TEACHR). Other clusters seem to bring together groups that, in terms of socioeconomic status or other characteristics, are not so different — for example, the cluster of agricultural workers, *rancho* dwellers, subsistence farmers, and workers of the eastern region, although this cluster also includes two middle-class groups, priests and government employees (CLERKS).

More puzzling perhaps is the cluster based on the evaluation of roles (Figure 7.4). Here, labor leaders (LABORL) and student leaders (STUDEN) are separated in an early stage of the cluster, which means that their evaluations are similar to each other but are quite different from the rest of the population. No apparent coincidence seems to exist between both sets of clusters (SYSTEM and ROLE); thus, from another point of view, the conclusion that people evaluate roles and systems somewhat

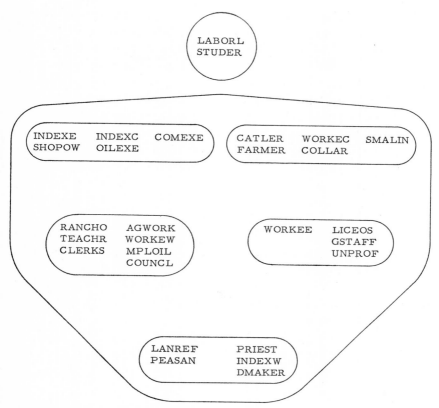

Figure 7.4   Clusters Based on Evaluation of Roles

independently is confirmed. Agreements of this kind therefore do not necessarily mean a consensus. For instance, it is true that labor leaders and student leaders assign the same rank to different roles; however, they were singled out as an outstanding example of groups having quite different evaluations of foreign influence. Labor leaders scorned Communists, whereas student leaders blamed capitalist influences primarily.

This chapter also has established that patterns of system evaluation greatly coincide with a critical attitude toward both the political system and the government, a strong attitude against military intervention in politics, and a desire for wider support of political parties, that is, placing party interest above and beyond any group interest. Such evaluations were found to be highly correlated both with perception of problems in sociopolitical systems, rather than in the economic or community areas, and with the choice of social and political measures over economic measures. Groups having this pattern of evaluation tended to be of high socioeconomic status, to have experienced quite a bit of change, to have a positive normative orientation, and to feel psychologically autonomous. They also were more likely to mention that all should be held responsible for the implementation of their recommended policies. Yet they were as likely as any other group to mention government as the principal agency of policy implementation.

Finally, a set of goal and instrumental priorities was examined, and certain interesting patterns were noted. From this particular analysis it may be inferred that specific priorities vary according to different criteria, but that institutional loci seem to be the most important homogenizing factor.

Whether differences or similarities in world view actually lead to establishment of antagonisms or consensus is something that cannot be considered yet. We need first to take into account degree of activism, political or otherwise, which is the factor that determines whether two groups ever confront their differences or similarities. This facet of the problem will be explored in the next chapter.

8   POLITICAL CAPACITY

Thus far we have been able to establish certain patterns of association among people's social location and experience of change; their political culture, psychological states, and the problems they perceive; solutions they recommend and agents they consider to be responsible for solving the perceived problems. Returning to the analytical plan set forth in Chapter 1, it now remains to examine the political capacity of Venezuelans.

This way of looking at politics is, of course, not new. In fact, it follows closely the classical model of political analysis. The idea that people make their decisions by considering the various alternatives, checking them against their beliefs, and then *acting* accordingly may be found in Aristotle. A more precise articulation of these ideas is to be found in such other classics as Marx, Rousseau, Smith, and Weber, although each of these authors gives particular emphasis to different aspects of the problem. These classical theories are well known, yet their authors were so prolific and the scope of their propositions was so encompassing that if a few words are not said to frame the discussion, the risk of obscuring the argument could outweigh the violence we do to these writers by summing up their ideas.

As Pool has suggested,[1] Aristotle defined the prerequisites that enable a society to make politically feasible what man desires: a set of procedures embodying the rule of law, ways of assuring the representation of the variety of interests present in society, the need to have a major sector more or less equal in its objective social location (middle class), and, finally, a set of attitudes that "valued the common good." It is this last

[1] Ithiel de Sola Pool, "The Public and the Polity," in Ithiel de Sola Pool, ed., *Contemporary Political Science* (New York: McGraw-Hill, 1967), p. 28

point that Rousseau carried almost to its logical conclusion. Adam Smith took an entirely different path by saying that the pursuit of personal interests leads to the benefit of society. Years later Marx stressed the role of organization and of collective endeavor for reaching the common good. De Tocqueville, and later Weber, also noted the role of intermediary organizations in the political process, but these thinkers convincingly argued that intermediary organizations, far from leading to instability, might indeed prevent it. Since then much has been written on the subject of political stability and political participation.

Pool has ably summarized the most relevant findings on the subject.[2] He argues that empirical research has helped toward better understanding of the problem to which classical thinkers addressed themselves. The main relevant findings may be grouped in three broad areas: the role of groups, relationship between leader and the public, and political alienation and politicization. We shall briefly mention those points which are most relevant here.

We note two kinds of group influences. One is that of pressure and interest groups, voluntary organizations, and the like, which actually make it possible to bargain and reach solutions in the interest of stability. Bargaining can be conflictive, but conflict, in this context, is no longer cumulative, and it may actually increase stability. Another kind of group influence is that of primary or face-to-face groups, which can be used effectively to induce individual loyalty to the nation or the society at large.

But if it is true that groups act as buffers between the leaders and the public, it is also true that such a relationship should continue to be considered of utmost importance. Here three points are worth noting. (1) Leaders can effectively help the integration of a fragmented or heterogeneous society; they can even change the political mood of a nation and induce new ways of acting when basic attitudes have not been modified. (2) In this sense, they function as respected reference individuals who under certain cultural conditions (3) may become unifying symbols or father figures. The role that mass communication plays in these processes is well understood in the developed nations; however, as was suggested in Chapter 4, the function of the mass media in the underdeveloped countries is not yet well established, although all research evidence presented here so far, as well as that of other studies, points to the fact that mass communication is related to a positive ethos for development.

[2] Ibid.

Finally, studies on politicization and political alienation also stress the point that "a participant civic culture comes in with modernity";[3] withdrawal from politics and nonallegiance to the political system are seen more as remnants of the past or of particular psychological states than as a result of industrialization and urbanization. However, political activism in the common man is far from being the most salient activity. This sort of participation (not too much but not too little) has been singled out as leading to political stability.[4]

Pool concludes his discussion by making it clear that political stability is not the only possible outcome from increased participation. He invokes as examples those places where "the politics of murder, terror, and revolution as ways to gain the good things of modern life" occur.[5] It is worth quoting a passage from this author at length because it clearly and briefly summarizes what recent research has contributed to the answer to a basic question:

> Why is it that participant politics can in one place so fully refute the classical fear of the turbulence of the masses and in another place so fully confirm it?
>
> The answers are not far to seek and have in recent years been increasingly spelled out in studies of political development. One way of summarizing what this new literature has told us is to assert that those revolutionary movements in the new nations are trying to achieve political participation in societies where many of the conditions of participation, listed in the preceding section of this chapter, are missing. They are seeking to achieve participation in the shaping of their nation's political destiny under conditions in which mobility is limited, where the wealth available seems like a fixed pie, where there is no clear prospect for steady progress toward a better life, where mutual trust outside the family hardly exists, where the average citizen feels thoroughly inefficacious, and where the degree of abstraction from and sublimation of personal goals into relatively broad political identification is rather low.[6]

Previous chapters in this study have made it clear that Venezuela historically has been a society in which acute conflicts have not been scarce. There is a long tradition of participation in armed movements, guerrilla groups (*cimarroneras*), and local battles, yet in the past forty years a truly mass-based politics has begun to develop, and the past ten years have been the most critical. Numerous coups d'état have been attempted, both by traditional army men and by young officers who have shared

[3] Ibid., p. 40.
[4] Gabriel A. Almond and Sidney Verba, *The Civic Culture*, especially chap. 15.
[5] Pool, "Public and the Polity," p. 46.
[6] Ibid.

progressive ideologies. Urban and rural guerrilla units have been organized, and although to the best of our knowledge they have been neutralized, there still remains a small group of devoted revolutionaries in the mountains of Venezuela. Yet, as we saw in Chapter 4, Venezuela is the only country in Latin America where the economy has had a steady and pronounced growth for the past forty years (with the exception of 1960–1962). Upward mobility rates are comparable with those of the most open countries of the world, and downward mobility rates are smaller than in many such places. Mobility is also subjectively high. Not only does the Venezuelan not perceive class barriers, but he is fully in touch with the world through some form of public communication. A significant proportion of even the backward subsistence farmers, who live in small villages, listen to the radio.

Venezuelans of all social levels were found to be incurable optimists. The future was perceived as promising by almost three of every four of the 5,500 individuals interviewed. From peasants to high government officials, from labor leaders to student leaders, every group felt confident that their future or their children's future would be better. The same radiant outlook was evident with respect to their family life by two of every three respondents, and about half of the interviewees claimed to be satisfied with the education they had received.

Objective social inequalities, however, have widened, and many individuals, especially in the petite bourgeoisie and low-status urban and rural groups, felt that their opinions had no importance politically; they showed paranoid symptoms, had no face-to-face intimate relationship with either a friend or a small group, and had the larger incidence of dissatisfaction. These people were more often found to have a less positive ethos for development. Yet they were less critical of both the polity and the government than any other group. The problems they perceived were linked mainly to the communities where they were living or to their personal economic conditions.

A description of priorities with respect to certain policies revealed that whereas the "have-not" groups gave primary importance to those policies which promised immediate gratification of their needs, the "have" groups notably favored those policies which promised gratification for the long run.

These findings attest that, at least in the case of Venezuela, political stability is a far more complex problem than either classical or empirical theories suggest. No rigorous test of such theories is likely to be performed until the problem of linking historical data with cross-sectional analysis is solved or longitudinal data of the sort analyzed here are gathered from more countries. We believe, however, that this theoretical introduction has served the purpose of setting a relevant frame of reference for the analysis of the Venezuelan's political capacity that follows.

Political Capacity among Venezuelans

Our conception of political capacity was briefly stated in *SRSP*: "the potential ability of actors to transmute . . . evaluations and particularly those that seem most stable into politically effective action. We look here to the political actor's present and past levels of participation, the capacity of the organizations to which he belongs, his position within them, his connections with other actors and organizations." [7] The detailed analysis of the political capacity of the Venezuelan elite that Bonilla makes in *The Failure of Elites* cannot be duplicated here. In this survey, however, we collected relevant information about the following variables: political participation, participation in voluntary organizations, interpersonal contacts, and the predisposition to cooperate. Let us examine each of them separately now and later bring them together in a general index of activism.

Political Participation

Formal enrollment in a party, attendance at party meetings, rallies, or public discussions, the writing of letters to representatives or public communiqués, or informal discussions of politics are examples of vehicles for mass political participation. The variety of such means for participating politically has as its only limit man's culturally bounded imagination. Each of these forms of participation defines styles and levels of involvement. The activist is likely to use as many vehicles as possible; at the other extreme, the apathetic individual will withdraw from politics. In the middle is the common citizen who will now and then discuss politics, vote, or attend a candidate's speech.

We attempted to measure the extent of political participation by means of the following set of questions:

1. Have you attended any meeting sponsored by a political party?
2. Have you participated in any labor union or professional association meeting?

[7] *SRSP*, p. 33.

3. Have you discussed politics with friends or acquaintances?
4. Have you actively worked for a party or candidate?
5. Have you participated in a strike?

It may seem inappropriate to some that participation in labor union meetings, professional organizations, or strikes is considered here as a form of political participation. These activities theoretically belong more to interest articulation than to interest aggregation. It is true that such participation usually involves issues that do not transcend the limits of the profession, the factory, or the community; yet in Venezuela such forms of participation must be considered political. Both labor unions and professional associations are strongly politicized. The election of members of the board, for instance, is inevitably a political issue. Electoral tickets (*planchas*) are formed primarily on the basis of party affiliation. The electoral turnouts in organizations such as the National Confederation of Workers, professional associations (*colegios*), the Venezuelan Federation of Teachers, the Federation of University Students, and even electoral results of high school student centers are considered indicators of the relative strength of political parties. The politicization of labor and professional organizations may be understood as a direct outcome of the historical fact that former members of the Venezuelan Student Federation, back in the 1930s, established the mass political parties. Subsequently these politicians established labor unions.

To build an index of political participation, we assigned a value of one to the "yes" responses and a value of three to the "no" answers. Then an average was computed based on the number of responses given by each individual. Those whose average was one or two were considered to be high participants because they would have said *yes* to at least three of the five questions listed here. The extremely high levels of political participation can be seen in Table 8.1. Except for the oil industry executives, who are "high," and for priests, who are "low," all cultural and political groups have 80 percent or more individuals who said that they participated in several ways. At the bottom (which here means less than 65 percent political participation), we find the lower-status groups, except the politicized land reform peasants (74 percent), industrial farmers, and the petite bourgeoisie. In the middle (between 65 and 80 percent), we find the industrial and commercial executives and the owners of cattle ranches.

Evidently, then, political participation is related to socioeconomic status. That greater incidence of political participation is likely to be found in those groups having a greater percentage of high socioeconomic status

TABLE 8.1   The Political Capacity of Venezuelans (percentages)

Sample Groups	POLPAR	SOCPAR	WORDOM	POLCAP
DMAKER	0.98	0.75	0.69	0.89
UNPROF	0.98	0.80	0.68	0.89
OILEXE	0.88	0.62	0.51	0.72
INDEXE	0.70	0.30	0.41	0.45
COMEXE	0.73	0.31	0.41	0.47
CATLER	0.74	0.20	0.66	0.57
FARMER	0.63	0.26	0.57	0.48
GSTAFF	0.90	0.46	0.54	0.68
LICEOS	0.89	0.53	0.62	0.72
PRIEST	0.62	0.30	0.67	0.55
STUDEN	0.98	0.26	0.95	0.94
COUNCL	0.91	0.24	0.87	0.85
SMALIN	0.61	0.09	0.49	0.42
SHOPOW	0.42	0.10	0.31	0.25
SCHOOL	0.84	0.23	0.49	0.53
CLERKS	0.60	0.13	0.30	0.29
LABORL	0.99	0.20	0.94	0.95
COLLAR	0.61	0.12	0.33	0.27
MPLOIL	0.62	0.25	0.44	0.45
WORKER	0.55	0.10	0.29	0.24
RANCHO	0.27	0.03	0.17	0.09
AGWORK	0.43	0.02	0.24	0.13
PEASAN	0.53	0.03	0.25	0.19
LANREF	0.74	0.07	0.26	0.26

individuals is indeed attested by the high rank correlation between both variables (tau = 0.50, $p < 0.00$). Although the group having a large proportion of politically active individuals is more likely to have a large proportion of persons with a positive ethos and who feel psychologically autonomous, those groups do not necessarily tend to have a larger proportion of individuals with a high experience of change.[8]

Participation in Voluntary Organizations

The political capacity of a country can be appraised in many ways. We have noted that one dimension of political participation can take many forms, from attending a political dinner to terrorism. Another dimension

[8] The tau coefficient between political participation and the variables mentioned in the test are A.MOOD = 0.67; ETHOS = 0.75, and CHANEX = 0.20. The first two are significant at the 0.00 level, and CHANEX has a probability of 0.17 that the association might be due to chance.

of such political capacity is participation in nonpolitical organizations. The introductory discussion in this chapter makes it clear that there is no common agreement on what functions these voluntary organizations perform for the polity. Classical theorists tended to consider the role of such organizations as leading to instability. The work of de Tocqueville and Weber, on the contrary, showed that they may effectively contribute to stability. Recent empirical findings point to the fact that either passive or active participation in nonpolitical organizations is, across national boundaries, associated with the kind of political culture that is congenial with a stable democratic process. Almond and Verba, generalizing for five nations, make this point clear:

> Membership in some association, even if the individual does not consider the membership politically relevant and even if it does not involve his active participation, does lead to a more competent citizenry. Pluralism, even if not explicitly political pluralism, may indeed be one of the most important foundations of political democracy.[9]

Hence, it seems that nonpolitical organizations increase the political capacity of a country at least in one important way, by increasing the political capacity of individuals. Let us see what the situation is in Venezuela.

In Chapter 7 we reported that when people were asked who should have the responsibility for solving certain problems that the respondents themselves had just mentioned, no more than 11 percent of most of the participant groups mentioned a voluntary association. The question was open-ended and therefore elicited spontaneous responses. About one out of every ten politically participant Venezuelans does not perceive such organizations as playing an important role in solving the problems that they consider to be most acute in either a national or an occupational locus.

This interpretation is confirmed further by the low levels of actual participation in such organizations. We asked the informants to tell us to which of a list of seven nonpolitical organizations they belonged.[10] In Table 8.1, we can see that an overwhelming proportion of university professors (80 percent) and of high government officials, about two out of every three oil industry executives, and one out of every two government technicians

---

[9] Almond and Verba, *The Civic Culture*, p. 322.

[10] The types of organizations listed were: social or sports club, the Rotary Club, the Lions Club, professional association, scientific association, charity organization, and cultural or artistic association.

and secondary school teachers reported belonging to at least one such organization. These high percentages, however, are mostly a reflection of their participation in professional associations. The rest of the groups show considerably lower levels of participation. The least participant of all are low-status individuals and members of the petite bourgeoisie who, in a proportion less than 12 percent, said that they belonged to some civic association or organization. Furthermore, not even when we specifically asked about membership in business organizations such as the Rotary Club and the Lions Club, which are widespread throughout the country, did a substantial proportion of industrial and commercial executives of large firms report being members of at least one voluntary association.

We also asked our informants if they had ever been officeholders in any of the listed voluntary organizations. The highest levels of active participation were found among oil industry executives and university professors, but each of these groups also rated high as active organizational participants in different fields. For example, one-third of the oil industry executives had been officeholders in social or sports clubs, and 39 percent of the university professors also had held office — but exclusively in professional organizations. Organizational activism in other groups varied but never reached those levels.

All these bits of evidence suggest that social participation, that is, participation in a nonpolitical organization, is restricted in Venezuela. Those who participate in civic organizations are likely to be upper class and tend to have experienced some amount of change. Organizational activism was also found to be closely related to normative orientation and psychological mood. Generally, the larger the proportion of organizationally active persons in a group, the greater the likelihood that the people in that group will have a positive ethos and tend to feel psychologically autonomous. Thus, social participation would indeed seem to be a process that enhances the political capacity of the society.[11]

Interpersonal Contacts

Among the many functions that social participation facilitates, one is of special interest here because of its relevance to political capacity. Voluntary organizational participation very often brings together, in close con-

[11] Tau coefficents between social participation and other characteristics are HIRSES = 0.77, CHANEX = 0.47, ETHOS = 0.74, and A.MOOD = 0.72. All of these coefficients are significant at the 0.00 level.

tact, people from different institutional spheres who have a common interest. This opportunity to engage in personal contact is important for the individual in many ways; the most important is that it increases the opportunity to influence and be influenced by others, depending on the subject and the characteristics of the persons. But personal influence, as it has been established by many studies, takes place in many situations outside of organizations.[12] In the household, work place, and the larger community, the role of personal influence for inducing change in attitude and behavior has been established clearly.

Personal communication is likely to have a greater impact than any other form of communication. Opinion leaders, as those persons have been called who are most influential on particular subjects, are likely to be of higher socioeconomic status, to be more innovative and cosmopolitan, and to have more personal contacts than any other persons. Personal contact, then, enhances the political capacity of a society because it facilitates what has been designated as the interaction effect, that is, the "process through which individuals in a social system who have adopted an innovation influence those who have not yet adopted it." [13] A society where key groups of the population have hardly any contact with other groups is less likely to adjust to change than one where there is a great deal of interpersonal contact.

In the questionnaire we included a question that gave us a measure of the number and frequency of personal contacts an individual had with the following types of persons: officials of the armed forces, big businessmen, peasants, workers, union leaders, student leaders, policemen, foreigners, and political leaders.[14] Responses were recoded, assigned values ranging from one (given to those who said "never") to seven (assigned to those who said "every day"). Those with an average of four or more would theoretically talk to each of the nine listed groups at least a few times a year. Most probably, of course, they talk more often to people socioeconomically similar to themselves or close to them. The percentage of individuals within each group averaging four or more can be seen in Table 8.1 (WORDOM).

[12] A good summary of the pertinent literature may be found in Everett Rogers, *Diffusion of Innovations* (New York: Free Press, 1962), chap. 8.

[13] Ibid., p. 215.

[14] The precise form of the question was, "How frequently do you have a chance to talk to each of the following types of people?" Responses were coded in the following categories: never, one or two times in my life, a few times in my life, a few times a year, a few times a month, a few times a week, and every day.

Again, cultural and political groups reported the highest rates of interpersonal contacts. The only economic group that is an outstanding exception (66 percent of the people having high interpersonal contacts) are the owners of cattle ranches. The lowest rates of interpersonal communication are found among the lower-status groups, whereas the petite bourgeoisie fluctuates between low and middle levels of incidence. But that socio-economic status is clearly related to the extent and degree of word-of-mouth communication is shown by the high tau coefficient between WORDOM and HIRSES (tau = 0.53, $p < 0.00$).

The literature suggests that the more cosmopolitan individuals are more often found to be the opinion leaders. From the data, we cannot tell if those persons high in word-of-mouth communication actually are opinion leaders. They certainly are not more likely to have had more experience of change than other Venezuelans (tau = 0.20, $p < 0.17$). Nevertheless, the larger the proportion of individuals in a group who said that they had some amount of personal communication with other groups, the more likely it is that we find a large proportion of positively oriented (ETHOS), autonomous (A.MOOD) individuals in that group.[15]

Cooperation

A high level of interpersonal contact does not mean necessarily that the political capacity of a social group is automatically enhanced. In fact, if such personal contacts are colored by distrust or are conflictual, the political capacity of the group may be hampered. This line of thought, as suggested in the introductory part of this chapter, is deeply rooted in the history of social thought.[16] From Plato and Aristotle to modern empirical research scientists, social theorists have emphasized the role of cooperation in achieving desired group goals. Even those theorists whose central theme is conflict or competition have acknowledged the role of cooperation within conflictive situations. The concept of class struggle could not exist if unity of action and purposes were not presupposed within the contending classes. The pursuit of self-interest would be impossible for the most rugged of the individualists without a cooperative infrastructure.

Durkheim made it clear that with what is now called development came a change in the kind of cooperation (from mechanical to organic solidarity),

---

[15] Tau coefficients among WORDOM, ETHOS, and A.MOOD respectively are 0.73 and 0.64, which are highly significant (0.00).

[16] Robert A. Nisbet, "Cooperation," in *International Encyclopedia of the Social Sciences,* vol. 3 (New York: Macmillan and Free Press, 1968), pp. 386–389.

not, as some unsophisticated Rousseaueans would like to believe, the substitution of cooperation for hostility. However, modern research has shown that even within the most organic settings, such as a large factory, spontaneous cooperation is so inexitricably intermeshed with the more formal organic rules of behavior that it notably affects productivity of labor.[17]

At a national level, it is now clear that social and political cooperation not only are present but are basic components of the political culture of the most competitive, capitalistic old democracies. Almond and Verba, after finding that general and social values and attitudes that foster cooperation with one's fellow citizens are more widespread in Britain and the United States than in Germany, Italy, and Mexico, offer an explanation that is important for its relevance here:

> Beyond that, these general social attitudes are more closely related to political attitudes in these two nations than in the other three nations. And this explanation adds weight to an interpretation we advanced earlier, of the meaning of the propensity to invoke one's primary group in time of political stress. This tendency to use primary associations in political influence attempts, we suggested, represented a close fusion of the basic primary group structures of society with the secondary structures of politics; a fusion that led to a more integrated political system.[18]

In Chapter 6 we dealt with those states of mind, such as feelings of trust and vindictiveness, which have been found to be closely associated with general attitudes of cooperation. Here we are more interested in the behavioral dimension of cooperation. Two questions in the survey were designed to identify the degree to which people perceived their environment as a cooperative one:

1. Do you find that people living around here help each other a lot, enough, little, or not at all?
2. Do you think that your fellow workers (or colleagues) help each other a lot, little, or not at all?

A measure of the extent to which people perceive their environment as cooperative is afforded by the percentage of people in each group who said that in both their neighborhood and among their fellow workers there was a lot or enough cooperation. Table 8.2 lists the percentage of individuals,

---

[17] The now-classic study in this area is Fritz J. Roethlisberger and William J. Dickson, *Management and the Worker: An Account of a Research Program,* conducted by the Western Electric Company, Hawthorne Works, Chicago (Cambridge, Mass.: Harvard University Press, 1949).

[18] Almond and Verba, *The Civic Culture,* p. 287.

TABLE 8.2   Cooperation in Venezuela (percentages)

Sample Groups	COONEI	COOWRK	COOP
DMAKER	0.32	0.93	0.31
UNPROF	0.37	0.65	0.25
OILEXE	0.61	0.87	0.56
INDEXE	0.47	0.77	0.38
COMEXE	0.40	0.76	0.35
CATLER	0.58	0.54	0.40
FARMER	0.45	0.49	0.33
GSTAFF	0.32	0.85	0.25
LICEOS	0.41	0.66	0.31
PRIEST	0.40	0.02*	0.01
STUDEN	0.36	0.52	0.20
COUNCL	0.51	0.61	0.35
SMALIN	0.41	0.25	0.14
SHOPOW	0.42	0.30	0.19
SCHOOL	0.51	0.77	0.43
CLERKS	0.33	0.74	0.27
LABORL	0.48	0.77	0.42
COLLAR	0.39	0.74	0.33
MPLOIL	0.58	0.77	0.50
WORKER	0.41	0.67	0.33
RANCHO	0.30	0.07	0.03
AGWORK	0.56	0.52	0.40
PEASAN	0.38	0.37	0.27
LANREF	0.50	0.52	0.45

* This question was not asked of priests.

by sample group, perceiving a cooperative environment in their neighborhood (COONEI), their work (COOWRK), and in both (COOP). The most evident finding is that, generally, cooperation at the community level lags behind the degree of cooperation among fellow workers, but that in both cases there are few groups who experience these types of cooperative relations. We found no relationship between perceiving cooperation in the community and perceiving it among fellow workers (tau = 0.10, $p < 0.49$).

High-status economic groups, and especially those working in oil firms, seem to experience more cooperative relations in both community and corporation than those who work in the political sphere. However, government officials of any level, municipal councilmen, and labor leaders do not report living, and above all working, in as uncooperative an environment as do the educators (except primary school teachers) and student leaders. Even the priests, to whom the question of cooperation at the place where they work was, for obvious reasons, not asked, mostly found themselves living in rather uncooperative communities.

Perception of cooperative relations in either community or work is not related to social status. Neither a high experience of change nor ETHOS and A.MOOD are related to cooperation, although there is a weak tendency on the part of the upper-status individuals to report experiencing cooperative relations among their fellow workers. The same is true for those who have experienced some change, have a positive normative orientation, and feel psychologically autonomous.[19] Thus, it seems that the level of cooperation in Venezuelan society is quite low, but the lowest levels are found in community life. However, this is but one dimension of political capacity. We shall now turn to the consideration of the interrelations among all dimensions of political capacity.

Interrelations among Dimensions of Political Capacity

We have presented in the preceding sections data that convey the idea that political participation, social participation, and interpersonal contacts follow a more or less similar pattern of distribution throughout the social structure. Cooperation, on the contrary, does not follow that pattern. This idea is supported by the tau coefficients in Table 8.3, where it is clear

TABLE 8.3   Intercorrelations among Dimensions of Political Capacity

Political Capacity Dimensions	COOP		POLCAP		WORDOM		SOCPAR	
	Tau	p	Tau	p	Tau	p	Tau	p
POLCAP	0.04	(0.31)						
WORDOM	−0.02	(0.88)	0.83	(0.00)				
SOCPAR	0.03	(0.85)	0.62	(0.00)	0.51	(0.00)		
POLPAR	0.15	(0.50)	0.83	(0.00)	0.70	(0.00)	0.53	(0.00)

that the larger the percentage of political participants in a group, the more likely it is that this group also will contain large percentages of individuals who are socialites as well as personal communicators. However, it is clear that they are no more likely than the less politically capable individuals to live in communities where the level of community cooperation is low,

---

[19] The highest tau coefficient among COOP and HIRSES, CHANEX, ETHOS, and A.MOOD was −0.07; the smallest coefficient among COOWRK and those variables was 0.22 ($p < 0.12$) and the highest was 0.30 (p < 0.05).

although at work, personal relations seem to be slightly easier for the participants.[20] Yet the likelihood that the participant will live and work where relationships among people are smooth is very small. Thus, in building a general index of political capacity we could not fuse cooperation with political participation, social participation, and personal contacts because empirically they seem to elicit entirely different dimensions of a conceptually similar area. The logic of analysis demands that we keep them separate. Hence, to build the index of political capacity (POLCAP), we COUNTED [21] the indexes that seemed to belong together. The percentage of people who were high on two or on all three indexes (political participation, social participation, and personal contacts) may be seen in Table 8.1. An examination of the percentage distribution of the politically capable individuals leads to the categorization shown in Table 8.4.

Table 8.4 suggests that working in the cultural or political spheres is a determinant of high political capacity, with the exception of low-level bureaucrats, low-level educators, and priests. In the economic sphere, only the executives of oil companies ranked high in political capacity. However, institutional locus is not the only correlate of political capacity. Socioeconomic status and experience of change are both highly and positively associated with political capacity. But it seems that the strongest association exists between political capacity, having a positive ethos for development, and feeling psychologically autonomous. It is clear, then, that activism is indeed a powerful force impelling one toward development, because it is more often found not only among those individuals whose political culture is believed to be more congenial with political and economic development but also among those whose personalities are more integrated in the sense that they show fewer paranoid reactions and signs of alienation. Yet such constructive political activism is carried out in a rather uncooperative environment, especially at the community level, and apparently it contributes little toward producing social relations of a more cooperative nature.

This gap between political capacity and cooperation and between cooperation and socioeconomic status, experience of change, positive ethos, and a feeling of psychological autonomy seems to be a crucial weakness in the political capacity of Venezuelan society, as will be shown later. We now turn to examine the influence of political capacity and cooperation on group

---

[20] Tau, on the one side, between perceived cooperation in community and among fellow workers and, on the other side, political capacity (POLCAP) are 0.04 ($p < 0.84$) and 0.31 ($p < 0.03$), respectively

[21] COUNT is an ADMINS command. See Appendix C, "A Note on the Analytic Tool,"

TABLE 8.4   Sample Groups by Political Capacity and Institutional Loci

Political Capacity Categories	Institutional Loci		
	Political	Cultural	Economic
High (POLCAP > 59%)	DMAKER GSTAFF COUNCL LABORL	UNPROF LICEOS STUDEN	OILEXE
Middle (59% > POLCAP > 44%)		PRIEST SCHOOL	INDEXE COMEXE CATLER FARMER MPLOIL
Low (POLCAP < 44%)	CLERKS		SMALIN SHOPOW COLLAR WORKER RANCHO AGWORK PEASAN LANREF

SOURCE: Table 8.1.

evaluations. The key questions here are: Do politically capable groups have a different world view than passive ones? Does living and working in a cooperative environment influence one's world view?

Evaluation of Systems and Roles

In the preceding chapter we showed that Venezuelans can be differentiated according to what system they perceive more frequently as being wrong. On the one hand, we noted that there were those who tended to focus on one set of five systems (EVSETB), namely, the family, education, polity, social behavior, and the Church. On the other, there were those individuals for whom economic or community problems were more salient (EVSETA). The social and psychological characteristics of both types of evaluators also tended to differ. Those for whom EVSETB problems were more salient tended to be of a higher socioeconomic status, to have experienced more change, to have a more positive ethos, and to feel psychologically more autonomous. We now wonder whether these different modes of evaluation are related to different levels of political capacity.

A look at Table 8.5 illuminates this matter. Those who are more active, in the sense that they participate more in politics and in voluntary organizations and are more often reported talking to many types of people, are more likely to perceive problems in the family, education, polity, social

TABLE 8.5 *Political Capacity and Evaluation of System and Roles*

System and Roles	Political Capacity			
	POLCAP		COOP	
	Tau	*p*	Tau	*p*
EVSETA	−0.30	(0.04)	0.20	(0.18)
EVSETB	0.77	(0.00)	−0.04	(0.76)
CULROL	0.85	(0.00)	0.02	(0.89)
POLROL	0.42	(0.03)	0.04	(0.77)
ARMROL	0.58	(0.04)	0.29	(0.05)
ECOROL	0.28	(0.05)	0.36	(0.02)

behavior, and religion (EVSETB) than in the community or the economy (EVSETA). Perception of a cooperative environment in both community and work, contrary to what might be expected, has a very weak relationship to saliency of community or economic problems and even less so with respect to other types of problems (EVSETB).

In Chapter 7 we also showed that no definite pattern emerged with respect to what people thought specific roles were contributing to the country. Such evaluations were mostly positive and could be explained only in terms of other evaluations. Apparently no characteristic was systematically and strongly associated with the particular way in which individuals in different occupations sampled by us perceived cultural, political, armed, and economic roles. For this reason, the data in Table 8.5 exemplify the key functions that activism performs in the shaping of people's evaluations. We can see that activism (POLCAP) is closely related to the evaluation of roles. In general, it may be said that the higher the frequency of activists in a group (POLCAP), the more likely it is that a large proportion of individuals in that group will tend to evaluate all types of roles positively. Moreover, those groups which tend to perceive more cooperation among neighbors and fellow workers also tend more often to evaluate the armed and economic roles positively. However, no relationship was found with respect to the evaluation of cultural or political roles.

The Political System

Later in this chapter we shall attempt to show the connection between differences in the evaluation of systems and roles and intergroup antagonism. But here we shall continue exploring the relationship between the distribution of political capacity among sample groups and their evaluations. Data in Table 8.6 throw further light on the role that political

TABLE 8.6   Political Capacity and Evaluation of the Political System

| Evaluation of the Political System | Political Capacity | | | |
| | POLCAP | | COOP | |
	Tau	*p*	Tau	*p*
BADPAI	0.42	(0.00)	0.02	(0.89)
IRRITG	0.62	(0.00)	—0.15	(0.29)
CIVICS	0.49	(0.00)	—0.04	(0.77)
WPARTY	0.51	(0.00)	—0.11	(0.45)
COMBAD	0.60	(0.00)	0.03	(0.85)
BADCAP	0.64	(0.00)	—0.14	(0.32)
CAPGD	0.57	(0.00)	0.08	(0.59)

capacity plays in shaping evaluations of the political system. The general finding is that those who are more active, but not necessarily those who perceive more cooperation among neighbors or fellow workers, tend more often to say that in Venezuela there is no political unity and that the system the constitution created is a bad one (BADPAI). Moreover, these individuals tend to report being often irritated with the government during the year previous to the interview and to say that there are foreign influences that determine what is happening in the country, be these prejudicial foreign influences, communism, or capitalism. This apparently contradictory fact is reconciled by what the coefficient of correlation reveals is a greater capacity of these groups to perceive foreign influences in general, whether prejudicial or beneficial. This is a concrete example of the cultural heterogeneity of politically active Venezuelans.

If we were to judge the preceding findings in the light of the republican history of Venezuela, we would have to conclude that these politically active, critical, irritated Venezuelans would favor military intervention. Perhaps many of the government officials, educators, student leaders, oil and manufacturing executives, bewildered by protests, government inefficiency and repression, oil pipe and factory burnings that make them critical of the political system — in dreams or in conspiratorial groups — secretly cherish the idea of military intervention in politics. Yet the data reveal that the larger the percentage of politically active individuals in such groups, the more likely were they to say, when asked, that they preferred the military to stay out of politics.

Perhaps more surprising for some, in view of the increasing political stasis of the country, will be the finding that the politically active Venezuelan, more than any other person, wishes that the political parties would respond to general rather than group interests. Yet it seems to us that it is precisely the awareness of such a lack of national unity that makes him foresee the need for the parties to fulfill a wider role, aggregating interests of wider sectors of the population rather than those of particular groups. Perhaps this attitude is fostered by the realization that cooperation among neighbors or fellow workers is not as widespread as it should be. However, we found no relationship between propensity to view politics in a critical way and the tendency to perceive cooperative relations (see Table 8.6).

Measures

The politically active individual presumably, then, is more likely to strive for the solution of family, political, educational, or social behavior problems or religious maladies because it is this set of systemic problems that he tends to perceive as most salient. Nevertheless, he believes that, in general, the problem is more a systemic one than a matter of bad performance of certain roles. In fact, he is more prone to judge as positive *all* types of roles, be they cultural, political, military, or (less so) economic. That the problems politically active individuals perceive are more encompassing than role performance is further illustrated by our questioning about the political system. We shall now explore whether these differences in world view between the active and the inactive groups are carried over to the solutions they propose.

Table 8.7 provides the opportunity to clarify this matter. There we clearly see that the larger the percentage of politically active individuals (POLCAP) in any given group, the more likely it is that we shall find a large

TABLE 8.7   Measures and Political Capacity

	Political Capacity			
	POLCAP		COOP	
Measures	Tau	*p*	Tau	*p*
DOPOLI	0.46	(0.00)	0.05	(0.73)
DOSOC	0.63	(0.00)	0.03	(0.85)
DOECON	−0.10	(0.50)	0.03	(0.87)
LONRUN	0.39	(0.01)	0.05	(0.73)
GOVERN	0.17	(0.26)	0.01	(0.93)
ALL	0.46	(0.00)	−0.18	(0.21)

proportion of persons recommending political (DOPOLI) or social (DOSOC) measures to solve the problems they perceive. More likely these measures will be of a type that produces gratification only in the long run (LONRUN). Economic measures, however, will either be neglected or at least will not be preferred more frequently by an active than by an inactive group. Again, those who perceive a cooperative community or work environment do not favor any particular type of measure.

Responsibility for Implementing Measures

Finally we shall try to answer the question of whom the politically active individual perceives as being responsible for solving the problems he identifies. As all the data have indicated, Venezuelans of all social positions and of all characteristics massively singled out the government. Some of them — probably the upper-status individuals who have had some experience of change, whose normative orientations are more congenial to development, and who feel psychologically autonomous — will in irritation point an accusing finger and say that the government did or did not adopt a certain policy to cope with (probably) a social or political problem. Others, like the campesinos or *rancho* inhabitants, will invoke the word government because they feel it is a new sort of pater familias to whom one turns in search of help for alleviating the pressing economic needs or community problems that torment their family, occupational, community, or national life. They rarely feel irritated by such a remote but powerful figure. Thus, any citizen, politically capable or not, feeling that he lives in a cooperative environment or not, is equally likely to point to the government as principally responsible for applying the measures he believes should be implemented.

The politically active individual is more likely than the more passive citizen to desire a wider involvement of the larger community in the solution of the occupational or national problem he confronts. This finding, on the one hand, suggests that the active individuals wish to overcome the very problems of disunity that they perceive. On the other hand, it suggests that they are not able to see any specific institution able to solve such deep-rooted problems. However, this community-oriented individual is not more likely than any other person to perceive interpersonal relations in the community where he lives, or in the place where he works, as cooperative.

Antagonisms

Recapitulating the data, we would like to call attention to a factor that may have been overlooked because the discussion has been focused on a search for patterns across the social structure. The most politically active groups very rarely achieved consensus on their evaluation of systems, roles, and measures. They certainly were more likely to favor one or another alternative than the less politically active groups, but it was only on a few occasions that they exceeded the 66 percent mark, which may be thought of as a rough measure of intragroup consensus. All groups showed consensus with respect to a few features, for example, the implementation agencies they favored (government or all); their evaluation of certain roles that were almost idyllically perceived, such as priests, teachers, and peasants; the importance that was attached by these politically active groups (except educators) to the creation of new industries; and the very low priority that all groups gave to the consolidation of the electoral system. But more often the opinion within the active group was split in a way that approached the maximum dissensus (50–50). To test whether these differences of opinion are really associated with political capacity, psychological states, normative orientations, experience of change, and social location characteristics would mean shifting radically the line of analysis we have been following so far. We shall here, by way of summary, explore the intergroup antagonisms based on differences of opinion about system and role performance.

A definition of intergroup antagonisms was developed for the VEN-UTOPIA model presented in *SRSP*.[22] This way of establishing antago-

[22] *SRSP*, pp. 350–351.

nisms among groups followed closely the measure developed earlier by Domingo and Varsavsky.[23] The computational formula is as follows:

$$\text{ANTAG}\,(\text{N,NN,I}) = (\text{SES}(\text{N}) + \text{SES}(\text{NN})^*\text{CORREL}(\text{N,NN,I})^*\text{CANT}$$

This formula tells us that the level of antagonisms between two groups (N and NN), with respect to an array of evaluations (I), is given by the difference of their evaluations (CORREL(N,NN,I)) weighted by their socio-economic status. In the formula CANT is a constant for antagonisms which was used to scale the output figures but to which some sociological meaning can be attached. For instance, when certain general conditions appear or disappear (revolutionary crisis or bonanza) the overall antagonisms may also be exogenously and generally increased or decreased. How the program operates was described in *SRSP*; thus we do not need to repeat it here, except for what is essential to clarify the discussion.

The indexes of evaluation of systems and roles for the use of VEN-UTOPIA were computed by following a technique different from the one described in Chapter 7. To build these indexes we used the same questions on which the discussion in that chapter was based. Two differences, how-ever, are worth mentioning. First, in the case of VENUTOPIA, system evaluations were computed by taking into consideration negative as well as positive evaluations of the system, whereas in this book, because we implicitly dichotomized every variable, we chose to emphasize only prob-lems.

Second, the technique used in VENUTOPIA allowed us to compute an ordinal value for each individual. This value ranged from -10 (the nega-tive extreme) to $+10$ (the positive extreme).[24] Based on the mean evalu-ation that each one of the 28 groups (for this computation executives and workers in large industrial firms were separated according to regional cri-teria: center, west, and east) made of seven systems and thirteen roles, the antagonism between every pair of groups was then computed. This pro-cedure yielded two matrices of figures which resembled correlation matrices, the only difference being that the greater the coefficient, the more acute the antagonism between groups in every pair.[25] These matrices were used as input to the clustering program described in Chapter 1. Figure 8.1 gives the results of the partitions based on the matrix of system antagonisms.

[23] Carlos Domingo and Oscar Varsavsky, "Un modelo matemático de la utopía de Moro," *Desarrollo económico*, vol. 7, no. 26 (July–September 1967), pp. 3–35.
[24] A description of the technique followed to compute these indexes may be found in *SRSP*, pp. 338–342.
[25] Ibid., pp. 358–359.

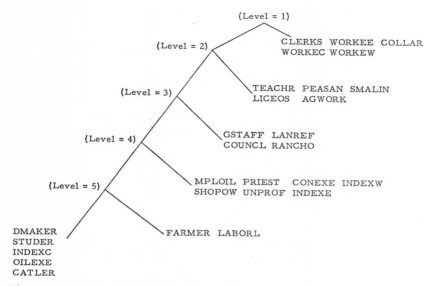

Figure 8.1   Clusters Based on System Antagonisms

Because of the way the program works (see Chapter 1), it may be said that those clusters defined earlier (lower-level figures) include groups among which antagonisms are less pronounced. Those pairs of groups whose levels of antagonisms were high will remain in the same cluster until the lowest specified level is reached. As is seen in Figure 8.1, no low-status group passed the third level of partition, and all high-status groups remained until the highest levels of clustering were completed.

Figure 8.2 shows the partitions based on role antagonisms. Except for the owners of agricultural enterprises, here also high-status groups reached the highest levels of clustering, indicating that antagonism among those groups is higher. However, the specific clusters defined for roles differ from those defined for systems. The only pairs of groups that figure in the same cluster both for systems and roles are high government officials and student leaders (DMAKER-STUDER) and university professors and priests (UNPROF-PRIEST).

Perhaps the best way to convey the significance of these clusters is to postulate that, if conflict were to start in Venezuela tomorrow, those groups at the bottom of the tree would be more likely to take an active role. Which particular groups would participate depends on the specific issue at stake because, as we have seen, for any group some issues are more salient than others. Nevertheless, it is important to note that analysis of

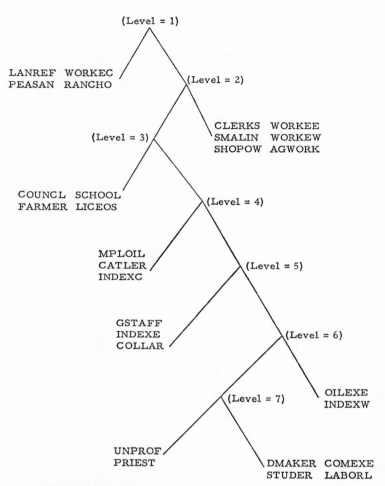

Figure 8.2   Clusters Based on Role Antagonisms

the evaluations has revealed that the groups that in this chapter are identified as potentially more antagonistic are also the groups likely to perceive
the same type of problems and to be the most politically active, which
indeed maximizes the possibility of a generalized conflict.

Although we have already shown some patterns of evaluations of groups
according to their characteristics, we have indicated only the relationship
between antagonisms and political activism. A test of the interconnection
between those two variables can be performed if we rank the sample groups
by their potentiality for antagonism. An index of such potentiality can be

constructed if we consider the cluster level as a way of ranking the groups according to their antagonism. The higher the level of the cluster, the higher the potential antagonism of the group. In Table 8.8 this operation may be appreciated.

TABLE 8.8   Level at Which a Cluster of Antagonistic Groups Was Defined (Systems and Roles)

Sample Groups	Systems	Level for Roles	Sum of Levels
DMAKER	4	7	11
UNPROF	4	7	11
OILEXE	5	6	11
COMEXE	4	7	11
INDEXE	4	5	9
INDEXW	4	6	10
INDEXC	5	4	9
FARMER	5	3	8
CATLER	5	4	9
GSTAFF	3	5	8
LICEOS	2	3	5
PRIEST	4	7	11
TEACHR	2	3	5
STUDEN	5	7	12
COUNCL	3	3	6
SMALIN	2	2	4
SHOPOW	4	2	6
MPLOIL	4	4	8
COLLAR	1	5	6
CLERKS	1	2	3
LABORL	5	7	12
RANCHO	3	1	4
WORKEC	1	1	2
WORKEE	1	2	3
WORKEW	1	2	3
AGWORK	2	2	4
PEASAN	2	1	3
LANREF	3	1	4

The high rank correlation coefficient between potential antagonism of a group and its level of activism ($Rs = 0.70$, $p < 0.00$) indicates that a high conflict potential is ever present in Venezuelan society. In other words, we can postulate that if one of these potentially antagonistic groups perceives an issue as conflictual, there is a fair possibility that other potentially antagonistic groups will perceive the same issue in the same way. Yet, as we have noted also, none of the potentially antagonistic groups is likely to have internal consensus on such an issue. Thus, if the potentiality of conflict is enhanced by the commonality of salience, the capacity of a group for handling such conflicts is diminished by intragroup dissensus. This complex interrelationship among characteristics, evaluations, and heterogeneity of the politically active groups is at the root of the political conflicts of the Venezuelan society. However, a recapitulation of the findings, to be undertaken in the next chapter, will demonstrate the futility of searching for some overarching explanatory factor.

9   SYNTHESIS

The central aim of the research program that CENDES started in 1963 was to devise a package of alternative strategies for economic development, assess the political feasibility of such strategies, and evaluate their probable impact on the distribution of the population with special reference to the problems of urbanization. The present volume is one more contribution to the realization of that program. Frank Bonilla, in *The Failure of Elites,* has carried the task of assessing the political capacity of Venezuelan society a long step forward. Whereas he was concerned with those men at the very top of the social structure, whose decisions affect the national society, the present study was conceived from the beginning as an assessment of the political capacity of the rest of the Venezuelans. It is still too early to judge whether the original aims have been achieved, for still pending is the work of bringing together the findings of these studies with the results of the economic simulations and of the urbanization study.

Such a perspective nevertheless demands a broad assessment of the scores of findings reported in this book. Venezuelan society emerges here as a complex social system in which permanent forces of change are at work, affecting groups of the population in so many different ways that the task of summarizing the findings coherently would be more appropriate for a team of social scientists. Nevertheless, in order to appraise the picture of Venezuelan society that these findings reflect, we decided to present two syntheses — each based on the same body of data, but using a different tool. The appraisal that follows immediately is a summary resting on the analytic power of ADMINS. The other synthesis seeks to overcome the main limitation of the first one — which stems more from the nature of the data (cross-sectional) than from the limitations of the tool itself — in order to treat the data in a dynamic way. It is our hope that both syntheses will complete the diagnosis of the Venezuelan political system.

First Synthesis: The Structure

In Chapter 4 we showed that, although Venezuelan society has changed tremendously in the past forty years, if the social structure remains unaltered, its present drift in the direction of more rather than less social and economic inequality will be intensified. The findings described in Chapter 6, however, indicated that the majority of Venezuelans nevertheless feel optimistic with respect to their future and have a fair level of satisfaction of their wants. It was established also that feelings of autonomy are positively related to higher social location and greater experience of change.

Consequently, many members of the middle- and upper-status groups have already acquired a set of orientations that, in the light of the criteria set forth in Chapter 1, are considered to be congenial with development (Chapter 5).

The degree of cultural heterogeneity both within groups and within classes, however, acts as a countervailing pressure against development. The highest degree of cultural heterogeneity was found among the middle-status groups, whereas the lowest degree was found in the lower-status groups.

Examination of the evaluations of the sample groups led to the establishment of two definite patterns: The first, to which the most privileged groups adhered, tended to perceive problems primarily in the family, education, polity, church, and social behavior, and to be utterly critical of the political system while at the same time wishing that political party interests were defined more in terms of broad aggregates than in terms of particular group interests. This type of evaluator was more prone to reject the role of the military in politics and to recommend social or political measures.

The priorities of this set of groups, however, were found to be heterogeneous with respect to broad goals such as maintaining the democratic system, redistributing wealth, or accelerating growth, although they showed a fair amount of agreement in setting as first priorities the creation of new industries and the improvement of the quality of education, and in relegating to the last position the consolidation of the electoral system. In general, these evaluators favor policies that supposedly would benefit all the population — in the long run. Finally, and significantly, these individuals, in spite of their high level of political capacity, assign the principal responsibility for carrying out the proposed policies to the government or to the nation as a whole. In other words, they accept no personal or intermediate responsibility for policy making or implementation. A convenient summary of where each group stands with respect to these tendencies is presented in Table 9.1, where groups who strongly share this pattern are indicated by a plus (+) sign.

The second pattern of evaluation, indicated by minus (−) signs in Table 9.1, was found more frequently among lower-status individuals of limited experience of change (SOCLOC), whose normative orientation was found to be less congenial with development, and who felt psychologically less autonomous (MEDISP). This type will perceive problems in the community and the economic areas (EVSETA) more often than in any other social system (EVSETB). Consequently, the measures more often recommended to solve such problems are of an economic nature (DOECON). Consistent with this finding, if asked to rank a set of policy alternatives, they tend to prefer those policies, such as housing for the poor or immediate improvement of the standard of living, which suggest an inclination to choose any alternative that will satisfy *their* present needs rather than those of the future population (LONRUN). But, inconsistent with this short-run view of what should be done, they are critical neither of the political system nor of the government. On the contrary, they seem to regard both country and government as satisfactory. Nevertheless, their attitude toward military intervention in politics is permissive. A significant proportion of them would accept such intervention even if there were no apparent justification for it.

Venezuelans characterized by this second pattern of evaluation do not feel that political parties should respond to the interests of the broader community; many of them will say that parties should respond to particular interests (CRIPOL). Consonant with this view is their disinclination to mention large aggregates such as "all the people" or "all the families" as responsible for implementing the measures they recommend to solve the problems they perceive (ALL). However, this does not mean that they perceive substitute agencies, because the majority of them (as was the case with the type of evaluators discussed previously) mention the government as the principal agent of responsibility (GOVERN). Finally, although this second type of evaluator has a much lower level of political capacity (POLCAP), he is just as likely as the other to live in a neighborhood or to work in a place where there are few cooperative relations.

In between these two types of evaluators, there are some individuals who

TABLE 9.1 Characteristics and Evaluations of Venezuelan Groups

Groups	SOCLOC	MEDISP	EVSETB	ROLES	CRIPOL	MEASUR	ALL	POLCAP	GOVERN	EVSETA	DOECON
DMAKER	+	+	+	+	+	+	+	+	+	o	−
UNPROF	+	+	+	−	+	+	+	+	o	o	o
OILEXE	+	+	+	o	+	+	o	+	−	−	−
INDEXE	+	o	o	o	o	+	o	o	o	o	o
COMEXE	+	+	+	−	o	+	o	o	o	o	o
CATLER	−	o	o	o	−	+	o	o	+	o	o
FARMER	−	o	o	o	o	o	o	o	+	o	+
GSTAFF	+	+	+	o	+	+	+	+	o	−	−
LICEOS	+	+	+	o	+	+	+	+	+	o	o
PRIEST	+	+	+	+	+	+	+	o	o	−	−
STUDEN	−	+	+	−	o	o	o	+	−	o	o
COUNCL	o	+	o	+	−	o	o	+	+	o	+
SMALIN	o	−	o	o	−	o	+	−	+	o	+
SHOPOW	o	−	o	o	−	−	o	−	o	o	+
SCHOOL	o	o	o	o	o	−	o	o	+	o	+
CLERKS	−	−	o	o	o	o	o	−	o	o	o
LABORL	o	+	o	+	+	+	+	+	−	o	o
COLLAR	−	−	o	−	o	o	−	−	o	o	o
MPLOIL	−	−	o	+	−	o	−	o	o	o	−
WORKER	−	−	−	o	−	−	o	−	o	o	o
RANCHO	−	−	−	o	−	−	−	−	o	+	−
AGWORK	−	−	−	+	−	−	−	−	−	o	o
PEASAN	−	−	−	o	−	−	−	−	−	+	o
LANREF	−	−	−	o	−	−	−	−	o	+	o
Mean	0.39	0.40	0.48	0.29	0.29	0.33	0.23	0.51	0.69	0.27	0.41

share characteristics of both types. These "mixed" evaluators are more likely to be found among industrial executives, upper-status rural groups, the petite bourgeoisie, municipal councilmen, primary school teachers, and lower-level employees in government, commerce, or the oil industries (see Table 9.1).

The tau coefficients presented in Table 9.2 reveal that there is a great deal of constraint within these two major patterns and that, considered across the social structure, they tend to be mutually exclusive. The only variables that do not lend themselves to pattern definition are the evaluations of roles (ROLES), the perception of government (GOVERN) as the implementation agency *par excellence*, and, as noted before, reports of having experienced cooperative relations both among neighbors and among fellow workers. Apparently, a positive evaluation of certain roles and holding the government responsible for the solution of all problems are attitudes as prevalent as the perception of cooperative relations is scarce. Hence, we are left with only one alternative interpretation of these pervasive phenomena: These characteristics, together with the widespread optimism reported earlier, are generalized cultural traits of Venezuelans.

Another and perhaps simpler way of conveying the results of the present study is shown in Figure 9.1, which closely follows the analytic scheme presented in Chapter 1 (Figure 1.2). To what has just been said, this representation adds a new and important element: the interconnection between groups' characteristics, patterns of evaluation, and the transformation of the world they live in. However, the dotted line in Figure 9.1 indicates that no empirical evidence could be established with respect to these points. Indeed, social science has yet to invent a way other than speculation of interrelating survey results with secondhand data about institutional processes. It seems fair, then, to suggest that the increasing inequality that was noted in the analysis of social location and the experience of change of Venezuelan groups (Chapter 2) is a consequence of the higher political capacity of the upper-status groups who, as indicated, give different answers to the questions "What is wrong?" "What is to be done?" and "Who should do it?" than do the lower-status groups.

In other words, the world the upper-status groups strive to achieve is different from that which the lower classes desire. But because both urban and rural low-status groups have a low political capacity, their only alternatives are to wait for a military figure to give them immediate gratification by making consumer goods or housing available or to wait for the government to do it.

TABLE 9.2 Intercorrelations among Characteristics and Evaluations

	POLCAP		GOVERN		ALL		DOECON		MEASUR		CRIPOL		ROLES		EVSETB		EVSETA		MEDISP	
	Tau	p	Tau	p	Tau	p	Tau	p	Tau	p	Tau	p	Tau	p	Tau	p	Tau	p	Tau	p
GOVERN	0.17	(0.26)																		
ALL	0.46	(0.00)	0.14	(0.35)																
DOECON	0.10	(0.50)	0.31	(0.04)	0.10	(0.50)														
MEASUR	0.59	(0.00)	0.07	(0.62)	0.53	(0.00)	0.32	(0.03)												
CRIPOL	0.69	(0.00)	0.00	(0.99)	0.59	(0.00)	0.29	(0.04)	0.67	(0.00)										
ROLES	0.03	(0.85)	0.12	(0.40)	0.03	(0.85)	0.02	(0.91)	0.09	(0.51)	0.18	(0.21)								
EVSETB	0.60	(0.00)	0.18	(0.21)	0.54	(0.00)	0.37	(0.01)	0.74	(0.00)	0.81	(0.00)	0.14	(0.34)						
EVSETA	0.22	(0.14)	0.11	(0.46)	0.46	(0.00)	0.28	(0.06)	0.46	(0.00)	0.47	(0.00)	0.19	(0.20)	0.51	(0.00)				
MEDISP	0.80	(0.00)	0.11	(0.46)	0.57	(0.00)	0.20	(0.17)	0.67	(0.00)	0.82	(0.00)	0.06	(0.69)	0.76	(0.00)	0.45	(0.00)		
SOCLOC	0.40	(0.01)	0.13	(0.36)	0.59	(0.00)	0.12	(0.42)	0.66	(0.00)	0.51	(0.00)	0.11	(0.44)	0.57	(0.00)	0.44	(0.00)	0.52	(0.00)

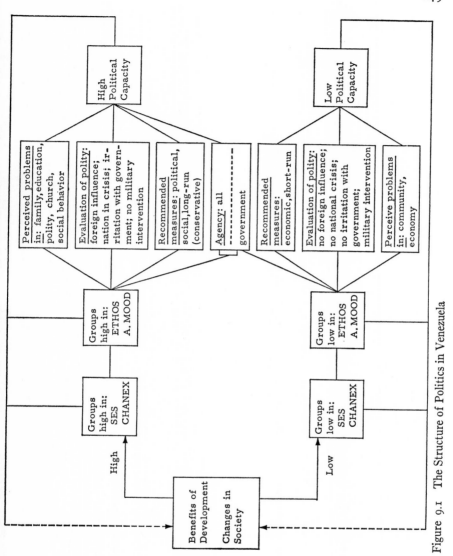

Figure 9.1   The Structure of Politics in Venezuela

It is true that labor organizations of workers and campesinos both are very strong in Venezuela. They perform a double brokerage function by actively transmitting the needs of the passive citizens to the higher echelons of authority, either government or enterprise, and by linking the latter to the party structure. However, one wonders about the efficiency if not the will with which labor leaders perform this brokerage function, because we know, as Table 9.1 clearly shows, that their mode of evaluation is actually closer to that of the upper-status groups, some of which are their masters, than to the mode of evaluation of their followers.

Thus, the passive citizen, who numerically constitutes the majority of the population of the country, is left with the meager hope that what those in the active roles do will trickle down to him. In the light of this evidence it seems reasonable to say that the Venezuelan social structure has a built-in conservative element that has led to a widening gap between the poor and the rich in spite of, or perhaps because of, the intense and widespread experience of change that most Venezuelans have had in the recent past.

It could be argued, of course, that the end product will be a more acceptable society because the more privileged groups, who are the ones riding the crest of change, have a normative orientation more congenial to development and feel psychologically autonomous. Moreover, as we have seen, not only is their appraisal of the situation a more sophisticated one but their priorities are of the sort that, economists tell us, are likely to stimulate growth. Apart from the time element involved, however (benefits will be long-run), two other facts cast some doubt on the probability that following this road to development will either produce the idea of democracy postulated in the Aristotelian model or bring about the economic advances demanded by other sectors of the society.

The first fact has already been mentioned: the condition of cultural heterogeneity noted in Chapter 5, and confirmed here for the mediating dispositions (normative orientations and psychological states). The only groups that have an overwhelming proportion of modern citizens are high government officials, university professors, student leaders, and labor leaders. In any of these groups are found 70 percent or more with a positive normative orientation and an autonomous state of mind. Oil, industrial, and commercial executives fluctuate between 40 and 60 percent in this measure. In this respect they resemble middle-status cultural and political groups except primary school teachers, 37 percent of whom possess such characteristics. In the remaining groups there are no more than one-third who share with the more active groups a positive ethos and an autonomous state of mind. Thus, the necessary predispositions that are likely to impel individuals to give significant support to the process of development have made but minor inroads in most of the middle-status groups and are practically absent from the majority of the population (lower-status urban and rural groups). Even among business executives (oil, industry, or commerce and agricultural entrepreneurs), men who are supposed to play a key role in the process of economic development, no more than 60 percent can be classified with high government officials or university professors.

Hence, any strategy for economic development is likely to be met with hesitancy, apprehension, and internal dissensus by the middle classes and by businessmen. It might, of course, be expected that high government officials, university professors, and student and labor leaders would support such developmental policies solidly, as a bloc, yet experience tells us that the situation is quite the opposite. It is within and among these groups where, for different reasons, the most active struggle has taken place in the last ten years. Why has this happened?

In *SRSP* we showed that high-level government officials wished to leave the bureaucracy because of the many psychological conflicts they were confronting.[1] One of these conflicts was ideological. The data in Table 9.3

TABLE 9.3 Ideology, Characteristics, and Evaluations

	Right		Left	
	Tau	p	Tau	p
SOCLOC	0.68	(0.00)	−0.66	(0.00)
MEDISP	0.42	(0.00)	−0.39	(0.01)
EVSETA	−0.51	(0.00)	0.51	(0.00)
EVSETB	0.53	(0.00)	−0.57	(0.00)
ROLES	−0.12	(0.42)	0.12	(0.43)
CRIPOL	0.41	(0.00)	−0.44	(0.00)
MEASUR	0.60	(0.00)	−0.57	(0.00)
POLCAP	0.29	(0.05)	−0.25	(0.09)

suggest that the sources of internal conflict among the more modern groups may well be of an ideological nature. In Chapter 5, we showed that university students, labor leaders, and university professors had the greatest

[1] *SRSP*, chap. 4.

proportion of leftists.[2] Data given in Table 9.3 indicate that leftists and rightists tend to have opposite patterns of evaluation. Therefore, because almost all members of these groups (90 percent or more) are active, it seems safe to infer that ideological heterogeneity (of conflictual ideologies) is the key factor behind conflicts involving these groups.

We may conclude, then, that any actions these groups may initiate — that is, actions radical enough to overcome the conservative element built into the social structure — are likely to be hindered by the opposition of high-status economic groups, who are rightists; by the indifference of the masses, who are passive; and, finally, by the ideologically based conflicts that are likely to emerge within and among these groups.

Admittedly, the synthesis presented up to now may have overlooked some of the logical conclusions that can be derived from all the propositions established in the previous chapters. Others may consider that the author has interjected some unjustified value judgments. The VENUTOPIA experiments to be described in the following section offer an alternative synthesis that can be objected to on many grounds, but *not* on these two.

Second Synthesis: The Dynamics

The experiments to be described here consist of exogenously changing certain values of the variables in the model so that these changes are the expression of a given policy. We then let the model run for a specified number of cycles and obtain a set of conclusions.[3] But before describing the experiments performed, we need to bring to the surface some of the assumptions behind the recurrent statements concerning the relationship between policy implementation and conflicts which were made in the preceding section.

A basic postulate of the general theory of planning is that the efficiency of any policy depends on both its realism and its feasibility. But contrary to what some planners would like to believe, realism and feasibility usually have a strong political dimension. An example might clarify the issue.

In mid-1967, the Venezuelan government quite unexpectedly submitted

[2] For a precise definition of "leftist" as used here, see the section on ideological orientations, Chapter 5.

[3] The model to be used here is a more refined version of VENUTOPIA I, which was described in *SRSP*. However, changes introduced involved recomputation of the parameters of some empirical laws, improving the output display, and the like, which in no way altered the structure of VENUTOPIA I. Therefore, we shall not describe the model again, but urge the reader to read Chapter 12 of *SRSP*.

two bills to Congress. One was aimed at increasing badly needed government revenues through an income tax reform. The other was a proposal for reforming the educational law. Both of these policy proposals immediately encountered wide opposition, not in Congress, where the government had the majority and was sure to win, but outside it and from different sectors. The government officials soon found that although they could have passed the bills in Congress, they could not carry their intentions any further because they found less support than expected in the population at large, and the political parties in the government coalition (AD and URD) could not mobilize the population in favor of their proposal. In short, government planners miscalculated the political resources (in this instance, support) available, and the political capacity on which they were counting to mobilize the needed support was lacking. Therefore, the proposals were neither realistic nor politically feasible. In general, then, if political realism and feasibility are, to a great extent, lacking, most probably the proposed policies are likely to be of low efficiency or never will be implemented.

One of the most crucial and difficult problems of social planning is to determine the political consequence of a policy package, whether it is economic, social, or political. Because politics is, among other things, the art of conflict resolution, it seems appropriate to evaluate the political realism and feasibility of a given program through its impact on social and political conflicts. The assumption here is that if conflict, anticipated or actual, surpasses certain limits, both the political realism and feasibility of a policy fade away. However, we do not regard conflict by itself as necessarily either prejudicial or beneficial. Nor do we wish to imply that all conflicts hinder the policy-making and policy-implementing processes. On the contrary, as some of the evidence for Latin America indicates, without conflict some policies would never have been carried out.[4] All we are suggesting is that when conflict reaches certain levels — levels that may vary for different areas — it usually hinders the applicability of a given policy.

The technique of numerical experimentation, as Varsavsky explained, allows the building of models in which such presuppositions can be made explicit.[5] In fact, the VENUTOPIA model follows closely the model of

[4] Albert O. Hirschman, *Journeys toward Progress.*

[5] Oscar Varsavsky, "La experimentación numérica," *Ciencia e investigación,* vol. 19, no. 10 (October 1963), pp. 340–347, and "Los modelos matemáticos numéricos como herramientas de decisión en problemas difícilmente cuantificables" (Introduction to an economic model elaborated by Arturo O'Connell and Oscar Varsavsky with the collaboration of N. Lugo, M. Malajovich, H. Paulero, J. Sabato, and V. Yohai), Instituto de Cálculo, Grupo de Economía de la Facultad de Ciencias Exactas y Naturales de la Universidad de Buenos Aires, *Boletín Interno,* no. 1 (August 1965).

UTOPIA,[6] which, although its principal emphasis was in the methodological aspects, was especially designed to take into account some of the considerations mentioned here.

The structure of the VENUTOPIA model may be summarized briefly as follows. It has 28 actors, the sample groups used throughout this study. Each one of these groups is described by its characteristics: social location, experience of change, normative orientation, psychological state, and political capacity. Each group evaluates seven social systems and thirteen roles. A description of the variables used may be found in Appendix A of this volume. For each one of these characteristics and evaluations, one empirical law exists which determines the amount of change that is to be expected in the dependent variable for each unit of change in the independent variables. Empirical laws have been computed for each variable and for six class aggregates (see Chapter 1). Thus, for example, the law that computes the variations in the level of education of the campesinos is different from the comparable law for the low-status urban groups.

Besides these empirical equations, the model has other laws that we have termed arbitrary laws. These are logical propositions that specify changes to be made in more global kinds of variables, such as heterogeneity, which apply to a whole group. These empirical laws also specify the behavior of the different groups when certain conditions are met. For instance, as Almond and Verba have suggested, social conflicts rarely involve all or many groups simultaneously.[7] By the same token, conflicts are seldom established around many systems. More often they involve a few groups disputing a single issue. In fact, when many groups are involved simultaneously in conflict over many issues, we can say that a revolutionary crisis exists.

In VENUTOPIA the law that determines the variation of conflicts over systems and roles is as follows:

Variation of conflict areas. The weight $[P(I)]$ of a conflict area will increase for a certain part (I) (role or system) if the more antagonistic groups evaluate it with a given magnitude of difference. A conflict area is defined or accentuated only if the degree of conflict is *high*.[8]

There are other laws of this type which compute the general level of

[6] Carlos Domingo and Oscar Varsavsky, "Un modelo matemático de la utopia de Moro."

[7] Gabriel A. Almond and Sidney Verba, *The Civic Culture*, pp. 479–487.

[8] *SRSP*, p. 347.

conflict, intragroup heterogeneity, polarization, and government action. However, to describe them all here would be to repeat what has been said elsewhere.[9]

The first experiment was, to put it in the planners' terminology, a prognosis. That is, we assumed that society would continue functioning as it has up to now. In the model, this implied letting it "run" without introducing any exogenous change. The second experiment assumed that the government applied a conservative policy; the third experiment involved the implementation of a liberal democratic policy. These last two policy packages, the conservative and the liberal democratic, are presented in comparative form in Table 9.4.

TABLE 9.4 Policy Sets Which Guided VENUTOPIA Experiments

1. Nonnationalist rightist in power.	1. Liberal democrat in power.
2. Censorship of information with a weak rightist ideological orientation in the information released by the government.	2. Control of information with a sweeping liberal logical campaign.
3. Economic policy favorable to the bourgeoisie, both national and foreign. Government allied with the upper bourgeoisie.	3. The application of radical economic, political, and foreign relations policies. These programs mass-oriented.
4. Centralization of power. Decrease of political participation.	4. Government continues to be decentralized and democratic, but the bourgeoisie loses influence.
5. Police and army strengthened. Become repressive.	5. Police and armed forces reformed. Become less repressive with the masses.
6. Educational policy becomes more elitist.	6. Education widespread and the more popular sectors given priority. Low-status groups increase in political participation.

More elaborate packages could have been devised and introduced in the model in different cycles. However, this is a task beyond the purpose of the present chapter.

Because of the volume of information produced by these experiments,

[9] *SRSP*, pp. 345–348.

we shall have to be selective here.[10] In Table 9.5 a concise summary of those results we considered to be most relevant are presented:

1. General levels of conflict over systems and roles are computed on the basis of the respective matrices of intergroup antagonisms.[11]

2. Levels of conflict are computed over each system and role.

3. Status congruence is the sum of each group's status congruence (congruence among education, income, and occupational prestige), weighted by its polarization potential.

A look at Table 9.5 allows us to observe the following:

1. Conflict is concentrated in a few areas; however, areas of conflict vary in the different experiments (words printed entirely in capital letters indicate systems):

STATUS QUO	CONSERVATIVE	LIBERAL DEMOCRATIC
CHURCH	EDUCATION FOREIGN RELA-TIONS	POLITY FOREIGN RELATIONS
government offi-cials communicators police priests	government officials police military	government officials

2. The highest level of general conflict occurs in the status quo alternative; nevertheless, it is interesting to note that most of it is due to conflicts over roles and not over systems, as is the case of the liberal democratic policy.

We shall now describe the impact of each alternative on intergroup

[10] For each cycle of each experiment the model produces an array of conflict values over each system and role; a 28-by-21 matrix of characteristics by groups; two 28-by-27 matrices of antagonism (one for roles and one for systems); a 28-by-20 matrix of group evaluations of systems and roles; an array of heterogeneity values (one for each group); two matrices (28-by-21 and 28-by-20) where the variations in both characteristics and evaluations are shown, and several lists that, if this is the case, tell which systems have been reformed by the government, which groups have been repressed, and which groups are bargaining over which issue. Then, when polarization occurs, messages are printed out defining the coalitions and the leader groups. Finally, the overall conflict values for systems and roles and a global measure of status congruence are printed out.

[11] For a description of intergroup antagonisms, see Chapter 7, pp. 180–187. However, a more complete version may be found in *SRSP*, p. 351.

TABLE 9.5 Evolution of Social Conflicts under Three Hypotheses of Social Policies

	Degree of Conflict						
	Status Quo			Conservative		Liberal Democratic	
Roles Evaluated	Cycle 1	Cycle 5	Cycle 9	Cycle 5	Cycle 9	Cycle 5	Cycle 9
Systems:							
Family	0.025	0.000	0.000	0.000	0.000	0.017	0.019
Community	0.000	0.000	0.000	0.006	0.168	0.000	0.000
Education	0.055	0.032	0.031	0.379	0.313	0.042	0.040
Polity	0.140	0 082	0.082	0.022	0.023	0.494	0.504
Economy	0.157	0.047	0.047	0.221	0.150	0.498	0.484
Church	0.267	0.374	0.373	0.153	0.154	0.074	0.070
Foreign Relations	0.410	0.208	0.207	0.318	0.318	0.532	0.526
All systems	1.053	5.016	5.015	1.060	0.989	4.025	4.057
Roles:							
Businessmen	0.044	0.066	0.066	0.143	0.174	0.012	0.011
Labor Leaders	0.000	0.000	0.000	0.000	0.000	0.000	0.000
Government Officials	0.045	0.000	0.000	0.012	0.013	0.059	0.063
Judges	0.069	0.067	0.067	0.090	0.096	0.038	0.037
Politicians	0.156	0.135	0.135	0.069	0.072	0.106	0.117
Primary Teachers	0.000	0.000	0.000	0.000	0.000	0.000	0.000
Priests	0.334	0.420	0.422	0.228	0.230	0.075	0.080
Students	0.076	0.143	0.142	0.039	0.033	0.025	0.026
Army	0.279	0.340	0.339	0.406	0.411	0.039	0.038
Police	0.444	0.442	0.443	0.384	0.395	0.063	0.069
Citizens	0.000	0.000	0.000	0.000	0.000	0.000	0.000
Communicators	0.268	0.341	0.340	0.180	0.183	0.042	0.037
All roles	0.972	11.842	11.719	0.859	0.892	0.428	0.428
Status congruence	6.187	6.290	6.171	6.218	6.174	6.216	6.518

conflicts: The status quo alternative opens with the opposition of student leaders and university professors who are demanding that the political, economic, and educational systems be reformed. Government implements some reforms but also represses the dissidents. A polarization takes place, in which we find on one side a coalition of student leaders, university professors, workers and labor leaders, *rancho* inhabitants, and campesinos. This coalition is headed by student leaders. On the other side, we find the government allied with the upper and petite bourgeoisie. Student leaders and university professors continue being repressed by government.

In the following cycle a traditional group, owners of cattle ranches, leads the antistudent coalition. Because this traditional group's evaluations are similar to those of the low-status groups, they draw the workers and their leaders, *rancho* inhabitants, and campesinos from the opposition coalition. Thus, student leaders and university professors are left alone in the opposition. Later on, in the next cycle, oil industry executives assume the antistudent leadership, but they now have the solid backing of almost every group against student leaders and university professors. Near the end, Cycle 8, we find priests leading a wide coalition against the rebellious student leaders and university professors, who remain stubbornly fighting alone in the opposition.

The conservative alternative evolves similarly. In the ten-cycle period for which the experiment was run, student leaders and university professors continually opposed government and other groups, only to encounter equally recurrent government repression. However, this time the rebels did not get support from any group, ironically, because the government was wise enough to make some of the reforms for which it was repressing the student leaders and university professors, thus attracting the dissidents' potential allies to its side.

The liberal democratic alternative elicits the most complex reactions on the part of the population. The first to protest are the bourgeois groups (executives and employees in oil industry, small businessmen, upper-status rural groups, industrial executives) and priests. The government meets some of their demands, but they are insistent in their opposition and because of that are repressed. However, polarization takes place only in Cycle 6. On one side we find a coalition led by university professors, with the backing of workers, campesinos, student leaders, educators, *rancho* inhabitants, small industrialists, and white-collar workers both in government and commerce. On the other side, oil industry executives head a coalition composed of oil industry employees, commercial and industrial executives, rural upper-status groups, and owners of small shops. This struggles continues until, in Cycle 8, university professors are left with the support of only educators, labor leaders, and government officials, whereas oil industry employees now act as leaders of the rest of the groups.

The most general interpretation that can be given to these "runs" is that, given the present sociopolitical structure, it is easier to implement a conservative than a liberal package of policies; but the most difficult one of all to maintain is the status quo, because this alternative generates the most conflict (see Table 9.5). Thus, if no structural changes are made by government, it is likely to become more and more conservative, because this is the mode of governing that allows it to minimize conflicts. We presume here that this process takes place quite unconsciously, with backward and forward moves, but with a steady drift toward conservatism.

These conclusions are, of course, applicable to the Venezuelan situation insofar as the model reflects the structure and dynamics of Venezuelan society. We give them only an experimental value; however, one is struck by the similarity of the results of the model and the conclusions derived from a more intuitive, but also data-based, analysis. Both of these analyses point to the fact that Venezuelan society has a conservative element built into its social and political structure; and unless changes in the rules of the game (that is, the structure of society) are implemented, the future development process is likely to follow a conservative path. On the basis of the evidence presented in this book, it can be said that liberal governments that hope to achieve a substantive amelioration of the condition of the masses, reduce social inequality, and, in short, make the benefits of development more accessible to workers, *rancho* inhabitants, and campesinos should either be prepared to find ways to make some structural changes — which undoubtedly will meet with the opposition of some of the most modern elements of the bourgeoisie — or be ready to recognize that their political programs are unrealistic, unfeasible blueprints.

Conclusions

It seems convenient at this point to reassess the alternatives that were identified in the hypotheses and defined in Chapter 3. The central option was signaled by the possibility of a new revolutionary crisis emerging by the 1980s. The reasons given were multiple and complex; we shall summarize them briefly. In the first place, there is the possibility that the happy stage of industrialization by import substitution may be completely exhausted — if, for political reasons, the very possibility of continuing industrialization along that path is not already closed. Successful industrialization implies that early phases should be accomplished efficiently, so that more complex phases (heavy industry) may be tackled, providing that there is a possibility of exporting the new industrial products. If this is not successfully accomplished, the prospect seems to be one of a long period of stagnation, like that in Chile and Argentina.

Historically (see Chapter 3), such crises always have been accompanied by profound political turmoil. In view of the ideological situation, the fact that by 1983 the main oil concession will end makes the prospects of such a political crisis more likely. There is no doubt that these conflicts will be stimulated by the dynamics of both processes, because both of them (exhaustion of import substitution and negotiations on oil policy) imply a greater involvement of the United States in the internal affairs of the country.

Our analysis of United States relations with Latin America leads to the conclusion that the United States government, through its multiple channels and agencies, always has actively intervened in the critical moments of various Latin American countries to favor the most conservative option of the moment. Such a possibility of intervening in Venezuela tends to become more and more real with the passing of time: in the first place, because North America shows a tendency to drift toward a neofascism that will probably accentuate the mechanism of domination of Latin America, a continent that is already becoming a satellite; in the second place, because the large U.S. multinational corporations' economic interests in Venezuela tend to increase rather than diminish. Some economists, linked to the government, like to think that import substitution will contribute effectively to the economic independence of the country simply because it will automatically reduce the importance of oil in the gross national product. The latter might be true, but what is not true is that such a process will increase economic autonomy. On the contrary, present tendencies in the industrial economy of the country give signs of an increasing denationalization of industry.

There are, of course, material reasons that explain denationalization: the increasing technological dependence on and control of enterprises by North American capital. The study reveals one additional sociocultural factor that helps to explain why such denationalization of industry is taking place. The Venezuelan bourgeoisie (industrial, commercial and agrarian entrepreneurs), as indicated in Chapter 5, do not possess the entrepreneurial capacity needed to undertake such a complex task as developing an autonomous heavy industry. Their capacity to defer gratification and their level of nationalism are so low that they will probably prefer to invest in speculative business and allocate to North Americans and "mixed" enterprises the realization of industrial development.

It also was pointed out, in both Chapter 1 and Chapter 3, that the process of becoming an economic satellite tends to be reinforced by an increasing cultural and military dependence. The words "ideological offensive" used to designate such dependency-producing designs are not mere propaganda; they correspond to the increasing overmilitarization of United States foreign policy. The target of this economic, cultural, and military combination is to create the economic base as well as the proper predispositions in the population which will make reality of what is now only a tendency toward submission.[12]

The findings reported by Bonilla in *The Failure of Elites*, Chapter 9, show this process in operation so clearly that it is worth summarizing them here: The most impressive results on the military and on what Bonilla finally called "the American community" is the extent to which socialization processes are being controlled by North Americans. Penetration is total in the army, including the new programs of "troop orientation." Selection and training of managers is a complete operation in which university graduates inside or outside the country are tracked down. The mobilization of the resident North American community, with the aim of bettering Venezuelan-United States relations, is based on the most primitive anticommunism; and right now, in alliance with local entrepreneurs and executives trained by them and linked to religious groups, an ambitious design for "cleansing" education at all levels is being mounted. At the same time, leftist groups feel depressed because their revolutionary message did not awaken consciousness in the masses. Although some awareness is found in the cultural sphere, there is no effort being made to analyze either the thinking of these groups or their own faults and failures to evolve a more effective intercommunication.

Whether this tendency is realized depends to a great extent on the Venezuelan capacity to face it. The first task is to become conscious of the denationalizing currents indicated here, because that awareness would make it possible to use the Venezuelan population's potentiality for change to negate the dependency-producing process by development that implies the realization of a more equalitarian social structure and a truly mass participatory political system.

The key question that we must ask is whether the present political system allows the achievement of such goals. The main conclusion derived from the preliminary analyses presented in *SRSP* clearly reveals that

If anything comes out clearly from our studies, it is that the personal experience of change and the desire for additional transformations in practically all

[12] Helio Jaguaribe, "Dependencia e autonomia na América Latina," mimeographed (Río de Janeiro: Instituto Universitario de Pesquisas do Río de Janeiro, August 1968).

spheres of life mark the thinking of Venezuelans of all social conditions. It is the technical and political capacity to channel and pace these energies that must rise to the occasion.[13]

Analysis and synthesis present in this volume reinforce and significantly expand such conclusions. On the one hand, they reveal the intricate social relations that determine and impel the social structure toward conservatism, and, on the other hand, they reveal that there exist in the population the seeds to overcome this situation. Consequently, to realign the present tendencies of national development it is necessary to take advantage of the potentiality for change of the Venezuelan masses, because this is probably the only alternative left to the dependency-producing tendencies mentioned here.

Advocates of elitist theories will probably say that these remarks go beyond the limits set by the data because groups included in this study, although important, are not really elites — that is, those men whose decisions affect the country as a whole — and will immediately add that such men could have the capacity to take advantage of the potentialities of the masses to transform the present social structure into a more equalitarian one. Nevertheless, the conclusions reached by Bonilla in his study of the elites negate such a possibility.

In Chapter 8 of his book Bonilla examines the ideology of the Venezuelan elite with respect to the masses and discovers two main currents of thought. The first one considers the mass as VICTIM of an unjust social structure. According to this ideology, the present state of ignorance, indigence, and exploitation in which most of the Venezuelan people live (peasants, *rancho* inhabitants, and workers) is a consequence of the unjust social structure; therefore, to change this situation, the elite are ready to propose and support such measures as agrarian reform, industrialization, and other structural changes. A substantial proportion of the elite holding these ideas would like to see profound changes take place, although the majority prefer gradual reforms. They would like to see these changes accomplished within a period that oscillates between five and twenty years. They believe that the country has enough resources to begin the task, but that it will be necessary to generate new resources in order to carry it on. Finally, they point out that the principal responsibility for change should be in the hands of the government or a responsible elite.

The second current of thought is a reactivation of pessimistic Latin

[13] *SRSP*, p. 370.

American sociology: The mass is a BURDEN because it is uneducated, savage, and primitive; therefore, the first need is to educate it, induce in it "decent" family habits, check its demographic growth, and, in short, contain it. The key word here is "caution," because at any moment the mass may become unruly, and then there will be chaos. These members of the elite favor only gradual changes, to be accomplished in the long run (more than twenty years). They are convinced that the main responsibility for effecting these changes should be in the hands of the economic elite.

The curious fact is that, whether VICTIM or BURDEN, both conceptions inevitably lead to the manipulation of the masses: that is, to work *for* the masses and not *with* them. Only a tiny minority of the elite interviewed was ready to recognize that the mass has a potentiality of its own for self-liberation. Obviously those who are more leftist are inclined to favor the VICTIM approach, whereas the rightists favor a BURDEN view. However, within each group — whether institutionally, politically, or ideologically defined — there is a substantial proportion of "dissidents." This heterogeneity means that the Venezuelan elite is caught in an impasse with respect to the realization of the objectives of autonomy and achievement of a more equalitarian society. In the light of all the other findings, this fact, as Bonilla points out, assures that the status quo will be the most costly alternative open to the country.

10 DEMOCRACY AND DEPENDENCY

The primary goal of the research project whose results are reported in this book was to analyze or, to use Ahumada's term,[1] to make a diagnosis of the Venezuelan political system; secondarily, the research was to produce enough accurate information to permit planning for development along lines less costly than in the past. Chapters 2 through 9 contribute significantly, although only partially, to these aims. The detailed analysis of the Venezuelan polity in those chapters reveals how the system operates. It reveals most strikingly, however, that the gap between the poor, the middle class, and the rich is widening, even though most levels of the society have experienced some change for the better.

However detailed and comprehensive this analysis may be, its findings become truly meaningful only when placed within a larger frame of reference. A hemispheric view of the dynamics in operation in Venezuela is necessary because many of the social conditions that exist there are significantly related to other, similar phenomena in Latin America as a whole. The most important of these is the dependency — economic, political, and cultural — of Latin America on the United States.

The purpose of this chapter is to sketch the historical roots, the present cultural framework, and the current character of this dependency. In order to do so, we shall be drawing on a literature that has only recently begun to appear. We shall first examine critically the common "consciousness" of today — that is, the prevailing ideology of Latin American development — and then look at its material base. Critical analysis of the underlying social, economic, and cultural dynamics of a society, as Karl Marx once observed, is a part of the universal human process of man's growing aware-

[1] Jorge Ahumada, "Hypothesis for Diagnosing Social Change," in *SRSP*, chap. 1.

ness of his environment, of its structure, and of its interrelationships. Included in this concept of the human environment, of course, is human society itself. Such a self-conscious examination will, we hope, open a path to its reform.

> The reform of Consciousness — Marx wrote to Ruge — is only a question of the world observing its own activity; the object is to make it stop dreaming about itself and explain to it its own activity. . . . Our motto, therefore, should be: reform of consciousness not by dogma but through an analysis of the mystic consciousness which is obscure to itself. . . . [It] will then become obvious that the world has long dreamed of things it has yet to realize in order to really possess them. It will be obvious that what is involved is not to draw a demarcation line between the past and the future, but to fulfill the ideas of the past. Finally, it will become obvious that mankind is not just beginning some new work but is consciously completing its old work.[2]

During the last twenty years a new ideology has emerged and spread through Latin America. At first confined to only a small circle of specialists, it later gained currency among the intellectual elite. Today it is central to the political debates of the country: *developmentalism*. Until recently, the most progressive sectors of the country were demanding industrialization, land reform, and other measures identified as aspects of the struggle for the "economic development of the country." Then the progressives picked up an unexpected ally when, in Punta del Este, Uruguay, in 1967, President of the United States Lyndon B. Johnson declared himself devoted not only to Latin American "development" but also to Latin American politicoeconomic integration. The progressives found it difficult to believe that the man who had sent the U.S. Marines into Santo Domingo and who had escalated the war in Vietnam could logically support what they meant by the term development. But, then, it would not be the first time in history that a popular term had been co-opted to legitimize activities and policies opposite to those implied by the word in its original usage.

Following rapidly on Johnson's Punta del Este speech, a new group in Venezuela became active in the political arena — a group composed of entrepreneurs who previously had termed themselves "neoliberals" but who abruptly changed their denomination to "developmentalists." Before this conversion they had been indifferent to the idea of Latin American integration; on the subjects of planning and developmentalist ideology

---

[2] Karl Marx, Letters in "Deutsche-Französische Jarbücher," cited in Jerzy Szacki, "Remarks on the Marxian Concept of 'False Consciousness,' " *The Polish Sociological Bulletin*, vol. 14, no. 2 (1966), p. 31.

they had been not merely indifferent but bitterly in opposition. Why, now, had they become its most fervent advocates?

The answer does not lie either in the entrepreneurs' response to U.S. humanitarian intentions or in their desire for "change." The phenomenon was merely a reflection of transformations now taking place in the ecomic base of a society, transformations that are the product of four centuries of domination, the end point of which is dependent capitalism.

Before setting out to show how the particular condition labeled underdevelopment came about in Venezuela as a historical product of the development of capitalism, we shall first examine briefly the ideology of developmentalism. Let us take as a starting point the most serious formulations, whose persuasiveness was, in the long run, responsible for the widespread acceptance of the ideology.[3] According to these formulations, underdevelopment is but a stage in the more-or-less long road to development. At the end of this road lies the affluent society, in which the most urgent needs of all are fulfilled; this is a society that today's conservatives would oppose as a serious danger to traditional social values — a welfare state. Clearly, then, the task before those espousing developmentalism was that of devising a series of steps — and developing political support for them — which would result in a country's active movement in the desired direction. What were those policies?

The endemic malady of Latin America, it has been said, arose from the fact that from its earliest colonial days it had grown "outward," because its economy was based on primary exports. This not only prevented modernization but also guaranteed that the centers of economic decision making would be located outside the country.

Logically, then, the believers in modernization advocated antifeudal and sometimes anti-imperialist movements. The most efficient way of modernizing, they said, was to industrialize the country by means of import substitution (the development of industry to manufacture consumer goods rather than import them), a radically different approach that would encourage internal growth. It was assumed that the building of a national industry would increase the growth of the economy, provide jobs for the growing marginal populations being driven from the rural areas by the crass inhumanity of the agrarian structure, and, finally, transfer decision-making power to groups within the national boundaries.

---

[3] There are two distinct techniques of developmentalist ideology: the first, technocratic and pure; the second, populist-nationalist. The second version is the one outlined here, because it is politically less naïve.

A national bourgeoisie was to emerge and would then become the active agent of industrialization. This national bourgeoisie, in developing the material base of the country, would in the process emerge as a ruling elite and fulfill its historical role: It would ally itself with the most modern sectors of the middle classes and of the proletariat.

Merged in multiclass parties, this group would take the reins of political power from the traditional ruling classes. It was assumed that once this heterogeneous developmentalist group had achieved real political power, the democratization of the country would be accelerated. Redistribution of income would be accomplished by means of programs such as land reform, radical expansion of education, and increased political participation. The struggle for better international trade terms would be facilitated once political power was affirmed securely. It would be possible to denounce commercial treaties with the United States and to supplant with domestic capital the international loans and foreign investments that were the initial compromises necessary to acquire the capital with which the program of internal growth and development could be initiated.

In the specific case of Venezuela, economic autonomy would develop almost automatically, because the share of oil in the gross national product would become relatively less as other industries developed. Oil, of course, would have to continue to be exploited with foreign capital, although competition would be established by setting up a national oil company. In this manner economic development could be achieved within not too many years.

The Reality

Even to the uninformed it is obvious that reality has proved the outlined hypotheses to be wrong. We need look only at the outskirts of the cities to see that marginal populations are increasing drastically; industrialization is superficial; and most of those who had been revolutionaries are now allied with the remodeled old dominant classes.

It is useful to analyze in detail what has happened in Latin America in general rather than confine the discussion to Venezuela, first, because the real process, as a product of the expansion of capitalist imperialism, is common to the entire continent and, second, because if we look even superficially at those countries in which the process is most advanced, we can see the options of Venezuela reflected in the mirror of history. In Argentina, Chile, and more recently Brazil, the process of import substitution has reached advanced stages. But the predicted takeoff toward development never has occurred. On the contrary, the process has shown three distinct stages. The first was economic growth up to a point; the second was economic stagnation; the third, in some cases, has been economic regression. Ironically, in those countries that have achieved the highest levels of economic diversification, we see the most acute demonstration of the *Latin American* crisis. That crisis is dramatically expressed in the progressive reduction of the growth rate of per capita income in Latin America as a whole.[4]

Why did the anticipated takeoff toward development never come about? What is wrong with developmentalist theory? There is no better way to expose a false theory than by analyzing the underlying reality.

The Process toward Underdevelopment

The general law that describes underdevelopment as a process has been briefly expressed as follows:

> Capitalism inserts, in a precapitalist structure, a foreign sector which gives origin to and fosters a deformed and dependent capitalist growth which generates the conditions for its own stagnation or involution.[5]

In order to understand this definition we must review history, though concisely, in order to lay bare the roots of the process. If we know how deep the roots lie, we shall better understand the enormous effort that must go into the uprooting.

Colonial Stage

What is today called Latin America was discovered when the European capitalist nations were expanding throughout the world in search of new

---

[4] The cumulative annual rate of growth of real per capita income in Latin America is as follows:

Period	Percentage
1950–1955	2.2
1955–1960	1.7
1960–1965	1.5
1965–1966	0.0

SOURCE: CEPAL, *Estudio económico de América Latina* (E/CN-12/696; E/CN-12/967), 1963, vol. 1, p. 3, and 1966.

[5] Adicea Castillo, "El sector agrícola y el desarrollo económico," mimeographed (Caracas: Facultal de Ciencias Económicos y Sociales, UCV, January 1969), p. 6.

trade routes, new markets, and primary resources. At that time, Spain and Portugal had some industry and carried on minor trade with other European countries, but they were in no sense dynamic centers of capitalism. They were, in fact, quite independent of the European centers of mercantilism. For this reason, the impact of their colonization policies was different from that of the countries which were to control the industrial revolution in Europe.

England and France, for example, permitted sizable emigration to their colonies not only to ensure supplies of raw materials but also to enlarge export markets. These markets could be maintained and broadened only if colonists to the new world were permitted reasonable latitude in the development of the lands they had occupied. Their purchasing power, obviously, depended on their own economic growth.

The economies of the Portuguese-Spanish colonies were organized on a different and extremely rigid pattern. The colonies were viewed by the mother countries as sources of wealth (gold) and raw materials, not as potential markets. Colonial policies were therefore tailored to ensure that the colonies would develop no national sense of their own. The forms of guaranteeing dependency were various. Both Spain and Portugal established intermediary centers (for example, Buenos Aires and Mexico City) between the colonies and the metropolis (the imperial states). This system guaranteed to Spain and Portugal both their monopoly of commerce and an effective control over the colonies.

The Spaniards, in this drive to maintain their colonies separate from, but dependent on, predetermined power centers, granted exclusive rights to carry on commerce to Spaniards sent out from the mother country. This policy was aimed also at maintaining the largest margin of profits possible for Spain. Their second major technique for averting any possible development of independent political structures in the colonies was to appoint only Spaniards in important political positions. Such arrangements effectively shut off the possibility that the criollos would be able to control their own destinies. Despite their Spanish descent and what would seem to have been their logical right to benefit from their economic activities and to control their political destiny, they were limited to agrarian activities — albeit on large plantations — and to minor political offices in the city. The situation might have been altered if there had been large-scale emigration from Spain and Portugal, but there was not. Instead, this dependent and atomized economy was firmly established, affecting not only the ecology of populated centers and the means of communications but also the distribution of products and the exercise of power.[6]

In Venezuela, which was a poor and therefore weak link in the chain of control, the *latifundista* class — criollo owners of large plantations — prospered, principally by cultivating cacao. What other agricultural products were grown were for local consumption. From its base of the cacao plantations, which were concentrated in the central region of Venezuela, the *latifundista* class emerged with enough power to challenge the Spaniards. This class gradually began to demand more participation in the economic and political control of the region. Antagonism between what had by then become two dominant classes therefore had two mutually reinforcing sources: first, hostilities between plantation owners and merchants and, second, those between criollos and Spaniards.

The social structure as a whole was conditioned by the mode of production of the latifundia, which had organizational characteristics similar to feudal modes of production but produced for a world capitalist market. Part of the labor force was slave, but most of it was made up of "free" workers of varying degrees of indenture. Meanwhile, a middle sector developed in the cities, composed of marginal whites and pardos (racially mixed persons) who worked in minor jobs but whose aspiration was to be incorporated into the total structure.

Two significant events helped to sharpen the conflicts between the dominant classes. First, the establishment and operation of the Compañia Guipuzcoana not only centralized and controlled the national market but also fostered the institutionalization of the organs of political control and made them more rigid. Second, at the end of the eighteenth century, the collapse of the cacao market seriously affected the volume of exports. A further factor was the weakening of Spanish control due to the French occupation of Spain.

All of the the events just described were among those leading to the wars of independence. With political independence came the possibility of transforming the colonies into autonomous centers, because finally the alternative of an indigenous development of capitalism was open. But this alternative was never adopted, because the criollos retained the economic and political patterns of the past.

[6] Some scholars maintain that there was a true interdependence of Latin American colonies based on a division of labor that maximized profits for the imperial countries. This hypothesis, however, has still to be proved.

The Formation of Nationality

The criollos, both during the war of independence and afterward, concentrated on keeping the economy linked with the world capitalist market through the exploitation and export of a new primary product, coffee, which was to substitute for the declining cacao.

First of all, it should be understood that Western political institutions were not created by chance. They were structured to meet the needs to administer, guide, and facilitate the development of the new capitalist relations of production and distribution being established throughout Europe. Thus, the development of industry created not only a new mode of work — "free work" — but also a new form of organizing production — a hierarchical system. This system is ultimately imposed on society through state bureaucracy. Along with the consolidation of markets, national boundaries were defined.

In Venezuela, as in most of Latin America, these stages of nationalization were not reached until the twentieth century, when an integrated national market had been established. Consequently, until recently Venezuela was not a nation in the conventional historical sense, because there had been no socioeconomic requirement for it to become one. Throughout the nineteenth century the region was basically an exporter of primary products; this condition helped to maintain the "islands" or regional centers, economically dependent on a world market but ruled by local caudillos who were constantly struggling with one another to gain central control.

At this stage, three dominant classes had developed: the *latifundistas,* the importers and their administrators, and the *latifundista* generals. Although they held considerable local control, they were still under a dependent structure, subordinate to decisions they did not control. The backwardness of the productive forces made organization of the masses almost impossible. Instead, they were used alternatively as soldiers or as semifree workers. The lowest classes, then, were subjected to both internal and external domination and profited not at all from their own work.

Toward the end of the nineteenth century a crisis in the world coffee market created a new and profound political crisis in Venezuela. The Andean region, where most of the important coffee plantations were located, suffered the most. Logically, the Andeans began a military invasion to the center. By the turn of the century they had gained national power. Meanwhile, foreign loans and investments increased, although not at the same pace as in other Latin American countries such as Argentina and Brazil. Nevertheless, the blockade of Puerto Cabello by foreign navies, as well as other international incidents, were political symptoms that the nature of dependency was changing.

Neocolonial Stage

Like the criollos after the wars of independence, the new Andean elite too showed no interest in changing the economic structure of the country; the entrepreneurs of those days were economically and culturally incapable of launching an industrialization program. Conditions such as this are perfect for establishing an economy of enclave. In Venezuela it was oil, which requires an accumulation of capital and a technological capacity well beyond that of the local entrepreneurs. Every Venezuelan petit bourgeois individual tried to grab a share of the enormous benefits the oil business was producing. Because of these factors the oil industry in its initial stages developed almost without national control. The companies exploiting the oil resources were able therefore to take advantage of all the facilities offered by an agrarian-based government elite and a dependent bourgoisie that saw, in urban land speculation and financial operations, unlimited opportunities for easy profit taking at small risk.

The peculiar character of the Venezuelan economic pattern of growth stems from this history. Its special consequence was that during the economic crisis of the 1930s, when other Latin American countries were pushing industrialization forward by means of import substitution, Venezuela kept growing outward. Its economic infrastructure was built on an untransformed dependent urban economy and agrarian structure. This phase of "simple growth," as Armando Córdova and Héctor Silva Michelena call it, had as its principal motive power the export sector of the economy.

Only during World War II did a few Venezuelan entrepreneurs, spurred by the trade limitations imposed by the war, begin to establish import-substituting industries. Thus, by 1950, when the world oil market was beginning to diminish its rate of growth, both national industry and the bourgeoisie were still at the primary level of development. The decision of the military dictator Pérez Jiménez to modernize the country through a program of public works — building magnificent highways, hotels, and so forth — was simply a variation of a system of dependent economic growth. The policy not only failed to generate a national, independent bourgeoisie but further engendered a bourgeoisie linked with and subordinated to the bourgeoisie of the dominant countries, especially of the United States.

Even so, what economic growth occurred did transform the conditions of existence of many Venezuelans of the middle sector, workers, and peasants. It also created a new phenomenon, a marginal population that was gradually but swiftly occupying the most visible — and least adequate for living — sites in and around the cities. Contrary to what had happened in the advanced capitalist countries, where the growth of the cities followed the growth of industry, Venezuelan cities took form before, and faster than, industry.

These economic facts, however, only rose to the surface, and therefore to the common consciousness of Venezuelans, between 1956 and 1959, when oil exports, and consequently fiscal revenues, decreased from 9 to 4 percent per year. This crisis forced both government and business to recognize the need to industrialize the country. With the inauguration of the democratic regime that deposed Pérez Jiménez, a crash program of import substitution was begun. This euphoric phase is already approaching its end. Almost all consumer goods, which are easy to substitute, are being produced internally. The process is now beginning to enter a new and more complex phase that requires more highly developed technology and more capital.

It is still too early to predict exactly what will happen. There are signs, however, that Venezuela is following the same course that was taken by Brazil and Argentina, that is, domination of industry by foreign capital — denationalization. Yet the key question here is why the Venezuelan bourgeoisie — now supposedly stronger and more class conscious — is incapable of conducting an autonomous national process of industrialization. There are several answers to this question, but we shall deal with the two crucial ones: the first is politicoeconomic; the second, technical.

The main thesis proposed here is that, as the process of import substitution continues, Venezuelan entrepreneurs are becoming weaker and less "Venezuelan." They are less Venezuelan in the sense that, with the increasing participation of large U.S. corporations in providing both capital and technology, control of the whole process of industrialization is moving into the hands of North Americans. Venezuelan entrepreneurs are less strong, because they lack the technical capacity, entrepreneurial spirit, and nationalism essential for an autonomous leadership (see Chapter 5). These are fatal weaknesses at a time when the industrializing process is becoming ever more complex and requires ever more complex technical training.

Again using Brazil and Argentina, where the process of denationalization is more advanced, as models for prediction, what can be anticipated for Venezuela? In the first phase, Venezuelan capital will merge with North American capital, with the latter rapidly gaining control of all light industries, such as rum, tobacco, and food. In a second phase, which might even be simultaneous with the first, medium and heavy industries will be established with more or less equal participation between local government and North American capital but relying heavily on North American technology. With such arrangements, we must assume that in this phase Venezuelan entrepreneurs will remain marginal. In the final phase, it is likely that the state will sell all the industrial complex, industry by industry, to large foreign corporations. Meanwhile, the Venezuelan bourgeoisie will retain control of the financial and commercial sectors, of construction and urban development, and of agricultural enterprises and will increasingly invest its profits in the New York stock market or place them in foreign banks.

Although loss of control of the key economic sector (industry) will make the Venezuelan bourgeoisie weaker as a force for economic nationalism, it will not become less important in internal politics. On the contrary, its own direct economic interests, together with its marginal participation in the heavy industry sector, already are being accompanied by an increasing political activity and class consciousness that is leading toward more open and effective use of special-interest organizations (particularly the Federation of Chambers of Commerce and Production, FEDECAMARAS) to exercise political pressure. These organizations are no longer merely defending themselves against government arbitrariness, as was the case in the late forties and early fifties; they are now geared toward guiding government economic policy. Their political philosophy, which underlies the economic process just described, as Frank Bonilla amply documents, might be expressed in a paraphrase of the statement that once rocked U.S. politics: "What is good for Fedecamaras is good for the nation." [7]

Let us assume, for the moment, that the Venezuelan bourgeoisie is culturally and politically able to confront and undertake the second phase of import substitution, industrialization, autonomously. What would be the likelihood of its success? To date, there is little if any capacity within

[7] Frank Bonilla, *The Failure of the Elites.*

Venezuela to generate the technology required to establish such industrial complexes. Inevitably, then, under the present form of political organization, it would have to adopt methods of production and forms of organization and control imposed by those who own the technology. Hence, it would continue to be subordinate to foreign capitalists.

Although a number of theorists recognize the risk of adopting technology produced in advanced countries, they feel that such use also has great advantages. Brazilian economist Celso Furtado recently pointed out the fallacy in this assumption.[8] Latin American entrepreneurs (assuming they have accumulated the capital and have the cultural disposition to do so) may choose from a wide spectrum of ready-made technology, which makes it unnecessary for them to invest in creating it. But how real is this advantage in the light of the needs of society? The technology of advanced countries is developed primarily around the goals of saving both labor and raw materials — perhaps the only abundant resources in underdeveloped countries. Thus the adoption of the technology tends only to worsen unemployment structurally — in terms of the classes in which it is the greatest problem — and to diminish the overall impact of new investments on the national economy. Furthermore, almost inevitably the adoption of a foreign technology is linked to dependence on those foreign groups that produce it, leading, in the end, to the denationalization of the economy.

Adoption of alien technology, however, has further consequences for underdeveloped societies. Armando Córdova, for example, points out that foreign technology imposes alien patterns of consumption, which, in turn, brake the development of national productive forces:

> Production not only provides materials to fulfill needs; it also provides needs for materials. . . . The need for an object that consumers experience has been created by perception of such object. . . . Thus production not only produces an object for a subject but also produces a subject for an object.[9]

Interdependently and dynamically, then, both processes reinforce the dependency of the peripheral country on a technologically and economically dominant one.

Furthermore, within the dependent country, the local bases of science and technology and, in general, of the culture consequent on developments in the productive process are judged according to foreign patterns and

---

[8] Celso Furtado, *Subdesenvolvimento e estagnacão na América Latina* (Río de Janeiro: Civilizacão Brasileira, 1968), chap. 2.

[9] Cited by Héctor Silva Michelena, "Neocolonialismo y universidad," unpublished manuscript, p. 14.

standards. This consequence not only reinforces the use of alien technology but also gradually closes down the possibility of developing an autonomous mechanism for producing the technological innovations that would liberate the potentialities for an indigenous technical structure of production. Moreover, because increments in productivity and therefore in personal income of the workers are linked to technological advances made in other countries, the workers tend to perceive dependency as necessary to their personal betterment. This idea is generally reinforced by the alien culture that is diffused through mass media. In this way the effects of alien — and alienating — technology are propagated through the productive process to social classes, culture, and society.[10]

Dependency is thus revealed as a particular form of relationship between advanced dominant capitalist centers and peripheral dependent capitalist economies. The foregoing analysis of this relationship was made from the standpoint of dependent countries. In order to have an overview of the phenomenon, however, we must examine, albeit briefly, the question from the viewpoint of the imperialist countries.

World Framework

Imperialism is an inherent and specific phenomenon engendered by capitalism. At each stage of capitalist development, however, the relations between the dominant and the peripheral countries have changed. A complete analysis of such changes is beyond the objective of this chapter. We shall concentrate therefore on the most recent phase of capitalist imperialism, which is characterized not only by the nature of its economic exploitation but also by its coordinated cultural, political, and military domination. The globalization of imperialism is a consequence of a political necessity of the hegemonic country, the United States, as well as an internal exigency of the tremendous development of the forces of production. The political necessity for the United States is to maintain an uncontaminated area of influence for the preservation of its own internal security.

The dissolution of the alliance between the United States and the Soviet Union after World War II was a consequence, of course, of the mutually recognized fact that the Soviet Union had emerged as the major world power antagonistic to the United States, which had become the principal power of the capitalist world.

Furtado recently described the dynamics of this process so clearly that

---

[10] Ibid., pp. 15–17.

it is worth summarizing his arguments here.[11] As the leader of the capitalist world, the United States was forced to abandon its comfortable isolation — that very isolation that had been the base of both its prolonged internal security and the rapid development that made it the hegemonic power of the Western hemisphere. The objective of the United States confrontation with the Soviet Union was not — as it was in the case of the capitalist countries in the 1920s — to make the socialist revolution fail but to *contain* the Soviet Union within its own borders.

The Soviet Union, as a result of its experience of intervention by foreign powers in its internal affairs and of its permanent insecurity, saw, as an existential need, Soviet control of the foreign affairs of the European countries on its borders in order to prevent further attempts at intervention. Out of this confrontation emerged the familiar Cold War, which was based on the premise that the world was politically bipolar and that it was necessary to forestall any shifts in that balance of power in the direction of further advantage to the Soviet Union.

In this world view, especially after the success of the Chinese revolution, instability and struggles in countries of the "third world" were considered to be a direct consequence of Russian Machiavellianism. The Soviets were seen not only as the beneficiaries of such third world revolutions but also as their creators.

This logic led North American generals to consider the possibility of waging an atomic war against, first, the Soviet Union, and, later, China. But, as pragmatist Hans Morgenthau recognized, dropping the bomb in Russia might have "solved" the problem of communism but not the problem of governing a radioactive territory covering one-sixth of the globe.[12] In the case of China — which U.S. military strategists believed could have been defeated by conventional warfare, assuming that the Soviet Union did not intervene — the problem was how to occupy a territory of such size and density of population. China, like the Soviet Union, considered it necessary to control neighboring territories in order to prevent operations against its own. The policy of the United States was to isolate China and create a permanent focus of threat and aggression by supporting Formosa, South Korea, and later South Vietnam.

Two events highlighted the fallacies underlying this U.S. policy of containment. In the first, Korea proved that political instability and wars

---

[11] Furtado, *Subdesenvolvimento e estagnação*, pp. 21–40.

[12] Hans Morgenthau, "A Reassessment of United States Foreign Policy." Cited by Furtado, *ibid.*, pp. 28–29.

of liberation arise from internal conditions in underdeveloped countries rather than from Russian manipulation. The Cuban revolution and the Vietnam war merely confirmed this reality. Another event, the invasion of Hungary in 1956, showed that the Soviet Union had by then firmly decided it would take whatever steps it deemed necessary to avert any reversal of its form of socialism. The United States, in turn, first in Cuba and later in Vietnam, made it clear it would barely tolerate present arrangements in the U.S. sphere of influence; in Santo Domingo, the United States demonstrated that it would not accept any new "reversals" in its sphere.

However, while the two poles were acting on this hard-line policy, the world became multipolar: on the one hand, Japan and Western Europe gained a considerable degree of political and economic autonomy; on the other, China was increasingly differentiating itself from the Soviet sphere of influence. Moreover, the pragmatic working out of peaceful coexistence between the Soviet Union and the United States made world politics quite different from that predicted by the early analysts of the Cold War. Nevertheless, both poles continued to deal with countries within their spheres of influence as if the world were still bipolar.

By 1957 it had become clear to the United States that economic development of the third world, and particularly of Latin America, was a vital need for its own internal security. All U.S. public statements about dedication to the preservation of freedom for the third world countries aside, a more candid and pragmatic view was expressed by President Eisenhower in his address to the nation on May 21, 1957:

> The common label of "foreign aid" is gravely misleading, for it inspires a picture of bounty for foreign countries at the expense of our own. No misconception could be further from reality. These programs serve our own basic national and personal interests.
> They do this both immediately and lastingly. In the long term, the ending or the weakening of these programs would vastly increase the risk of future war. And, in the immediate sense, it would impose upon us additional defense expenditures many times greater than the cost of mutual security today.

He proceeded to summarize briefly the sufferings and costs of wars waged by the United States during this century and concluded:

> Plainly, we must seek less tragic, less costly ways to defend ourselves. We must recognize that, whenever any country falls under the domination of communism, the strength of the free world — and of America — is by that amount weakened and communism strengthened. If this process, through our neglect or indifference, should proceed unchecked, our continent would be gradually

encircled. Our safety depends upon recognition of the fact that the Communist design for such encirclement must be stopped before it gains momentum, before it is again too late to save the peace.[13]

The loss of Cuba strengthened the argument for this policy, which later was intended to be realized on a large scale for Latin America through the Alliance for Progress. The aim was to maintain U.S. influence intact in all nearby areas. The economic development of backward countries therefore became a central interest of U.S. foreign policy. The theory that informed this policy was elaborated principally by W. W. Rostow, who conceived economic development as a process characterized by stages. All that had to be done was to help the *developing* countries (a euphemism for *backward*) to develop further through foreign aid and reorientation of internal expenditures and investments.

Time and reality have effectively demonstrated the poverty of Rostow's theories. The Alliance for Progress and other foreign aid programs were not enough to placate the discontented in Latin America. It became necessary to establish a military aid program in which, between 1953 and 1966, a total of $135.8 million was expended.[14] Along with these military expenditures, a program was launched for training and modernizing Latin American armies. North American military missions did not confine their advice to warfare techniques; through direct translation of U.S. Army manuals and instructions, anti-Communist ideology generated to meet Cold War needs was introduced into Latin American troop indoctrination. In this way, by means of a subtle mechanism of transfer, the Latin American military have come to identify national liberation struggles as a threat to the nation and to their military establishment. Thus, they believe that they are protecting their national interests when they are in fact simultaneously helping to reaffirm dependency and defend U.S. internal security and other interests. U.S. military concepts of "counterinsurgency" also were vigorously impressed on the cadres of Latin American armies. Because of this, Latin American armies tend to resemble occupation forces rather than national armies.

Recent developments have shown, however, that neither foreign aid nor military assistance is sufficient to ensure the rapid economic development of Latin America and to eradicate discontent or subversive (i.e., nation-

---

[13] Dwight D. Eisenhower, "Address to the Nation, May 21, 1957," *The Department of State Bulletin,* June 10, 1957.

[14] Compiled from U.S. Department of State, AID, Statistics and Report Division, "U.S. Overseas Loans and Grants" (Special Report Prepared for the House Foreign Affairs Committee, March 17, 1967), pp. 26–52.

alist) activities. To bolster economic and military programs, a new U.S. policy of economic and cultural imperialism is being put forward, the latter bearing the significant name of the "ideological offensive."

The new policy proposes to foster economic integration of Latin America under the domination of the large North American corporations. In a first phase, integration would be carried out regionally, for example, in the Andean region. In a second phase, Latin America as a whole would be integrated into the U.S. economy. This policy is now being pursued vigorously. Its proponents expect that, as was the case in the United States, the intrinsic dynamism of the large U.S. corporations will induce a rapid rise in the standard of living of the population of the subject region and ultimately of the continent as a whole. The potential for internal subversion thereby would be eliminated. Furtado sarcastically notes that, according to this scheme, Latin American governments, relieved of their political functions, would be able to dedicate themselves to the administration of things rather than men, realizing in this way — though in inverse order — the ancient ideal of Saint-Simon.

Meanwhile, as the North American theorists foresee the future, mass communications will create a new social supraconscience suitable to the development of a populace sufficiently consumption oriented to handle the productive capacity of the new supercorporations. The new social supraconscience also will conveniently establish that degree of loyalty to the United States that will psychologically repress any desire to rebel against its domination of the southern half of the hemisphere. The efficiency of mass communications will be enhanced enormously in a few years. Today programs are broadcast throughout Latin America by means of local radio and television stations using "Latinized" versions of U.S. programs. Tomorrow, artificial satellites will make it possible to create a communications fallout onto every Latin American rooftop without the intermediate stages that might stray into the wrong hands. Thus the Orwellian nightmare of absolute control over minds is becoming technically feasible and, in the light of current world political trends, by no means a moral impossibility.

The new superimperialism, however, is not without its basic flaws. In the first place, the huge corporations, by virtue of their own technological exigencies, tend to generate problems in the national economy which may in turn become the source of their own destruction. Automation makes the corporations incapable of absorbing growing demands for employment of an expanding population because to do so would lower rates of profit below the point of acceptability to the owners. Thus large corporations tend to increase the inequalities in distribution of income. Both trends — unemployment and gross income inequities — tend to create an explosive revolutionary potential.

In the second place, once that revolutionary potential becomes a day-to-day reality, the question arises whether a modern, mechanized army can achieve decisive victory over a population intent on conducting guerrilla warfare. The lessons of Vietnam suggest that the answer to this question favors the guerrillas: If the mechanized army does not win, it loses; if the guerrillas do not lose, they win. As a consequence, it will become necessary under the new imperialism for the state to adopt increasingly repressive measures that will only heighten social tensions and slow down or stop whatever progress is made in economic development. This trend could presumably serve to entrench even further both the repressive role of local government and the revolutionary determination of larger and larger groups of the population to resist the local government as an agent of the super-corporate intrahemispheric system.

Much of what is depicted here as possibly occurring in the future depends, of course, on the political capacity of Venezuelans of different social levels and ideologies to direct the course of events in one or another direction.

APPENDIX A: List of Variables

No.	Symbol	Index	No.	Symbol	Index
1	AGE	Age	25	STUDEN	Evaluation of university students
2	OCPRES	Occupational prestige			
3	YRSEDU	Years of education	26	SOLDIR	Evaluation of soldiers
4	INCOME	Monthly income	27	POLICE	Evaluation of police
5	FATHED	Father's education	28	CITIZN	Evaluation of citizens
6	EDUMOB	Educational mobility	29	DK	Index of those who answered "don't know" to evaluation questions
7	GENMOB	Intergenerational occupational mobility			
8	OCCMOB	Intragenerational occupational mobility	30	MASMED	Frequency of use of mass media
9	FAMILY	Evaluation of family	31	LEVINF	Level of information
10	BARRIO	Evaluation of the community	32	WORDOM	Communication or personal contacts with other groups
11	EDUCAT	Evaluation of education			
12	POLITY	Evaluation of politics	33	POLPAR	Political participation
13	ECNOMY	Evaluation of the economy	34	OPTPES	Optimism-pessimism
			35	POLEFF	Political efficacy
14	CHURCH	Evaluation of the church	36	NATION	Nationalism
15	FOREL	Evaluation of international relations	37	PROLEF	Proleftism
			38	PRORIG	Prorightism
16	BUSNES	Evaluation of businessmen	39	URBANX	Life experience in urban environment
17	PEASAN	Evaluation of campesinos	40	LOCALM	Residential mobility from town to town and state to state
18	LABORL	Evaluation of union leaders			
19	GOVOFF	Evaluation of government	41	RELIG	Religiousness
			42	RANGEV	Number of functions evaluated
20	JUDGES	Evaluation of judges	43	INTERP	Interpersonal relations
21	POLTCO	Evaluation of politicians	44	COOP	Cooperativeness
22	TEACHR	Evaluation of primary school teachers	45	GETS	Achievements
23	TALKER	Evaluation of controllers of mass media	46	SATISF	Satisfaction
			47	SECULR	Secularity
24	PRIEST	Evaluation of priests	48	WANTS	Aspirations

APPENDIX B: Sources for Figure 3.1

TABLE B.1   Exports of Cacao

	Year	Amount in Fanegas (1 fanega = 110 pounds)
(1)	1630	946
	1640	3,352
	1650	4,148
	1660	7,486
	1671	3,499
	1680	10,960
	1690	9,120
(2)	1701	20,721
(3)	1721	34,017
(4)	1731	33,000
(5)	1750	58,793
	1760	56,819
	1764	66,118
(6)	1775	58,923
(7)	1816	30,000

SOURCES: (number in parentheses indicates reference for the years following).
(1) Eduardo Arcila Farías, *Economía colonial de Venezuela*, pp. 96–98.
(2) F. Brito Figueroa, *La estructura económica de Venezuela colonial*, p. 238.
(3) Arcila Farías, p. 178.
(4) This figure was obtained by averaging figures cited by Arcila Farías, p. 178 for 1730, and Brito Figueroa, p. 240 for 1733.
(5) Arcila Farías, p. 257.
(6) Ibid., p. 270.
(7) F. Brito Figueroa, *Historia económica y social de Venezuela*, vol. 1, p. 221.

TABLE B.2   *Nominal Value of Petroleum Exports*

	Year	Value (in millions of bolivares)
(1)	1921	12
	1929	594
(2)	1936	684
	1941	1,000
	1948	3,340
(3)	1950	3,760
	1951	4,372
	1952	4,616
	1953	4,553
	1954	5,337
	1955	5,901
	1956	6,646
	1957	7,286
	1958	7,084
	1959	7,144
	1960	7,394
	1961	7,450
	1962	8,058
(4)	1963	8,378
	1964	8,713
	1965	9,062
	1966	9,424
	1967	9,801
	1968	10,193

SOURCES: (number in parentheses indicates reference for the years following).

(1) International Bank for Reconstruction and Development, *The Economic Development of Venezuela* (Baltimore: Johns Hopkins Press, 1961), p. 482.

(2) A. Uslar Pietri, *Sumario de economía venezolana: Para alivio de estudiantes* (Buenos Aires: Imprenta López, 1960).

(3) D. F. Maza Zavala, *Venezuela: Una economía dependiente* (Caracas: Imprenta Universitaria, 1964), p. 341.

(4) Author's estimate. Hypotheses of a 4 percent growth rate.

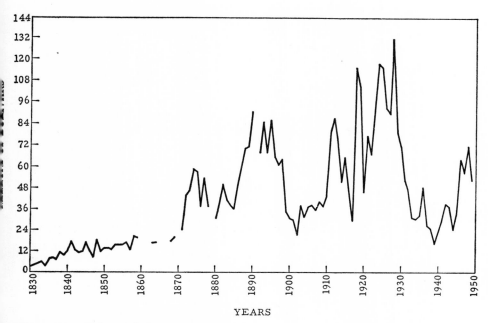

Figure B.1   Value of Coffee Exports

SOURCE: Eduardo Arcila Farías, "Evolución de la economía en Venezuela," p. 420.

APPENDIX C: A Note on the Analytic Tool

Descriptions of method in sociological or political science books usually appear in appendixes (largely at the insistence of publishers, who are convinced that such technicalities in the opening pages will automatically destroy a book's sales potential). I would have preferred to break this convention because, although the CONVEN study described in this volume involved the use of some familiar analytic tools, the amount of data from which this profile of a nation was drawn demanded the use of a less well known but unusually powerful analytic tool. It seemed only fair to the reader that this tool, which was the major instrument for analyzing the data presented (particularly in Chapters 4 through 9) be described somewhere (if not in advance) so that he might have a clearer understanding of how it was possible to handle the amount of detailed data from which these chapters were written. In deference to the public, this note has been relegated to the back of the book.

Analytic Methods

Political science survey research has become an ever more complex operation, both in design and in the amount of data gathered. A one-country study based on a national sample is a relatively simple operation in comparison to other surveys now in the planning stage or being analyzed. This trend toward complexity is likely to continue for the next few years, because the need for comparative research has been firmly established and because there is a growing awareness that the bases for comparison (whether of nations, groups, or institutions) must be more finely differentiated. Relevant to this consideration is the increasing demand for social scientists as policy counselors in public and private operations. Policy recommendations, to be more than platitudinous, must be very specific, thus increasing the need for more differentiated research designs. Forces of a different nature, also compelling political scientists toward more complex approaches, were described recently by Karl Deutsch in terms of

. . . a large increase in the resources for political research that have become available. There has been an increase in the range, diversity, and effectiveness of empirical methods of investigation; an increase in the amounts, variety, and accuracy of quantitative data; and an increase in the breadth, versatility, and power of the available mathematical and statistical methods of data analysis and interpretation.[1]

All of these resources, he goes on to say, have been enhanced by the greater availability of electronic computing soft- and hardware facilities. Moreover, the product of the many types of studies being undertaken is an ever more attractive and increasing pile of data. Deutsch estimates that by 1970 there will be a data stock of about 29 million IBM cards or the equivalent.[2] By virtue of the few data banks that exist, it now becomes possible to test longitudinal hypotheses, to develop models of change processes, and so forth.

Yet the political scientist working with the large survey frequently wishes that the era of the countersorter had not faded away. In the two and one half years that I was a visiting social scientist at M.I.T., I heard such complaints from some of the most sophisticated survey analysts of the Cambridge community. The analyst is told by programmers, or experts of the existing data-handling systems, that almost anything he can think of can be done within the time limits of his study. Spurred by the richness of his data, by the desire to contribute to theory, and by his unfenced imagination, he readily falls into the temptation to attempt complex analysis, only to experience repeated frustration. Eventually things do get done, even if it means expending 50 to 100 percent and more of the original time and money budgeted. One contemplates, not without despair, how some of the best ideas soar upward, only to fail, like Icarus, just when the desired objective of searing truth has almost been reached.

Because experience shows that a large survey requires the investment of five to ten years of one's life, and funds do become exhausted, it is pertinent to ask whether a more efficient system of analysis could readily be designed to solve at least some of the basic problems of data handling: (1) the possibility of enough flexibility to combine responses to different questions and different kinds of data in both an empirically and a conceptually meaningful way; (2) the possibility of instant interaction with the data to test hypotheses and hunches as the analyst goes along; (3) facilities for arranging and rearranging the data for handling and display purposes; (4) capacity to store and easily retrieve the information created; and (5) capacity to work simultaneously with many different surveys (data sources).

No data management system is likely soon to solve all the problems of data analysis that the survey analyst now faces. However, the closest approximation I have seen to a solution is the ADMINS system currently being developed at

---

[1] Karl W. Deutsch, "Recent Trends in Research Methods in Political Science," in James C. Charlesworth, ed., *A Design for Political Science: Scope, Objectives, and Methods,* Monograph 6 (Philadelphia: American Academy of Political and Social Science, December 1966), p. 149.

[2] Ibid., p. 156.

288

M.I.T. by Stuart McIntosh and David Griffel.[3] As an introductory note on the methods used for the analysis this volume presents, it is pertinent to describe, in a nontechnical fashion, the experience I have had using this system. For purposes of comparison I shall refer to the cross-tabulation system available at the M.I.T. Computation Center, which is at least as good as any other such system. This is a survey of about 5,500 respondents, who were distributed in different samples.[4]

Preanalysis

Perhaps the best plan is to proceed through the different stages of a survey after the data have been punched on cards. The researcher wants first to be able to check for punching errors. Using a verifying machine is helpful, but experience tells us that it is not enough. Once we discover the errors, usually after the first tabulations, they are seldom numerous enough to ruin a question or to justify going through the pains of modifying the original cards.[5] However, every time we use the information containing the error, it sticks like a fishbone in the throat. For instance, what can I do with this peasant who is classified as having a university degree? This is one of many problems that may be called *input* problems. The ADMINS system has a set of tools for checking the input to see if it coincides exactly with what is expected; the system then gives one the opportunity to alter the source data according to the original questionnaire. It offers the additional advantage of outputing a new item file that is stored in a disk for later usage, and resequencing or recoding the original data in what may be a more logical, easy to handle, or meaningful way.

The ADMINS system has facilities for taking different kinds of data (BCD, Binary, Column Binary, and so forth). This is done through a format declaration that is simple enough for a nonprogrammer to understand. In contrast, not only does the cross-tab program have no way of checking whether the input data corresponds with expectations (the codebook), but it accepts data only in a BCD format (that is, there are no multiple responses in a single column). Therefore, a specific editing subroutine is available that is supposed to convert multiple-response data to a format acceptable to cross-tabs. However, this is an operation that can be done only by a trained technical assistant. In the case of the Vene-

[3] This is an on-line (interactive) data management system. Basically it comprises four main programs: (1) ORGANIZER, which prepares a machine-readable codebook; (2) PROCESSOR, which brings together the organized codebook and the data; (3) INVERTER, which takes individuals of the item file produced in the processing and puts them in category files; and (4) ANALYZER, which allows building of indexes, making of cross-tabulations, and other data analysis techniques. For a description, technical and otherwise, of the system, see the following memoranda: David Griffel and Stuart McIntosh, "ADMINS — A Progress Report" (January 1966), and Ithiel de Sola Pool, J. Beshers, Stuart McIntosh, and David Griffel, "Computer Approaches for the Handling of Large Social Science Data Files," report to the National Science Foundation on Grant GS-727 (Cambridge, Mass.: Center for International Studies, M.I.T., 1967).

[4] For a description of the survey, see *SRSP*.

[5] As will be discussed later, we are assuming that the data have to be prepared for inputing into the cross-tab program. This requires investment of both time and money.

zuelan survey it took a programmer about three months and almost two hours of computer time (IBM 7094) to prepare the data. The programmer had to stand the existing program on its head because I had a multisample survey. In the process of editing I had to lose some information because the program did not accept certain coding sequences used in the data.

Thus, for instance, instead of having the respondent's father's place of birth classified by region, state, district, county, and town, it had to be recoded into rural and urban (the most likely use of this specific information). By the same token, information about the educational experience of respondents and their fathers was lost because of the lack of flexibility of the input recoding routine. No such restrictions exist in ADMINS.

Once the errors in the data have been corrected, the analyst usually wants to see the "marginals," that is, distribution of responses for each question. In any survey questionnaire there are questions that require a different type of marginals. For most of the questions, of course, an X-ray (frequency and percentage for each punch of a given column of the card) of the input will suffice. However, quite frequently the respondents are asked to rank a list; in this case the more meaningful marginal will be the average. In other cases two questions are linked together or are followup questions, for example, "What did you study, that is, in what department or specialty?" and "How many years of study did you complete in this department?" The desired marginals in this case are a cross-classification of the responses to the two questions. Still another type of marginal, as when we ask for the exact age or income of a person, are frequencies by intervals. Only the X-ray type can be obtained using a regular cross-tab program. Besides offering the opportunity of outputing different kinds of marginals, the ADMINS has greater facilities for labeling and computing percentages. This can be seen in Table C.1, which shows the type of marginals obtained from the cross-tab program, and Table C.2, showing those obtained from the ADMINS.

Analysis

Most surveys are meant to test hypotheses that may be more or less explicitly or formally stated. The more refined and explicit the statement of these hypotheses, the more swiftly the analyst can proceed. To be brief, I shall continue the discussion assuming the case in which some general hypotheses are explicit statements, and some are only more or less vague descriptions of expected relationships among variables loosely defined.

Because there are perhaps as many ways of analyzing survey data as there are analysts, we cannot expect any system of data management to take into account all the individual idiosyncrasies; even less can we expect that the system will, by some automatic procedure, actually make the analysis plan. The ADMINS system, however, seems to be flexible enough to accommodate almost every individual; furthermore, it provides the opportunity to test and retest the initial assumptions of any plan for the analysis of survey data. This is, in fact, quite a radical departure from the most common procedures forced on the analyst by the limitation of the cross-tab programs. A key difference between the ADMINS and

*TABLE C.1   Marginals from the Cross-Tabulation Program (Student
Leaders)*

Grp. No.	22	0	0	4	44	45	47	49	1	1	6	0	0	0	0	197
Percentage		0.0	0.0	2.03	22.34	22.84	23.86	24.87	0.51	0.51	3.05	0.0	0.0	0.0	0.0	100.00

*TABLE C.2   Marginal from ADMINS System, Same Group, Same
Question, but with Codes Conceptually Resequenced*

020A	1.000	1.000	197	FATHER ABANDON FAMILY
1	0.000	0.000	0	APPROVE
2	0.020	0.020	4	NOTHING
3	0.000	0.000	0	DK
4	0.228	0.228	45	NONVIOLENT NONINSTITUTIONAL SANCTION
5	0.223	0.223	44	ADVISE
6	0.030	0.030	6	DEPENDS
7	0.239	0.239	47	INSTITUTIONAL SANCTION ONE
8	0.249	0.249	49	INSTITUTIONAL SANCTION TWO
9	0.005	0.005	1	MODERATE VIOLENCE
10	0.005	0 005	1	EXTREME VIOLENCE
11	0.000	0.000	0	ATYPICAL ANSWER
12	0.000	0.000	0	REFUSAL

the cross-tab approach is that the latter mass-produces tables that take a long time for the analyst to digest, whereas ADMINS opens the possibility of inter-acting with the data and thus testing ideas as one builds them up. Let us scrutinize both of these strategies.

In both cases, from a careful examination of the marginals, the analyst begins to know his people. In the case of multisample surveys, he identifies gross differences and similarities among his sample groups. This will allow him to describe his subject of study more accurately than before. However, it is most likely that none of the hypotheses with which the survey started really can be tested. At most, the analyst can expect to refine some of them and perhaps to be able to suggest new ones. But the real usefulness of the marginals is that cutting points can be picked up for identifying the "highs" and "lows" in the distribution of responses to each question. Once this is done, the real difference in approaches begins to show up.

The cross-tab-minded analyst will want to know which "controls" should be used to neutralize the effects of certain variables when testing for the relationship of two or more other variables. For instance, if he knows that sex and political participation are associated, in testing for the relationship between political participation and optimism he would test males and females separately to be sure that the results are not actually the consequence of sex differences. Most commonly, sex, education, age, income, and occupational prestige are used as "hard" data, as opposed to the "softer" opinion and attitude types of data. In practice, this means that the seasoned analyst will order a run in which he will cross-tab-ulate those five "hard" questions by all others, and then sit down and digest a roomful of cross-tabs. In the case of the CONVEN survey such an approach would have meant producing some 54,000 tables.[6] If it is assumed that this *can* be digested, looking at such an output would require, with only a minute devoted to each table, about 125 eight-hour days! Clearly, then, a shortcut is necessary.

Paradoxically, another aim of mass-producing tables in such a way is precisely to find a shortcut for the final analysis: to test for variables that may form an index (grouping of several questions which have some conceptual relationship). In this case, however, the output could be more limited. We need to cross-tab-ulate only those variables that may form an index. This, of course, presupposes hypotheses that are not always specified a priori. Useful as it is, the cross-tab system is very limited for index building (a user-prepared MAD subroutine) both in the number of variables that can be combined and in storing the index pro-duced for later usage.[7] Thus we need to use another technique, different from the cross-tabulation, for that purpose.

Afew such techniques for which programs exist (Guttman, Factor Analysis, and so forth) are available. These programs, however, are seldom readily usable. They must be adapted to the data and the available machine. We were lucky enough to get a copy of a Guttman scale program. After three months of work the programmer finally made it work, only to discover that there was a "bug" in the program which was very difficult to locate because of its tremendous size. We had a factor analysis index-building program specially made for the data. However, this was designed for an IBM 1620, and in order to make it work for an IBM 7094, a complete reprogramming had to be done. Because we had already used this program and had some doubts about its applicability to survey data,

[6] Five "hard" variables times some 300 questions in the questionnaire times 36 samples in the study.

[7] The following paragraph, taken from a report based on the use of the cross-tabs program of M.I.T., illustrates the limitations, for index building, of the "Boolean" tool:

"To conclude the discussion of methodology, three problems should be discussed which arise from the techniques used. First, in classifying one response level for a ques-tion as modern and another as traditional (selecting "cutting points"), we attempted to come as close to a 50/50 split as possible without being overly arbitrary. Moreover, questions were chosen which would be classified as having a reasonably balanced split. This was done so that a resulting index, made up of several such questions, would include a substantial portion of the samples. However, it presents the danger of having an arbitrary result. (The reader should note that the relatively high cutting points for the cognitive variables reflect the high level of communication and information of the Venezuelan middle and upper classes.)

"Second, in using a single question to represent an entire dimension (such as secularism or innovation), we ran the risk of choosing one which was unrepresentative. Ideally we would use an index composed of all questions appropriate to the dimension; unfortunately, this technique proved to be too cumbersome to handle with our compu-ter program."

Janice Perlman and Philip Raup, "Style of Evaluation of the Middle and Upper Classes," mimeographed (Cambridge, Mass.: M.I.T., May 1966), p. 6.

we decided to make a different program, following the techniques used by Sewell. It was only after a year that we had 300 questions reduced to about 50 indexes. Had we followed the cross-tabulation approach, we would have had to order some 5,400 tables (three independent variables that later might be used as controls — socioeconomic status, sex, and age — times 49 indexes, times the 36 sample groups).

At this stage, the order of magnitude of the task has been reduced, but it is still a sizable job. From here on it is less clear, or more idiosyncratic, how the analyst proceeds. It depends mainly on how explicitly the study's hypotheses were stated at the beginning, how compulsive the analyst is in pursuing hunches and new hypotheses and, more than anything, an intangible element, the experience of the analyst.

The process described so far is not without "bugging" details so trivial that no investigator dares mention them even in explanatory notes or in a hidden corner of his report. Methodology textbooks usually do not mention them, yet these details are more responsible for the usual lags in producing the final report than anything else. In the end, most of these difficulties are due to lack of an easy form of storing and retrieving the information produced.

How do we proceed in an interaction system like ADMINS? The approach is radically different. We do not mass-produce tables, but we proceed according to a previously defined plan of analysis. For instance, families of concepts such as background, experience of change, political capacity, evaluations, and the like may be defined a priori. Then we can concentrate independently, at first, in such areas. The aim here is to build two or three social science indexes that then can be "carried over" in order to look for relationships with other such indexes in other conceptual areas. An example may clarify the procedure.

Suppose that we want first to analyze data on background characteristics (income, education, occupational prestige, and so forth) and experience of change (vertical mobility). Figure C.1 is a graphic representation of the analysis plan. Because the system allows interaction with the data, we can start from Level 1, that is, from the raw data; from there we proceed to higher levels of aggregation in snowball fashion. In this way, we can "control" several variables at a time, without the annoying problem of running out of respondents, as in the cross-tabulation technique. We shall follow one particular variable all the way through.

Figure C.2 shows the ADFORM statements and marginals for income and occupational prestige of respondents. We have, of course, an a priori notion about which occupational prestige category should be assigned each one of the 98 occupations in which respondents first were coded. Nevertheless, in order to build a socioeconomic status index that reflects the empirical groupings, we can easily, in the analyzer, build as many indexes to income as we wish to have categories and then ask for a frequency distribution of occupational codes under each income category. After seeing the results, we can immediately proceed to UNION (an ADMINS command), those occupational codes which were classified under similar income categories. This can then be reproduced in the ADFORM in order to store it in the disk for later usage (see Figure C.2).

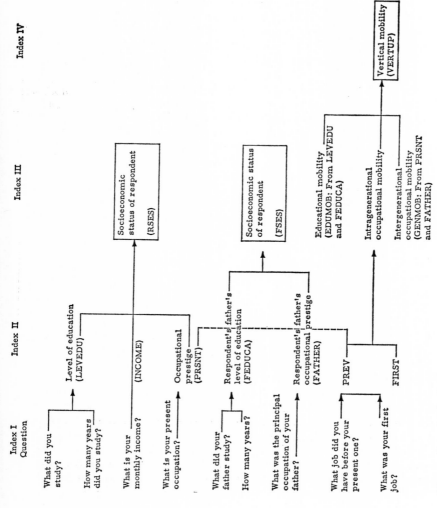

Index I
Question

Index II

Index III

Index IV

What did you study?

How many years did you study?

Level of education
(LEVEDU)

Socioeconomic status of respondent
(RSES)

What is your monthly income?
(INCOME)

What is your present occupation?

Occupational prestige
(PRSNT)

What did your father study?

How many years?

Respondent's father's level of education
(FEDUCA)

Socioeconomic status of respondent
(FSES)

What was the principal occupation of your father?

Respondent's father's occupational prestige
(FATHER)

What job did you have before your present one?

PREV

What was your first job?

FIRST

Educational mobility
(EDUMOB: From LEVEDU and FEDUCA)

Intragenerational occupational mobility

Intergenerational occupational mobility
(GENMOB: From PRSNT and FATHER)

Vertical mobility
(VERTUP)

Figure C.I Analysis Plan

	Percentage Based on Total No. of Respondents in the Survey	Percentage Computed on Raw Marginals	Raw Marginals	

```
N=VN36.
FMT=1,61,A1.
D=INCOME
        /10000  OR MORE
        / 6000  TO  9999
        / 3000  TO  5999
        / 2000  TO  2999
        / 1000  TO  1999
        /  800  TO   999
        /  600  TO   799
        /  400  TO   599
        /  200  TO   399
        / LESS THAN 200
        / DK/RFL.
RSC=$1$-$9$+$0$+$X$+$Y$ PERMIT $$.
E=12,1,0 ..
```

VN36	.90	1.00	4950	MONTHLY INCOME
1	.01	.01	38	10000 OR MORE
2	.02	.02	104	6000 TO 9999
3	.13	.15	745	3000 TO 5999
4	.10	.11	531	2000 TO 2999
5	.17	.19	930	1000 TO 1999
6	.08	.09	464	800 TO 999
7	.11	.13	630	600 TO 799
8	.09	.10	505	400 TO 599
9	.11	.12	593	200 TO 399
10	.05	.05	262	LESS THAN 200
11	.02	.02	84	DK
12	.01	.01	64	RFL

```
N=PRSNT.  New Name
FMT=VN30(N).  Name Given to the Present Occupation of Respondent in Level I ADFORM Which Be-
comes the New Format Statement
D=OCCUPATIONAL PRESTIGE/I/ II/ III /IV/V/VI/SAME AS BEFORE.  (Description)
RC= IF VI E   1 O VI E 26 O VI E 27 O VI E 32 O VI E 33
    IF VI E   3 O VI E  5 O VI E  6 O VI E  7 O VI E 28 O VI E 36 O VI E 45    Recode
    IF VI E   2 O VI E  8 O VI E 16 O VI E 17 O VI E 21 O VI E .3              Statement
    O VI E 34 O VI E 40 O VI E  4                                             in Which
    IF VI E   4 O VI E  9 O VI E 10 O VI E 11 O VI E 12 O VI E 18             Similar Codes,
    O VI E 29 O VI E 31 O VI E 35 O VI E 39                                   as Shown by
    IF VI E 13 O VI E 22 O VI E 24 O VI E 30 O VI E 37                        Previous
    IF VI E 14 O VI E 15 O VI E 19 O VI E 20 O VI E 25 O VI E 38             Analysis, Are
    O VI E 41 O VI E 42 O VI E 43 O VI E 46 O VI E 48 O VI E 50              Grouped
    IF VI E O.
E=7,1,0...
```

PRSNT	.91	1.00	5039	OCCUPATIONAL PRESTIGE
1	.00	.01	27	I
2	.24	.26	1301	II
3	.17	.19	942	III
4	.21	.23	1146	IV
5	.12	.13	670	V
6	.17	.19	940	VI
7	.00	.00	13	SAME AS BEFORE

Figure C.2 ADFORM Statements and Marginals for Income and Occupational Prestige of Respondents

Through this process we can generate empirically significant indexes (using the Fisher Exact Test as a criterion). Then tables can be printed either on- or off-line in which, in this case, the rows contain sample groups and the columns, those indexes of interest. These indexes may or may not be mutually exclusive and from different categories; up to nine columns are accepted for off-line tables, up to fourteen for on-line tables. Once the table is produced (and stored on the disk), it can be used for performing any statistical test, provided the table and the test have been properly interfaced. For instance, we have a statistical package that allows one to compute Kendall tau correlation coefficients among all columns of the tables, gives a matrix showing the significance level for each tau, builds new variables based on the ranks of the columns, computes coefficient of concordance, rho average, and chi square tests.[8] Other such subroutines can easily be interfaced.

[8] These statistics have been used throughout this book.

Once we are sure that the indexes built give the information desired, they can be reproduced for later use either through a higher level ADFORM or, if appropriate, can be COUNTED directly into the disk. This last command puts into the disk category files that can be indexed immediately, using relational operators so as to be able to put together all those who answered to more (less or equal) than a specified number of the indexes being COUNTED. Figure C.3 gives an example

```
        count rmeed rmepr rmein = mesesr

-               0         1         2         3
TVEN
EXACT         1923      1561      1392       647
CUM.          5523      3600      2039       647


MESESR        TVEN CONSTRUCTED.


5             1x mesesr g 2 = mesesr middle. ses. respondent
```

Figure C.3   Construction of an Index and Category File of Respondents of Middle Socioeconomic Status Using the COUNT Command

of COUNTing the persons who have middle-level education, prestige, and income. As can be seen, 2,039 persons coincide in more than one of the three indexes, whereas only 1,392 individuals responded in the same way to exactly two indexes. All of this information is stored in the disk in a category file that can be used immediately or later. The same procedure can be followed for building all other indexes until we end up with the final high-level social science indexes specified in the analysis plan (see Figure C.1): socioeconomic status of respondents and of their fathers, and vertical mobility. Then we can put them in the columns, put the sample groups in the rows, and produce a table with the appropriate tests of significance (see Table C.3 and Figure C.4). To do in the analyzer what has been described would take about two hours of the analyst's time and about six minutes of computer time in the M.I.T. time-sharing system.

Conclusion

The present trend toward multination and/or multisample surverys in political science is likely to continue in the future. This requires, more and more, new tools for analysis if we want something beyond a huge and increasing stock of unexploited data. The ADMINS system being designed at M.I.T. is one such set of tools. Its main advantages are (1) the ability to provide the analyst with a compact and integrated set of tools for checking thoroughly and swiftly the information gathered; (2) capacity for inspecting the data coupled with instant index-building capabilities; (3) facilities for producing tables in a much more flexible way; (4) statistical tests including the possibility of easily interfacing

TABLE C.3   Example of Tabular Output of ADMINS System

GROUPS TVEN POP = 5523

GROUPS 4927 ITEMS

#	Group			HIPRES 2270	HI.INC 1418	HI.ED 2759	HIRSES 3123	HIFED 2658	HIFPR 907	HIFSES 3437
1	High Government Officials	RAW	100	100	98	93	100	87	26	97
		SIG		1.00	1.00	1.00	1.00	1.00	.99	1.00
		PC/ROW	1.00	1.00	.98	.93	1.00	.87	.26	.97
2	University Professors	RAW	190	173	176	188	190	163	83	180
		SIG		1.00	1.00	1.00	1.00	1.00	1.00	1.00
		PC/ROW	1.00	.91	.93	.99	1.00	.86	.44	.95
3	Oil Executives	RAW	224	174	205	188	220	158	44	193
		SIG		1.00	1.00	1.00	1.00	1.00	.89	1.00
		PC/ROW	1.00	.78	.92	.84	.98	.71	.20	.86
4	Industrial Executives	RAW	200	175	93	152	192	140	40	167
		SIG		1.00	1.00	1.00	1.00	1.00	.90	1.00
		PC/ROW	1.00	.88	.46	.76	.96	.70	.20	.83
5	Commercial Executives	RAW	176	165	104	138	172	109	37	152
		SIG		1.00	1.00	1.00	1.00	1.00	.94	1.00
		PC/ROW	1.00	.94	.59	.78	.98	.62	.21	.86
6	Owners of Cattle Ranches	RAW	178	137	107	45	142	75	43	99
		SIG		1.00	1.00	0.	1.00	0.	1.00	0.
		PC/ROW	1.00	.77	.60	.25	.80	.42	.24	.56
7	Agricultural Entrepreneurs	RAW	174	83	67	43	97	67	17	84
		SIG		.96	1.00	0.	0.	0.	0.	0.
		PC/ROW	1.00	.48	.39	.25	.56	.39	.10	.48
8	Staff in Government	RAW	162	147	154	147	161	128	37	154
		SIG		1.00	1.00	1.00	1.00	1.00	.98	1.00
		PC/ROW	1.00	.91	.95	.91	.99	.79	.23	.95
9	Secondary School Teachers	RAW	183	146	89	183	176	139	65	161
		SIG		1.00	1.00	1.00	1.00	1.00	1.00	1.00
		PC/ROW	1.00	.80	.49	1.00	.96	.76	.36	.88
10	Priests	RAW	193	191	5	185	190	127	29	147
		SIG		1.00	0.	1.00	1.00	1.00	0.	1.00
		PC/ROW	1.00	.99	.03	.96	.98	.66	.15	.76
11	Student Leaders	RAW	197	14	4	197	177	175	56	187
		SIG		0.	0.	1.00	1.00	1.00	1.00	1.00
		PC/ROW	1.00	.07	.02	1.00	.90	.89	.28	.95
12	Municipal Councilmen	RAW	152	99	29	68	96	63	18	93
		SIG		1.00	0.	0.	.95	0.	0.	0.
		PC/ROW	1.00	.65	.65	.45	.63	.41	.12	.61
13	Small Industrialists	RAW	200	175	31	61	121	88	32	130
		SIG		1.00	0.	0.	.86	0.	0.	.77
		PC/ROW	1.00	.88	.15	.30	.60	.44	.16	.65
14	Small Shopowners	RAW	179	156	31	34	96	68	16	92
		SIG		1.00	0.	0.	0.	0.	0.	0.
		PC/ROW	1.00	.87	.17	.19	.54	.38	.09	.51
15	Primary School Teachers	RAW	202	0	0	191	174	125	41	147
		SIG		1.00	0.	1.00	1.00	1.00	.92	1.00
		PC/ROW	1.00	0.	0.	.95	.86	.62	.20	.73
16	Government Employees	RAW	141	1	2	102	86	84	26	115
		SIG		0.	0.	1.00	.84	1.00	.71	1.00
		PC/ROW	1.00	.01	.01	.72	.61	.60	.18	.82
17	Labor Leaders	RAW	220	124	38	81	139	90	33	134
		SIG		1.00	0.	0.	.98	0.	0.	0.
		PC/ROW	1.00	.56	.17	.37	.63	.41	.15	.61
18	White-Collar Workers in Commercial Enterprises	RAW	180	9	11	117	76	84	23	132
		SIG		0.	0.	1.00	0.	0.	0.	1.00
		PC/ROW	1.00	.05	.06	.65	.42	.47	.13	.73
19	Oil Industry Employees	RAW	211	13	20	72	88	77	18	102
		SIG		0.	0.	0.	0.	0.	0.	0.
		PC/ROW	1.00	.06	.09	.34	.42	.36	.09	.48
20	Independent Workers	RAW	666	15	19	205	109	210	83	345
		SIG		1.00	1.00	0.	1.00	0.	0.	0.
		PC/ROW	1.00	.02	.03	.31	.16	.32	.12	.52
21	*Rancho* Dwellers	RAW	258	2	0	19	36	65	24	94
		SIG		1.00	0.	1.00	1.00	0.	0.	0.
		PC/ROW	1.00	.01	0.	.07	.14	.25	.09	.36
22	Wage Workers in Agriculture	RAW	168	3	3	4	7	19	13	31
		SIG		0.	0.	1.00	1.00	0.	0.	0.
		PC/ROW	1.00	.02	.02	.02	.04	.11	.08	.18
23	Peasants	RAW	182	6	0	1	0	16	8	22
		SIG		0.	0.	1.00	1.00	0.	0.	1.00
		PC/ROW	1.00	.03	0.	.01	0.	.09	.04	.12
24	Land Reform Peasants	RAW	191	0	0	1	1	25	10	37
		SIG		1.00	0.	1.00	1.00	0.	0.	0.
		PC/ROW	1.00	0.	0.	.01	.01	.13	.05	.19

W 2244.9
EXECUTION.
KENDALL TAU GENERATOR.
WHAT IS INPUT FILE NAME
backg Tables
THIS IS CATEGORY TYPE TABLE.
READY FOR COMMANDS...
Tau print tape 1 / sigtes print / rsav consol / newvar consol 1 / execut

BEGIN EXECUTION
INPUT TABLE HAS 8 COLUMNS AND 24 ROWS.
PLEASE TYPE NVAR CONTROL CARDS. (C6,1013)

4
Exchan 3 4 5 8 9
PLEASE TYPE RSAV DATA CARDS (C6,1013)
THE LAST ONE MUST BE AN 'END'

5
rsav 3 4 5 6 8
W = .5529 RSAV = .4411 CHISQU = 63.5840 SAMPLES USED = 24 VARS USED = 5
PLEASE TYPE RSAV DATA CARDS (C6,1013)
THE LAST ONE MUST BE AN 'END'

2
rsav 1 6
W = .8558 RSAV = .7115 CHISQU = 39.3650 SAMPLES USED = 24 VARS USED = 2
PLEASE TYPE RSAV DATA CARDS (C6,1013)
THE LAST ONE MUST BE AN 'END'

2
rsav 6 9
W = .9561 RSAV = .9122 CHISQU = 43.9800 SAMPLES USED = 24 VARS USED = 2
PLEASE TYPE RSAV DATA CARDS (C6,1013)
THE LAST ONE MUST BE AN 'END'

0
end

KENDALL TAU RANK CORRELATION MATRIX CORRECTED FOR TIES

	EXCHAN	NEWSTA	NOCHEX	CHANEX	HORMOB	FOREX	VERTUB	HIFSES
NEWSTA	.48							
NOCHEX	−.78	−.58						
CHANEX	.78	.58	−1.00					
HORMOB	.51	.17	−.49	.49				
FOREX	.52	.10	−.46	.46	.43			
VERTUB	.55	.36	−.42	.42	.11	.24		
HIFSES	.34	.44	−.51	.51	.23	.19	.08	
HIRSES	.33	.43	−.50	.50	.25	.22	.13	.72

RESULTS OF 2-TAIL TEST.

	EXCHAN	NEWSTA	NOCHEX	CHANEX	HORMOB	FOREX	VERTUP	HIFSES
NEWSTA	.00							
NOCHEX	.00	.00						
CHANEX	.00	.00	.00					
HORMOB	.00	.25	.00	.00				
FOREX	.00	.51	.00	.00	.00			
VERTUP	.00	.01	.00	.00	.45	.10		
HIFSES	.02	.00	.00	.00	.11	.20	.61	
HIRSES	.02	.00	.00	.00	.09	.13	.38	.00

ALL TABLES HAVE BEEN GENERATED. THIS IS CATEGORY TYPE TABLE. READY FOR COMMANDS...

Figure C.4   An Example of the Kendall Tau Generator

ADMINS-produced data or tables with any statistical subroutine or, for that matter, any algorithm; (5) possibility of storing for instant use the information produced so that we can, literally, build on it; (6) possibility of working comparatively with multisource files (that is, surveys done in different nations, censuses of various years, and so forth).

Other capabilities that exist, but which I did not need to use, include input of serial alphabetic codes; direct questionnaire input; modeling by having the analyzer execute computational algorithms on data-producing data results that are further usable; and linking files related by inclusion relationships (for example, peasant file and village file).

The next version of the system is now being designed; current ADMINS has, like a new pair of shoes, many inconveniences. But if we can imagine the system once completed, we can foresee that its main weakness is also its greatest virtue: that of forcing the social scientist radically to change his way of analyzing surveys.

BIBLIOGRAPHY

Acosta Saignes, Miguel. *Estudios de etnología antigua de Venezuela.* Caracas: Imprenta de la Universidad Central de Venezuela, 1961.

Ahumada, Jorge. "Conferencia No. 5, Teoría del desarrollo económico." Mimeographed. Caracas: CENDES, September 25, 1964.

———. "Hypothesis for Diagnosing Social Change: The Venezuelan Case," *International Social Science Journal,* vol. 16, no. 2 (1964).

Akzin, Benjamin. *States and Nations.* Garden City, N.Y.: Doubleday, 1966.

Alexander, Christopher. *Notes on the Synthesis of Forms.* Cambridge, Mass.: Harvard University Press, 1964.

Almond, Gabriel A., and Powell, G. B. *Comparative Politics: A Developmental Approach.* Boston: Little, Brown, 1966.

Almond, Gabriel A., and Verba, Sidney. *The Civic Culture: Political Attitudes and Democracy in Five Nations.* Princeton, N.J.: Princeton University Press, 1963.

Angarita, Isaías Medina. *Cuatro años de democracia.* Caracas: Pensamiento Vivo, 1963.

Apter, David E., ed. *Ideology and Discontent.* New York: Free Press of Glencoe, 1964.

Arcila Farías, Eduardo. *Economía colonial de Venezuela.* México: Fondo de Cultura Económica, 1946.

———. "Evolución de la economía en Venezuela," in *Venezuela independiente.* Caracas: Fundación Mendoza, Editorial Sucre, 1962.

Benedict, Ruth. *Patterns of Culture.* Boston: Houghton Mifflin, 1934.

Betancourt, Rómulo, *Venezuela: Política y petróleo.* México: Fondo de Cultura Económica, 1956.

Blalock, Hubert M. *Social Statistics.* New York: McGraw-Hill, 1960.

Bonilla, Frank. *The Failure of Elites,* vol. 2 of *The Politics of Change in Venezuela.* Cambridge, Mass.: M.I.T. Press, 1970.

———. "Occupation as a Unit of Cross-National Political Analysis." Paper prepared for the joint ESOMAR-WAPOR Conference, August 20–24, 1967,

Vienna, Austria. Cambridge, Mass.: Center for International Studies, M.I.T., June, 1968. B/68-1.

———, and Silva Michelena, José A., eds. *A Strategy for Research on Social Policy*, vol. 1 of *The Politics of Change in Venezuela*. Cambridge, Mass.: M.I.T. Press, 1967.

Briceño-Iragorry, Mario. "Discourso de recepción como individuo de número de la Academia Nacional de las Historia, in Germán Carrera Damas, ed., *Historia de la historiografía venezolana*. Caracas: Imprenta de la Universidad Central de Venezuela, 1961.

Brito Figueroa, Federico. *La estructura económica de Venezuela colonial*. Caracas: Imprenta de la Universidad Central de Venezuela, 1963.

———. *La estructura social y demográfica de Venezuela colonial*. Caracas: Ediciones Historia, 1961.

———. *Historia económica y social de Venezuela*, vol. 1. Caracas: Imprenta Universitaria, 1966.

Calder, Nigel. *The World in 1984*, 2 vols. London: Penguin Books, 1964.

Carrera Damas, Germán. "Apuntes de clase." Mimeographed. Caracas: CENDES, 1968.

———. "La conciencia nacional como meta," in Elena Hochman, ed., *Venezuela primero*. Caracas: Imprenta de la Universidad Central de Venezuela, 1963.

———. "La sociedad colonial: Formación y dinámica." Mimeographed. Caracas: CENDES, January 1968.

Castillo, Aldicea. "El sector agrícola y el desarrollo económico." Mimeographed. Caracas: Facultad de Ciencias Económicos y Sociales, UCV, January 1969.

Center of Development Studies of the Central University of Venezuela (CENDES). *Estudio de conflictos y consenso: Serie de resultados parciales*, 15 vols. Caracas: Imprenta Universitaria, 1967–1968.

———. *Muestra de ganaderos y empresarios agrícolas: Resultados parciales*. Caracas: Imprenta Universitaria, 1967.

CEPAL. *Estudio económico de América Latina* (E/CN-12/696; E/CN-12/967), 1963, vol. 1, and 1966.

Charlesworth, James C., ed. *A Design for Political Science: Scope, Objectives, and Methods*. Philadelphia: Monograph 6, American Academy of Political and Social Science, December 1966.

Clarke, Arthur C. *Profiles of the Future*. New York: Harper & Row, 1962.

Córdova, Armando. "Consideraciones acerca del tipo de desarrollo alcanzado por la economía venezolana," *Economía y ciencias sociales*, vol. 5, no. 2 (April–June 1963).

———, and Gardicochea, Manuel Felipe. "Inversiones extranjeras y desarrollo económico, primera parte." Mimeographed. Caracas: Publicaciones del Instituto de Investigaciones de la Facultad de Economía, 1966.

———, and Silva Michelena, Héctor. *Aspectos teóricos del subdesarrollo*. Caracas: Imprenta Universitaria, 1966.

Cotler, Julio. "Visión panorámica del proceso histórico social de Venezuela." Mimeographed. Caracas: CENDES, 1963.

De Vries, Edgar, and Medina Echeverría, José, eds. *Aspectos sociales del desarrollo económico en América Latina*, vol. 1. Paris: UNESCO, 1963.

Domingo, Carlos, and Varsavsky, Oscar. "Un modelo matemático de la utopía de Moro," *Desarrollo económico*, vol. 7, no. 26 (July–September 1967).

Eisenhower, Dwight D. "Address to the Nation, May 21, 1957." *The Department of State Bulletin*, June 10, 1957.

Fagen, Richard R. *Politics and Communication.* Boston: Little, Brown, 1966.

FALN. "Our Errors," *Studies on the Left*, vol. 4, no. 4 (1964).

Fals Borda, Orlando. *La subversión en Colombia: El cambio social en la historia.* Bogotá: Tercer Mundo, 1967.

Freedman, Robert, ed. *Marx on Economics.* New York: Harvest Books, Harcourt, Brace, 1961.

Frey, Frederick. *The Mass Media and Rural Development in Turkey*, Report no. 3, Rural Development Research Project. Cambridge, Mass.: Center for International Studies, M.I.T., 1966. C66-2.

Furtado, Celso. *Subdesenvolvimento e estagnacão na América Latina.* Río de Janeiro: Civilizacão Brasileira, 1968.

Gabor, Dennis, *Inventing the Future*, 2 vols. New York: Knopf, 1964.

García Ponce, Guillermo. *Política y clase media.* Caracas: Editorial Muralla, 1966.

Germani, Gino. "Clase social subjetiva e indicadores objetivos de estratificación." Mimeographed. Buenos Aires: Instituto de Sociología, 1963.

Gil Fortoul, José. *Historia constitucional de Venezuela*, vol. 2, 5th ed. Caracas: Ediciones Sales, 1964.

Gorer, Geoffrey. *The American People: A Study in National Character.* New York: Norton, 1948.

———. *Exploring the English Character.* New York: Criterion Books, 1955.

Hauser, Philip R., ed. *Seminar on Urbanization Problems in Latin America.* New York: International Documents Service, 1961.

Hess, Robert D., and Torney, Judith. "The Development of Basic Attitude Values toward Government and Citizenship during the Elementary School Years," part 1. Multilith. Chicago: University of Chicago Press, 1965.

Hill, G. W., Silva Michelena, José A., and Hill, R. O. "La vida rural en Venezuela," *Revista de sanidad y asistencia social*, vol. 24, nos. 1 and 2 (Caracas, January–April 1959).

Hirschman, Albert O. *Journeys toward Progress: Studies of Economic Policy-Making in Latin America.* New York: Twentieth Century Fund, 1963.

Horowitz, Irving L., ed., *The New Sociology: Essays in Social Science and Social Theory in Honor of C. Wright Mills.* New York: Oxford University Press, 1964.

Huntington, S. P. "Political Development and Political Decay," *World Politics*, vol. 17, no. 3 (April 1965).

———. "Political Modernization: America vs. Europe," *World Politics*, vol. 18, no. 3 (April 1966).

Hurley, Neil P. "Satellite Communications," *America*, August 27, 1966.

Hurtado, Héctor. *Etapa difícil y compleja del desarrollo industrial.* Caracas: Imprenta Nacional, 1966.

International Bank for Reconstruction and Development. *The Economic Development of Venezuela.* Baltimore: Johns Hopkins Press, 1966.

Jaguaribe, Helio. "Dependencia e autonomia na América Latina." Mimeographed. Río de Janeiro: Instituto Universitario de Pesqúisas de Río de Janeiro, August 1968.

Jouvenel, Bertrand de. *Futuribles.* Geneva: Droz, 1963.

Kahl, Joseph, ed., *La industrialización en América Latina.* Mexico: Fondo de Cultura Económica, 1965.

Klapper, Joseph T. *The Effects of Mass Communication.* Glencoe, Ill.: Free Press, 1960.

La Palombara, Joseph G., ed. *Bureaucracy and Political Development.* Princeton, N.J.: Princeton University Press, 1963.

Lanz, L. Vallenilla. *Escrito de memoria.* Paris: Imprimerie Lang Grandemange, 1961.

Lasswell, Harold D. *Power and Personality.* New York: Norton, 1948.

――――. *Psychopathology and Politics.* New York: Viking, 1930.

――――, and Lerner, Daniel, eds. *World Revolutionary Elites.* Cambridge, Mass.: M.I.T. Press, 1965.

Lenski, Gerhard E. *Power and Privilege.* New York: McGraw-Hill, 1966.

Leoni, Dr. Raúl (Constitutional President of the Republic). "Second Message to the Congress," March 11, 1966.

Lerner, Daniel. *The Passing of Traditional Society.* Glencoe, Ill.: Free Press, 1958.

Levy, Marion, Jr. *Modernization and the Structure of Societies.* Princeton, N.J.: Princeton University Press, 1966.

Lewis, Oscar. *La Vida.* New York: Knopf and Random House, 1968.

Lindzey, Gardner, ed., *Handbook of Social Psychology,* vol. 2. Cambridge, Mass.: Addison-Wesley, 1954.

Lipset, Seymour Martin. *Political Man.* Garden City, N.Y.: Doubleday, 1960.

――――, and Bendix, Reinhard. *Social Mobility and Industrial Society.* Berkeley: University of California Press, 1959.

――――, and Solari, Aldo, eds. *Elites in Latin America.* New York: Oxford University Press, 1967.

Liscano, Juan. "Aspectos de la vida social y política de Venezuela," in *150 años de vida republicana (1811–1961).* Caracas: Ediciones de la Presidencia de la República, 1963.

Luttenberg, Norman R., ed. *Public Opinion and Public Policy: Models of Political Linkage.* Homewood, Ill.: Dorsey Press, 1968.

McAlister, L. N. "Recent Research and Writings on the Role of the Military in Latin America," *Latin American Research Review,* vol. 2, no. 1 (1966).

McClelland, David C. *The Achieving Society.* Princeton, N.J.: Van Nostrand, 1961.

McIntosh, Stuart, and Griffel, David. "ADMINS: A Progress Report." Mimeographed. Cambridge, Mass: Center for International Studies, M.I.T., January 1967.

Mangin, William. "Latin American Squatter Settlements: A Problem and a Solution," *Latin American Research Review*, vol. 2, no. 3 (summer 1967).

Marrero, Levi. *Venezuela y sus recursos*. Madrid: Editorial Mediterráneo, 1964.

Martz, John D. *Acción Democrática: Evolution of a Modern Political Party in Venezuela*. Princeton, N.J.: Princeton University Press, 1966.

Maza Zavala, D. F. *Venezuela: Una economía dependiente*. Caracas: Imprenta Universitaria, 1964.

Mead, Margaret, "National Character," in *International Symposium on Anthropology*. New York, 1953.

Miller, S. M. "Comparative Social Mobility," *Current Sociology*, vol. 9, no. 1 (1960).

Mills, C. Wright. *The Sociological Imagination*. New York: Oxford University Press, 1959.

Ministerio de Fomento, Dirección General de Estadisticas y Censos Nacionales. *Venezuela: Indicadores socio-económicos*. Caracas: Ministerio de Fomento, 1968.

Nisbet, Robert A. "Cooperation," in *International Encyclopedia of the Social Sciences*, vol. 3. New York: Macmillan and Free Press, 1968.

Osgood, Charles E., Suci, George J., and Tannenbaum, Percy H. *The Measurement of Meaning*. Urbana, Ill.: University of Illinois Press, 1957.

Osorio, Alejandro M. *Factor limitante del desarrollo agropecuario*. Caracas: Imprenta Nacional, 1966.

Ossowski, Stanislaw. *Class Structure in the Social Consciousness*. New York: Free Press of Glencoe, 1963.

Packenham, Robert A. "Approaches to the Study of Political Development," *World Politics*, vol. 17, no. 1 (October 1964).

Parsons, Talcott. *Essays in Sociological Theory*. Glencoe, Ill.: Free Press, 1954.

———. *The Social System*. Glencoe, Ill.: Free Press, 1951.

———. *Societies: Evolutionary and Comparative Perspectives*. Englewood Cliffs, N.J.: Prentice-Hall, 1966.

Pascuali, Antonio. *El aparato singular*. Caracas: Imprenta Universitaria, 1967.

Pérez Guerrero, Manuel. *Petróleo y hechos*. Caracas: Imprenta Nacional, 1965.

Perlman, Janice, and Raup, Philip. "Style of Evaluation of the Middle and Upper Classes." Mimeographed. Cambridge, Mass.: M.I.T., May 1966.

Picón Salas, Mariano. "La aventura venezolana," in *150 años de vida republicana (1811–1961)*. Caracas: Ediciones de la Presidencia de la Republica, 1963.

Pool, Ithiel de Sola, ed. *Contemporary Political Science*. New York: McGraw-Hill, 1967.

———, Beshers, James., McIntosh, Stuart, and Griffel, David. "Computer Approaches for the Handling of Large Social Science Data Files." Report to the National Science Foundation on Grant GS-727. Mimeographed. Cambridge, Mass.: Center for International Studies, M.I.T., January 1967.

Pye, Lucian. *Aspects of Political Development*. Boston: Little, Brown, 1966.

————, ed. *Communications and Political Development*. Princeton, N.J.: Princeton University Press, 1963.

————, and Verba, Sidney, eds. *Political Culture and Political Development*. Princeton, N.J.: Princeton University Press, 1965.

Quintero, Rodolfo. *Sindicalismo y cambio social en Venezuela*. Caracas: Imprenta Universitaria, 1966.

————. "Las bases económicas y sociales de una aristocracia obrera en Venezuela," *Economía y ciencias sociales*, vol. 5, no. 2 (April–June, 1963).

Rangel, Domingo Alberto. *Los andinos en el poder*. Mérida: Talleres Gráficos Universitarios, 1965.

Roethlisberger, Fritz J., and Dickson, William J. *Management and the Worker: An Account of a Research Program*. Cambridge, Mass.: Harvard University Press, 1949.

Rogers, Everett. *Diffusion of Innovations*. New York: Free Press, 1962.

Rokeach, Milton. *The Open and Closed Mind*. New York: Basic Books, 1960.

Rosenstein-Rodan, Paul. "Latin American Development: Results and Prospects." Mimeographed. Cambridge, Mass.: M.I.T., 1967.

Rustow, Dankwart A. *A World of Nations: Problems of Political Modernization*. Washington, D.C.: Brookings Institution, 1967.

Santoro, Eduardo. *"Los medios de comunicación de masas."* Mimeographed. Caracas: Escuela de Psicología, Trabajo de Ascenso, 1967.

Searing, Donald D. "Elite Socialization in Comparative Perspective." Mimeographed. Chapel Hill: University of North Carolina, March 1968.

Silva Michelena, José A. "Desarrollo cultural y heterogeneidad cultural en Venezuela," *Revista Latinoamericana de sociología*, February 1967.

————. "Satisfaction, Personal Adjustment, and Incongruencies in Venezuelan Society." Mimeographed. Cambridge, Mass.: Center for International Studies, M.I.T., 1966.

Silva Michelena, Héctor. "Neocolonialismo y universidad." Unpublished manuscript.

Silvert, Kalman H. *The Conflict Society: Reaction and Revolution in Latin America*. New Orleans: Hauser Press, 1961.

————, ed. *Expectant Peoples: Nationalism and Development*. New York: Random House, 1963.

Silvert, Kalman H., and Bonilla, Frank. "Education and the Social Meaning of Development: A Preliminary Statement." Mimeographed. New York: American Universities Field Staff, 1961.

————. "The Process of National Development." Mimeographed. M.I.T., Course 14.925, 1965.

Siso Martínez, J. M. "Ciento cincuenta años de vida republicana," in *150 años de vida republicana (1811–1961)*. Caracas: Ediciones de la República, 1963.

Smelser, Neil, and Lipset, Seymour Martin, eds. *Social Structure and Mobility in Economic Development*. Chicago: Aldine, 1966.

Soares, Glaucio, and Hamblin, Robert L. "Socio-economic Variables and Voting for the Radical Left: Chile, 1952," *American Political Science Review*, vol.

61, no. 4 (December 1967).

Sorel, Georges. *Reflections on Violence.* New York: Free Press, 1950.

Soublette, Carlos. "Objecciones hechas por el poder ejecutivo al proyecto de ley sobre Instituto de Crédito Territorial," in Laureano Villanueva, *Ezequiel Zamora* (Caracas, n.d.).

Staley, Eugene. *The Future of Underdeveloped Countries.* New York: Harper & Row, 1954.

Sullivan, Harry Stack. *The Interpersonal Theory of Psychiatry.* Helen Swick Perry, Mary Ladd Gowel, and Martha Gibbon, eds. New York: Norton, 1954.

Sutton, F. X., Harris, S. E., and Tobin, J. *The American Business Creed.* Cambridge, Mass.: Harvard University Press, 1956.

Szacki, Jerzy. "Remarks on the Marxian Concept of 'False Consciousness,' " *The Polish Sociological Bulletin,* vol. 14, no. 2 (1966).

Tumin, Melvin, and Feldman, Arnold S. *Social Class and Social Change in Puerto Rico.* Princeton, N.J.: Princeton University Press, 1961.

Turner, John C. "Asentamientos urbanos no regulados," *Cuadernos de la sociedad venezolana de planificación,* no. 36 (December, 1966).

———. "La Marginalidad urbana: Calamidad o solución?" *Desarrollo económico,* vol. 3, nos. 3 and 4 (1966).

United States Department of State, AID, Statistics and Report Division. "U.S. Overseas Loans and Grants." Special Report Prepared for the House Foreign Affairs Committee, March 17, 1967.

United States House of Representatives, Committee on Foreign Affairs, Subcommittee on International Organizations and Movements, Behavioral Sciences and the National Security, Report No. 4 on Winning the Cold War: *The U.S. Ideological Offensive.* Washington, D.C.: Government Printing Office, December 6, 1965.

URVEN study data. Caracas: CENDES, 1968.

Uslar Pietri, Arturo. *Sumario de economía venezolana: Para alivio estudiantes.* Buenos Aires: Imprenta López, 1960.

———. *Del hacer y deshacer de Venezuela.* Caracas: Publicaciones del Ateneo de Caracas, 1962.

Varsavsky, Oscar. "La experimentación numérica," *Ciencia e investigación,* vol. 19, no. 10 (October 1963).

———. "Los modelos matemáticos numéricos como herramientas de decisión en problemas dificilmente cuantificables." Introduction to an economic model elaborated by Arturo O'Connell and Oscar Varsavsky with the collaboration of N. Lugo, M. Malajovich, H. Paulero, J. Sabato, and V. Yohai. Instituto de Cáculo, Grupo de Economía de la Facultad de Ciencias Exactas y Naturales de la Universidad de Buenos Aires, *Boletín Interno,* no. 1 (August 1965).

Vekeman, Roger, S. J., and Segundo, J. L. "Tipología socioeconómica de los países latinoamericanos," *Revista interamericana de ciencies sociales,* special issue, vol. 2 (1963).

VENELITE. Interview 138.163.

Venezuela, Plan de la Nación, 1966–1968. CORDIPLAN.

Ward, R. E., and Rustow, Dankwart A., eds. *Political Modernization in Japan and Turkey*. Princeton, N.J.: Princeton University Press, 1964.

Weber, Max. *The Protestant Ethic and the Spirit of Capitalism*. New York: Scribner's, 1958.

――――. *The Theory of Social and Economic Organization*. Glencoe, Ill.: Free Press, 1947.

Wood, Bryce. *The Making of the Good Neighbor Policy*. New York: Columbia University Press, 1962.

Zamansky, Harold S. "Paranoid Reactions," in *International Encyclopedia of the Social Sciences*, vol. 11. New York: Macmillan and Free Press, 1968.

Zeitlin, Maurice. *Revolutionary Politics and the Cuban Working Class*. Princeton, N.J.: Princeton University Press, 1967.

INDEX

Acción Democrática, 58, 62–64, 68–70, 190, 253

Activism, index of, 221

AD. *See* Acción Democrática

Adjustment, personal, 155–169
  index of maladjustment, 159–163
  interpersonal, 156–157, 172
  paranoid reactions, 156–158
  powerlessness, 156, 158–159
  satisfaction level, 156, 163–169
  want-get balance, 156

Agrarian system, 5

Agriculture
  importance of, 36, 49, 53, 64–66, 78
  modernization of, 72

Ahumada, Jorge, v, 11, 16, 78, 116, 146, 157, 264

Alexander, Christopher, 20, 21

Alfaro, Eloy, 4

Alienation, 116
  political, 218, 219
  of white Venezuelans, 40

Alliance for Progress, 279

Almond, Gabriel A., 2, 115, 124, 150, 173, 174, 224, 228

Analysis
  approaches of, 2
  plan of, 16–32
  tool for, 286–298

Andes (mountain region) and Andeans, 45, 51, 56, 72, 271, 272, 280

Angostura, 36n

Antagonisms, 11, 15, 39–41, 63, 270. *See also* Conflict
  intergroup, 237–242

Anti-Communism, 59

Apathy, of Venezuelans, 52, 121

Aranda, Francisco, 113

Argentina, 3, 4, 6, 66, 74, 125, 259, 267, 272–274

Aristocratism, 145. *See also* Elites, failure of

Aristotle, 217, 227

Armed Forces of National Liberation (FALN), 69, 70

Army, national, 5, 50, 52, 71
  institutionalization of, 58, 64
  political role of, 190–193

Artisans, 54

Authority, rationalization of, 2–10 *passim*

Banco Agrícola, 54

Banco Central, 48

Banks, and bankers, 48, 51, 65

Barinas, 36n

Barquisimeto, 42

Barranquilla (Colombia), 48

Batista, Fulgencio, 4

Batlle y Ordoñez, J., 4

Bermúdez (military commander), 44

Betancourt, Rómulo, 68–70, 110, 206

BND. *See* National Democratic Block

Bogotá, Colombia, 44

Bolívar, Simón, 44, 47

Bolivia, 4

Bonilla, Frank, 84, 156, 157, 161, 221, 243, 261–263, 272

Bourgeoisie. *See* Criollos

Boves, army of, 42

Brazil, 4, 6, 267, 272–274

Buenos Aires, 269

Cacao and cacao estates, 38, 47, 48, 50, 72, 73, 113, 270, 271
  exports of, 283

Capitalism, 144, 145, 197

Capitanía General de Venezuela, 36

Caracas, 36n, 38, 39, 42–44, 46, 69, 89, 90

Carías, Tiburcio, 4
Carlos V, 37
Carrera Damas, Germán, 37
Carúpano, uprising in, 71
Castro, Cipriano, 45, 48, 50–52, 57, 195
Castro, Fidel, 69, 197
Catholic Church and Catholicism, 46, 47,
    56, 125, 145
Cattle industry, 47, 130
Caudillismo, 5
Caudillos. *See* Dictators
CENDES, research program of, v, 243
Change
    experience of, 79, 102–106, 117, 172
    impact of, 78–112
    political, 13–14
Chile, 3, 4, 7, 66, 74, 125, 259, 267
China, 277, 278
Christian Democratic movement, 56
Cimarrones, 38
Citizen (civic) responsibility, 124, 126
CIVICS defined, 191
Class barriers, 126. *See also* Social classes
Cochran, Thomas C., 145, 146
Coffee, 48, 50, 54, 72, 73, 271
    exports of, 285
Colombia, 3, 4
Committee of Democratic Defense, 58,
    58n
Committee of the Independent Electoral
    Political Organization (COPEI),
    63, 68, 70
Communication variables, 79. *See also*
    Mass media
Communism, 68, 173, 196, 197
Communist Manifesto, 80, 124
Conditions, external and internal, 6
Conflict, 16, 17, 70, 132. *See also* Antag-
    onisms; Venezuela, dynamics of
Construction industry, 72
Contacts, interpersonal, 221, 225–227,
    230
CONVEN, 18
Converse, Philip E., 175
Cooperation, role of, 221, 227–230
COPEI. *See* Committee of the Independ-
    ent Electoral Political Organization
Córdova, Armando, 272, 275
Coro, 36n, 42, 45, 51
Costa Rica, 3, 4
Criollos (bourgeoisie), 41, 42, 82, 131,
    270, 271
Cuba, 4, 68, 173, 278, 279
Culture. *See* also Venezuela, social struc-
    ture of
    heterogeneity of, 11, 116, 154, 264
Cumaná, 36n

Delgado Chalbaud, Carlos, 57n
Democracy
    and dependency, 264–281
    world framework of, 276–281
Democratic National Party (PDN), 58,
    59
Dependency, stages of, 82, 83
Development, theme of, 1–2, 6
Developmentalism, 265–268
Diagnostic approach in social sciences, 1–
    33
Díaz, Porfirio, 4
Dictators, 3–5
    last of military, 64–68
Differentiation, structural, as sociopolit-
    ical process, 2, 5, 10, 11, 33, 58
Domingo, Carlos, v, 17n, 238
Dominican Republic, 4, 7
Ducharne, Alejandro, 51
Ducharne, Horacio, 51
Duvalier, F., 4

Economic growth, 13, 53, 54
    characteristics of, 47, 60
Ecuador, 4
Education, 13, 49, 56, 63–66, 79
Eisenhower, Dwight D., 278
Eisenstadt, S. N., 9
El Bloque, 58n
Elites. *See also* Aristocratism
    failure of, 156, 221, 243, 261
El Salvador, 4
Employers' organizations, 67
Encomiendas, 36
Engels, Friedrich, 124
England, 52, 82, 151, 228, 269
Entrepreneurs, value orientation of, 145
Equality, 7, 8, 45
Ethnic discrimination, 63
Evaluation, style of, 14–17, 32, 116–119,
    121, 127, 140, 144, 146, 149, 172
Evaluations, 172–216. *See also* Venezuela,
    social structure of
    of the polity, 187–199
        foreign influence on, 195–199, 202
        government, 189–190, 213
        political parties, 193–195
        political role of army, 190–193
    recommendations, 199–212, 235–237
        economic, political, and social, 200–
        205
        implementations of, 210–213, 224,
        236–237
        priorities of, 205–210
    of roles, 180–187, 213, 232–234
    of systems, 175–180, 232–234

Falcón, Juan Crisóstomo, 45
Fals Borda, Orlando, 10, 11
Familism
    deferment of, 144–151, 154
    index of, 149
Federalism, 42
Federal War, 42. *See also* War of Federation
Federation of Chambers of Commerce and Production (FEDECAMARAS), 67, 71, 274
Federation of University Centers, 193
Federation of University Students, 222
Fombona, Blanco, 51
Foreign influence, 195–199
France, 52, 269
Frei, Eduardo, 7
Frente Nacional Democrático (FND), 70n
Frustration, 116
Furtado, Celso, 275–277, 280

Gallegos, Rómulo, 56–62 *passim*
García Ponce, Guillermo, 131
Germani, Gino, 87–88
Germany, 151, 228
Gil Fortoul, José, 43, 46
Gómez, Juan Vicente, 4, 45–59 *passim*
Gorer, Geoffrey, 150
Goulart, João, overthrow of, 7
Government employees, 56
Gracias al Sacar, 40
Gran Colombia, 42, 44, 46
Gratification, deferment of, 144–150, 154
Great Britain. *See* England
Groups
    changes in, 35
    key, 10–11
    role of, 33, 218
    sample, 15, 20–27
Guardia, Tomás, 4
Guatemala, 4
Guayana, 46, 51, 52, 110
Guipuzcoana Company (Compañia Guipuzcoana), 39, 48, 270
Guzmán Blanco, Antonio, 42–43, 47, 48, 56

Haiti, 4
Hernández, Maximiliano, 4
Herrera, Martin de, 39
Hirschman, Albert O., 9–11
Holland, 52
Honduras, 4
Hurley, Neil, 77

Identification, national, 120, 121, 125

Identity, as sociopolitical process, 2–10 *passim*
Ideology, 116, 117, 137
    interest theory of, 138–139, 159
    orientations of, 138–144
    and psychic states, 140
    strain theory of, 139
    types of, 140–142
Immigration, encouraged, 65
Imports, role of, 72, 266, 267, 272, 273
Income, distribution of, 64
Inequalities, 64
Information
    level and sources of, 117–118
    redundancy of, 21
Innovativeness, 117, 118
Institutional locus, 84, 85
Integration, social, 3
Intendencia del Ejército y Real Hacienda, 36
Interest theory. *See* Ideology, interest theory of
Israel, 101
Italy, 91, 151, 228

Jérez, Martin, 39
Jesuits, 56
Johnson, Lyndon B., 265
Judicial system, 65, 66

Labor force, distribution of, 55
Labor organizations (unions), 58, 60, 61, 63, 70, 85, 128, 132, 143, 160
La Guajira, 52
Land, importance of, 34, 36
Land Credit Institute, 113, 114
Lander, Luis, v
Landowners, 53, 54
Lanz, Vallenilla, 63n
La Salle, Brothers of, 56
Las Casas, Fray Bartolomé de, 37
Latifundia, and *latifundistas*, 50, 83, 145, 270
Leaders, relationship with public, 218
Legalism, 146, 154
Leguía, A. B., 4
Leon, Juan Francisco de, revolt of, 39
Lerner, Daniel, 15, 163
Levy, Marion, Jr., 8
Lewis, Oscar, 124
Life styles, 12, 83–85
Linares, Vicente, 88–89
Lipset, Seymour, 145
Llaneros, 45, 47
Llanos, 45, 48
    Rule of the, 41
López Contreras, Eleázar, 45, 57, 60, 69

McClelland, David C., 145
Maladjustments, personal, 159–163. *See also* Adjustment
    structural, 64, 65
Mantuano revolutionaries of 1810, 43
Maracaibo, 36n, 42, 58n
Mariño (military commander), 44
Martinez, Ortega, 51
Marx, Karl, 1, 8, 80, 81, 84, 124, 138, 139, 155, 217, 264, 265
Mass media, role of, 106–108, 111, 117, 118, 130, 132, 218
Mediating dispositions, role of, 114–115
Medina Angarita, Isaias, 45, 58–60
Merchants, 54
Mérida, 36n, 46
Mexico, 3, 4, 6, 38, 151, 228
Mexico City, 269
Migration. *See also* Mobility
    rural to urban, 5, 13, 53, 66, 67, 101
Military aid, 279
Military power, 44, 56. *See also* Army
Militia, national, 44
Mobility, 220
    educational, 99–100
    horizontal or residential, 78, 79, 88–104 *passim*
    index of, 117
    mental, 106–112
    occupational, 96–104 *passim*
    social, 5, 49
    vertical, 88, 95–104 *passim*
Modernization. *See* Development
Monagas, Domingo, 45, 51
Morales, army of, 42
More, Sir Thomas, 1
Moreno, García, 4
Morgenthau, Hans, 277
Morillo, Pablo, pacification policy of, 42
Movement of the Revolutionary Left (MIR), 68–69
Movement of Venezuelan Organization (ORVE), 58n
Municipal government, 65

National Association of Laborers (ANDE), 58n
National Confederation of Workers. *See* Venezuelan Confederation of Workers
National Democratic Block (BND), 58n
Nationalism, 13, 116–127, 140, 146, 149, 154
    defined, 7
    index of, 126, 127, 149
Nationality, formation of, 271–272

National Republican Union (UNR), 58n
National Union of Public Employees (UNEP), 71
Negroes. *See* Slavery
Nepotism, 5, 65
Nicaragua, 4
Nuñez, Rafael, 4

Occidente, 44
Occupations, 115
    as social criterion, 84, 96–99, 102, 103
Oil and oil companies, role of, 34, 50–56, 58n, 61, 64, 65, 68, 72, 73, 75, 78, 84, 91, 104, 119, 130, 173, 196, 203, 229, 272, 273
    exports of, 284
Opinion, range of, 117, 118
Optimism, 116
Orientations
    ideological, 138–144
    normative, 11, 113–153
Oriente, 44
Ownership, not a criterion, 85

Pablo, Juan, 51
Páez, José Antonio, 42–45
Panama, 3, 4
Paraguay, 4
Paranoid state, variables of, 162
Pardos, 40–42
Parsons, Talcott, 125
Participation
    political, 2–10 *passim*, 61, 65–67, 128–129, 217–242
    social, 230
Patriotism, defined, 7, 121
PDN. *See* Democratic National Party
Peasants and peasant organizations, 61, 70, 94, 128, 135, 174
Peñalosa, Manuel, 51
Pérez Jiménez, Marcos, 45, 57, 67–69, 89, 133, 146, 272, 273
Personalismo (personalism), 5, 145
Peru, 4, 38
Petroleum. *See* Oil and oil companies
Plato, 1, 227
Political efficacy, 13, 116, 127–132, 140, 146, 149, 154. *See also* Venezuela, dynamics of
Political parties, 63, 70, 193–195
Political system, 234–235
Pool, Ithiel de Sola, 217–219
Portales, Diego, 4
Portugal, 82, 91, 269
Powell, G. B., 2

Power
  changes in, 33
  dissociation of, from army, 57–64
  national concentration of, 50–57
Prestige, as variable, 79
Priests, 91, 100, 130, 160
Progressive Republican Party (PRP), 58n
Protestant ethic, 144, 145
Provincialism, role of, 41n
Psychology, social, normative styles of, 113–153
Public works, 114
Puerto Cabello, 36n, 71, 195, 272
Puerto Rico, 85, 95
Punta del Este, 265
Punto Fijo, pact of, 68

Rancho dwellers, 85, 90
Rationalization. *See* Authority, rationalization of
Real Audiencia de Caracas, 36
Recommendations. *See* Evaluations, recommendations
Regional factor, 45, 57
Remón, José, 4
Repartimientos, 36
Revolts, Venezuelan, 43, 71
Revolution, possible future, 71–77, 259
Riera, Gregorio, 51
Rokeach, Milton, 172, 174
Rolando, Nicolás, 51
Ron, Hernández, 51
Roosevelt, F. D., 59
Rosas, Juan Manuel de, 4
Rostow, W. W., 279
Rousseau, Jean Jacques, 217, 218, 228

Saint-Simon, Duc de, 280
Sanctions, style of, 116, 137, 138, 140, 144
San Javier, Count of, 39
Satisfaction, level of, 116, 171. *See also* Want-get ratio
Searing, Donald D., 101, 115
Secession, 42
Secularism, 46, 117, 125, 126
Silva Michelena, Héctor, 272
Self-affirmation, as goal, 8
Silvert, Kalman H., 3, 4
Slavery, 33–45 *passim*
Smith, Adam, 217
Social classes, 5, 38, 79–112. *See also* Status; Venezuela, social structure of
  criteria for, 33, 80, 85
  experience of change in, 86–88
Socialization, lag of, 13
Somoza, A., 4

Solagnie, Amabile, 51
Sophistication, as a normative orientation, 146, 154
Sorel, Georges, 132–133, 135, 138
Soublette, Carlos, 44, 113–114
Soviet Union, 276–278
Spain, 82, 91, 269
Staley, Eugene, 163
Standard of living, 146
Status, class
  criteria for, 7, 45, 80, 81, 84
  sample groups of, 87
  socioeconomic, 84–86, 98, 102, 103, 109, 132, 172
Strain theory. *See* Ideology, strain theory of
Strategy for Research on Social Policy, A, v
Strikes, general, 132, 133
Stroessner, Alfredo, 4
Student Federation of the Central University of Venezuela, 56
Student Federation of Venezuela (FEU), 58n
Student movements, 56–58, 60, 85, 130–132, 143, 160, 174
Subversion, 10
Suffrage, universal, 60, 62
Synthesis, 243–263
Systems, evaluation of, 175–180

Táchira, 53, 57, 72
Tactical Combat Units (UTC), 69
Teachers, 100, 130, 160
Timoto-Cuicas, 34
Tobacco, 47
Tocqueville, Alexis de, 218, 224
Torres, Crespo, 51
Tovar, Manuel Felipe de, 39
Trujillo, R. L., 4

Ubico, Jorge, 4
Underdevelopment
  defined, 81
  process toward, 268–276
    colonial stage, 268–270
    formation of nationality, 271–272
    neocolonial stage, 272–276
Unemployment, high, 69, 104
United States, 101, 151, 228
  influence of, 6–8, 32, 51, 52, 59, 76, 82, 85, 191, 197, 260, 261, 264–281
University professors, 130
Urbanization, 66, 84, 85
URD (Unión Republicana Democrática), 68, 70, 253
Uruguay, 3, 4

Valencia, 38, 44
Vargas, Getulio, 4
Variables, list of, 282
Varsaky, Oscar, 238
VENELITE, 18
Venezuela
  dynamics of, 252–259, 264, 276–277
  economic structure of, 78
  employment structure of, 78
  first republic, 41
  government structure of, 62–63
  history of, 33–49, 50–77, 264
    colonial, 34–41, 268–270
    war period, 41–42
    Republic to 1900, 42–49, 272–276
    twentieth century, 50–77
  mood of citizens, 170–171
  political capacity in, 221–230
  political ethos in, 150–153, 170
  political system of, 234–235
  population of, 35, 36, 48, 66, 78
  psychological states in, 154–172
  social structure of, 244–252
  suffrage in, 41
Venezuelan Association of Executives, 71
Venezuelan Campesino Federation, 193, 206
Venezuelan Confederation of Workers, 188, 193, 206, 222
Venezuelan Corporation of Guayana, 75

Venezuelan Democratic Party (PDV), 59
Venezuelan Federation of Peasants, 135
Venezuelan Federation of Teachers, 193, 222
Venezuelan Independent Association (AVI), 71
Venezuelan Petroleum Company, 75
Venezuelan Student Federation, 222
VENUTOPIA, 18, 237, 238, 253–258
Verba, Sidney, 2, 115, 124, 150, 173, 174, 224, 228
Vidal, Zoila, 51
Villalba Jóvito, 59, 69
Violence, 77, 132–138, 146, 154, 190, 219
Vivas, Ezequiel, 57
Voluntary organizations, participation in, 221, 223–225

Want-get ratio, 15, 16, 156, 163–169
War of Federation, 42, 45, 89, 114
Wars for independence, 48, 89
Weber, Max, 80, 81, 144, 145, 217, 218, 224
Women, in labor force, 55
Workers, industrial, 104
Workers' Front, 58
Workers' National Front, 58
Working class, future of, 74

Zamansky, Harold S., 157–158

DATE DUE

AP 27 '88			